Cross-Platform Mobile Application Development

A Beginner's Guide Using Solar2D

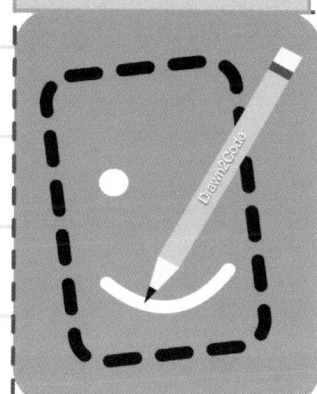

John R. Carlson, Ph.D.

Cross-Platform Mobile Application Development
A Beginner's Guide Using Solar2D

Copyright © 2021 John R. Carlson (LillipelliLabs)
All rights reserved.

This book and any contents may not be reproduced in any manner without the prior written consent of the author, except for brief quotations allowed by copyright law for noncommercial uses.

Although every effort has been made to ensure the accuracy of the information presented in this book, it isn't perfect. It is virtually certain to contain errors and, if such a thing is possible, to also contain omissions. This book should not be used as a flotation device. The writing's also a bit spotty. As such, no warranty, express or implied is given.

Printed in the United States of America.

Version 2.0
January 2021

Acknowledgments

This book exists because of the fantastic Solar2D platform (previously the Corona SDK), which provides a powerful, easy-to-use software development kit for building cross-platform mobile apps. In turn, Solar2D (and therefore this book) rely on the efficient and easy to learn Lua scripting language (www.lua.org).

Images used in the book may contain portions of the solar2d.com and coronalabs.com websites, Solar2D/CoronaSDK product, icon or logo and are used with permission. Such materials are copyright Solar2D and CoronaLabs ("Corona") with all rights belonging to Corona or Solar2D respectively.

Text in this book includes trademarks owned by third parties such as Apple, Google, and Microsoft. Likewise, screenshots of running apps may include elements copyrighted by these same parties. In such cases, all rights are reserved by the original rights holder. Usage in this book does not indicate that the rights holder sponsors or endorses any of the contents.

In addition to the fonts **Futura** and **Marker Felt**, which are bundled with Apple Pages, this book uses Baskerville (en.wikipedia.org/wiki/Baskerville), `Liberation Mono` (en.wikipedia.org/wiki/Liberation_fonts), and HamletOrNot (designed by CybaPee Creations). Many thanks to the creative work of these artists.

Drawn2Code (the prototype IDE bundled with this book) is written in Java and uses some cool icons from flaticon.com. Screenshots of *Drawn2Code* used in this book may include these icons.

The contents of this book have been "field tested" across eight semesters of beginning mobile development students, beginning in 2013. For many of these students, this material was their first real exposure to programming. Issues that caused any confusion have been identified and reworked, with the explicit goal of making the book friendly and approachable to beginners. Many thanks to all of the students who have provided this valuable feedback.

Contents

Preface 1
    What should I expect? 2
    Why Lua and Solar2D? 3
    Lua and Solar2D: What's the diff? 3
    The thing about games 4
    The book's theme 4
    Can only "ace" coders create a mobile app? 4
    References 5

Chapter 1: Download & Setup 7
    Let the downloads commence 7
    Downloads: What, Why, and How 8

Setup	9
Solar2D	9
ZeroBrane Studio (ZBS)	11
Drawn2Code	15
Hello World	17
ZeroBrane Studio (ZBS)	17
Drawn2Code	18
Summary	21
End-of-chapter exercises	22

Chapter 2: Introduction 25

What is "programming"?	25
Programs	27
Input	28
Variable naming rules	28
Process	30
Math	31
Strings (text)	32
Boolean logic	32
Branching & looping	34
Functions	36
Output	37
Solar2D	38
The development process	38
Code that isn't input, process, or output	39
Key programming skills	40
Summary	41
End-of-chapter exercises	41

Chapter 3: The Screen & Intro to Text 45

Devices and their many shapes and sizes 45

Table of Selected Device Screen Resolutions 46

Comparative Screen Resolutions 47

The Solar2D Simulator 48

    Hello World 2 48

    Using the simulator 50

Defining the content area using "config.lua" 51

    The content area 52

Your device 54

Fonts 56

    Solar2D font limitations 57

Screen size & location 58

    But where is (x,y)? 59

Aligning text (and other display objects) 60

    Setting anchors 60

    Text anchoring playground 61

Colors 63

Device status bar 65

The flow of execution: Top to bottom 65

    Order is everything 66

    Location is everything too 66

The period and the colon 67

Summary 67

Chapter resources 68

End-of-chapter exercises 69

Chapter 4: Display Objects & Touch ... 71

- Beyond text: Shapes & images ... 71
  - Locating your shape ... 72
  - Defaults ... 72
- Example: Basic shapes ... 72
  - Line ... 73
  - Rectangle ... 74
  - Rounded rectangle ... 74
  - Circle (that can be stretched into an oval) ... 74
  - Polygon ... 75
  - Image ... 75
    - Scaled image files ... 76
- Changing the colors ... 77
- Gradients ... 78
- A little wild ... 79
- A function to simplify your code ... 80
- Adding text (the MOB DEV logo) ... 82
- Groups and fun things to do with them ... 83
  - Notes ... 84
  - Using the group ... 84
  - Your first transition ... 85
- Touch & sound ... 86
  - Notes ... 87
- Flow of execution: Top to bottom & functions ... 88
- Summary ... 88
- Chapter resources ... 89
- End-of-chapter exercises ... 89

Chapter 5: Buttons & Logic 91

Your first widget 91

Events 91

 The event cycle 92

Get the widget library 93

Buttons 93

 Syntax notes 96

 Making the button do something 96

Shape buttons: When words alone aren't enough 97

 Notes 98

A button using images (finally) 98

 The images 99

 The syntax 99

 The transition effect 101

Using logic to control the flow 104

 Flowcharts 104

 Touch event phases 104

 An example: "button_sound" 105

  Limiting an action to a specific event phase 106

 A second example: "button_sounds" 106

 A third example: "multiple_buttons" 107

  Syntax note: using "dot dot dot" 109

Advanced: A function to make buttons for you 110

A simple counter 113

 Button event-handler (code box #8) 116

 Flowcharting the increment/decrement logic 117

 That's an app! 118

Summary 118

Chapter resources 119

End-of-chapter exercises 119

Chapter 6: Text Fields & Loops 123

Your second widget 123

The native library 123

Text fields 124

    Basic setup 124

        Text fields produce multiple event-phases 126

        Simulator and platform issues 127

The logic of loops 129

The 'for' loop (a known number of repetitions) 130

    Situation #1 131

The 'while' loop (repeat zero or more times) 132

    A 'while' loop that uses a counting index 133

    Situation #2 133

The 'repeat until' loop (repeat one or more times) 136

    Simple counting with a 'repeat until' loop 137

    Situation #3 138

Breaking out of a loop 139

A game of dice 140

    A 'while' loop works 140

    But a 'repeat until' works better 141

An example with buttons and a text field 142

    1. Setting up the UI 145

    2. Button event-handler 145

    3. Text field event-handler 147

    That's Simple Counter 2! 148

Summary 148

Chapter resources 149

End-of-chapter exercises 149

    Warning 150

Chapter 7: Sliders & Functions 153

Your third widget 153

Functions 154

Sliders 154

    Event data 155

    Change the starting value 157

    Change the range (minimum and maximum values) 157

        Displaying and updating the value 158

    Note 159

Putting the algebra in a function 159

    Note the four requirements of the function syntax (code box #6) 160

A better function 162

    A few notes on this function 164

Slider playground 164

An app with a bit of actual utility? Egads! 166

    Multiple sliders 166

    A settings screen 167

    Sharing your awesome color 168

    Slider misalignment ("shifty sliders") 169

        Fixing the shift 169

Summary 171

Chapter resources 171

End-of-chapter exercises 172

Chapter 8: Coding & Debugging 175
Bugs 175
    Bugs can include 176
    Keep these in mind while coding (the "three laws of debugging") 176
Proactive strategies 177
    1. Define 178
    2. Modularize 178
    3. Incremental build 178
    4. Test & debug as you go 179
Reactive strategies 180
    1. Look for clues 180
        a. Look for warning from the IDE 181
            Emors involving "M" 182
        b. Look at the Lua console 182
        c. Observe what appears 183
        d. Get more information 184
    2. Isolate the error 185
    3. Reproduce the error 186
Summary 187
Chapter resources 187
End-of-chapter exercises 187

Chapter 9: Dragging & Collisions 189
Tapping, images & sounds 189
    Playing "background" music 190
    A note on sound file formats 191
Listening for and handling a drag 192

More sophisticated drag handling	194
Basic collisions	195
Requirements	195
Detecting overlap	197
Sound effect	198
The complications	198
Timers	200
Timed galleons	201
Ten galleon timer	201
Galleon jump	202
Extending a display object with additional attributes	203
Notes	205
Tables	205
Tables of your own	205
Datasets	207
Table advantages	208
Not just coins	209
Thirty Taps	210
Making loops that contain script objects	212
Summary	214
Chapter resources	214
End-of-chapter exercises	214

Chapter 10: Switches & Segments 217

New widgets	217
Platform differences	218
Basic platform detection	219
What up, switches?	220

- Checkboxes 220
    - Adding a text label 221
        - Issue: Centered text 222
        - Issue: Tappable text label 223
    - A complete example 224
- Radio buttons 225
    - Defining a radio button group 226
    - Radio button event handler 226
    - A complete example 227
    - Issues 228
- On/off slide (toggle) switch 229
    - Issues 231
    - A complete example 232
- Segmented control 232
    - A complete example 235
- Switch playground 238
    - Enabling and disabling widgets 238
    - Alert dialog pop-up 239
- Summary 241
- Chapter resources 242
- End-of-chapter exercises 242

Chapter 11: Tabs & Tables 245
- Tab bar 245
    - Tab bar versus segmented control 246
    - Syntax and requirements 246
    - Notes and glitches 249
- Table view widget 251

Scroll view widget 254

    Scrollable image: Calendar 255

    Scrollable text: Team information.. 255

    Scroll view notes 257

Spinner widget 257

    Image sheet 258

One more thing 260

Summary 260

Chapter resources 261

End-of-chapter exercises 262

Chapter 12: Physics I 265

It's built in 265

A bouncing ball 266

    Types of physics bodies 267

    Bounciness 268

        Playing with the bounce 268

    Other attributes 269

Using images rather than basic shapes 270

Having multiple physics bodies 271

Irregular shapes 272

    Hybrid draw mode 273

    The solution.. 274

        Finding the points 274

        Potentially an easier way 275

Making the ball roll 276

    Friction and sliding 276

    Explore the settings 277

Fun with loops and timers 278
 Using timers in place of loops 279
Game basics: Runtime and enterFrame 280
 The ball drop (stacked_boxes_vs_10_balls) 281
  Additional considerations 281
Game basics: Runtime and Touch 283
 Step-by-step 283
Using both together 285
 Everything moves 286
Summary 286
Chapter resources 287
End-of-chapter exercises 287

Chapter 13: Physics II: Collisions 289

Collisions: Already happening 289
 Adding the listener 290
 The collision event 291
  Information about the collision 291
 Adding the listener to the Runtime object 293
 Comparing the two approaches 294
  Where to Add the Listener 295
Eye on the ball 296
 Making your own sound effects 296
  bfxr 297
 Adding a tint 297
 The result 298
Damaging the lockboxes 299
 The lockbox as a display group 300

    Tinting and untinting the correct lockbox(es) take II 301

    Calculating damages 302

    Adjustable damages 304

Summary 305

Chapter resources 306

End-of-chapter exercises 306

Chapter 14: Physics III: Explosions 309

An exploding iron box 311

Dropping a bomb 313

An iron box that takes proximity damage 316

Applying a blast force 320

    Where to apply the force 322

    Lines of force 323

    Drawn2Code: More of a game 323

    Keeping your eye on the iron box 324

    Alternate approaches 325

A pallet of boxes 326

    Using the blast radius 327

    A landscape app 327

Summary 329

Chapter resources 330

End-of-chapter exercises 331

Appendix A: Android Build & Test 333

Building for Android 334

    Upload the APK file 335

Download & set up the Android Studio 336

Using the Android Emulator 338

    Start your Android device and download the app 338

Real Android devices 341

Appendix B: iOS Build & Test 343

Install Xcode 343

Building for iOS 344

Installing on an iOS device 346

Appendix C: Corona Project Management 349

Beyond main.lua 349

    Constants 350

    Functions 350

Basic UML 353

Extending to the display 354

A more complex example 356

    A buggy encore 356

    UML 358

    Scope & privacy 358

    Analyzing the code 359

    Chapter resources 360

Index 363

Preface

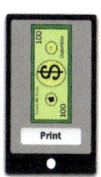
Mobile apps have become tremendously popular over a surprisingly short period of time. Developing these apps has been called the new "Gold Rush" and many people view them as a path to **fame and fortune**. Although they certainly *can* be that, most apps are not huge financial successes. But that doesn't mean that an app you develop can't make a difference, help land an interview or a job, or be loads of fun to make. Of course, it may make money too.

Apps that run on mobile devices such as phones and tablets have become a huge part of the software landscape and there is no sign that this will change any time soon. Some quick statistics: Over 60% of all U.S. mobile phones are now so-called "smart phones" [1] and these devices are kept within arm's reach by over 90% of owners [2]. There are 5X as many mobile devices in use as there are PC's [2]. Mobile internet usage surpassed desktop usage in early January, 2014 [3]. Apple (iOS) app developers earned over $20 billion in 2016 (up 40% from 2015) [5]. According to CNNMoney, "mobile applications developer" is the **best job in America** (ranked #1 out of 100 jobs with the best pay, growing opportunities, and job satisfaction in 2017) [6]. Certainly, your interest in this field is warranted.

My focus in this book is on you, the aspiring mobile app developer. Although some who read this (perhaps many) will have some prior development experience, the material is provided in a sequence and pace that enables **everyone to learn**. This book is not meant to be a reference guide to any particular programming language or framework. Rather, this book introduces you to these while you learn fundamental programming concepts.

Developing mobile apps requires many of the same skills as building desktop apps, although there are a number of key differences:

1. Mobile screens are *smaller* than modern desktop screens.
2. The Mobile UI paradigm is distinct in at least two ways:
    i. Mobile devices are generally touch sensitive and don't use a mouse.
    ii. Instead of desktop icons and pull-down menus, users expect mobile apps to be rich and interactive.
3. Mobile device users are sensitive to the energy that apps drain from their batteries.
4. Many mobile devices offer apps access to unique hardware features such as high-quality cameras, motion, tilt, and acceleration sensors, haptic feedback controllers, GPS and location data, and so on.

So, while you may bring some development experience along with you (or not), there's a lot to learn to master mobile applications.

What should I expect?

If you have no prior experience creating software, trying to explain what it will be like is akin to explaining to your cat how to play Minecraft: You'll annoy the cat and there's a non-zero chance that the cat will be better at it than you (which would be humiliating). Maybe the better analogy is to say that learning to program is like **learning a foreign language**. But, the foreigner you are learning to speak to is *exceptionally* literal, alternates between acting brain-damaged and then brilliant, and occasionally seems to hate you.

While it is certainly possible to **spin code into gold**, realistically, mastering the material in this book may only be a step towards such an ambitious goal. In addition to reading the chapters, doing the end of chapter exercises — even if you aren't reading this book as part of a college course — is tremendously important. You simply can't learn to program without writing programs.

Each app you make is like a small voyage of discovery. Some trips will be short and swift, while others may be long and more difficult. In either case, learning something new, especially something effortful, builds your talent reservoir and expands your possibilities. This journey is possible for anyone reading these words. Expect to become good at mobile development, because with time and practice, you will.

Why Lua and Solar2D?

Picking a language for a new developer **isn't as easy as it might seem**. Initially, given that Java is the top language (overall) and can be used in Android development, that seemed like a safe choice. However, since Java apps won't easily run on iOS devices, that path never seemed optimal given Apple's lead in developer interest and revenue. However, the main alternative to Java would be to focus on Objective C and/or Swift for iOS development. However attractive that may be, that path would require readers to have and use a Macintosh computer, leaving Windows and Android users out in the cold. Moreover, both Java and (especially) Objective C are reasonably difficult to learn, which can be off-putting.

I had a few of **key goals** that I thought were essential for the development platform:
1. It should support both iOS and Android devices and stores.
2. It should support both Mac and PC users for the development platform.
3. It should support the easy creation of rich, interactive, beautiful apps.
4. It should be free.
5. It should have good tools and reference materials.

So, long story short, the Solar2D platform (formerly the "Corona SDK") was **the only one** I found that met all of these requirements. Solar2D is based on the Lua scripting language. Luckily, Solar2D is also awesome and Lua is much easier to learn than the alternatives above. It's a win-win.

Lua and Solar2D: What's the diff?

Lua is a "scripting" language and not a full, general purpose language. That's good, because scripting languages are easier to learn. Solar2D is a "software development kit" (or SDK). But what is an SDK? An SDK is a set of tools and structured software libraries that programmers can use to create apps. Specifically, Solar2D provides developers with high-level graphics and animation libraries, a library of GUI widgets, libraries to interface with the device's capabilities (like touch), and so on, along with tools to build their code into runnable apps. You can access all of this via the Lua scripting language and "Lua-like" syntax to access features of Solar2D.

Although it may sound like a confusing combination of syntaxes, in practice you don't really notice any difference (especially if you are unfamiliar with Lua and/or Solar2D). You will learn basic Lua/Solar2D syntax without the need or requirement to distinguish between them in any way. Working with them will seem natural and, for the most part, easy.

The thing about games

As soon as you start to look at the Solar2D website (Solar2D.com) or the available reference material, you'll see that there is an emphasis on **gaming apps**. Gaming apps have also been huge money makers, so it makes some sense to see them promoted. However, that doesn't mean you can't build non-game apps as well (i.e., apps that aren't primarily designed for entertainment). Nor are such apps any better or worse. It just means that, using Solar2D, you have the *option* to make non-game apps that are rich and interactive. And you can make games too. This book is your introduction to both.

The book's theme

In order to create some unity between the various and many examples, demonstration apps, and end-of-chapter exercises — and just for fun — this book lightly applies the theme of a "magic" or "wizarding" school. If you are a fan of J. K. Rowling's "Harry Potter" books or Ursula K. Le Guin's "Earthsea" series, this will be even more fun. We will use available online graphics, fonts, and sounds to create simple apps based on this theme (note that these extra resources are not distributed with this book, but download links are provided where appropriate). That said, this theme is applied sparingly, so as not to become tiresome.

Can only "ace" coders create a mobile app?

Seriously, no. Reading the chapters closely and working through the end-of-chapter problems are the real key to success. If you are motivated to learn this, that's how you do it. Each chapter will introduce a new set of topics and build within you a new set of capabilities. Incrementally, you will master more and more.

Do you know the kind of high-school or college class in which you could show up intermittently and the material being discussed on any particular day still made sense? Or, if you got behind, you could easily get caught up simply by reading the chapters you've skipped, over a long weekend perhaps?

This would **not** really be that kind of class.

This material builds, one topic upon another. Each step will add to your knowledge and understanding of Lua, Solar2D, and mobile development. You can't easily jump ahead to an advanced topic and you can't quickly catch up several chapters by cramming over a weekend.

You know the kind of course in which you work hard but love it? In which you learn more than you thought you could? In which knocking out exercises is fun? Where you amaze yourself and your friends with what you are able to do?

This would be that kind of course.

Your journey starts in Chapter 1.

References

[1] http://www.entrepreneur.com/article/236832

[2] http://www.forbes.com/sites/cherylsnappconner/2013/11/12/fifty-essential-mobile-marketing-facts/

[3] http://searchenginewatch.com/sew/opinion/2353616/mobile-now-exceeds-pc-the-biggest-shift-since-the-internet-began

[4] http://techcrunch.com/2013/11/26/half-of-all-pcs-shipped-in-2014-will-be-tablets-cost-friendly-androids-65-of-them-apple-30-and-most-profitable/

[5] http://www.apple.com/newsroom/2017/01/app-store-shatters-records-on-new-years-day.html

[6] http://money.cnn.com/pf/best-jobs/2017/list/index.html

NOTES

Download & Setup

Let the downloads commence

You have a few items to download before you can start setting up. You may **already have** some of the software you need, however, let's double-check (see table "Downloads: What, Why, and How"). Most of these items are free; however, some do cost money depending on how you plan to use them. You'll see the terms "SDK" and "IDE" used below:

SDK: A "software development kit" is a set of programs that provides the tools to enable development for a particular platform. Solar2D, Java, and Android all have such development kits. Java calls it the "Java Development Kit" (JDK) while Apple provides the same tool, but calls it "Xcode".

IDE: An "integrated development environment" is a set of tools for entering, testing, and debugging applications on a particular programming language. At a minimum, an IDE provides a simple programmer's editor linked to separate testing and debugging tools for one or more platforms. In the case of Android and Apple, a complete IDE is provided with the download. For Solar2D (and Java, but we aren't programming in Java), you will need to select and download one.

Software	Why Needed	URL's
Solar2D (Free)	This SDK is required to create mobile apps using Solar2D.	https://github.com/coronalabs/corona/releases
Drawn2Code (beta demo bundled with book)	Lightweight IDE designed to support this book. Use code "getbetademo" to open the download.	http://lillipellilabs.com/mobiledev/w/drawn2code/
Chapter Resources	All of the programs and *Drawn2Code* designs from this book (and more!).	http://lillipellilabs.com/mobiledev/download/chapter_resources.zip
ZeroBrane Studio (Pay what you think it is worth).	A nice little IDE which works with Solar2D.	http://studio.zerobrane.com
Fonts: Google Roboto font (Mac/Win), Helvetica Neue (Windows)	Windows and Mac developers wishing to use the default iOS/Android fonts during development may need to download and install one or both.	https://material.io/guidelines/resources/roboto-noto-fonts.html http://www.freefontsdownload.net/free-helveticaneue-font-74318.htm
Apple Xcode (Free)	This is Apple's complete iOS development environment, which we aren't going to use, however, it is required for actual iOS device builds or publishing to the iOS App Store. It also contains the official *iOS Device Simulator* (useful for testing).	https://developer.apple.com/xcode/ (**Mac only**; you may also get this in the Mac App Store)
Android Studio (Free)	This is Google's SDK and IDE for Android development and includes the *Android Emulator* (useful for testing).	http://developer.android.com/sdk/index.html
Java JRE/JDK (Free)	If you get to the point that you want to build an app for an Android device, you need the **full JDK** ("Java development kit").	https://adoptopenjdk.net

Downloads: What, Why, and How

To start, the first three rows are **essential** to get going. If you wish to be able to test your app in the official Android Emulator (i.e., a mobile device simulator), you'll need to download the

Android Studio in addition to the Java JDK. Apple Xcode is a free download, but is Mac only. If you are using Windows, you can still use the Solar2D simulator to test your code, but you can't actually load it on your personal iPhone, test it on the Xcode device simulator, or publish it to the iOS store.

Solar2D is **completely free**, which is a great price. There is a marketplace of free and low cost plug-ins that you can add to your apps (https://solar2dmarketplace.com), but none of these are required in this book. The Solar2D Simulator does require a reasonably up-to-date computer (see the requirements here: https://docs.coronalabs.com/guide/start/systemReqs/index.html).These requirements are probably the most stringent of all of the tools, so if your computer meets them, you should be set to install everything correctly.

Setup

The Java installs only require you to download the installer and run it, so there's not really any setup. The Xcode install is even easier (especially if you get it from the Mac App Store). So, the focus here is on the download and setup of Solar2D, ZeroBrane Studio, and Drawn2Code.

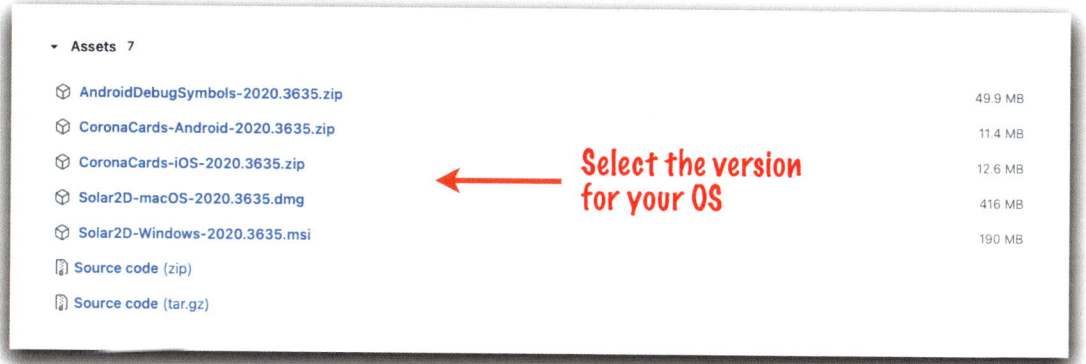

Solar2D Downloads on GitHub

Solar2D

When you click the link above for the Solar2D download, you'll be greeted with a list of available versions, based on the type of computer you use (see screenshot). Select the version that matches your OS and download it. Once downloaded, double-click on the dmg (for the Mac) or msi (for Windows) file in your downloads folder.

The first thing you may notice after opening the download is that it says "Corona Labs" and "install Corona", etc., on screen. Now is a good time to note that Solar2D still uses the "Corona" and "Corona Labs" name and nomenclature in many places. Some documentation is still hosted on the coronalabs.com website. I assume that the naming will be migrated at some point to "Solar2D", but for now, don't let it confuse you. Solar2D can be thought of as the most up-to-date version of Corona and it is okay to refer to it using either name.

Not that Solar2D still uses the Corona name and badge in many places

On the Mac

The Mac download will (by default) place a new "dmg" (disk image) file in your "Downloads" folder. Just open the dmg, agree to the licensing terms, and drag the orange folder to the (alias to) your "Applications" folder (see "Mac install (drag and drop)"). That will copy the Solar2D SDK in place and you are done.

Mac install (drag and drop)

On Windows

The Windows download is an "msi" (Microsoft installer) file, which you should save and then run. You will then need to go through a standard Windows installer wizard (see "Windows install (next, next, next, etc.)"). Once again, you may need to accept the license terms and then select a folder to install it to. The Solar2D simulator may launch after the installation completes (which you can close).

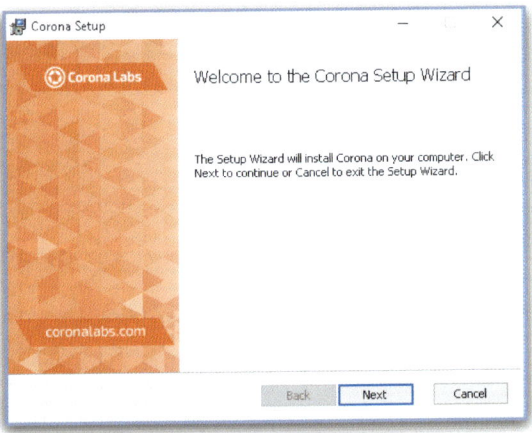

Windows install (next, next, next, etc.)

On either OS you may be prompted to approve the installation, which you'll need to do, obviously, for the installation to take place. There is nothing more to do with Solar2D install. All of our interaction with it will generally be via our IDE (e.g., ZeroBrane Studio, Drawn2Code, or something else).

Next, let's install one or more IDE's.

ZeroBrane Studio (ZBS)

Click the link in the table above to load the website for ZeroBrane Studio. After reading the introductory text, hit the "download" button at the top. You will be taken to a page that gives you the opportunity to pay "what you want" for the software, which is quite generous.

If you wan't to pay nothing (at least when trying it out), click the small "**take me to the download page this time >>**" link. This will take you to the download page, which looks something like the screen shot below. Click to download the IDE for your platform.

ZeroBrane Studio Download Page

Obviously, if you end up using ZBS, you should consider supporting the project to ensure continued development and support.

On the Mac

After download, installation of the Mac version proceeds as with the previous software (see "Mac ZeroBrane Drag-and-Drop"): Double-click to open the dmg file and then drag and drop the app into the applications folder). You may then eject the disk image and open ZBS.

Mac ZeroBrane Drag-and-Drop

On Windows

Windows users have the option of downloading a zip file (which can be unzipped and the contents copied into your programs folder) or a full installer (see "Windows ZeroBrane Installer"). In either case, Windows users need to install ZeroBrane as an administrator.

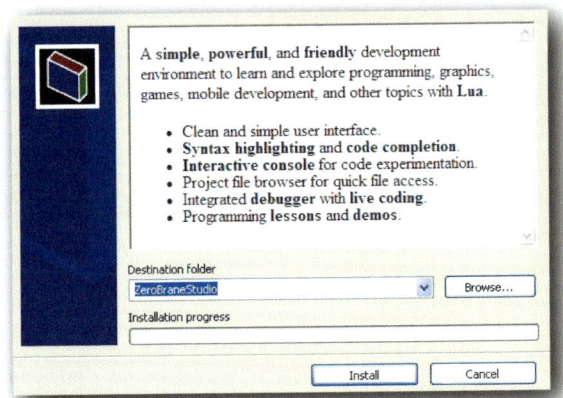

Windows ZeroBrane Installer

Tutorial

Once you start ZeroBrane Studio, there is a short tutorial window open (see screenshots below). If you select "ZeroBrane Studio basics" it will load an introductory tutorial that is pretty quick, encompassing just 10 short screens.

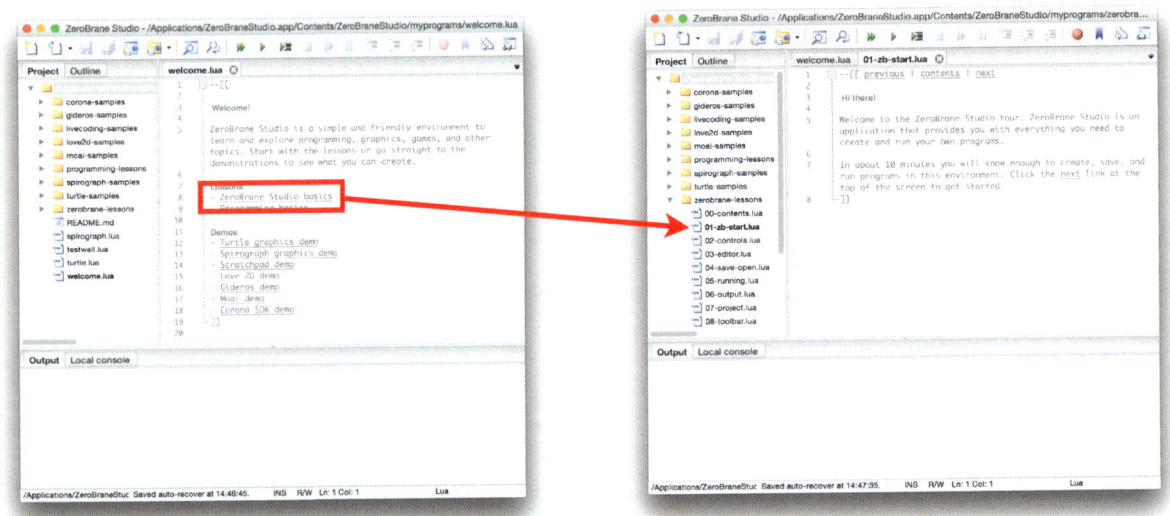

ZeroBrane Studio Tour

There is an additional "getting started" guide online here: http://studio.zerobrane.com/doc-getting-started.html and an introductory screencast here: http://notebook.kulchenko.com/zerobrane/debugging-and-live-coding-with-corona-sdk-applications-and-zerobrane-studio.

Configuration

You need to set the Lua Interpreter to "Corona" so that ZBS will use Solar2D (rather than the default Lua interpreter). To do so, pull down the "Project" menu and select "Lua Interpreter", then choose "Corona". This should only need to be done once.

lillipellilabs.com/mobiledev/w/drawn2code/

Drawn2Code

Click the link above to access the download page. There are separate downloads for Mac or Windows (either an encrypted disk image or zip archive). In either case, you'll need an activation code to access the download. Follow the installation instructions on the download page. Note that *Drawn2Code* is in active development and has glitches and missing features. Keep you eye on the download page for newer versions, but keep you older version on hand as a backup.

Drawn2Code is in active development and may have glitches & omissions

Drawn2Code isn't designed to be a programmer's editor (i.e., like *ZBS*). Instead, it allows you to visually design your app and generates the required code for you. You may save your designs (as ".d2c" files) and reopen them later to work on.

Drawn2Code Toolbar

Configuration

There are just a couple of things to do to set *Drawn2Code* up for use. First, double-check whether you want to make changes to any of the default settings. You may access the settings by hitting the "Settings" button, which has a gear icon.

First up, there are several options that you may select with regard to how *Drawn2Code* handles files. You probably should start with the default settings, but you may adjust them at your discretion.

File Options

By default, *Drawn2Code* will save generated files (including the "main.lua" file) into the project folder when you save your current design. The project folder is wherever you save the *Drawn2Code* design you are working on; in general, each app you design should be in its own design folder. *Drawn2Code* will also copy sounds and image assets to this folder for you as well, which makes organizing and exporting your work easier. You may select to see a confirmation dialog each time you save your design, although this may become tedious. Finally, you may control whether *Drawn2Code* generates the needed "config.lua" and "build.settings" files, and optionally remove older versions of these that may be present in your project folder.

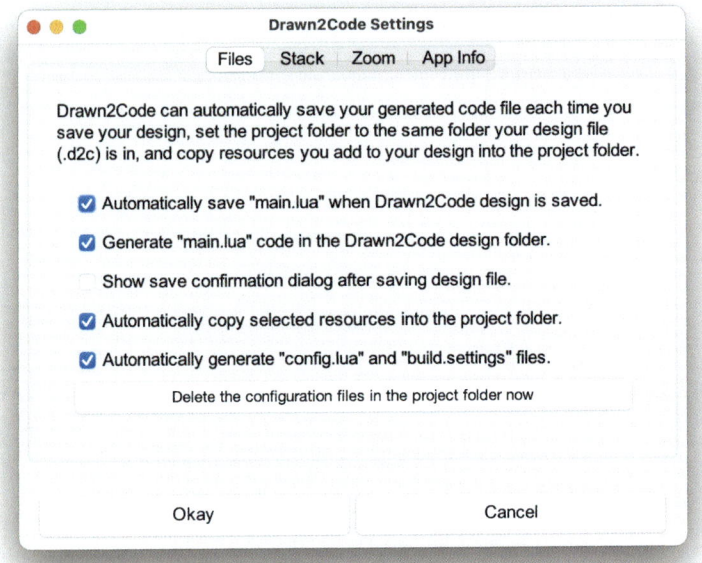

File Options

Stack Options

The stack options are limited, but you may optionally display line numbers in the stack and change the object numbering for new script objects. The line numbers are useful to allow you to easily find the selected script object in the generated code, but that information takes

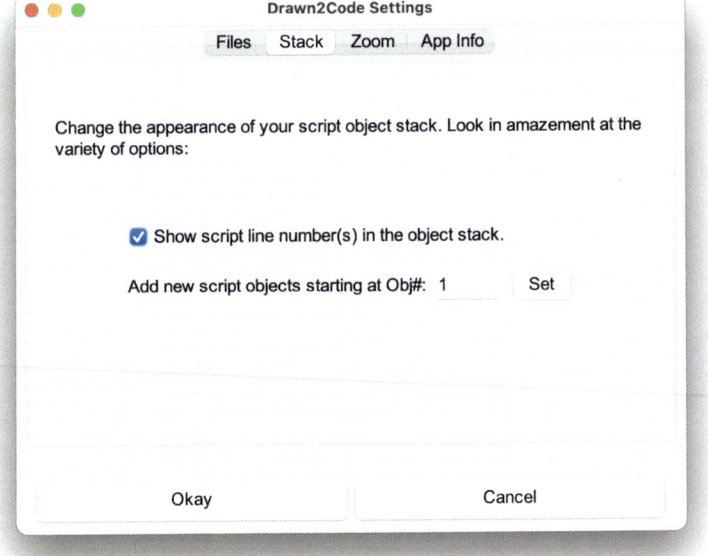

Stack Options

14

up space and might seem to clutter the stack.

Zoom Options

You'll want to determine whether the app fits well on your screen or not. Use these settings to scale the UI to better fit your needs. Note that these settings will be applied the next time you start *Drawn2Code*.

The UI components were originally designed to fit on smaller, lower resolution laptop screens. However, this is really too small for larger, higher resolution screens. So, play around with the zoom and find a setting that works for you. Note that the smallest size is the original (100%) size. It can be scaled up quite a bit to take advantage of more screen real estate.

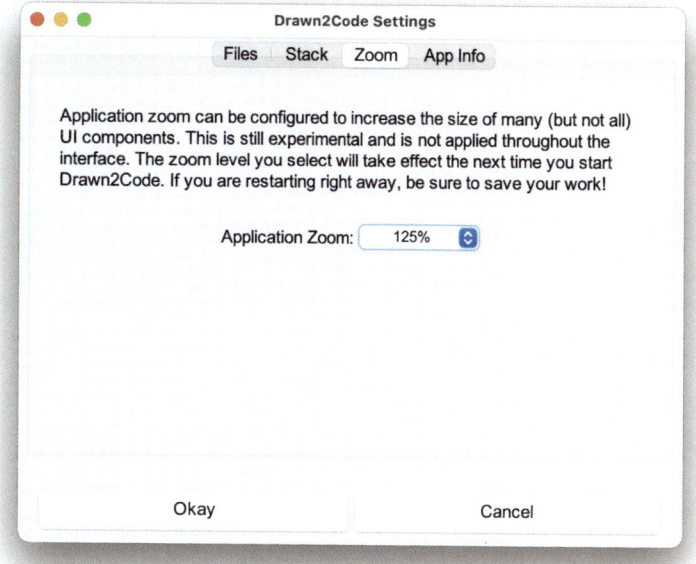

Zoom Options

App Info

Finally, you can check the version of *Drawn2Code* that you have and confirm that it is the latest update be hitting the "App Info" tab. If an update is available, you can be taken to the download page to look at the new features (and fixes) that are available and decide whether to get the new release. You should keep your old copy of *Drawn2Code* as well, in case the new version does something you don't like.

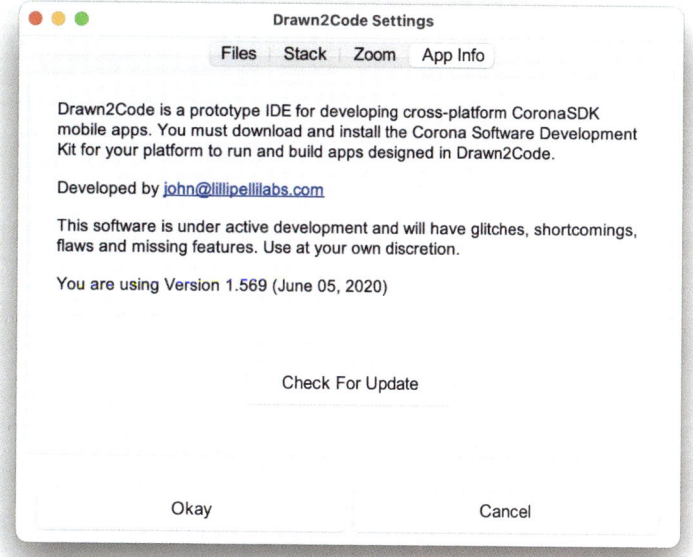

App Info (Update Check)

Windows Only: Finally, if you are using Windows, you'll need to show *Drawn2Code* where to find your Solar2D installation. You can use *Drawn2Code* without Solar2D, but you won't be able to test your app outside of the design window.

This is found in the generated code window. Hit the "Code" button (with the little factory icon) to open that window.

You should see this toolbar at the top of the generated code window (again, this is Windows only):

Link to Solar2D Simulator (Windows Only)

Hit the button that looks kind of like the sun to load a file dialog box. Find the location of the "Corona SDK" folder and select the "Corona Simulator.exe" file. You only have to do this once (the app will remember the location). If you can't find it, look at the footnote on page 18.

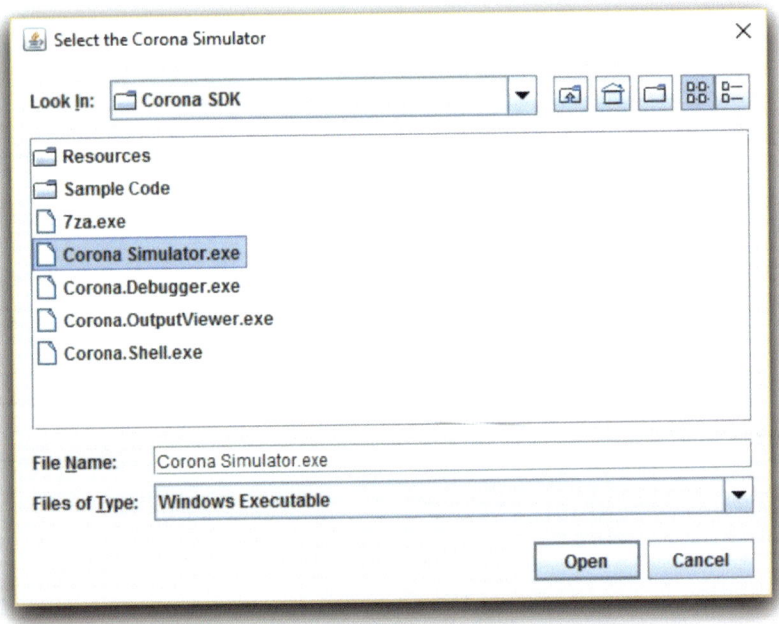

File Selection Dialog

Note that, as of January, 2021, the folder and simulator still use the "Corona" naming, although the simulator will load as the "Solar2D Simulator". If you can't find the "Corona SDK folder, try looking for a "Solar2D" folder! After that set up, the "Run" button will enable.

You are new ready to try your new tools out!

Hello World

Okay, after all of this download and setup, I am sure you are ready to learn how to run a basic "hello world" app. The purpose of this app is mainly to test that you have your IDE and SDK set up correctly. If it works, your app should say "hello world" to you.

Zerobrane Studio (ZBS)

In *ZBS*, create a new empty document using the toolbar ( ), the File menu (i.e., File…New), or the keyboard (ctrl-N or ⌘-N). A new tab named "untitled.lua" will be created into which we can type this code:

```
print("hello world!")
```

Make sure to save your script as "main.lua" in a folder of your choice

Importantly, we do not want the file named "untitled.lua" and, as with all of our apps, it *must* be named "main.lua". So, save the file and select a good place for it and be sure to name it "main.lua".

Before we can successfully run this simple app, you must set the project folder, which tells ZBS where to run the "main.lua" file from. This will be the folder you just saved the "main.lua" file to. The easiest way to set the project folder is to hit the button "set project directory from current file" ( ). This will need to be done **any time** you want to run a new "main.lua" script. Now, you should be ready to run your app. Hit the run button or choose "Project…Run".

After that, the *Solar2D Simulator* should open.*

---

* If you get an error that ZBS can't find Solar2D, you'll need to *rename* the folder Solar2D is installed in to match the location in the error message.

With **some excitement** you may now be looking at a mobile device simulator, which looks just like an actual mobile device, but completely flat. As you stare at it, giddy with anticipation, waiting for "hello world!" to appear, you may begin to wonder why nothing is showing up.

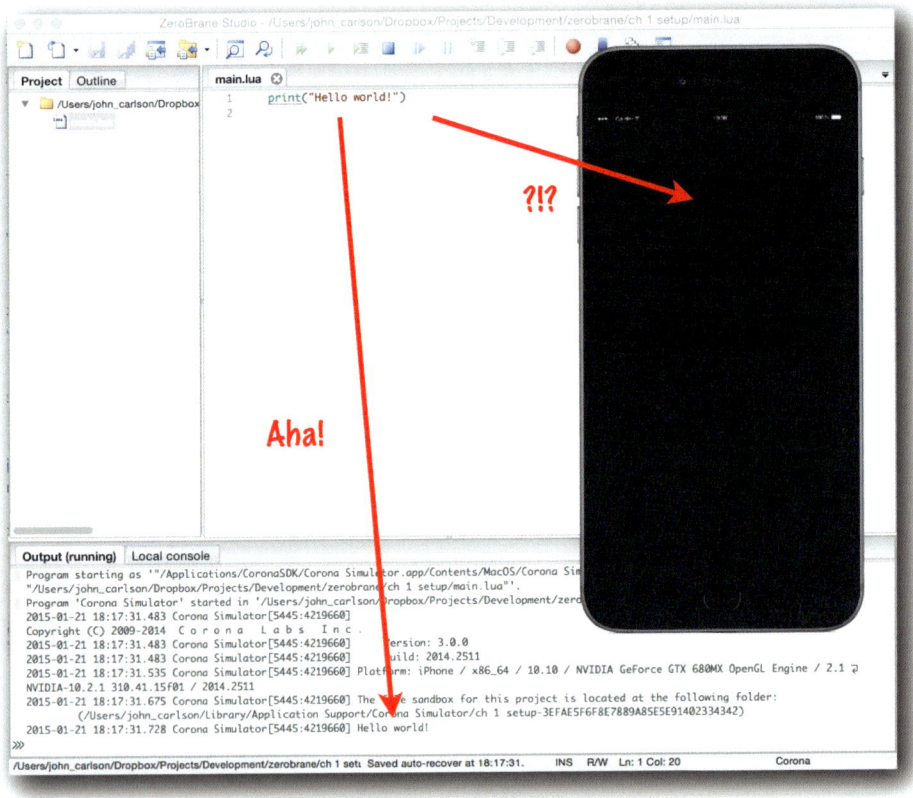

ZeroBrane Studio: Hello World!

Before your excitement turns to despair, look to the IDE console (the text output window at the bottom of the IDE). There, in the console, you should see a well-deserved salutation. Now, crack open a fresh root beer and celebrate.

Drawn2Code

If *Drawn2Code* isn't already running, then start it up. Although *Drawn2Code* is designed mainly to build apps with a GUI, you can also use it to enter and test the basic "hello world" app. To do so, change to the "Snippets" palette (in the "Add Objects" palette on the left) and hit the "New Snippet" button (see "Drawn2Code: Hello World Snippet").

A Beginner's Guide Using Solar2D

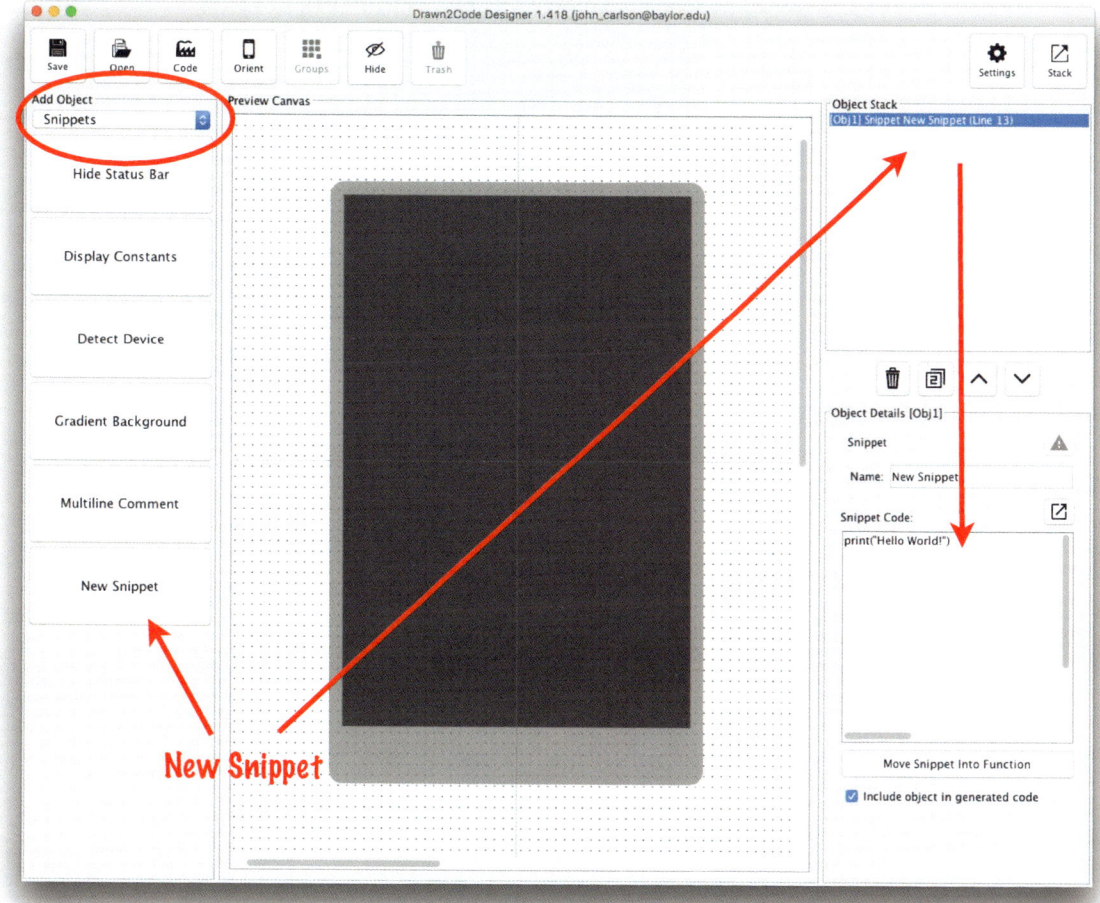

Drawn2Code: Hello World Snippet

You should see a new "script object" (a program element that *Drawn2Code* allows you to control) added to the "Object Stack" on the right (an ordered list of script objects that compose an app). This script object is given the identifier "Obj1". Since it is automatically selected when you create it, the "Object Details" panel at the bottom right contains the elements of the script object that you can manipulate.

Type your "hello world" code into the "Snippet Code" code window in the "Object Details" panel (in the lower right of the app, below the object stack):

```
print( "hello world!" )
```

Save your design and call it "Hello World". This will save a file named "Hello World.d2c" to the folder you select (which is now the "project folder").

19

This design file can be reloaded later to continue working on your masterpiece. You can open a saved designed file in several ways: After launching *Drawn2Code*, use the "Open" button or use the "File Open" menu selection; choose the file from the "Open Recent" list in the File menu; drag-and-drop a .d2c design file onto the Design Canvas (in the center of the app); or double-click a .d2c file in your file browser.

After that, hit the "Code" button in the toolbar (the one that looks like a little factory), which will launch the "Generated Code" window. You should see your "hello world" code as the only statement in your app (the lines above are simply comments). Note that you **can't run your app yet** (the "run" button is disabled).

To launch your app in the *Solar2D Simulator*, you'll **need to save** the generated "main.lua" file. The default location is your design folder (if you've saved your design above) or the documents folder (if you haven't). If you don't want it saved in either of these locations, hit the project folder button first and select where you want this project code to reside.

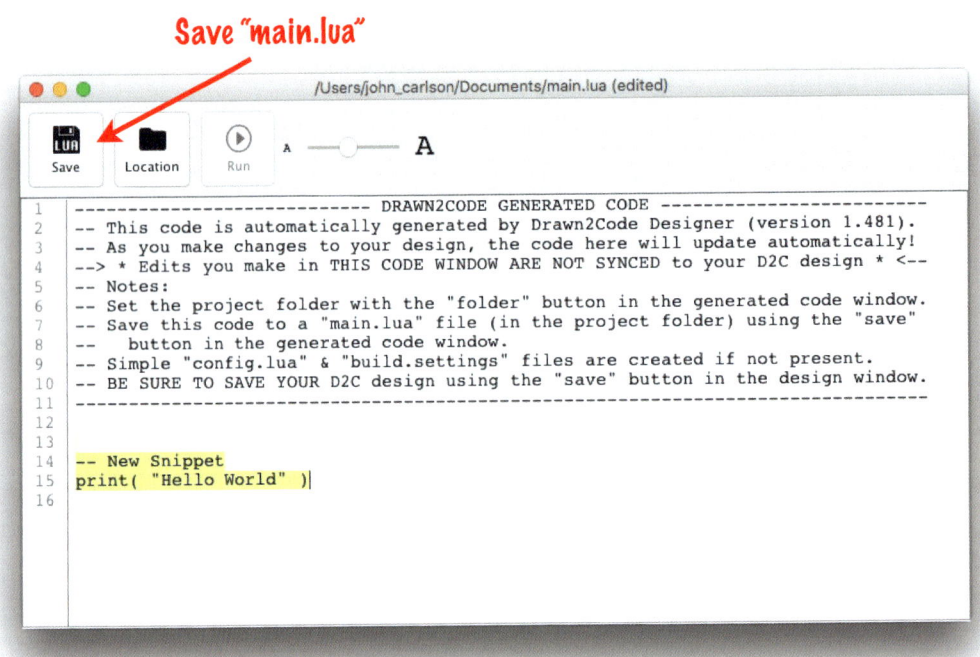

Drawn2Code: Generated Code Window

After saving the generate code, you should see the "Run" button enabled— hit it and the *Solar2D Simulator* (also called the "Corona Simulator") will launch and **run your app**. Once again, you should see an "empty" simulator window. Look at the Solar2D Console to see your salutary text.

Note that, in both of these IDE's (as well as any others), when you make a change to your code and save it, the *Solar2D Simulator* will offer to reload the app for you. In general, you will want it to do this, since it makes testing your code much easier.

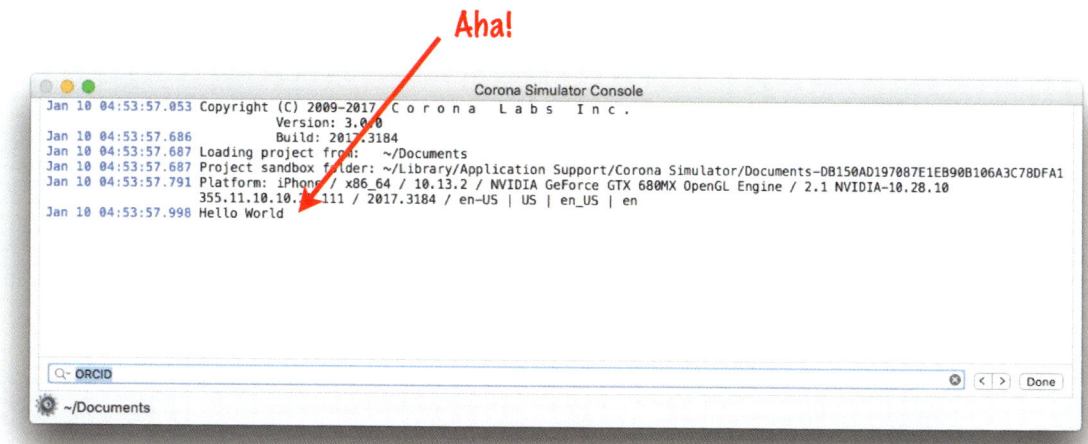

The Solar2D Console

Summary

Creating a mobile app requires the use of a variety of tools, most of which are free. These tools also rely on your "development machine" (i.e., your laptop or desktop computer) meeting certain requirements and being set up correctly. Not all of the tools discussed need to be installed right away. At a minimum, you'll need Solar2D and some sort of editor in which to write your script.

If you want a more sophisticated IDE, such as *ZeroBrane Studio* or *Drawn2Code*, you'll need to download and install that as well. Solar2D offers a plugin marketplace that can be used to enhance your app or ease the development process for certain features. In addition, when you get to a point in the development of your app that you want to test it in the *Xcode Simulator* and/or *Android Emulator*, you'll need to install one or both of those tools.

Solar2D is in the midst of transitioning from the "Corona SDK", so you will see both terms until this process is complete.

End-of-chapter exercises

1. Download and install Solar2D SDK.

2. Download and install *Drawn2Code* and/or ZeroBrane Studio (or another IDE of your choice). Work your way through the welcome and customization steps.

3. In one or both IDE's, enter and run the "Hello World!" app described in this chapter.

4. Describe in your own words what the "print" script statement does.

5. In a new project (folder), create a version of #3 that changes the text ("string") to use your name (i.e., displays your name at the console).

6. Using ZBS, create a new project called "Hello Me". In a new "main.lua" file, enter this line of code (where <<your name>> is *your actual name*):

    ```
    display.newText("Hi <<Your Name>>", display.contentCenterX,
            display.contentCenterY, native.systemFont, 48)
    ```

    Run this in the Solar2D Simulator and see what happens.

7. Using *Drawn2Code*, create a new design and add a text display object (in the "Display Objects" palette) to your app. Customize the text and run it in the *Solar2D Simulator*.

NOTICE

Upon completion of these activities, you are now a programmer (if you were not already)! Henceforth, you should use the term "string" in everyday conversation to refer to text. When someone says something stupid about technology in your presence (including calling a string "text"), you may now snort derisively and mutter "*user!*" in such a way that it clearly rhymes with *loser*. Be prepared also for unexpected cravings, including nacho cheese Doritos, fruit-flavored sodas containing no actual fruit, and anything microwaveable at 7/11.

< MOB DEV

NOTES

NOTES

Introduction

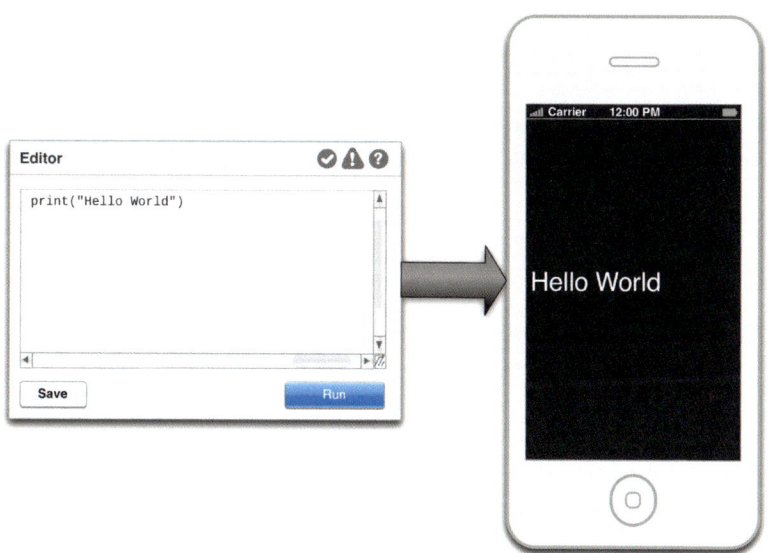

What is "programming"?

Programming is the art and science of telling computers (including any computing device, such as a mobile phone or tablet) what to do. Not like when you scream at Siri for not recognizing what you've said or at autocorrect for making you look dumb. Instead, it is like writing your device a long note, detailing something you'd like it to do for you.

Interestingly, the devices we work with "speak" a variety of languages. Unfortunately, none of them is English. Of course, there are spoken-language interfaces that allow simple commands and queries, but to make anything sophisticated, you need to learn a language that is native to the computer or computer-based device.

We write to the device using one of a number of well-defined "programming" or "scripting" languages. The history behind these is interesting (and actually predates electronic computers), but the modern languages have taken shape based on a variety of theories and beliefs about how to best communicate complex ideas to a computer. As such, each of the programming languages looks a bit different.

For example, the first program you made (after getting all of your tools downloaded and installed) was called "hello world". In fact, in most languages, it is customary to write a "hello world" app as the first program you code. Here's what it looks like in Lua, Java, and Malbolge (en.wikipedia.org/wiki/Malbolge):

Lua
```
print("Hello World")
```

Java
```
public class Hello {
  public static void main (String[] args) {
    System.out.println("Hello World");
  }
}
```

Malbolge
```
('&%:9]!~}|z2Vxwv-,POqponl$Hjig%eB@@>}=<M:9wv6WsU2T|nm-,jcL(I&%$#"
 `CB]V?Tx<uVtT`Rpo3NlF.Jh++FdbCBA@?]!~|4XzyTT43Qsqq(Lnmkj"Fhg${z@>
```

I know you are probably thinking, "Wow, Malbolge looks *interesting*. I wish we could study it instead of Lua." Alas, there are no Malbolge textbooks as yet, nor does the potential market for such books make economic sense. Why do the languages look so different? Well, Lua is a scripting language designed to be "easy to learn". Java is a general-purpose language that is "object oriented" to the core, so that even a simple "hello world" app has to be OO. Malbolge is, well, *evil*.

Moreover, saying that Lua is "easy to learn" doesn't mean that it is *actually* easy to learn. That's why it's in quotes. It is as difficult as learning any new language and much of the difficulty, as is often the case, lies with knowing *what you want to say* rather than *how* to say it.

The purpose of this chapter is to provide a basic introduction to programming concepts and terminology. We will return to each of these topics in detail in future chapters.

Programs

A computer program consists of the commands (or "statements") for the computer to execute along with any necessary resources required (such as sound files, graphic and icon files, database tables, XML files, and so on). Programs may be written in one of the languages mentioned (or of the hundred others), or even be a mix of languages. Statements are typically entered in a text file, which is later either compiled or interpreted to actually run.

In concept, programs are something like **recipes**. A typical recipe will tell you everything you need to do to create a meal of some sort. That includes a description of the meal, the ingredients, and the procedure you need to take (in the order you need to take them) to get the correct meal output (see recipe example for, well, let's call it "root beer").

Looking over this recipe (or any recipe) we can see it breaks into three components:

1. Input (the ingredients)
2. Process (the procedure)
3. Output (the result)

This can be depicted visually as a simple **systems diagram** (below). The "inputs" are the ingredients. They must be given a *name* and an *initial value* (or amount). The "process" is the step-by-step instructions that tell the cook what to do with the ingredients. The steps must be specified in the *correct sequence* (as taking actions out of order may spoil the result). The "output" is, one hopes, the desired meal (or drink).

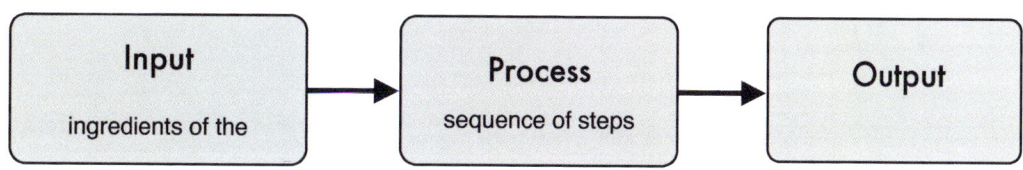

Basic Systems Model

Programs are much the same. Let's look at these three elements in turn using this recipe as a context.

Input

So, how do we "feed" the computer information? The "input" can include various types of data, such as <u>numbers</u>, <u>text</u> (we call it "string" data in programming), <u>boolean</u> values (true/false), and data that has been structured in some way (like a list or <u>table</u>). Lua supports each of the underlined types.

In addition, data of these types may be stored in **named variables**. A variable is simply a named storage location for data values you need to work with. These can be numbers, text, booleans, or tables. The name stays the same, but the value stored can change as needed in your program.

Variable naming rules

Variables may be named (or "identified") using letters, numbers, and the underscore ("_") character, however, they **must start with a letter or an underscore** and may not contain any spaces. Lua variables are also **case-sensitive**, so "nameOfHop" is different from "NameOfHop". Finally, you may not use any words reserved by Lua or Solar2D (such as `local` or `function`).

Note also that, in general, all entities in your app have **unique identifiers** (names). Having two variables with the same name in the same chunk of code won't work.

So, in our recipe program, we will want to store the data in variables for use later (in processing). Here are three examples to get you started (DME is "dry malt extract", a common ingredient in "root beer"):

```
poundsOfDME = 9
nameOfHop = "Cascade"
bottleCondition = true
```

These three lines create three variables and assign to them a number, a string, and a boolean. The *syntax* (structure and rules that define a valid expression or statement in a programming language; en.wikipedia.org/wiki/Syntax_(programming_languages)) of assignment is pretty simple:

```
[variable name] = [literal, variable, or valid expression]
```

You might have also noticed that the "assignment operator" (the symbol or symbols used to tell Lua we are putting a value in a variable) is the single equals sign ("="). In the three examples above, we created three variables and assigned literal (actual) values to them. We could have assigned a variable to store instead, e.g.,:

```
addPrimingSugar = bottleCondition
```

or assigned the result of an expression to the variable. For example, if we wished to double the amount of an ingredient, we could use a simple expression to do that:

```
poundsOfDME = 2*poundsOfDME
```

More examples of expressions can be found later in this chapter.

The **difference** between literals and variables is this: literals *are* values while variables *store* values.

> **Variables store literal values such as "Hi" or 4.0**

In all of these examples, note that we didn't need to do anything special to "set up" any of these variables. We **just use them**. Lua is very flexible in allowing you to mix data of different types. No special declaration or initialization is necessary.

You may have noticed that I haven't provided an example of a Lua table. Tables are a bit more complex than the first three examples, but not completely inscrutable. Here's an example:

```
hopsTable = {["cascade"] = 2, ["chinook"] = 4}
```

We'll cover tables in more detail in Chapter 7. But, briefly, this table is storing 2 "key-value" pairs, each pair separated by a comma (which, in this case, means 1 comma). The keys, in this table, are 2 strings which happen to be names of hops. The values represent the ounces of each hop, based on the recipe above. This "style" of table is sometimes called a *dictionary*.

To get data out of a table, we use the name of the table and the key (the first item in the key-value pair) we want to access:

```
firstHopOunces = hopsTable["cascade"]
print(firstHopOunces)
```

If we run this 3-statement sequence, we will see "2" at the console (without the quotes).

Interestingly, the key can be any type of data, **except for `nil`**, and you can **mix keys of different types** in the *same* table. Nil, the final data type we are covering here, is equivalent to "null" in Java and means "nothing". A `nil` variable is empty (no value has been assigned to it).

Process

> All of the variable declarations above are simple statements.

In processing, we tell the computer **what to do** with the various inputs and **what order** these steps are to be taken in. In most cases, just as with recipes, the steps are executed in a defined order, typically read from **top to bottom**. The most basic step in a process is a "statement" (which can be described as an expression which constitutes a valid line of code), which tells the computer to do one thing. Processing, then, is accomplished by **executing a series of statements.**

Here's an example of a statement involving a bit of math:

```
poundsOfDME = 7*lightDME + 2*amberDME
```

Let's "zoom in" on this statement to break it down into the *key language elements* we've been discussing (we'll cover the operators "=" and "*" in the following section):

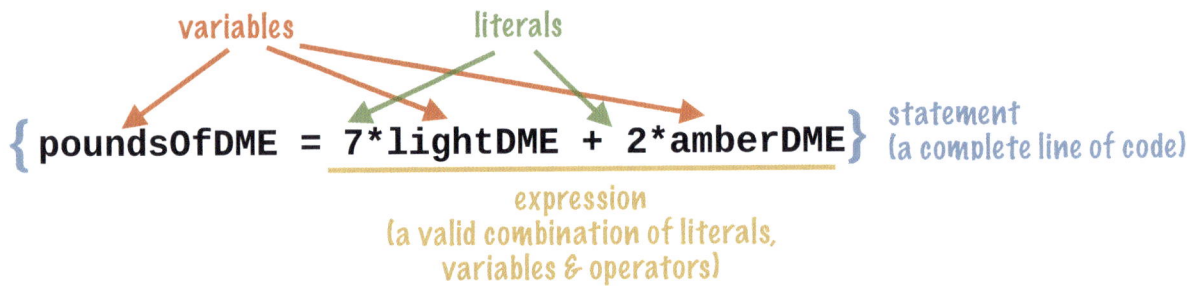

You can see that this statement uses 3 variables, 2 literals, 2 distinct arithmetic operators, and the assignment operator. The right-hand side of the statement (the expression) is evaluated first. The values stored in the variables are looked up and the math is performed to find a result. Finally, the result is assigned into the variable `poundsOfDME` and the computer moves on to the next statement.

In addition to performing <u>mathematic</u> operations on input, statements also include manipulating <u>text</u> characteristics of input, and testing input (using <u>boolean logic</u>) and controlling the flow of execution (i.e., where, whether, when, and in what sequence steps are executed). Let's look at a quick example of each of these in Lua.

Operator	Description
+	Addition
-	Subtraction or negation
/	Division
*	Multiplication
^	Exponentiation

Arithmetic Operators

Math

Lua understands the same basic operations that your calculator or spreadsheet does. The table "Arithmetic Operators" provides a short list of arithmetic operators Lua understands. And, of course, Lua follows the correct order of operations (exponentiation, then multiplication/division, then addition/subtraction). You can override this order using parenthesis if you need to. Some examples:

```
totalDME = 7 + 2
daysOfConditioning = monthsOfConditioning * 30.42
```

I can't think of any good reason to do this from the standpoint of the recipe, but I need an example for exponentiation:

```
amountOfDMESquared = totalDME^2
```

A note on spaces: spaces in simple expressions like these are typically ignored, so the first example above is equivalent to:

```
totalDME=7+2
```

or,

```
totalDME=  7        +2
```

and so on.

However, you still **may not** have spaces *in* the variable name; so, this line of code:

```
total DME= 7 + 2
```

is **not valid**. Likewise, spaces you add to strings will become part of the string (e.g., "Wizard" and "Wiza rd" are different strings).

With practice (and the excellent instruction provided here), you'll learn to write valid expressions that you find easy to read and understand.

Operator	Description
..	Concatenation

String Operator

Strings (text)

We will learn to do quite a bit with text as our skills develop, however, one easy thing to learn is string **concatenation** (putting two pieces of text together). This is done by connecting the text (variables or literal values) with two periods: "..".
For example:

```
ourSDK = "Solar".."2D"
print(ourSDK)
```

or, using variables (and inserting a comma in the middle),

```
hop1 = "Cascade"
hop2 = "Chinook"
hopList = hop1..", "..hop2
print(hopList)
```

If you ran these two sequences, you would see "Solar2D" and "Cascade, Chinook" (without the quotes) at the Lua console.

Boolean logic

You will often find yourself needing to know something about a variable, such as whether it has reached some predetermined value, is below some acceptable value, or is above some threshold or maximum value. These all require the use of logic which, in programming, we call "Boolean" logic after the inventor of this type of work (en.wikipedia.org/wiki/

George Boole). If you are familiar with writing tests and comparisons in a spreadsheet, this is very much the same. The Boolean operators are displayed in the table "Boolean Operators".

Operator	Description
==	is equal to
~=	is not equal to
>=	is greater than or equal to
<=	is less than or equal to
>	is greater than
<	is less than
and	logical AND
or	logical OR
not	logical negation

Boolean Operators

The result of any Boolean comparison (or "condition") is the Boolean value `true` or `false`. For example, if we had a timer (call it `boilTimer`) set up to keep track of how long we were boiling the ingredients (in step 6 of our recipe) and wanted to figure out if it was time to turn the stove off, the syntax might look like this:

```
timerDone = boilTimer >= 90
```

If the timer was currently at 60, then the expression would be evaluated this way:

```
timerDone = 60 >= 90
```

and finally,

```
timerDone = false
```

That is, the Boolean comparison `60 >= 90` is made and, since `60` is not greater than or equal to `90`, the result of `false` is assigned to the variable `timerDone` (i.e., it is not time to turn the stove off).

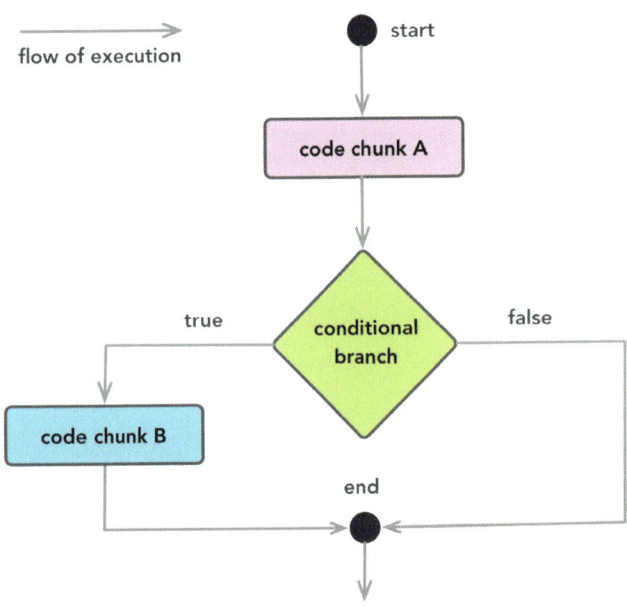

Using Boolean Logic to Branch

Branching

This sequence of statements that a program executes is called the **flow of execution**. In simple programs, the flow of execution is a simple path (from top-to-bottom), however, in more complex programs the flow may be branched into alternate paths, looped to repeat a particular path, or jumped to a particular place in the code (i.e., with a function).

Boolean logic is usually employed to **control the flow** of your application — to branch the flow of execution so that the correct code executes dependent on the exact circumstances present or to repeat a segment of code to achieve a desired result.

For example,[1]

```
timerDone = boilTimer >= 90

if timerDone == true then
        -- code runs only when timer is done:
    shutOffStove = true
end
```

---

[1] Or, more simply: if timerDone then

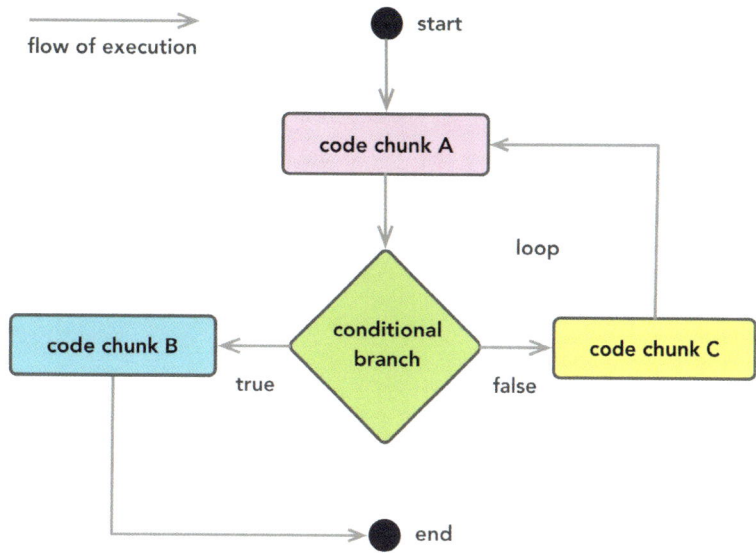

Using Boolean Logic to Branch and Loop

We will delve into the exact syntax and options of 'if' statements in a later topic, but this simple example should be easy to understand. The Boolean condition is evaluated and, if it is `true`, then the code after `then` and before `end` is executed. If the expression is `false`, then the code is skipped. This decision point creates a **branch** in the code (in one branch, the variable `shutOffStove` is modified, in the other branch it isn't).

Referring to the figure above, code chunk A is the statement setting the boolean value of `timerDone` (`timerDone = boilTimer >= 90`), and the "conditional branch" is the test of `timerDone == true`. The line of code inside the if-then statement (i.e., code chunk B) is `shutOffStove = true`.

Looping

The other way we control flow is when we need to **repeat** a section of code (sometimes called a "chunk" or "block" of code) more than once. Although there are a few ways to do this, a while-loop is quite like a repeated if-statement:

```
while not timerDone do
    -- keep stirring the pot:
    stirThePot()
    timerDone = boilTimer >= 90
end
```

So, again referring the the figure above, the repeated chunk of code (code chunk C) is a call to the function `stirThePot()`. Presumably, this function will run a motor that stirs the boiling pot. Now, while that is a valid loop, it would run as fast as the microprocessor could handle. It would constantly check `boilTimer`, as fast as possible, which is not really necessary in this context. Checking every minute or so would make more sense.

Functions

Finally, a good deal of processing is done by **functions**. In other languages these are called methods, procedures, routines, subroutines, and perhaps several other identifiers. You will frequently use functions that are **built-into Lua and/or Solar2D**. For example, the `print()` statement we have used a few times is a Lua function. When we call a function, the **flow of execution** jumps to the code inside the function (which may be defined elsewhere in the code, even in a different source code file).

Functions give the programmer the ability to easily bundle sequences of code that they expect to reuse. Later, when the programmer needs to use the code, it may be recalled (or "called") by simply giving the name of the function. The syntax for creating your own function is pretty straightforward. For example, a function that added together the amounts of the different types of hops in our recipe might look like this:

```
function addAllHops(h1oz, h2oz)
    total = h1oz + h2oz
    return total
end
```

Calling a function of your own design is no different from calling a built-in function. You need to know the name of the function (which should be easy, since you named it) and any data you need to pass to it (again, this should be easy). The `addAllHops()` function requires two pieces of data (the ounces of each of the two hops in the recipe). You might use this in your code something like this:

```
totalHops = addAllHops(5,3)
print(totalHops) -- will display 8 at the console
```

or, using the table created above:

```
totalHops = addAllHops(hopsTable["cascade"], hopsTable["chinook"])
print(totalHops) -- 6
```

A more useful version

You may be looking at this sample function and thinking: "Why don't we just pass the hopsTable *itself*, rather than individual values?". That's a really good thought. That way you could have **any number of hops**, not just two (or, any number of whatever you wanted to do some math on).

The addAllHops() function could be made much more useful with only a slight increase in complexity by passing a table of numbers to it, rather than just two numbers. To do this, you need to revise the syntax as follows:

```
function addAllHops(t)
      total = 0
      for k,v in pairs(t) do
        total = total + v
      end
      return total
end
```

Okay, that might seem more than a "slight" increase. In this version, we pass a single parameter (a table), then use a 'for' loop to go through the table item by item, adding the values together (we'll cover using loops in detail in Chapter 6). Using the table would look like this:

```
totalHops = addAllHops(hopsTable)
print(totalHops) -- also 6
```

This will display 6 at the console as well. Note that this function isn't perfect. For example, it doesn't deal with the possibility that the user sends it data that isn't in a table. We will cover the ins and outs of functions in Chapter 7.

Output

The output of our recipe will be a refreshing and well-deserved root beer. A program's output can take a variety of forms, however, it will rarely involve food. In these examples today, we have simply written results out to the Lua console (or, really, we've pretended to do that, since we haven't set our development environment up yet). However, output could also be directed to the screen, speakers, buzzer/vibrator (or another haptic module), a social network, a file or database, a printer, or any other computer-controlled device.

Solar2D

If Lua provides the underlying programming syntax for input, processing, output, expressions and statements, how does Solar2D fit in?

Although you can write complete programs in Lua, however, they are **strictly console based**. To access device features (like the screen), you need a library of tools designed to do that, which is where Solar2D fits in, adding features necessary to create mobile apps.

You can view this as a pyramid of sorts, with Lua as the foundational language and Solar2D as a framework which rests on top of Lua. Solar2D relies on Lua for basic scripting functionality, but adds powerful features to support mobile app development. Finally, the mobile app that you've created rests on the combined foundation provided by Lua and Solar2D, enabling you to make wonderful things.

Mobile App

Solar2D
touch features
multimedia capabilities
animation effects
access to hardware features
file/database I/O
Social networking support
Widgets
...

Lua
variables (*numbers, strings, and booleans*)
data structure (*table*)
boolean expressions (*to branch or loop the flow of execution*)
arithmetic expressions (*calculations*)
functions (*modularization*)
library tables (e.g., math constants and built-in functions)

Foundation of Your Mobile App *

The development process

One does not simply sit down at their computer and write a complex program any more than one would pick up a camera and begin shooting a feature film. It takes planning. Sometimes months or even years of planning and preparation, during which the goals of the project are defined, the needs of the users are divined, and the design of the program refined.

---

*Underneath Lua? It's turtles all the way down.

There are many different ways to *think about* the development process, but perhaps the most enduring is called the "waterfall" model, which breaks development into a sequence of stages, each to be completed before moving to the next. It can be arranged visually to look something like water flowing down a series of steps (hence the name).

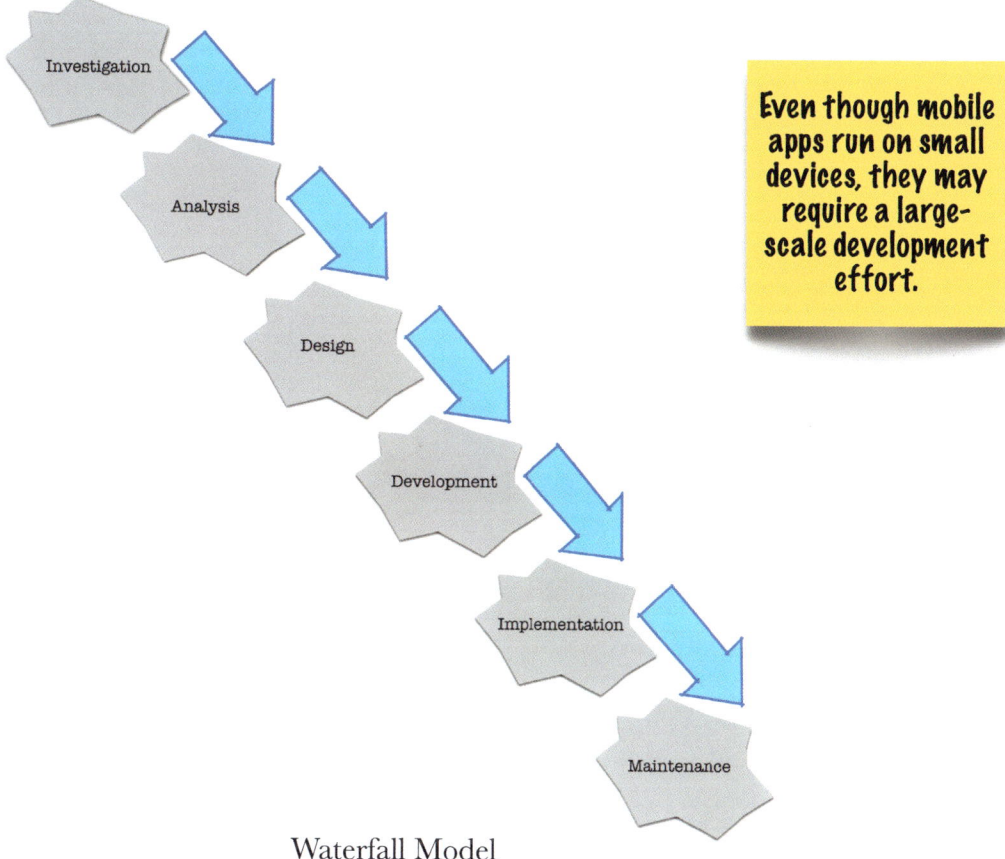

Even though mobile apps run on small devices, they may require a large-scale development effort.

Waterfall Model

Our focus here is on *system development*, but you should understand that development takes place as part of a larger process, and the success of any project will hinge on the work done across all of the stages.

Code that isn't input, process, or output

There is actually **crucial code** that doesn't perform an input, process, or output task: **Documentation**. Documentation encompasses several practices, but **commenting your code** is the first step. You are allowed to place text in your source code which isn't executed, but instead describes your code in a helpful manner.

Basic comments can be placed anywhere by preceding the text with two hyphens (as with AppleScript):

```
-- this is a Lua comment
print("hi") -- so is this
```

Other commenting styles will be introduced later in this book. It is considered good practice to comment your code as you go. It doesn't have to be elaborate, but it should be sufficient to allow a teammate to pick up the code and make sense of it quickly. It can also help you remember code you wrote weeks, months, or years ago.

Key programming skills

Among the skills you will develop as you learn to program, three of the most important will be understanding and controlling the **flow of execution**, **decomposing** complex tasks into sequences of statements, and **modularizing** code into reusable chunks such as functions.

Understanding and controlling the flow of execution is something you'll learn in several chapters of this book, but it starts with knowing that your script statements are processed by the computer starting at the top of your code and moving down, one statement at a time. We can control the flow more directly using logic and repetition (Chapters 5 and 6).

Ultimately, programming is more about *thinking* than *syntax*. Decomposition is the process of breaking a task into the detailed steps that need to be carried out to accomplish the task. We can't simply tell the computer to "make root beer". It doesn't know how to do that. You (the programmer) have to break it down into discrete, ordered steps that the computer can understand. This is a skill that you'll develop throughout this book.

Finally, modularization involves finding ways to break code into smaller sequences that can be worked on, at least to some extent, separately. Functions are one way to modularize your code and are covered in Chapter 7.

Summary

In this chapter you've seen the basic concepts that enable computer programming along with syntax examples in the Lua scripting language. You will see each of the basic concepts again as you work your way through this book and have the opportunity to see them in action (via code examples) and put them to use (via end-of-chapter exercises).

End-of-chapter exercises

1. What Lua statement would display (print) <u>your name</u> at the console?

    a) Statement: _____

    b) Enter this statement (e.g., as a new "code snippet") and test it!

2. What script statements would display (print) your <u>first name</u> then your <u>last name</u> at the console?

    a) First name: _____

    b) Last name: _____

    c) Enter these statements in a new script and test it in either ZBS or *Drawn2Code*!

    d) Swap the order of these lines and re-test the script. What effect does the order have?

3. Put the following line of code (e.g., as a new "code snippet") in a new script:

    ```
    monthsOfConditioning = 2
    daysOfConditioning = monthsOfConditioning * 30.42
    ```

    a) Identify the *key language elements* (the statements, expression, assignments, literals, variables, and operators) as comments.

    b) What statement would display (print) the result (e.g., the value in `daysOfConditioning`) in the console?

    _____

c) Add (b) to your script and test it in either ZBS or *Drawn2Code*!

4. Using 2 lines of code, write the statements that would store <u>your name</u> in a variable called `myName`, then use this variable to display `"hi "` concatenated with <u>your name</u> at the console.

    a) Variable `myName`: _____

    b) Display greeting: _____

    c) Enter these 2 statements in a new script and test it in either ZBS or *Drawn2Code*!

5. Starting with `hop1` and `hop2` as defined in this chapter, create a third variable named "hop3" and set it equal to "Amarillo". Extend this statement:

    `hopList = hop1..", "..hop2`

    to add `hop3` to the comma-separated list and display (print) the result in the console.

6. Which of the following proposed variable names (identifiers) are valid in Lua?

Proposed Name	Valid?
firstPayment	
lastPayment	
2ndPayment	
_total21	
hops[]	
t	
local_t	
customerName$	
while	
avgDaysInMonth	
total daysInYear	

7. What is the difference between "=" and "=="? Give an example and add a comment to each statement.

_____

_____

_____

_____

8. Determine where each of the following capabilities comes from: in Lua itself or in Solar2D:

Capability	Lua	Solar2D
Math (Calculations)		
Named Variables		
Text Field (Widget)		
Sound Effects		
Table (Data Structure)		
String (Text) Processing		
Game Physics		
Console Read/Write		
Animation		
Boolean Operations		
Drawing Elements (On Device Screen)		
Posting on Facebook		
Modularizing Code in Functions		

NOTES

The Screen & Intro to Text

Devices and their many shapes and sizes

The various mobile devices you might target for your app all generally have at least one thing in common: a **rectangular screen** which is a certain number of **pixels** wide and tall. However, the similarity ends there. Devices by different manufacturers may use different screen technologies, physical sizes (i.e., inches across diagonally), and screens of differing pixel resolution. The pixel resolution (mainly the pixel width and height of the display) most significantly impacts mobile programming.

Mobile apps also must **typically run full screen** and also be aware of the device's portrait/landscape **orientation**. This isn't often the case with desktop apps, where you can code your app to look great at, say 800x600, and allow users to move your app window around their desktop. If you don't want users to be able to resize your desktop app, you can just disable that feature. Lots of desktop apps are restricted this way, and users see it as completely normal. And if the user tips his/her monitor on its *side*? Well, that would just be odd.

Device	OS	Screen Dimension (Portrait)	Scale	Screen Size (Inches)
iPhones up to 3gs	iOS	320x480	1x	3.5"
iPhone 4/4s	iOS	640x960	2x	3.5"
iPhone 5/5s/5c	iOS	640x1136	2x	4"
iPhone 6/6s/7/8	iOS	750x1334	2.34x	4.7"
iPhone 6/6s/7/8 Plus	iOS	1080x1920	3.375x	5.5"
iPhone X/XS/11 Pro	iOS	1125x2436	2.17x	5.8"
iPhone XR/11	iOS	828x1792	2.16x	6.1"
iPhone 12/12 Pro	iOS	1170x2532	2.16x	6.1"
iPhone XS Max/11 Pro Max	iOS	1242x2688	2.16x	6.5"
iPad up to 2	iOS	768x1024	2.4x	9.7"
iPad 3/Retina/Air/Air 2	iOS	1536x2048	4x	9.7"
iPad mini	iOS	768x1024	2.4x	7.9"
iPad mini 2/3	iOS	1536x2048	4x	7.9"
iPad Air	iOS	1536x2048	4x	9.7"
iPad Pro	iOS	2732x2048	1.33x	12.9"
Google Nexus 1	Android	480x800	1.5x	3.7"
Google Nexus 4	Android	768x1280	2.4x+	4.7"
Motorola (Google) Droid	Android	540x960	1.7x	4.3"
ASUS Transformer/Prime	Android	800x1280	2.5x	10.1"
HTC (various)	Android	540x960	1.7x	4.3"
Samsung Galaxy S III	Android	720x1280	2.5x	4.8"
Samsung Galaxy S 5	Android	1080x1920	3.4x	5.1"
Samsung Galaxy Tab 1/2/3	Android	800x1280	2.5x	10.1"
Samsung Galaxy Tab S	Android	1600x2560	5x	10.5"
Amazon Kindle Fire 7"	Android	600x1024	1.88x	7"
Amazon Kindle File 8.9"	Android	1200x1920	1.6	8.9"

Table of Selected Device Screen Resolutions

This isn't the case with mobile apps, which are expected to fill the entire screen. Even worse, **the definition of how many pixels constitute full screen differs based on the device** (see "Table of Selected Device Screen Resolutions"). Moreover, not only do the screen resolutions change, but the **aspect ratio** of the devices vary quite a bit (from 16:9 on the iPhone 5 to 4:3 on the iPads, and 3:2 on older iPhones, for example).

You might have also noticed that the screen resolutions are often multiples of older resolutions. For example, the early iPhones were 320x480, while the iPhone 4/4S exactly doubled that, to 640x960. The iPad 1/2/mini have screens of 768x1024, while the iPad 3+ also exactly doubled that to 1536x2048. This scaling will make it somewhat easier for us to code apps, at least for iOS, that run on multiple devices.

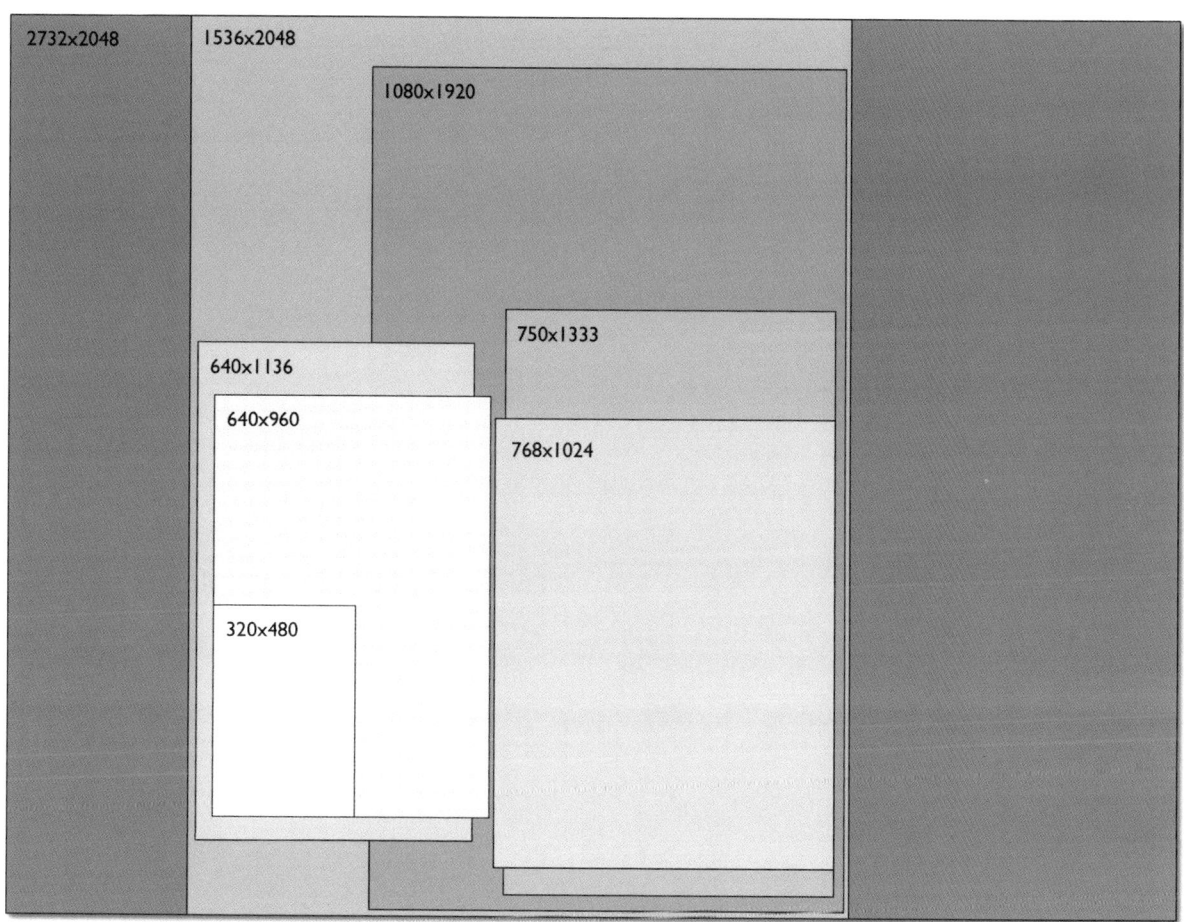

Comparative Screen Resolutions

Visually, these various resolutions span quite a range (see "Comparing Screen Resolutions"), however, since devices may use different pixel densities, these don't correlate to physical sizes. However, these **differences still matter**. Imagine designing a logo for your app and making it 200x200 pixels. It would look great on smaller resolution devices, but on larger resolution devices it would either be physically small or scaled up and blurry.

The Solar2D Simulator

An essential part of Solar2D is the **Solar2D Simulator**, which runs your code and displays it in a window which *simulates* a mobile device (hence, the name). The simulator currently supports 21 device options, including: iPhone 4s/5/6/6 Plus/X, iPad, iPad Air/Mini/Pro, Apple TV, HTC Sensation, Samsung Galaxy S3/S5, Kindle Fire HD 7"/9", Amazon Fire TV 720/1080, Ouya 720/1080 (see "Simulator Devices", below).

You entered and ran a really basic "hello world!" app in the previous chapter — and it was fun — but it didn't actually put the words on the device simulator. It just spit them out at the *console*. So, although it still counts, it doesn't count very high. Let's use the Solar2D Simulator instead.

Hello World 2

Hello World 2

Create a new project folder in your IDE and in an empty "main.lua" script file, add this code*:

```
display.newText("Hello World!", 150, 150,
    ➡ native.systemFont, 24)
```

After you run the app, you should see the Solar2D Simulator launch and display "Hello World!" on a simulated device screen (see the "Hello World 2" screenshot. This works by using a feature in Solar2D (i.e., something not available in a "plain" Lua install): The `display` table (docs.coronalabs.com/api/library/display/).

---

* Note that the "➡" symbol indicates that the statement continues here (i.e., this line is still part of a single instruction).

The `display` table has a number of functions in it, including functions to perform basic drawing (including text and various shapes). Each drawn component is created syntactically by calling a function inside the table with a period ("dot"), such as ".newText()". The basic syntax for the `newText()` function is:

```
DISPLAY NEWTEXT SYNTAX

display.newText(string, x, y, font, fontSize)
```

Using this syntax will create a Solar2D "display object" (docs.coronalabs.com/api/library/display/newText.html) and render it on the device screen with the settings you specify for the string, location, and font.

However, the object created above doesn't have a *name* (it is an "anonymous" object) and therefore would not be addressable later in your code. This means that if you wanted to edit or move this text, say, later in the program, you would have no way to do so.

The solution is simply to call the `newText()` function and assign the resulting display object to a variable:

```
myTxt = display.newText("Hello World!",
    ↪ 150, 150, native.systemFont, 24)
```

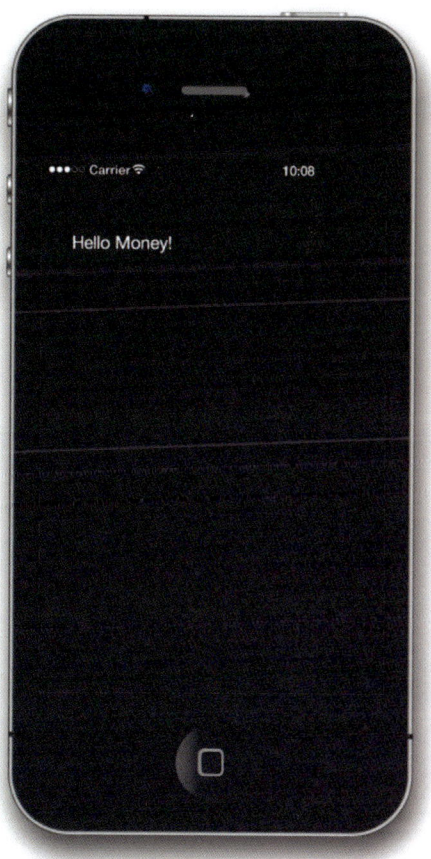

Now, you have a "handle" to use to identify and work with this display object. So, for example, if you wanted to change the text in the `myTxt` display object at some later point, you could do so by editing the "text" property of this object:

```
myTxt.text = "Hello Money!"
```

If you add this line after the line above, what you'll see is shown in the screenshot "Hello Money". If you run this, notice that you don't ever even see "Hello World!", since the text is modified so quickly. If you want to be able to

Hello Money

see text change, you'll need to use *transitions* (which you'll learn in Chapter 4).

Using the simulator

Once your app is running, you can switch the device that the simulator is simulating by pulling down the "Window" menu and selecting "View As…". This will display a submenu with 22 different devices (see the screenshot "Simulator Devices"). You can switch to a different device in this menu just by selecting it. If you have "Hello Money" running, switch to the iPhone 6 Plus and see what happens.

If you look at the screenshot "iPhone 6 Plus", you'll see that, in addition to the device appearance changing, the text has apparently **shrunk quite a bit**. If you switch to the Samsung Galaxy S 5, the text also looks quite small. However, switching to the iPad mini results in text that is quite readable (see screenshot "iPad mini").

So, what is going on?

> **Text that you size the same can appear in different sizes on screen!**

The answer is actually in the "Simulated Devices" screenshot: These devices have different screen resolutions (i.e., the number of pixels horizontally and vertically). The text you are displaying (either "Hello World!" or "Hello Money!") is displayed with a font size of 24, which is measured in **pixels**. So, the same text will appear in different sizes when displayed on devices with differing resolutions in pixels-per-inch. It isn't a matter of the text "shrinking," but rather of the screen packing in more pixels-per-inch, squeezing those 24 pixels into a smaller amount of screen real estate.

Simulator Devices

While higher resolution screens are — at least up to a point — better for consumers, these varying sizes and resolutions will make it difficult for your apps to render a consistent UI across such varied devices.

Fortunately, Solar2D has a solution built-in: the "config.lua" file.

A Beginner's Guide Using Solar2D

iPhone 6 Plus

iPad mini

Defining the content area using "config.lua"

Instead of writing code to deal with these varying physical screen resolutions, you can define a common virtual "content area" and allow Solar2D to scale your app to appear consistently across devices. You'll write your code to work in the content area and Solar2D will do the rest!

Although there are a lot of settings you can place into your "config.lua" file, the most basic is the content area and scaling method:

```
1  application =
2  {
3      content =
4      {
5          width = 320,
6          height = 480,
7          scale = "letterbox"
8      }
9  }
```
1

The content width and height (i.e., 320x480 in the example configuration shown in box 1) defines the content area for your app, while the scale setting ("letterbox") tells Solar2D how to deal with device screens with incompatible resolutions. This content size (320x480) has been the default for most development projects since several devices are exact multiples of this resolution (or, at least, close to it).

The content area

The content area is a rectangle that has the dimensions defined in the "config.lua" and forms an (x,y) coordinate system with (0,0) located at the top-left corner (see "Content Area".

All of your drawing, image, object and widget placement will use the coordinate system of the content area to define position and size. **You will use this content area regardless of the device your app is running on**. Solar2D will automatically scale the content area to fit the screen, allowing your code to work correctly without having to customize it for every possible device. That's a really nice feature.

Content Area

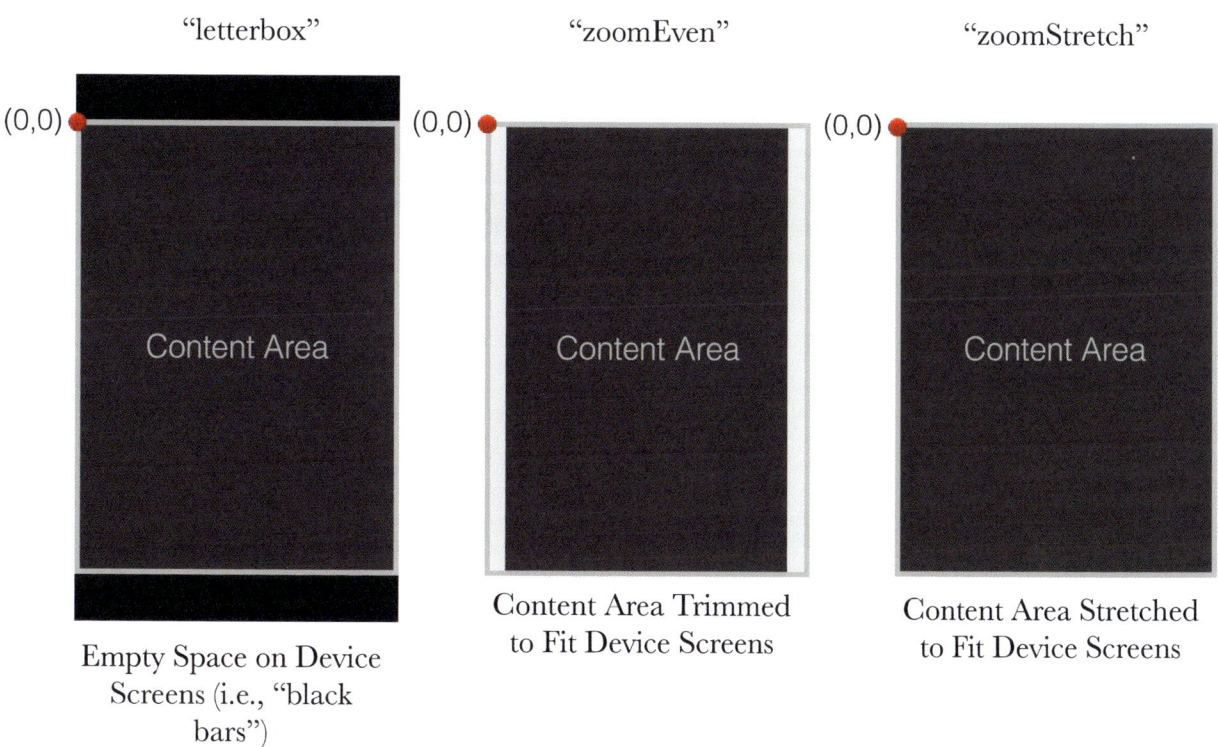

Empty Space on Device Screens (i.e., "black bars")

Content Area Trimmed to Fit Device Screens

Content Area Stretched to Fit Device Screens

However, given the variety of devices and screen resolutions, you have a choice to make about how Solar2D should scale your app when the shape of your content area (i.e., the rectangle) doesn't fit the shape of the device screen. You have three options: "letterbox", "zoomEven", or "zoomStretch".

In most cases, the "letterbox" technique is the most useful, since it won't trim or distort aspects of your UI.

If you add the "config.lua" file described above to the folder containing the "Hello World 2" app, you'll find that the "Hello World!" (or "Hello Moncy!") text now displays in a visually appropriate size. That means that it will scale bigger on larger devices (like tablets) to remain proportional to the content area.

If you are watching closely, you'll notice that the text is actually twice as large as it was without the configuration file. Why is that? Well, the content area you defined was *half* the resolution of the iPhone 4 screen size you are using in the device simulator. If you wanted it to be identical, you could half the font size to 12 or double the resolution of the content area.

You will learn more about the "config.lua" file in the following chapters. If you are using LuaGlider, the one automatically generated will be fine. Otherwise, you can omit this file (for the time being) or use a default one such as shown above.

Your device

You can easily figure out information about the device your app is running on and what its screen size is, just by asking. If your IDE isn't already running, then start it up. Create a new "main.lua" file in a new project or folder. Let's start by looking at the model, size (screen resolution), and scale of the device you are using.

Add these `print()` statements at the top of this new script file (box 2):

```lua
print("model = "..system.getInfo("model"))
print("width = "..display.contentWidth)
print("height = "..display.contentHeight)
print("scale = "..display.pixelWidth / display.actualContentWidth)
print("- - - - - - - - -")
```

Remember, the ".." is a string operator that joins (or "concatenates") two strings together. Although this is only marginally more exciting than the "hello world" app (from the previous chapter), it should report some useful information in the console:

```
model = iPhone
width = 640
height = 960
scale = 1
- - - - - - - - -
```

If you are using the iPhone 4 device in the simulator, you should see the model name "iPhone" and the 640x960 dimension reported. Obviously, if you are using a different device, you will see different values at the console. Take a moment to switch through some of the devices in the *Solar2D Simulator* and see the different models and screen resolutions reported. In each case, however, the reported scale should be 1.

Here's what it looks like for the various iPhone devices:

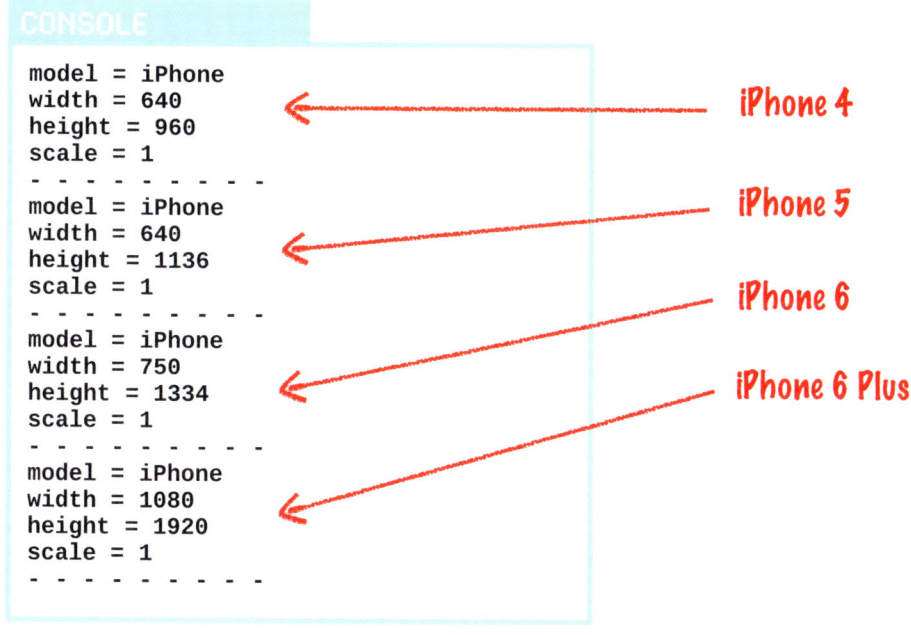

No "config.lua"

Now, place a copy of the basic "config.lua" file into this project folder and see what happens. Here are the same devices with the content area set to iPhone 4 size (640x960):

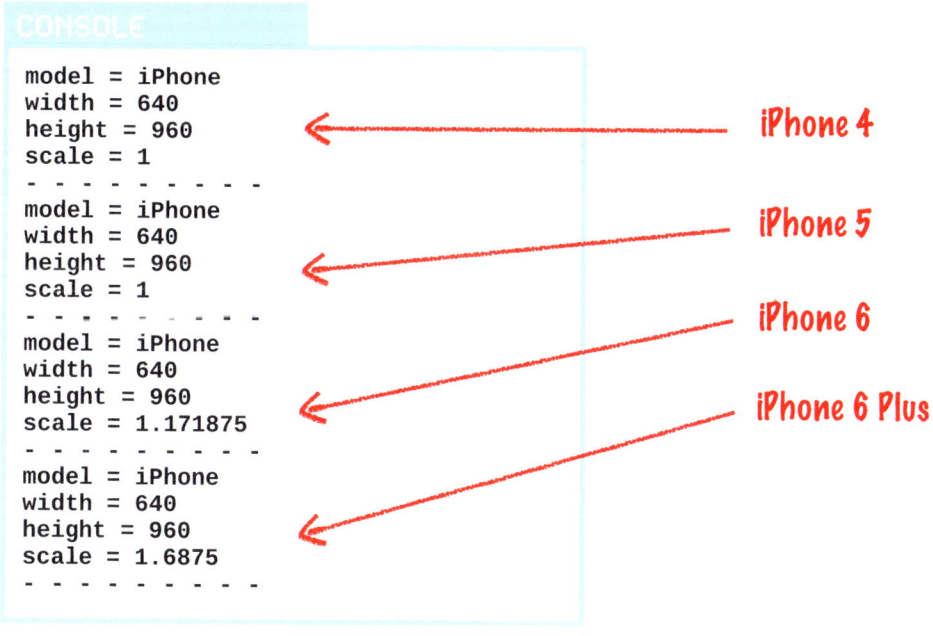

Content area set at 640x960 in "config.lua"

Notice now that the reported resolution is now fixed to the content area defined in the "config.lua" file and the scale adjusts based on what Solar2D needs to do to automatically make the content fit the screen. The scale for the iPhone 5 is the same as the iPhone 4 because Solar2D will letterbox the output based on your setting.

Note that you don't have programmatic access to the **physical size** of the screen (i.e., inches) for iOS devices, although it is possible to get that data for Android. A wealth of information can be read about your device using the `system.getInfo()` function (docs.coronalabs.com/api/library/system/getInfo.html).

Fonts

You have access to all of the fonts on the device, which can be as few as three or so to dozens. The iosfonts.com list contains over 80 distinct fonts that you can count on being available on any recent and up-to-date iOS device.

The situation on Android is somewhat more difficult (as seems to generally be the case). There are three original fonts (fonts.google.com/specimen/Roboto) that should be present on all devices: "normal" (or Droid Sans), "serif" (or Droid Serif), and "monospace" (or Droid Mono). Newer devices should also have Google's Roboto font installed (fonts.google.com/specimen/Roboto). If you are planning to develop for Android devices, you should at least download and install the Roboto font family on your development machine(s) (Mac or Windows).

How do you know what fonts you can (or at least might want to) use? Well, for starters, you can list the fonts that the simulator sees to the console using this code (box 3):

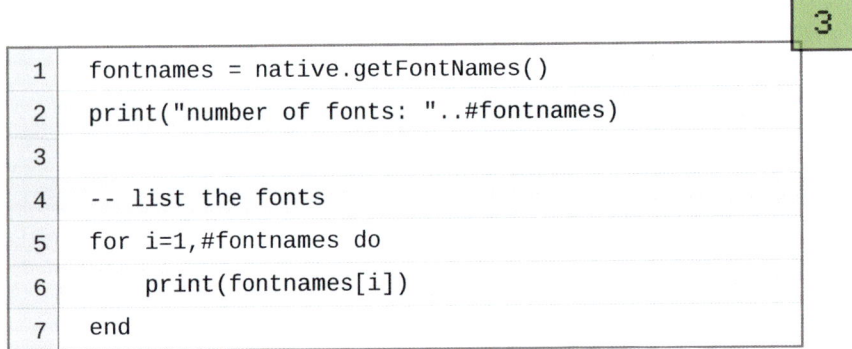

```
1  fontnames = native.getFontNames()
2  print("number of fonts: "..#fontnames)
3
4  -- list the fonts
5  for i=1,#fontnames do
6      print(fontnames[i])
7  end
```

You can set the font for text display objects in the line that creates the text. However, note that it is not currently possible to *change* the font after the text display object has been created. To set a particular font, you just need to know its name.

For example, if the font "Monaco" is available, you could use it like this:

```
display.newText("Do you know where Prince Albert
  is?", 50, 50,"Monaco", 28)
```

Which would look like the screenshot to the right, running in the simulator, assuming you have the font "Monaco" installed on your machine. "Prince Albert" is in folder "3" of the resource download.

But do you have Prince Albert in a can?

Solar2D font limitations

Note that Solar2D can see all of the fonts installed on your development machine (i.e., your Mac or PC), even if those fonts are not typically present on mobile devices. That can be

There are several limitations

misleading. Picking a font that isn't present on the mobile device(s) you are developing for will lead to typographically disappointing results. You can run the included Font Viewer app (look in folder "3" of the resource download) to see the fonts graphically, although running this on an actual device will require you to refer to an appendix.

As a work-around, note that both iOS and Android apps may bundle their own fonts, to be distributed as part of the app itself (requiring no additional steps by the user), if you have the proper license to bundle them.

In addition, there doesn't seem to be any way of **styling text within a text object** (e.g., like underlining or *italicizing* a particular word in a sentence). Although there are

A Font Viewer (main.lua)

57

workarounds for this, it is a significant disadvantage at this point. In general, anything other than plain text is **difficult**. Although you can include symbols not found on the standard alphabet (but that are part of the en.wikipedia.org/wiki/UTF-8) there is, regrettably, no easy way to type them in.

It may be possible to *drag-and-drop* symbols into your IDE from a character palette (this works with LuaGlider and ZBS). However, this approach has **two key limitations**. First, **only certain characters work**. In general, the black-and-white ones do, while the ones with color (like Emoji) don't. You can drag-and-drop the "bad" ones as well, but whatever shows up in the IDE won't be displayed on the device. Second, not all of the symbols will work **across platforms** nor will they necessarily survive sharing the code with a teammate). See the supplied app "Trouble_With_Symbols" (in folder "3" of the resource download). So, bottom line, symbols are — at this point — best left to graphics files.

Screen size & location

You saw earlier that it is possible to get the size of the screen your app is running on using `display.contentWidth` and `display.contentHeight`. Remember that these dimensions are driven by values in the "config.lua" file (and not by the device being simulated). You can also get the center of the screen programmatically using `display.contentCenterX` and `display.contentCenterY`.

To place a text object containing the screen size in the center of the display you could do this:

```
res_txt = display.newText(
    display.contentWidth
    .."x"
    ..display.contentHeight,
    display.contentCenterX,
    display.contentCenterY,
    "Courier", 24)
```

Running that code will look a lot like the "Screen Resolution" screen shot to the right.

Screen Resolution

But where is (x,y)?

Where is the (x,y) location in the text object? Center? Top-left? That is one of the big changes Solar2D made with the "Graphics 2.0" upgrade. Now, the (x,y) location for most display objects defaults to the **center of the object** (even for text). This makes centering objects really easy.

You can visually confirm the location of (x,y) by drawing a set of "cross-hairs" at the location of the text object. To draw a line, you will use the `newLine()` function in the `display` table, and pass it four parameters: The (x,y) location of one end of the line and the (x,y) location of the other end. For example, to draw a **diagonal line**, this code:

```
diagonal = display.newLine(0, 0,
    → display.contentWidth,
    → display.contentHeight)
```

will display a line running from the *top-left* corner to the *bottom-right* corner of the content area.

For **cross-hairs**, if you want a horizontal line running across the display (from 0 to `contentWidth`) at the level of the y-value for the `res_txt`, the statement is:

```
h_line = display.newLine(0, res_txt.y,
    → display.contentWidth, res_txt.y)
```

Likewise, if you want a vertical line running top to bottom through the x-value of `res_txt`, the statement is:

```
v_line = display.newLine(res_txt.x, 0,
    → res_txt.x, display.contentHeight)
```

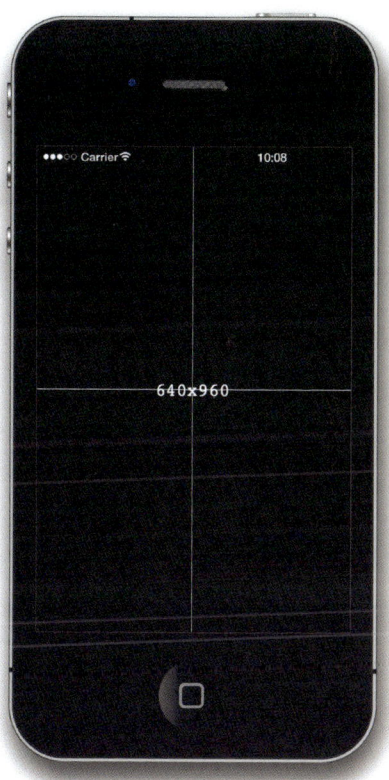

Position Lines

As you can see in the screenshot, the lines cut **right through the center of the text object**. So, the (x, y) location of the text object is in its center, which makes it easy to center on screen. However, what if you don't want the text (or other display object) centered?

59

Aligning text (and other display objects)

If your display objects (at least those with a single x,y location) are located via their center, how would we, for example, align some text to the left? That's a somewhat common thing to do. Luckily, the solution is pretty easy. You need to set the horizontal (docs.coronalabs.com/api/type/DisplayObject/anchorX.html) and vertical (docs.coronalabs.com/api/type/DisplayObject/anchorY.html) "anchor" values for the object.

Anchor value	anchorX	anchorY
0	Left align	Top align
0.5	Center align	Center align
1	Right align	Bottom align

Alignment Using Anchor Values

Setting anchors

There are two anchor values for any display object: anchorX (controlling the horizontal alignment) and anchorY (controlling the vertical alignment). Each anchor property can take three values: 0, .5, or 1. See the table "Alignment Using Anchor Values" for the meaning of these values.

So, if you want to *left align* some lines of text, say, we'll need to set the anchorX value on the text display objects to 0. Code box #4 shows example of using anchor values to achieve this alignment.

Notice that each of the lines of text has had its anchorX value set to 0 which, as you can see in the table above, means that it will now be positioned using its left edge, rather than the center. This means that the text will be drawn to the right of the x,y location, rather than being centered around it.

Anchoring Text

```
1  f = native.systemFont
2  line1 = display.newText("I like fonts", 50, 200, f, 32 )
3  line1.anchorX = 0
4
5  line2 = display.newText("I like colors", 50, line1.y + 32, f, 32 )
6  line2.anchorX = 0
7  line2:setFillColor(1,0,0) -- you will learn about colors below!
8
9  line3 = display.newText("I like symbols", 50, line2.y + 32, f, 32 )
10 line3.anchorX = 0
11
12 top_left_txt = display.newText("I'm in the top left!", 0, 0, f, 24)
13 top_left_txt.anchorX = 0
14 top_left_txt.anchorY = 0
15
16 bottom_right_txt = display.newText("I'm in the bottom right!",
↳          display.contentWidth, display.contentHeight, f, 24)
17 bottom_right_txt.anchorX, bottom_right_txt.anchorY = 1, 1
```

The anchorX and anchorY settings can be used in combination to orient display objects by their corners. For example, if you wanted to put some text at the top-left corner of the device, you would set its anchorX value to 0 and anchorY value to 0.

Text anchoring playground

There are, of course, other combinations of {anchorX, anchorY} that can be used to change the way a text object is positioned around its (x, y) point. In fact, there are 9 possible parings of anchorX and anchorY values (3^2).

> You can set the font and horizontal alignment easily using Drawn2Code

These can be visualized like this (where the numbers in the braces are the anchorX and anchorY values):

Anchor defines	Right edge of text	**Center of text**	Left edge of text
Bottom edge of text	{1, 1}	{0.5, 1}	{0, 1}
Center of text	{1, 0.5}	**{0.5, 0.5}**	{0, 0.5}
Top edge of text	{1, 0}	{0.5, 0}	{0, 0}

How {anchorX, anchorY} Defines the Location of Text

Remember that the default value for the anchors is {0.5, 0.5}, which places the (x, y) position in the horizontal and vertical center of the object (bolded in the table above).

It can be a bit tricky to visualize the effect of changing these anchor values, so you can run the "Text Anchoring Playground" app to see how a sample text object (in the center) is affected (see the screenshot to the right).

Notice that the (x, y) position of the text is *fixed* at the center of the screen (which you find using `display.contentCenterX` and `display.contentCenterY`). This position is highlighted with a red dot.

The key thing to understand is that changing the anchor does not move the (x, y) location of the text; instead, it changes the meaning of x and y.

When you run the app, notice how the red dot *never moves*, but the text moves around it. The dot starts out in the vertical and horizontal center of the text, which is the default.

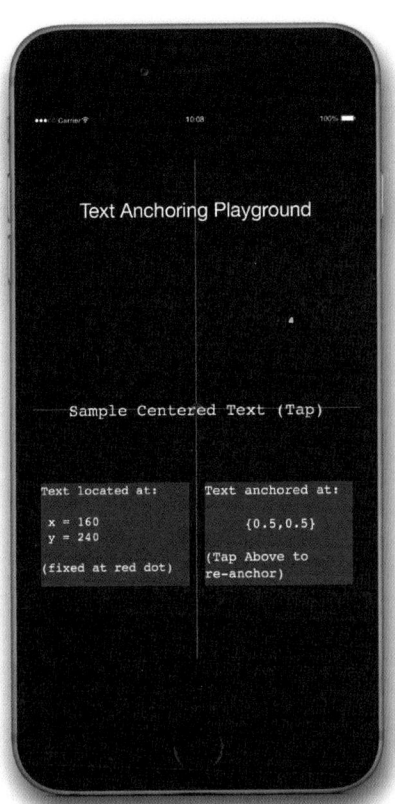

Text Anchoring Playground

As you tap the text, you can watch the anchorX and anchorY values change through all 9 possibilities while the text jumps around the dot *based on what x and y mean.*
Although this technique and syntax isn't necessarily the most intuitive, it does work and gives you (the programmer) the flexibility to locate a text object (or any object) anywhere you please

and easily align it with other onscreen objects (this app is available in the download as "anchor_playground"). Like that red dot? Awesome segue.

Name	Color	RGB Value
Red		1,0,0
Orange		1,.65,0
Yellow		1,1,0
Green		0,.5,0
Blue		0,0,1
Indigo		.3,0,.5
Violet		.92,.5,.92
Brown		.65,.16,.16
White		1,1,1
Light Grey		.8,.8,.8
Grey		.5,.5,.5
Dark Grey		.4,.4,.4
Black		0,0,0

RGB Values of Common Colors

Colors

Perhaps, in addition to changing the text or location of a display object, we'd like to change its color. By default, the color of all of the display objects we've been using is white, which shows up nicely against a black display. To modify the color of a display object, you'll learn to use the setFillColor(), setTextColor(), and setStrokeColor() functions.

For text, unsurprisingly, you use `setTextColor()`:

> **SET TEXT COLOR FUNCTION**
>
> `[display object]:setTextColor([r],[g],[b])`

Where [r][g][b] is the RGB code for the desired color (see the table "RGB Values of Common Colors" for a short list). RGB values must be specified between 0 and 1. White, the **default color** is specified as (1,1,1), while black is (0,0,0).

For example, if you have a text object named "myText", you can show it in **red** using:

```
-- red, for example:
myText:setTextColor(1,0,0)
```

Any color can be represented in RGB by finding the desired values for red, green, and blue. A fairly complete list is put out by the w3 (www.w3.org/TR/SVG/types.html#ColorKeywords). In addition, you can add a fourth parameter to the function to customize the *alpha value* of the color and make use of two more color setting functions (coming soon in Chapter 4).

The alpha value of a color defines the degree to which the object is transparent. An alpha value of 0 means it is *completely transparent*, while an alpha value of 1 means it is *fully opaque*.

Unfortunately, Solar2D **does not have named colors built-in**. So, there is no simple way to set color to "blue" or "green". While I am on the subject of limitations, there is apparently **no way to change the *font*** for an existing (on screen) text object (you would have to replace it with a new text object in the new font you desire).

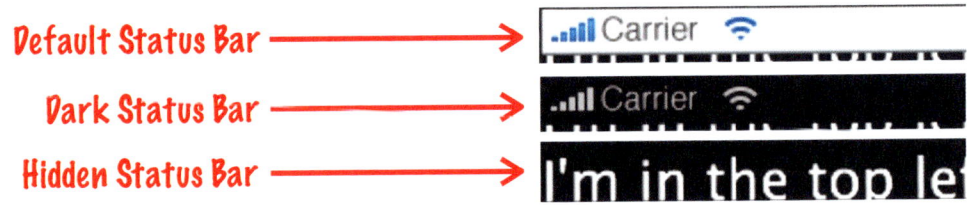

Status Bar Options

Device status bar

The "status bar" is the rectangular information panel that sits at the top of the device screen. Did you notice that the status bar was **missing** from the Font Viewer example app (above)?. In some of the other examples, the device's "status bar" (at the top) is bisecting the text at the top of the screen, which looks odd. Luckily, it is easy to show and hide the status bar (docs.coronalabs.com/api/library/display/setStatusBar.html):

```
-- hide the device status bar:
display.setStatusBar( display.HiddenStatusBar )
-- show the device status bar:
display.setStatusBar( display.TranslucentStatusBar )
```

You can also set the status bar to "default" (which is not translucent) or "dark" (which is, well, dark and not translucent). You can see what these options look like in "Status Bar Options" (on the facing page).

In some of your apps you may want to hide the status bar so that it doesn't obscure your content. However, this should be done with some caution, as users rely on having that information at the top of their devices, so hiding it unnecessarily could be more annoying than leaving it in place.

The flow of execution: Top to bottom

Important

Remember that your code executes from **top to bottom**. In general, this means that display objects will be drawn in the order that their code appears in the app (we'll do a lot more drawing next time). So, items that are drawn later in the code may be drawn *over* (or "on top" of) previously drawn objects. This allows you to build up more complex shapes from layers of simpler shapes. Although this does also allow you to hide a display object behind another one, which can be confusing. We'll cover drawing and overlapping shapes in Chapter 4.

Changes to the *properties* of the display objects, such as their location and color, change the object that is drawn on screen. Moreover, even if you make the change dozens of lines of code later, the change will typically appear right away.

For example, if you want to change the color of `bottom_right_txt` at the bottom of your code to blue, after it has already been put on the screen in white, you'd use this syntax:

```
bottom_right_txt:setTextColor(0, 0, 1) -- now it's blue
```

This will **immediately change** to blue. As with changing the text (string) content, you may never even see the text displayed in white.

Order is everything

Note however, that you can't make changes to a display object (or any other Solar2D entity) *prior* to creating it. Until you take the step of defining it, it does not exist. So, if you placed the above "set color" statement at the top of your app, you'll get an error because `bottom_right_txt` hasn't been defined yet. This is true for variables as well.

For example, if you try to use this statement:

```
count = count + 1
```

without having *first* defined the variable "count" (e.g., using a statement like "count = 0") on a prior line, you will also get an error about trying to use an undefined variable (specifically: "Attempt to perform arithmetic on global 'count' (a nil value)".

Location is everything too

Although you haven't learned much about functions yet, it is also important to know that the entities like variables and display objects that you define *inside of a function* will **only be visible** *inside of that function*. The "scope" of a variable is the area of code in which you may see and use a variable. In general, the scope is below the line of code that defined the variable or entity, but is further restricted by the placement of the declaration inside of a function. In this case, the scope is restricted to the body of the function itself, below the line that contains the definition.

The period and the colon

If you looked at the line of code above closely, you might have noticed a somewhat unexpected use of the colon (":") where you might have thought a dot (".") would be. In Lua, the dot is used to access table elements such as the "text" *property* of a text display object. In contrast, when executing table *functions* (i.e., functions that are stored in tables such as the "display" table), we will more commonly use a colon, as you see above to access the `setTextColor()` function.

Important

However, this isn't universally the case and exceptions to this rule will be pointed out as you are introduced to them.

Summary

Mobile device screens are sized using pixels to form a 2 dimensional (x, y) grid with horizontal and vertical axes (this is, by the way, how larger computer displays work as well). Mobile devices also include a *status bar* that you may configure. You can switch the Solar2D Simulator between different (emulated) devices with potentially different dimensions and appearances. The problem of needing to support so many devices can be addressed by configuring a *content area* in a file named "config.lua". The *content area* acts as a virtual screen that you write your script to support, then Solar2D takes care of sizing and scaling for all of the different devices (however, you may customize how this is accomplished).

Text can be displayed onscreen using a Solar2D text *display object*, in the display library. To do so, you need to specify the text itself, the (x, y) location where you want it displayed, and information about the font. The text is displayed onscreen centered around the specified (x, y) location. For Solar2D entities (like text display objects), you can override this default centering behavior by setting the *anchorX* and *anchorY* values. Finally, you learned the basics behind using RGB colors to change the color of the text displayed.

Last, you learned about the **top-to-bottom** *flow of execution* and its impact of the script you write, along with the concept of variable *scope* and how the **location** in which you define a variable (or other program entity like a text *display object*) will affect where you can use it. In general, variables may only be used after they have been defined (i.e., in statements that are below the line in which the variable is defined). Moreover, variables defined **inside of**

functions are additionally scope restricted to that function and aren't available to use outside the function. You will continue to learn about scope and flow of execution in future chapters. You will create your first function in Chapter 4.

Chapter resources

In the chapter resource download for this book (www.lillipellilabs.com/mobiledev/download/chapter_resources.zip), you'll find the following app in folder "3":

1. Hello World 2 (without a config.lua)
2. Hello Word 2 (with a config.lua)
3. Print display information (without a config.lua)
4. Print display information (with a config.lua)
5. Prince Albert
6. Font Viewer
7. Trouble With Symbols
8. Cross-Hair
9. Text Alignment
10. Text Anchoring Playground

End-of-chapter exercises

Confirm

1. Display your name on the device simulator, centered.
   a. Add "cross-hairs" to locate the (x, y) position of your name. Cross-hairs are just two line display objects, one vertical and the other horizontal. Cross them at the (x, y) position of your name.
   b. Change your name to appear in your favorite color (that is, as long as your favorite color isn't "white").
   c. Make the font size as large as it can be to fit your name onscreen (i.e., roughly edge-to-edge).

2. Put your first name in the top-right corner, and your last name in the bottom-left corner.

3. Modify #1 or #2 to remove the status bar.

4. Create a **Wizarding School** "nickname" for yourself and display it in between your first and last name, in quotes.
   a. Change the color of your text to your favorite color (that is, as long as your favorite color isn't "white").
   b. Make the font size as large as it can be to fit your text onscreen (i.e., roughly edge-to-edge).

5. Place a line display object under your name (i.e., to "underline" it). Unfortunately, that's the way you underline text in Solar2D. (As a work-around you could render the text as an image first, or perhaps use an underlined font).

Challenge

6. Download a fancy **Wizarding School** font (e.g., www.fontspace.com/cybapee-creations/hamletornot or www.fontspace.com/dave-howell/magicmedieval) and use that to display #1, #2, or #4.

7. Modify #4 to use this font as well and to make it so that <u>only your nickname</u> has the non default color (i.e., your first and last names are either white or a unique color).

8. Create a short rhyme or limerick and display it on screen. Set the color and font of each line uniquely.

NOTES

 # Display Objects & Touch

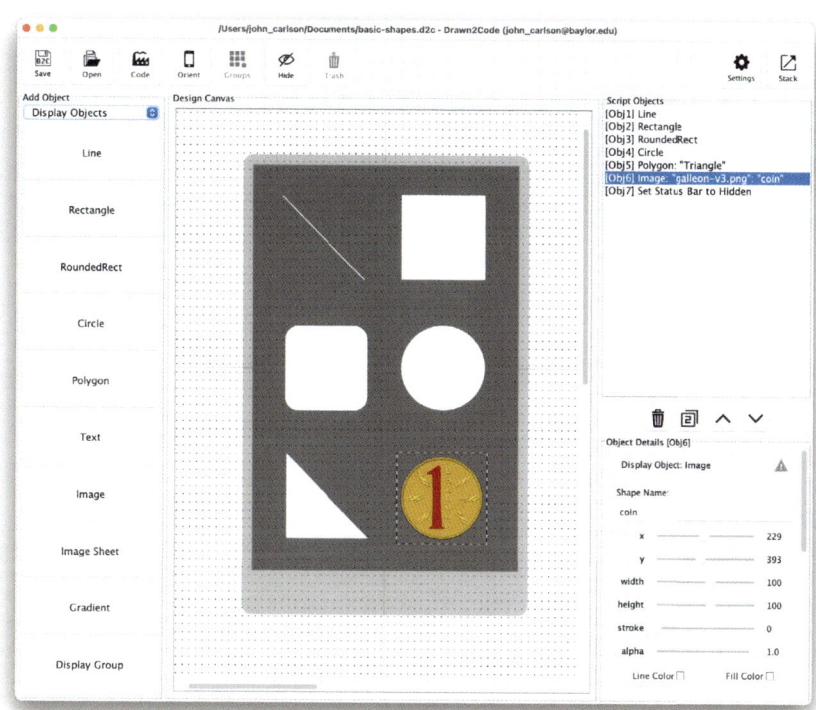

Display Objects in Drawn2Code

Beyond text: Shapes & Images

In addition to the (wonderful) text you created in the previous chapter, you can create other display objects in the form of lines, rectangles, rounded rectangles, circles (ovals), polygons, and images (docs.coronalabs.com/api/library/display/index.html). The construction of these objects follows the same basic syntax you learned last time (for text and lines):

> **DISPLAY OBJECT SYNTAX**
>
> ```
> lua_identifier = display.new[Something]([parameters])
> ```

In each of these cases, you can *locate* and *size* the display object as you wish, and set *colors* and outline *stroke width* to values that you want (the syntax for setting colors is covered below, after an introduction to color). In *Drawn2Code*, you can add these display objects easily from the "Display Objects" palette (see "Display Objects in Drawn2Code"). The "basic-shapes" design above will look like this on a device:

Locating your shape

Each shape you want to draw is located and sized using pixel values. The location is specified using (x, y) values, with the coordinate system starting in the top-left corner of the device. Except for lines, the position will locate the **center of the shape**. Also, except for lines, you'll use width and height values (in pixels) to size your shapes. The line just uses 2 (x, y) values to define the endpoints.

Defaults

By default, none of the objects has a surrounding line (or, perhaps more accurately, the size of the **stroke is initialized at 0**). If you want to see a line *outlining* the shape, set the strokeWidth to something positive. Also, both the fill color and stroke color **default to white**, so if you want to actually *see* the surrounding line, you'll need to change one of the colors.

Basic Shapes

Example: Basic shapes

• •

The first app today puts one of each of these types of display objects on screen. Coding by hand (e.g., using ZBS) will require you to provide location and size values that put these shapes where you want them. If you are using *Drawn2Code*, the **syntax** for each of these will be written for you. Open the "Generated Code Window" to see what it looks like.

A Beginner's Guide Using Solar2D

```
1   Obj1 = display.newLine(35, 35, 135, 135)
2   Obj1.id = "Obj1"
3   Obj1.strokeWidth = 1
4
5   Obj2 = display.newRect(230, 85, 100, 100)
6   Obj2.id = "Obj2"
7
8   Obj3 = display.newRoundedRect(90, 240, 100, 100, 16)
9   Obj3.id = "Obj3"
10
11  Obj4 = display.newCircle(230, 240, 50)
12  Obj4.radius = 50
13  Obj4.id = "Obj4"
14
15  Obj5_vertices = {
16    0, 0,
17    100, 100,
18    0, 100,
19  }
20  Obj5 = display.newPolygon(90, 391, Obj5_vertices)
21  Obj5.id = "Obj5"
22  Obj5.name = "Triangle"
23
24  -- image "galleon-v3.png"
25  Obj6 = display.newImageRect( "galleon-v3.png", 100, 100 )
26  Obj6.x = 229
27  Obj6.y = 393
28  Obj6.id = "Obj6"
29  Obj6.name = "coin"
30  display.setStatusBar( display.HiddenStatusBar )
```

Basic Shapes: Generated Code

Line

A straight line can be created by using the `display.newLine()` function. The four values in the parentheses represent the (x, y) locations of the line's *endpoints* — e.g., (x1, y1) and (x2, y2). These values are used inside the `newLine()` function to draw the line.

```
Obj1 = display.newLine(35, 35, 135, 135)
```

Note that the line created here — named "Obj1" — has a default width of 1 pixel. You can see how *thin* the actual line is in the screenshot on the previous page ("Basic Shapes"). If you want to add some thickness to the line, you can set the `strokeWidth` to some value greater than 1. For example, adding this setting will create a noticeably thicker line:

```
Obj1.strokeWidth = 4
```

Rectangle

A basic rectangle can be created by using the `display.newRect()` function. The four values passed represent the center of the rectangle — named "Obj2" — (i.e., the x, y location) along with its `width` and `height`.

```
Obj2 = display.newRect(230, 85, 100, 100)
```

This creates a new rectangle display object named "rect_obj" sized at 100x100 pixels, placed on the device screen 80 pixels (i.e., 20 + 60) down from the top (to the center of the rectangle) and horizontally centered.

Rounded rectangle

The rounded rectangle is a rectangle with — wait for it — rounded corners. To get one, you use the `display.newRoundedRect()` function. The function takes 5 parameters, with the first 4 being the same as the rectangle. So, the major customizable setting is the pixel radius of the rounding, which you provide as the 5th parameter (in the example below it is 16). The higher the number, the bigger the rounding effect at the corners. This creates such a shape with the name "Obj3":

```
Obj3 = display.newRoundedRect(90, 240, 100, 100, 16)
```

Using the same value for centerX as above, this code also calculates a y position for the rounded rectangle which leaves a 10 pixel gap between it and the rectangle above.

Circle (that can be stretched into an oval)

Tired of being a square? Looking for a more rounded life? Now you too can draw a perfect circle, or other oviform object! It's easy. You use the `display.newCircle()` function. The `newCircle()` function takes 3 parameters: The (x, y) location of the center and the radius. If you want the circle, named "Obj4", to appear below the rounded rectangle and have the same 10 pixel gap, we'll need to recalculate y in the same manner as above:

```
Obj4 = display.newCircle(230, 240, 50)
```

Note that there isn't a `display.newOval()` function (which is **kind of odd**). Instead, you can create a circle and then adjust the scale (discussed below) to *stretch* it vertically or horizontally into an oval.

Polygon

Triangle *aficionados* may have noticed the glaring lack of an ability to draw triangles. Fortunately, it is also possible to create **polygons**, using as many points as you desire and possessing the capability to be filled. To do so, we'll use the `display.newPolygon()` function, which takes 3 parameters: The x location of the center, the y location of the center, and the list (actually a table) of (x,y) points ("vertices") to construct the polygon. A simple triangle can be created as a polygon like this:

```
Obj5_vertices = {
    0, 0,
    100, 100,
    0, 100,
}
Obj5 = display.newPolygon(90, 391, Obj5_vertices)
```

Polygons, like other display objects, default to filled, white shapes.

Image

Working with images in Solar2D is no more difficult than any other display object. Solar2D understands several file formats, although it seems that most developers **prefer to use PNG** files due to their cross-platform compatibility. Images don't have a surrounding line and, although they may have a fill color, it is blended with the image to create something like a tint. It's kind of cool.

To create an image display object (in this case named "Obj6"), the `display.newImageRect()` function takes 3 parameters: The *image file name* and the `width` and `height` values to use in sizing the image. Somewhat oddly, the x and y values must be set separately. For example,

```
Obj6 = display.newImageRect("galleon-v3.png", 100, 100)
Obj6.x = 230
Obj6.y = 393
```

Scaled image files

Solar2D will also scale any image resources you use in your app, however, that can make your artwork appear blurry or stretched if you aren't careful. The solution? Let Solar2D select the appropriately pre-scaled image by adding extra information to your "config.lua" file (see code box 1).

The various `imageSuffix` settings (lines 10-12) allow Solar2D to select appropriate graphics, based on some multiple of the specified content area (i.e., 320x480 in the example configuration). For this to work, you must have created these graphics and scaled them correctly *beforehand*.

While this technique doesn't necessarily cover each and every device *exactly*, it does get us close and avoids having Solar2D attempt to resize a poorly fitting image. If you weren't planning to support devices as small as 320x480, then you could change the specified width and height in the "config.lua", keeping in mind such a change would alter the resolution of the scaled values as well.

Let's take a look at the "MOB DEV" logo used in this book.

Standard (base) size
60x80 pixels
file: "logo.png"

Double size
120x160 pixels
file: "logo@2x.png"

4X Size
240x320 pixels
file: "logo@4x.png"

The Same Image in Three Resolutions
(Standard, Double, Quad)

If you wanted to display the "MOB DEV" logo image *crisply* on multiple devices, you would provide it in several resolutions, changing the name of each file using the defined suffixes as shown.

Using this technique, when you supply the image resources using the naming system you define in "config.lua", Solar2D will automatically select the correct image for the device your app is running on.

```
1   application =
2   {
3       content =
4       {
5           width = 320,
6           height = 480,
7           scale = "letterbox",
8           imageSuffix =
9           {
10              ["@2x"] = 2,  -- x2 resolution devices
11              ["@3x"] = 3,  -- x3 devices (iPhone 6 Plus)
12              ["@4x"] = 4,  -- x4 devices (iPad Air)
13          },
14      }
15  }
```

Changing the colors

Although white is the default color, you have complete control of the colors that the shape is drawn (i.e., filled) and outlined (i.e., the stroke color) in. Except for lines, which don't have a filled area. All of the display objects have a function `setStrokeColor( )` to, as you might guess, set the color of the line. All display objects but line also have `setFillColor( )` to set the color of the interior of the shape. As an example, to set the colors on a display object "Obj9" to green fill with a gold outline:

```
Obj9:setStrokeColor(1.0, 0.8, 0.2, 1.0)
Obj9:setFillColor(0.0, 0.6, 0.0, 1.0)
Obj9.strokeWidth = 7
```

These color functions accept RGBA color settings that specify how much **red**, **green**, and **blue** colors are used, along with the alpha (or transparency) of the color onscreen. Also, as noted above, to actually *see* the gold outline, you'll also need to set the `strokeWidth` to some positive number (since the default is 0).

Gradients

If you'll glance at the screen shot on the facing page, you may notice that the background isn't black! Instead, I created a rectangle to fill the display, and gave it a gradient fill (to make it look cool). Doing this is fairly simple and can be accomplished easily. You just need three things: a display object (any of the shapes except the line), a gradient, and a statement to set the gradient as the fill color of the shape (in our case, a rectangle).

To create a gradient you need 4 items: The type ("gradient"), the starting color ("color1"), the ending color ("color2"), and the direction of the gradient ("up", "down", "left", or "right").

```
-- create and apply the gradient:
Obj8 = {type = "gradient",
            color1 = {.8,.8,.8},
            color2 = {.4,.4,.4},
            direction = "down"
        }
Obj9:setFillColor( Obj8 )
```

For example, if you add a new gradient object to the design we are working on in *Drawn2Code*, it will be Obj8. I've set the colors to a light gray ({.8, .8, .8}) and a darker gray ({.4, .4, .4}). These will be blended vertically downward, toward the bottom of the rectangle. Then, I've created a new rectangle display object (Obj9) and set its fill color to the gradient (Obj8). In *Drawn2Code*, press the option (alt) key on the keyboard when hitting the fill color button to apply an available gradient.

This example is in the resource downloads as *basic-shapes-gradient-background.d2c*.

Attention

Note that code statements and objects in your *Drawn2Code* stack **are executed in order**, top to bottom. This is important to remember because, for example, if you tried to set the fill color on Obj9 prior to creating the gradient Obj8, your code wouldn't run. *Drawn2Code* lets you easily move script objects up and down your stack, but always keep in mind any dependencies before doing so.

A little wild

The display objects we've created look fine, but they are kind of *boring*. Let's adjust the colors, the alpha (transparency), and the outline (stroke) colors. And, let's make them **random**, just for fun. See "That's So Random" for one possible output. Every time you run the app, it is a completely new experience!

When using math.random(), it is a good idea to set a random "seed" to reset the sequence of pseudorandom numbers generated (so that each time you run the app you get results that appear to be random). This is generally done once, before any random numbers are generated:

```
math.randomseed(os.time())
```

You can generate random numbers using the math.random() function. This function generates a **random integer** between any two parameters you pass it (inclusive). So, for example, if you wanted a random playing card between 1 and 52, you could get that number using:

```
math.random(1, 52)
```

That's So Random

However, to create an RGB color you need *decimal* numbers between 0.0 and 1.0 (inclusive), so the statement to get a random R, G, or B value is just:

```
math.random( )
```

79

However, you'll need to do this for all 3 color components. The alpha value ends up being a bit trickier, because having the color "too transparent" makes it impossible to see. So, I end up using a random number between 0.5 and 1.0 so that the color is at most 50% transparent.

To set the fill color as well as the stroke color and thickness, and to randomize all of the colors, you can plug your random number statement in like this (for the rectangle Obj2):

```
1  Obj2:setFillColor(math.random( ), math.random( ),
        math.random( ), math.random(50, 100)/100)
2  Obj2:setStrokeColor(math.random( ), math.random( ),
        math.random( ), math.random(50, 100)/100)
```

You are using the functions setFillColor() and setStrokeColor() to randomize the colors of the rectangle and the outline. Of course, you have to take **the same steps for all of the display objects** (although the image doesn't have a separate outline stroke).

A function to simplify your code

One thing you might have noticed is that there is a **tremendous amount of repetition** in the color randomization code. That is a **red flag** that should prompt some added attention. Any time you find yourself copying and pasting (or, gasp, *retyping*) the same code over and over, you might be **better off using either a function or a loop**. In this case, a function that returns a random color could simplify your code quite a bit.

In the case with the app above, it has a recurring need to generate a random color. In each case, the code used to generate the random color is identical:

```
math.random( ), math.random( ), math.random( ), math.random(50, 100)/100
```

That is, you need four random numbers separated by commas. The first three vary between 0.0 and 1.0, while the fourth varies between 0.5 and 1.0 (so that no display objects are invisible). Instead of retyping or pasting this code every time you need it, you could define a function to produce it (box 3):

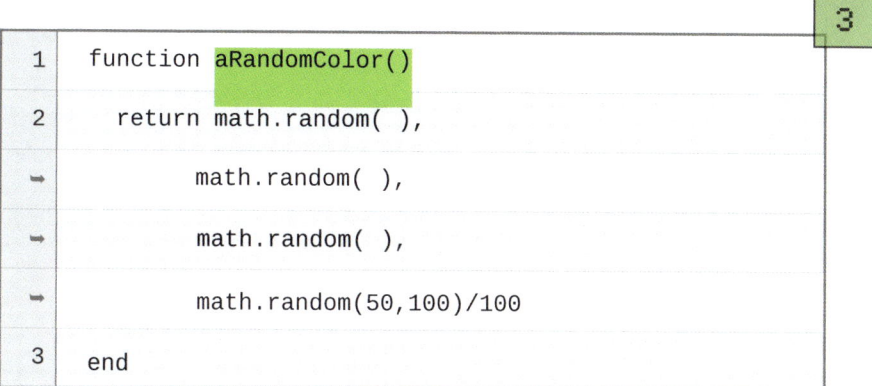

```
1  function aRandomColor()
2     return math.random( ),
         math.random( ),
         math.random( ),
         math.random(50,100)/100
3  end
```

The function really only contains a single line of code (although it is broken into three lines so we can see it here), which starts on line 2 (box 3). This code (lines 2-3) simply generates and returns the **same data** we were previously generating. If you place this function toward the top of your code, prior to any line of code that uses it, it can simplify your work quite a bit. Now, you can just call the function rather than cutting and pasting the code.

For example, if you set up the colors for the circle display object(Obj4), the code becomes:

```
Obj4:setFillColor( aRandomColor() )
Obj4:setStrokeColor( aRandomColor() )
```

Wow, that's easy! You'll learn more about functions in Chapter 7, but this is a good start.

Adding the function in *Drawn2Code* is also straightforward: There a "Functions" palette at the left, from which you can select "New Function" (at the bottom of the list). This will create a new object in the stack (Obj10). Enter the function information as shown to the right, then move this object up to the top of the stack.

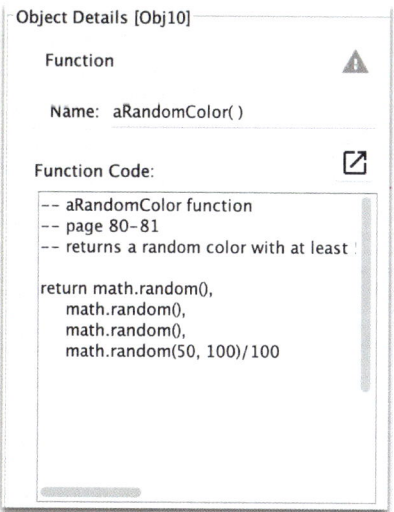

Second, you'll need a bit of code to set the fill colors using this function. Head to the "Snippet" palette and hit the "New Snippet" button at the bottom. In this case, the snippet is Obj11 (although the object id doesn't matter) and contains the function calls for each of the shapes.

Adding the code shown to the right will do the work of randomizing all of the colors. Don't move this snippet to the top of the stack! It needs to stay below the creation of objects 1 through 5 so that references to them work.

This example is in the resource downloads as *basic-shapes-random-colors.d2c*. There's no screenshot because it looks identical to the previous app, with this modification just having simplified the code.

Snippet to Randomize Colors

Adding text

None of these display objects have a text component. If you want text to appear on (or "inside") one, you have to **add a separate text object** (or objects). These are added using the `display.newText( )` syntax (or by adding a text object in *Drawn2Code*).

To create the "MOB DEV" logo to the right, you will need nine display objects:

- ☑ Two rectangles:
  - ▸ Filled green logo background
  - ▸ Gray frame
- ☑ Two text objects:
  - ▸ "MOB"
  - ▸ "DEV"
- ☑ Four circles (for the small white buttons).

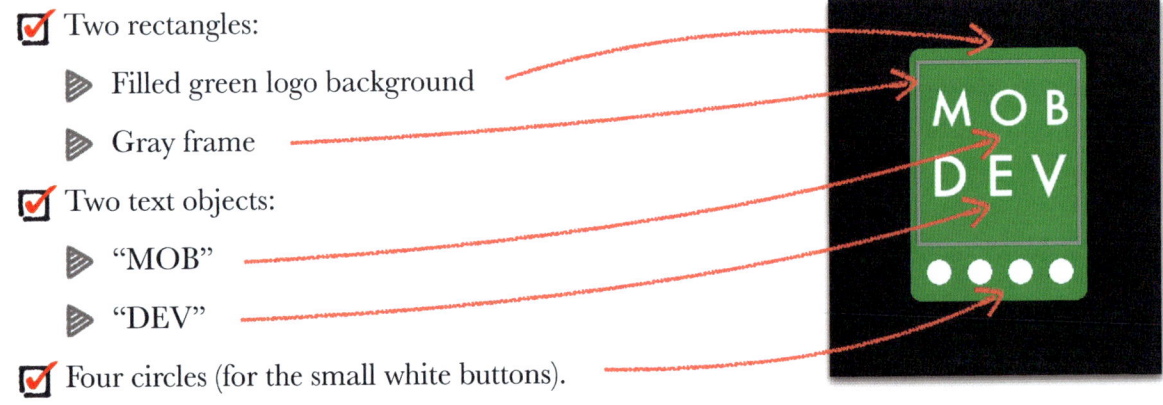

Mob Dev Logo

Although the logo looks pretty simple, the code required to generate it is a bit more complex than prior examples. A "hand-coded version can be found in the resource download, but it is much easier with *Drawn2Code*.

These 8 display objects can be aded to a new *Drawn2Code* stack (see "Mob Dev Logo Stack"). You have full control over the appearance of text via the object's settings panel (see "Text Settings Panel").

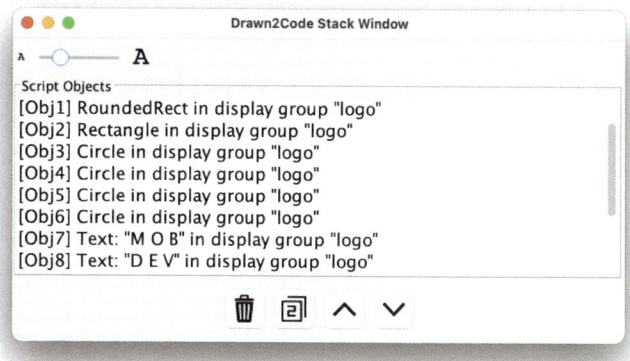

Mob Dev Logo Stack

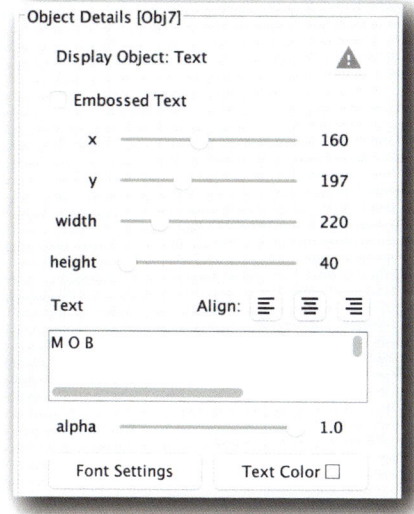

Text Settings Panel

Note that these have been added to a display group to get ready for the next topic.

For very fussy designs, you may need to place and size each character individually or, of course, use an image instead.

In *Drawn2Code*, hover over each of the positioning sliders for keyboard shortcuts to, for example, center a display object onscreen (command + left/right arrow keys to shift from left, center, and right aligned).

Groups and fun things to do with them

The logo looks great, but **what if you don't want it centered?** Do you have to perform the trial and error procedure for every position you may want to draw it in? No. Here's where Solar2D **display groups** come in handy. You can add your display objects to a display group, and then perform operations such as movement on the group, rather than individually on each item in the group.

You create a new display group using the `display.newGroup()` constructor (just as you do with any display object), then add items to it using the `insert()` function. For example, to create the "logo" group and add the rounded rectangle Obj1 to it, the syntax would be:

```
1  logo = display.newGroup()
2  logo:insert( Obj1 )
```

In *Drawn2Code*, add a "Display Group" script object from the "Display Objects" palette and give it a name like "logo". Then, for each display object you wish to add, select the display object and hit the "Add To Display Group" button:

After hitting that button, you'll get a list of optional display groups (i.e., one's that you've already created). After adding that display object to your display group, keep doing this for any other display objects you wish to put in the group.

Notes
Display objects can only be added to 1 group. After adding a display object to a display group, that button changes to "Change Display Group". If you wan't to remove it from all groups, hit "Change Display Group" then select "Remove Group Membership".

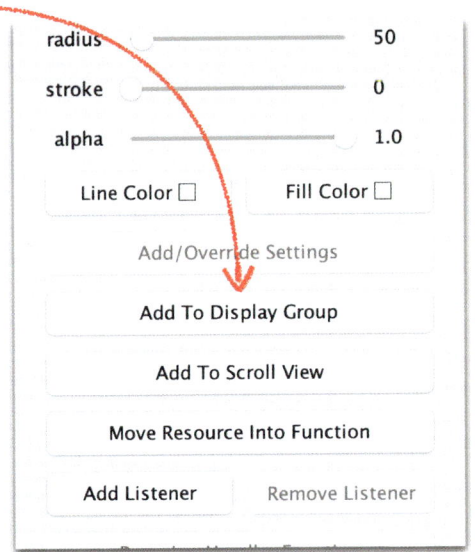

Adding to a Display Group

Using the group
Now that your drawing is in a group, you can easily reposition it using the settings panel for the group (to the right).

In addition, you can perform other operations on the group that aren't directly supported in *Drawn2Code* by using a snippet. For example, although you like your logo, you might like it 50% more if it were 50% bigger. You use the `scale()` function to adjust the horizontal and vertical size. A value of 1.0 means no change. Values less than 1.0 scale the group smaller, while values greater than 1.0 scale it larger. So, with one line of code:

```
logo:scale(1.5, 1.5)
```

You don't have to worry about scaling fonts or adjusting the pixel locations for anything. In theory, the `scale()` function takes care of everything.

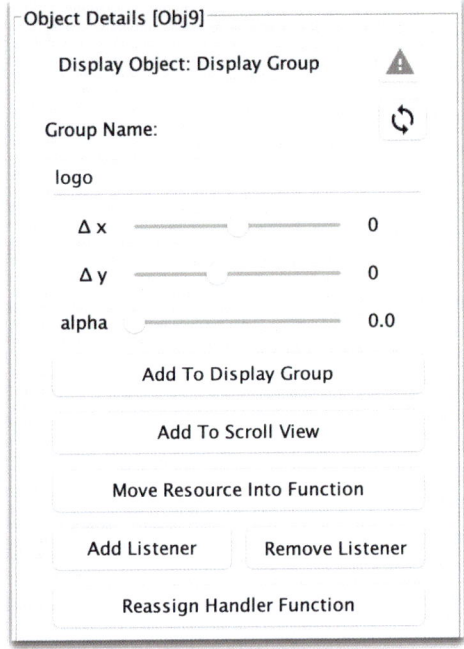

Display Group Settings

Attention

In practice, rescaling compound display objects (i.e., groups of objects) can have unanticipated consequences. In some cases, the rescaled object is also *moved*. In addition, once we learn to use the physics engine (covered in Chapter 12), we will avoid display groups because they don't work well together.

Your first transition

Another cool thing you can do with display objects (including the logo group) is to add a bit of **animation**. Solar2D makes it easy with the `transition.to()` function. We'll use this to do several things during the semester, but let's start out by having it fade your class logo in. You can do this by starting the group off with an alpha of 0 (completely transparent -- i.e., invisible) and animating it up to an alpha of 1 (completely opaque -- i.e., fully visible).

To do this, you only need to add two lines of code:

```
logo.alpha = 0
transition.to(logo, {time = 2000, delay = 500, alpha = 1.0 })
```

That's it! A fade-in animation in **two lines of code**. The first line makes the group transparent (i.e., not visible on screen), while the second performs a transition effect to make the group slowly appear by becoming more and more opaque (all the way up to 100% visible). The transition effect spans 3 seconds (2000 milliseconds) and starts after a delay of ½ second (500 milliseconds).

To do this in *Drawn2Code*, follow these two steps: make the logo transparent by sliding its alpha value to 0.0 (see the bottom screenshot to the left where it is already at 0.0). Then, add a "Transition" action (from the "Actions" palette) and set the target as the logo group. In the transition settings panel (to the right), slide the alpha to 1.0 and check the checkbox. That's it!

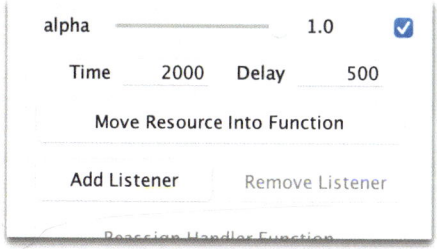

Transition Settings

You will learn to use transitions extensively to animate display objects in a variety of different ways. You can even run multiple transitions at the same time, giving you the power to create wonderful eye-candy in your apps.

Touch & sound

Okay, wouldn't it be cool if you could touch something we've drawn on your device and have it *react*? Let's create an app using the "logo" display group and play a sound when the user taps it. To do this, you'll need to learn three more things:

1. How to load a sound
2. How to tell your app to "listen" for taps on the display object
3. How to play the sound when the tap occurs

Let's tackle these in order. To load a sound, the syntax uses the `audio` table, which contains a `loadSound()` function. In *Drawn2Code*, add a "Load Sound" action to your stack and select the sound file ("Magic-wand-sound-effect.mp3"). Note that this only loads the sound, it doesn't actually play it (that is a separate action). You only need to load sounds once (but you can play them as many times as you'd like).

Magic Sound!

```
Obj14 = audio.loadSound("Magic-wand-sound-effect.mp3")
```

Next, add the "tap" listener to the logo display group. In the logo settings panel, hit the "Add Listener" button and select "Tap". This will add a new function to "handle" the taps in your stack called "Obj9TapHandler" and place it above the logo group script object.

Finally, you'll need to create a play sound action, set it to play the magic wand sound, and move it into the new function. After creating the "Play Sound" action, hit the "Move Resource Into Function" button on its settings panel and select the highlighted function. In the screenshot of the full stack, you'll see this is Obj 15.

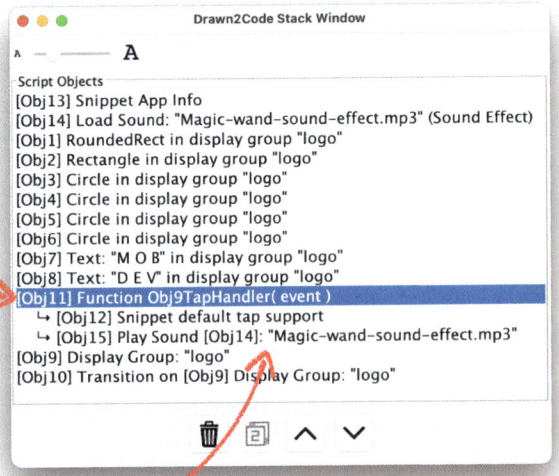

The Full Stack

The syntax to "listen" for the user tapping on `logo` is:

```
logo:addEventListener("tap", Obj9TapHandler)
```

Note that the name of the event handler (**Obj9TapHandler**) is generated by *Drawn2Code* and is unique to the object that it is attached to. If you are hand-coding this, you should feel free to create a more descriptive name (like "logoTapHandler", or whatever you like). The syntax for the function itself looks like this:

```
function Obj9TapHandler( event )
      Obj15 = audio.play( Obj14 )
end
```

This function only contains one line of code, a call to the play( ) function in the audio table. That's it! Save it to reload it in the device simulator and tap away!

Every time the user taps the logo, the code inside the tap handler will execute. If there's anything else you want to do when the user taps the logo, just create those script objects and move them into the tap handler.

Notes

As always, the order of these statements in your code is important. If you are using *Drawn2Code*, the order of the script objects in your stack drives this. For this tap-based app to work, the event-handler function must be placed **above** (or prior to) the line (or script object) that adds the event listener. In this example, since the listener is added to Obj9, the handler Obj11 has be be above it in the stack (which it is). More on this below.

Remember, to run this app you need to have the **image and sound file in the same project folder.** If everything is in place, when you tap the image, you should hear the "magic wand" sound. I've also created a version with a bit of code to make it more fun. This bonus version (*logo-tap-with-sound-bonus.d2c*) moves the `logo` display object to a new random location each time it is tapped. We'll build this "game" out a bit more in future topics.

Flow of execution: Top to bottom & functions

As noted, your scripts will execute **top to bottom**, line by line, as they are typed in the script file (e.g., "main.lua"). In *Drawn2Code* the script objects in your stack will also execute from the top down, except for functions. When Solar2D finds a function defined in your app, it reads the function in, but does not execute (run) it.

Functions are only executed either in response to a listened-for event (such as a user "tap") or when you (the programmer) call (or "invoke") the function by name. For example, the `aRandomColor()` function described above is only executed when it is used in a subsequent statement such as `Obj1:setFillColor( aRandomColor() )`, while the `Obj9TapHandler()` function is only executed when the user "taps" the `logo` display object.

In most cases, the function needs to be defined prior to actually calling it in a statement. As such, most functions will be defined towards the top of your code, *above* their actual use.

Summary

You have learned how to draw basic shapes in this chapter, including how to set their fill and outline colors (including random colors). In addition to positioning and sizing these shapes, you may also set the thickness of the line that outlines the shape (the "stroke"). In drawing multiple, overlapping shapes you are gaining an appreciation for the "top down" nature of script execution. In your drawings, shapes that you draw below (i.e., later in your code) will appear over (on top of) shapes drawn earlier (i.e., above in your code). Finally, you learned how to group multiple shapes together into a single display group.

You are also now handy with the "tap" listener and are able to react to (or "handle") user taps on display objects of your choosing. Finally, you've learned how to load and play a sound file at an appropriate time (i.e., in response to a tap).

Chapter resources

In the chapter resource download for this book (www.lillipellilabs.com/mobiledev/download/chapter_resources.zip), you'll find the following app in folder "4":

1. basic_shapes: The basic stacked display objects, the gradient background, and the random colored ("wild") version.
2. mob_dev_logo: The class logo app, the creation of the "logo" display group, and the version with the dramatic fade-in (transition) effect.
3. touch_and_sound: The fun app that detects touches on the image, plays a sound, and the bonus version that moves the image to a new random location each time it is tapped.

End-of-chapter exercises

1. Display a rounded rectangle in the center of the display.
   a. Choose any color and border you would like (as long as you don't only like "white"), but be sure the outline stroke is visible.
   b. Add the "tap" listener to the display shape and play a **magical sound** when it is tapped.
   c. Randomly change the colors of the shape when tapped.
2. Create a display group with a circle display object with your **Wizarding School** nickname in it (i.e., drawn on top of it) in a **magical font**. Make your group *fade into view* using a transition when the app loads.
3. Modify #2 by adding the "tap" event listener to your display group.
   a. Play a **magical sound** of your choice when the user taps the group.
   b. Use a transition to make the display group *fade out* when tapped.

Confirm

4. Find or create a **magical image** of some sort and make an app to display it.
   a. Give the app a nice gradient background.
   b. Add a **magical sound** when the image is tapped.
   c. Use the aRandomColor( ) function to randomly tint the image (using setFillColor( )) when it is tapped.

Challenge

5. Using a polygon display object, draw a **wizardly** lightening bolt in the center of the screen. When tapped:
   a. Add an appropriate sound effect.
   b. Use a transition to move the lightening bolt to a new, random (x, y) location on screen.
   c. Use the aRandomColor( ) function to randomize the colors of the lightening bolt.

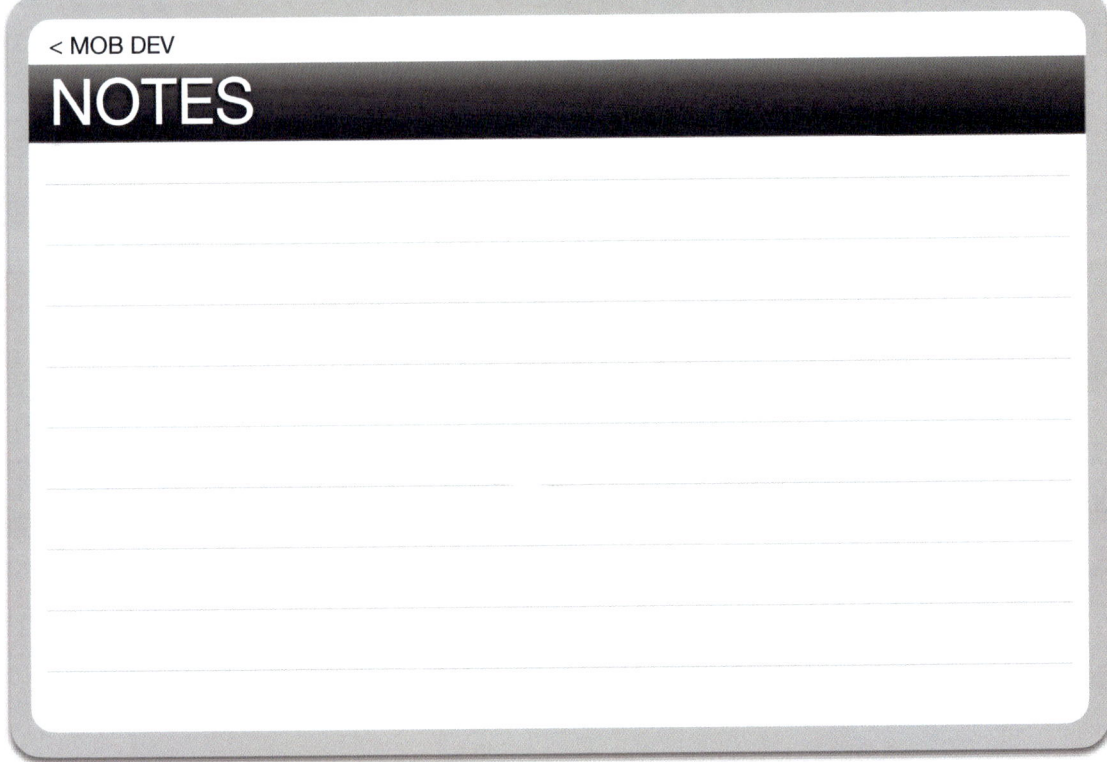

Buttons & Logic

Your first widget

It is almost hard to believe **how much you've learned to do** without using *any* widgets. No buttons, textfields, sliders, lists, etc. So far, you've just drawn what you wanted to appear on the screen, or used images, as appropriate. In fact, you've set up images and drawn items to listen for the user "tapping" on them (so that you might play a sound, for example). Essentially, in doing that, what you've done is created *your own* button widget. In this chapter you'll learn how to use the widget library to create buttons more easily and build more complex event-driven apps. You will also learn how to build apps with multiple buttons and introduce the *if-then logic* you may use to work with them.

Events

Apps that respond in some way to an action taken by the user — touching the screen, for example — are called "event-driven". An event in your app is something like an event in real life: it is something that occurs that affects us, perhaps something that you were expecting and that you were watching and waiting for. It is something of enough importance that you *pay attention* to its coming and *take some action* when it arrives. Your **next paycheck**, for example, may be an event. Or an upcoming **birthday**, or even a **flat tire**. Each of these events would, to some extent, interrupt your normal routine, requiring a response that is appropriate to the event itself.

Apps that contain widgets of some sort (buttons, sliders, text fields, etc.) are *always* event-driven.
In addition, apps that listen for events on an image or drawing you have made (such as the momoney image used in the previous chapter) are also event-driven.

The event cycle

When you write a simple event-driven app, you set the UI up and then your app *waits* for some user action. When the user touches the screen on an object you are watching (e.g., on an image or widget), then the app executes the code you've placed in a function to deal specifically with such an event.

This process is called the "event-cycle" (see figure), which describes the setup, monitoring, and execution required to react to user events.

Note that you (the programmer) don't have to write any code to force your app to *wait*. Once your script has executed all of the statements you've written, it automatically enters this mode if you've added any event listeners.

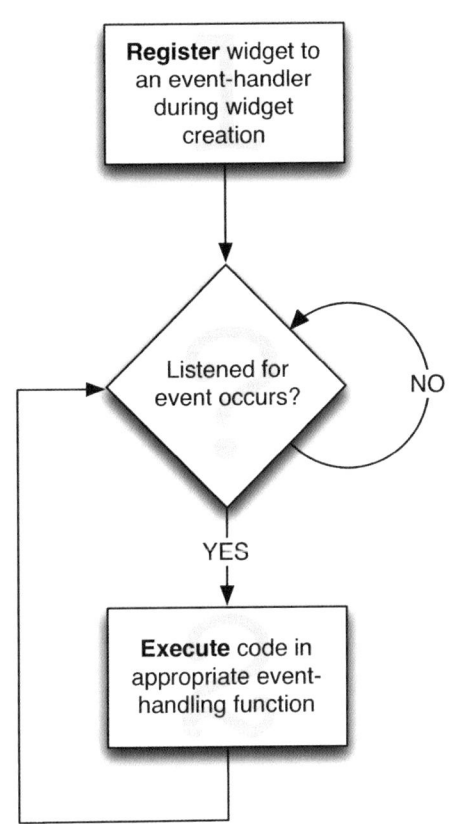

The Event Cycle

All event-driven apps will have a few things in common:

1. Something (an "object") the app is listening to (e.g., a widget, drawing, or image). Or, of course, a combination of such objects.

2. The type of event(s) the app is waiting for (e.g., "tap", "touch", or widget-specific event such as a button "press" or "release").

3. Function(s) written to "handle" events for the listened-to object(s). Such functions are referred to as "event handlers". Within the event-handler you may need to utilize some Boolean logic (i.e., 'if-then' or 'if-elseif-then' statements) to execute the proper code based on the source or nature of the event.

Okay, enough theory. Let's jump into an example.

Get the widget library

You will get your widgets from one of two Solar2D libraries: `widget` and `native` (everything but text fields are in the widget library). So, you'll use `widget` to create (also called "construct" or "instantiate") a button object. When coding by hand, to gain access to libraries that Solar2D doesn't load by default, you need to use the "require" statement:

```
widget = require "widget"
```

The keyword "require" is used to link your script to extra resources

After that, you can access with widget library using the identifier "widget". In this chapter, specifically, we'll use `widget.newButton{}` to create buttons.

Note that, in *Drawn2Code*, this require statement is **added automatically**, whenever you add your first widget script object.

Buttons

Button widgets are highly configurable, but much of the configuration is optional. There are three basic ways to use the button widget: (1) create default "text" buttons, (2) create buttons with visuals drawn using a display object such as a rounded rectangle, and (3) create buttons using an image or images. A basic button widget can be as simple as this (code box #1):

```
Obj1 = widget.newButton
{
    label = "Button Text",
    x = display.contentCenterX, -- optional but needed
    y = display.contentCenterY, -- optional but needed
    onPress = Obj1OnPressHandler
}
```

This creates a default button, which is designed to mimic the look of either iOS or Android buttons. As of iOS 7, buttons are "flat" text and/or icons, without any skeuomorphic (e.g., en.wikipedia.org/wiki/Skeuomorph) styling. That is, something like this:

Button Text

Notice that the button is configured via a table of key-value pairs. For the button to work, it needs a **label** (which is the text it displays) and a hook-up to an **event handler** (these two lines are bolded in the code box above on lines 4 and 9).

In *Drawn2Code*, you'll just hit the "Button (Text)" button at the top of the widgets palette. This will add 4 script objects to your stack: the require statement, the event handling function with a default snippet inside, and the button declaration itself (i.e., the code from box #1).

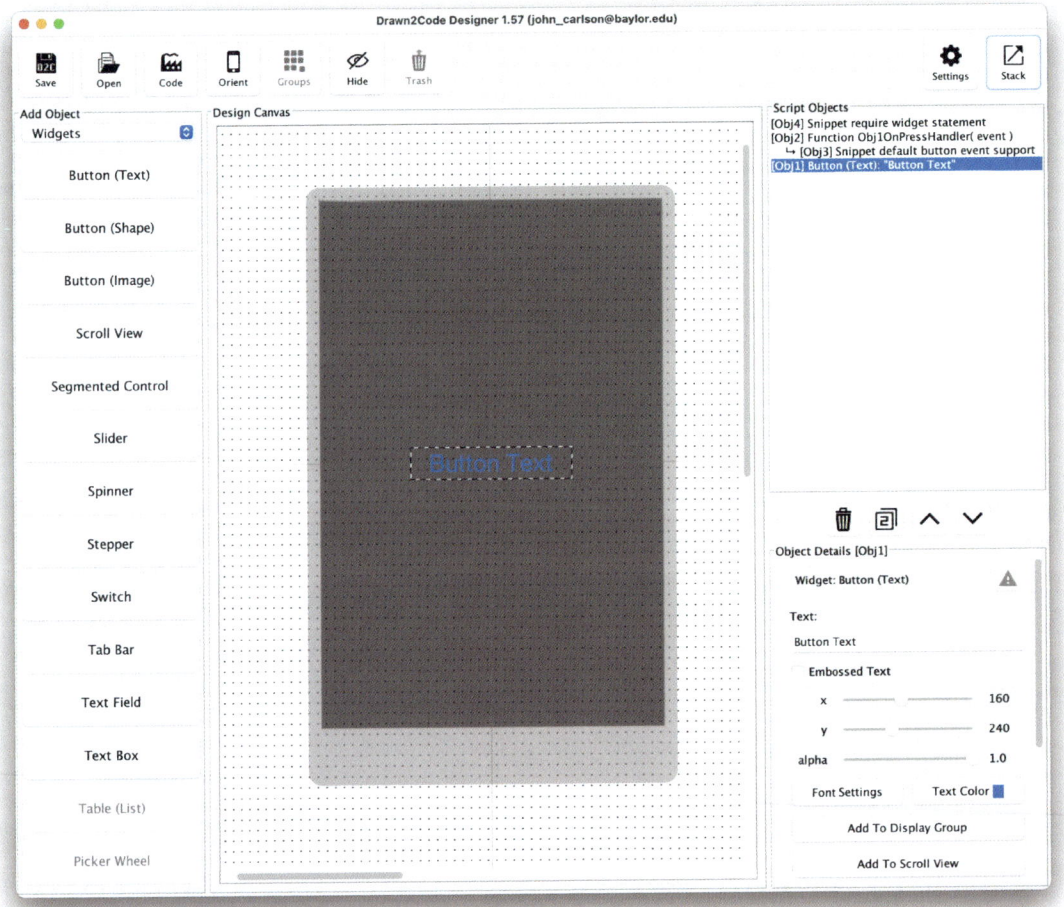

Your First Button

In this case, the *button widget* is paired to an event-handling function named "Obj1OnPressHandler". When coding by hand, you can call the event handler anything you want (assuming what you want is a valid Lua identifier), however, you have to supply a function with that name (e.g., code box #2). In *Drawn2Code*, this function has already been supplied (see Obj2 in "Adding Your First Botton"). Syntactically, it looks something like this:

```
function Obj1OnPressHandler( event )
    print("button pressed")
    -- here's where you would put the code
    -- you want to run when the user presses
    -- the button
end
```

This drawn to code stack will run and produce a black screen with the "Button Text" displayed. Try to contain your enthusiasm. This is in the chapter download as *your-first-button.d2c*.

Syntax notes

When coding by hand, there are are at least two potential "gotchas" here:

1. Be sure to notice that the `widget.newButton` code is surrounded by **curly braces** ("{ }"), not by parentheses, which is a bit of a shift in syntax (in code box #1). You may put parentheses around the curly braces, if you wish, but they don't do anything.

2. **Place the event-handling function** (box #2) **prior to (above) the widget** construction. The code will appear error-free either way, but if the function isn't "on top" of the widget, then it won't be hooked up when you construct the button (and the button won't work).

Gotchas

Making the button do something

If you want the button to do something (beyond just printing information to the console), you'll want to place that code into the event handler. For example, if you want the button to change some text displayed on screen, you'll add that text display object (let's call it Obj5) and access it in the event handler.

In *Drawn2Code*, if you add Obj5 and move it so that it isn't overlapping the button, you'll be able to work with it easily and see the result. Change the text object to say something like "Press the button", so that the app will look like the device on the left:

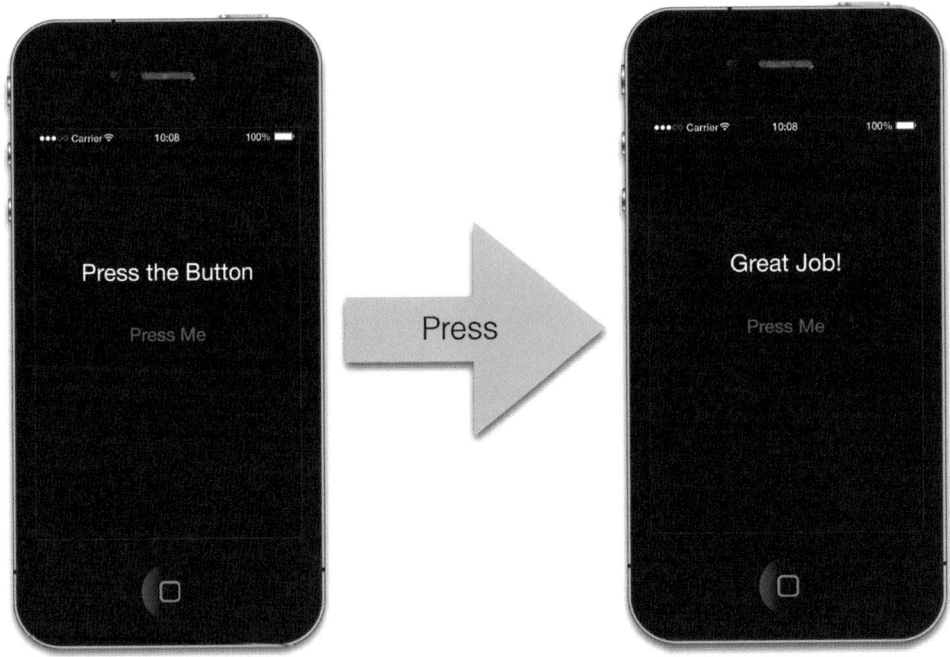

Button With Changing Text

Inside the event handler, add this bit of code to modify the text:

```
Obj5.text = "You pressed the button!"
```

When you press the button, you should see the result in the device on the right (above). This is in the chapter resources as *button-with-changing-text.d2c*.

Finally, I've included a **bonus app** in the download that adds a little extra feature: it uses a multiline text display object to prompt you to press the button, praises you when you successfully do, and then switches the text back to the original. So, how do you achieve these miraculous features? Have a peek at the design and see! Briefly:

1. There is a transition script object that changes the text.

2. Why use a transition? Because you can call another function when the transition completes.

3. That second function changes the text back to the original after a delay.

4. Also note that the text in this example spans multiple lines. You can create a multiline text object by doing two things: break lines using a newline ("\n"), and you set a width (100) and height (80) for the object. Note: If a width and height aren't set, Solar2D will **ignore the newlines**.

After pressing the *button widget*, you will see the text change to a congratulatory message. You should feel good about your button pressing skill. This is in the chapter download as *button-with-resetting-transition.d2c*.

Shape buttons: When words alone aren't enough

Although the plain (flat, text only) *button* presented by **default is fine**, depending on your app, you may want to see a more traditional button, that is, one with a visible outline and/or background that defines an area that can be touched (beyond just the text) to activate the button.

These are called "shape" buttons in Solar2D and are an easy extension of the plain ("flat") button. When creating a *shape button*, you'll be able to specify whether the button should be rectangular, rectangular with rounded corners (i.e., a rounded rectangle), circular, or a more complex polygonal form using the "shape" attribute. These buttons use the display table to draw the shapes for you, making these easy to set up and use.

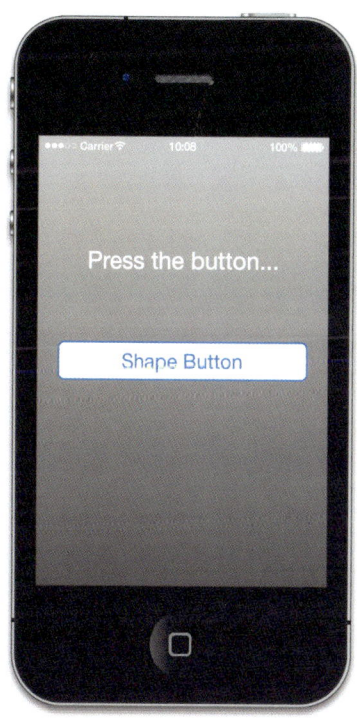

Here's the syntax to see a rounded rectangle:

```
shape = "roundedRect"
```

Shape buttons allow you to provide the user with a **larger area to press or tap**, beyond just the text (label) on the button. See the "Shape Button" screenshot (above) for an example.

For a more **intuitive effect**, you want the button to change (visibly) when pressed, to give the user additional feedback

Shape Button:
Bigger and Easier to Press

97

and confirmation. This can be done setting the "fillColor" button attribute and specifying two values: One configured as the "default" color and other other as the "over" (or *pressed*) color. For example, to keep the default (white) color, but darken it when the user presses the button, the added setting looks like this:

```
fillColor = {default={1}, over={.8}}
```

In *Drawn2Code*, you can add a button with a rectangle or rounded rectangle shape easily by hitting the "Shape Button" button in the widgets palette. The default is a rectangle with slightly rounded corners, but you can adjust the rounding in the settings panel. Move the slider to 0 if you want squared off corners. You can also expand or remove the stroke, which starts with a default value of 4 pixels. *Drawn2Code* also adds a default shading to the button when it is pressed.

Drawn2Code gives you control over the color of the shape and the color of the text. If you have a stroke outline (for the shape), it will be drawn in the same color as the text.

This first shape button app, which has the simple text switching, is available in the chapter download as *shape-button.d2c*. There is also a **bonus version**, with the transition back-and-forth described above called *shape-button-transition-d2c*.

Notes

Unfortunately, as of the latest Solar2D early (2021), it does not appear possible to fill shape buttons with gradients (i.e., in place of "flat" fill colors).

A button using images (finally)

In some cases, and perhaps more than that, these plain buttons won't do for the app you are designing. In these cases, you may move to a widget button that uses one or more images to create the look that you want. However, to do this, we'll need to create the image files using a tool like Photoshop or one more focused on button creation.

At a minimum, you need two images: one for the "default" (i.e., not pressed) button and a second image for the "pressed" (or what Solar2D calls the "over") button. Solar2D also supports buttons with more image "slices", if your needs are more sophisticated.

The images

I've made 2 images for you to start with. Notice that the buttons are "empty" (i.e., without a text label). The **label will be added on top of the image** by the button widget, so if you put any text there it would be in the way. These files are named *button.png* and *pressed.png* (and are included in the download for this chapter). If you are going to use these images in a different project (which is fine), you'll need to copy them into your project folder so that your app can find them.

Advanced Tip: In a project you are planning to distribute, remember to create versions in higher resolutions and to append the "@2x", "@4x", etc., image suffixes on them. Then, Solar2D will select the best fit for the device your app is running on (as discussed in Chapter 3).

Okay, so how do you *use* these files? It is actually **easy**.

A Button Widget with Images

The syntax

The hard part is *making the images* in the sizes and styles you need (i.e., the prior step). Now that you have them, there are just two properties of the widget button you need to set: "defaultFile" and "overFile". For example, here's a snippet of the settings table for the image button example app (see "A Button Widget with Images"):

```
defaultFile = "button.png",
overFile = "pressed.png",
```

The first one, clearly, is the default button (i.e., the top one, above). The second one is the "pressed" version, even though the property key is "overFile" and *not* "pressedFile". This does't really make sense, since mobile devices don't yet detect if you finger is hovering *over* a button (it only knows when you've touched it).

So, the syntax for setting up an image button is basically the same as for setting up a regular text or shape button, which some differences in the settings table. If you are coding by hand, entire settings table from the image_button app is shown in code box #3, which the major differences highlighted.

```
1  Obj1 = widget.newButton
2  {
3      id = "Obj1",
4      label = "Image Button",
5      font = "HelveticaNeue-Light",
6      fontSize = 16,
7      x = display.contentCenterX,
8      y = display.contentCenterY,
9      width = 300,
10     height = 36,
11     strokeWidth = 2,
12     emboss = true,
13     defaultFile = "button.png",
14     overFile = "pressed.png",
15     onPress = Obj1OnPressHandler
16 }
```

Note the two highlighted key-value pairs discussed above (lines 13 & 14) are defining the image files you are using (i.e., the ones downloaded with the chapter or others that you've created). Note also that the text is **embossed**, which looks a bit nicer on image buttons.

Now, the widget will appear as in the screenshot ("A Button Widget with Images"), offering potentially **great-looking buttons** that are also somewhat easy to use.

If using *Drawn2Code*, you'll just hit the "Button (Image)" button and then specify the two files in the settings panel. Note that, when you first add the image button script object to your stack, it will show up in the design canvas with a big red "X" through it:

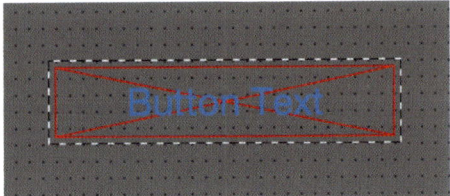

100

This "X" is just to remind you that the app won't display an image button until you've selected both of the required images. Once you do, the button will show up "correctly" in *Drawn2Code*. In the device simulator, just press and hold the button down to see the "pressed" image.

The transition effect

If you have run any of the **bonus apps**, you'll have noticed that the text doesn't actually just switch, but rather it *transitions* (beautifully) from one message to the other, and then back. This is relatively easy to do using the transition table that comes in Solar2D, which you were introduced to in Chapter 4.

As you might suspect, to perform two transitions, we'll use two `transition.to()` statements (if coding by hand) or a transition display object (in *Drawn2Code*).

The first transition will fade the congratulatory text out slowly (over 1 second). The second, which is unnamed, will fade the original text back in, after a delay of 2 seconds (2000 ms). See code box #4 for a version of a slightly simplified version of the event-handler. You can find the first transition on line 12.

There are a couple of important points to make note of. First, when the button is pressed, any ongoing transition is stopped (lines 3), and the congratulatory text is (re)displayed (lines 8 — 9), after which the animated transition restarts. This allows the user to hit the button as often as they like, each time seeing the inspirational message immediately reappear. Stopping and then restarting the transition effect allows the fade out / fade in to occur as intended.

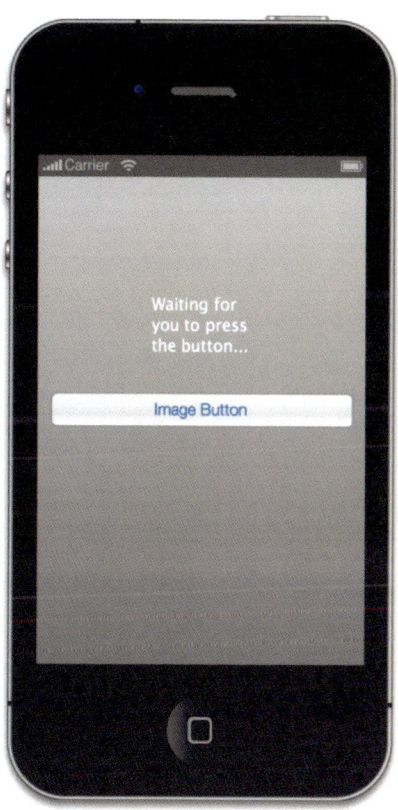

The Transition Effect

The second transition, which restores the original text (the "waiting" message) by fading it in, is started by using the "onComplete" attribute in the transition Obj8's settings table. This allows you to specify a function (any function) to run when your transition has — you might have guessed this — completed.

```
1   function Obj1OnPressHandler( event )
2       -- stop any ongoing transitions:
3       transition.cancel( Obj8 )
4
5       -- set the congratulatory text:
8       Obj6.text = "You pressed the button!\n\nGreat job."
9       Obj6.alpha = 1
10
11      -- fade txt out and back to the original text:
12      Obj8 = transition.to(txt, {delay=2000, time=1000, alpha=0,
            onComplete=Obj8OnComplete})
13  end
```

Here's the function specified from the app ("Obj8Oncomplete")

```
1   function Object8OnComplete()
2       Obj6.text = "Waiting for you to press\nthe button..."
3       transition.to(Obj6, {delay=500, time=1000, alpha=1})
4   end
```

Finally, note that this function needs to be placed somewhere above Obj8 in the app. Also, since Lua allows functions to be placed inside of other functions, you could actually place "Obj8OnComplete( )" **inside of** the "Obj1OnPressHandler( )" function (so long as it is placed above Obj8.

In *Drawn2Code*, much of this syntax will be written for you. After creating the image button (Obj1) and the text display object (Obj6), you'll create the first transition (Obj8) and move it into the button's event handler (Obj2). See it highlighted in the stack to the right ("Stack With

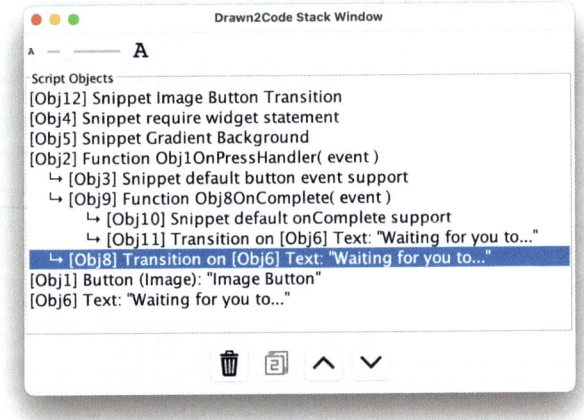

Stack With Transitions

Transitions"). The gradient background (Obj5) you see in my stack is just eye-candy and isn't required.

To create the the function that runs when the first transition completes, you'll add a listener to the transition Obj8 itself. To do so, select the transition object in the stack, and hit the "Add Listener" button in the settings panel. You'll see a pop-up dialog that allows you to choose what type of listener you want. You need to select "onComplete" to call a function when the transition ends.

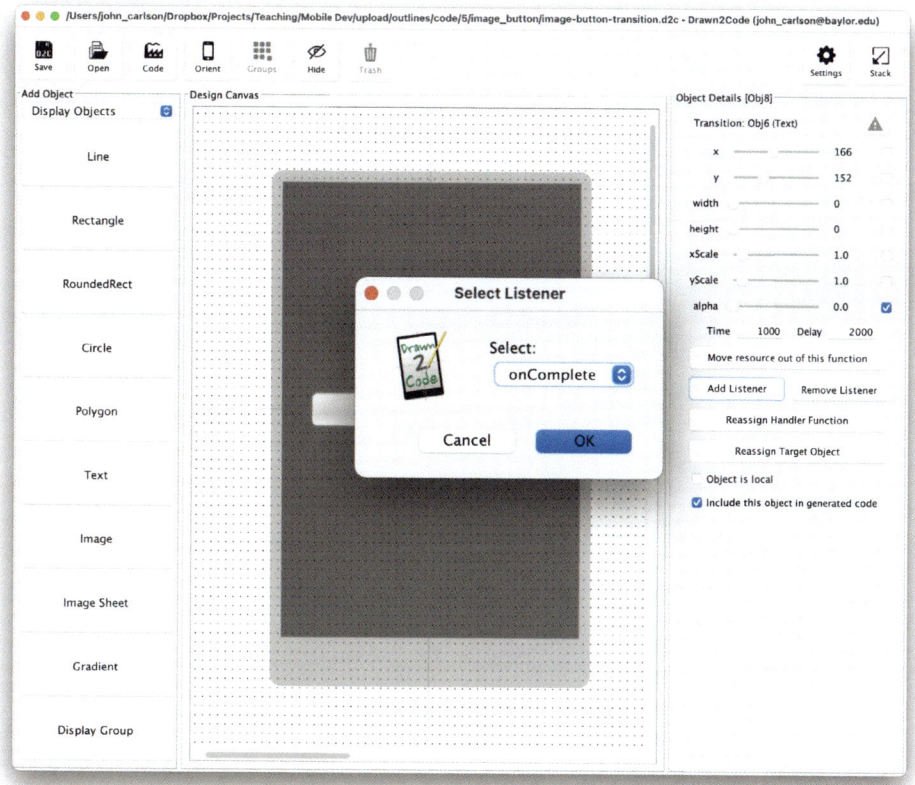

Adding an onComplete Listener to a Transition

Drawn2Code will create all of the syntax for you, including the function to handle the on complete event.

Next, you'll create a snippet to switch the text back to the initial prompt (or add to Obj10 which is already there) and a second transition (Obj11 in my stack) to fade that text back in. This is obviously more complex than it needs to be, but I hope that you'll have fun playing around with transitions as you learn about configuring button widgets!

Using logic to control the flow

We'll need to use conditional branching (or, more simply, 'if-then' logic) to create more sophisticated apps. At its most basic, a simple 'if-then' statement can be flowcharted (see "A Conditional Branch") to visually diagram the **branched flow of execution**. The "branching" or "conditional" logic allows the programmer (i.e., you) to specify code to be executed only under certain conditions. You write these conditions using Boolean logic, often involving testing for equality, or whether some value is greater than or less than another.

Flowcharts

Program logic is frequently diagrammed using **flow charts** like these which provide the programmer with a visual way to design, refine, and communicate the inner workings of their code, especially with less technical stakeholders. A chunk of Lua/Solar2D script may be close to indecipherable to some end-users, while a visual depiction of the logic may be readily understandable.

Flowcharts will have a defined beginning ("start") and end (usually labelled "end" or "stop") and use a variety of fairly standard symbols, including the **diamond shape** to represent a conditional branch, and rectangles to represent lines or blocks of code (Lua refers to standalone blocks of

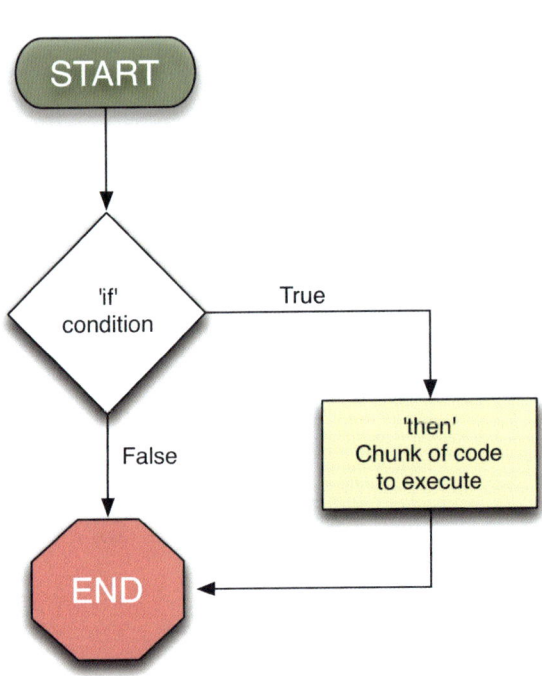

A Conditional Branch ('if-then' Logic)

code as "chunks"). Additional symbols are available to represent database access, report printing, and many other common app tasks. The arrows represent the **flow of execution**, that is, the path that the app takes when executing script statements. Although the default flow of execution is *top to bottom*, the path can be controlled via conditional branches and functions (for example).

Touch event phases

When you touch a button it actually can produce three distinct event phases: "began", "moved", and "ended". While these phase names are essentially self-defining, it may seem strange to some that a **single touch** onscreen can yield **three separate events**. In some apps, it makes sense to listen for all of these phases and react to them appropriately. So far, we have avoided the need to do so by limiting our attention to the "press" phase by only attaching the "onPress" listener to the button. There's nothing wrong with that and it has been appropriate for our apps to this point. However, what if we wanted to play a sound when the user pressed the button and a separate sound when they released the button?

In these examples, you'll learn how to listener for all of the event phases and react appropriately using a single event-handler. To do that, these examples use the "onEvent" listener rather than the more restrictive "onPress" listener.

Touch events correspond to the moment the user's finger *touches* the device screen, as it *moves while touching* the screen, and when it is *lifted* from the screen. What this means is that every time a user touches a button, the event-handler will be called (executed) **at least two times**. If the user moves their finger while pressing, the event-handler will be called **continuously**, as they move, pixel-by-pixel. Some apps will require this detailed information about what the user is doing to operate as desired. In other apps, as is the case today, such fine-grained control is unnecessary.

An example: "button_sound"

So, when will this come in handy? Well, right now! This app shows you how to add a sound effect to the button press and to play only on a specific phase ("began", in this case). If you don't limit the sound to the desired phase, you will hear it **multiple times** (quite a few, if the user drags their finger while pressing the button). That's not what you want!

Limit Chunk to Single Event Phase

Loading a sound: Firstly, you'll need a sound effect of some sort. The one included in the download is named "click-on.mp3" and identified as "clickSND" in the app. It is an MP3 file downloaded from a free online repository[1]. Sound effects are loaded using the audio table (introduced in Chapter 4).

---

[1] Sources and attributions are included in the script itself.

Here's the basic syntax:

```
clickSND = audio.loadSound("click-on.mp3")
```

Limiting an action to a specific event phase: So, how do you limit the sound effect to the "began" phase of the touch event, so that it plays just once when the user pushes the button? Conditional logic, of course! You'll use an 'if-then' statement to limit the sound effect to the "began" phase of the event:

```
if event.phase == "began" then
        audio.play(clickSND)
end
```

This conditional logic can be flowcharted as shown ("Limit Chunk to Single Event Phase"). See the complete app in the chapter download: *button-click-sound.d2c*.

A second example: "button_sounds"

Did you notice that is says "sounds" rather than "sound"? That's right, you are going to play **separate sounds**, tied specifically to the "began" and "ended" phases. To make it simple, this app uses the same "press" sound and just adds a "release" sound:

```
releaseSND = audio.loadSound("click-off.mp3")
```

To create an app with distinct button "press" and "release" sounds, based on these distinct touch event phases, you'll also need to use conditional logic, but this time the 'if-elseif' syntax. This can be visualized in a flowchart as well (see "Limit Chunk to Specific Event Phases" on the facing page). The Lua/Solar2D syntax is also easy and looks like this:

```
if event.phase == "began" then
        audio.play(clickSND)
elseif event.phase == "ended" then
        audio.play(releaseSND)
end
```

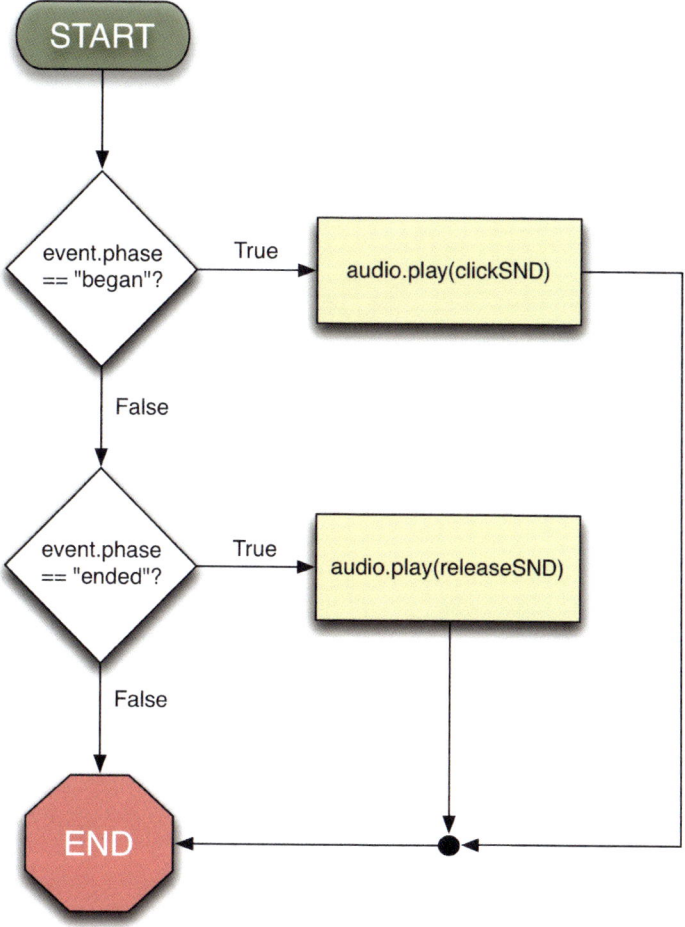

Limit Chunk to Specific Event Phases

See the complete app in the book resources: *button-click-sounds.d2c*

A third example: "multiple_buttons"

Frequently, one button is not enough. Given the requirements of your app, you might find that you need multiple buttons (of whatever type). In such an app, you (the programmer) will want to know which button the user pressed to allow you to take appropriate action.

One way to handle this is to link each button to its own event handler (as is done in the *Drawn2Code* version), however, when coding by hand it may be easier to use conditional logic to branch the flow of execution to the code handling each of the buttons (see the flowchart "Limit Chunks to Specific Event Phase and Button ID" for a visual depiction of the logic).

You'll code this inside the event handler (i.e., the function often named "onButtonEvent( )", or similar, shown in box #6). Note that these buttons only react to the "began" phase, so the

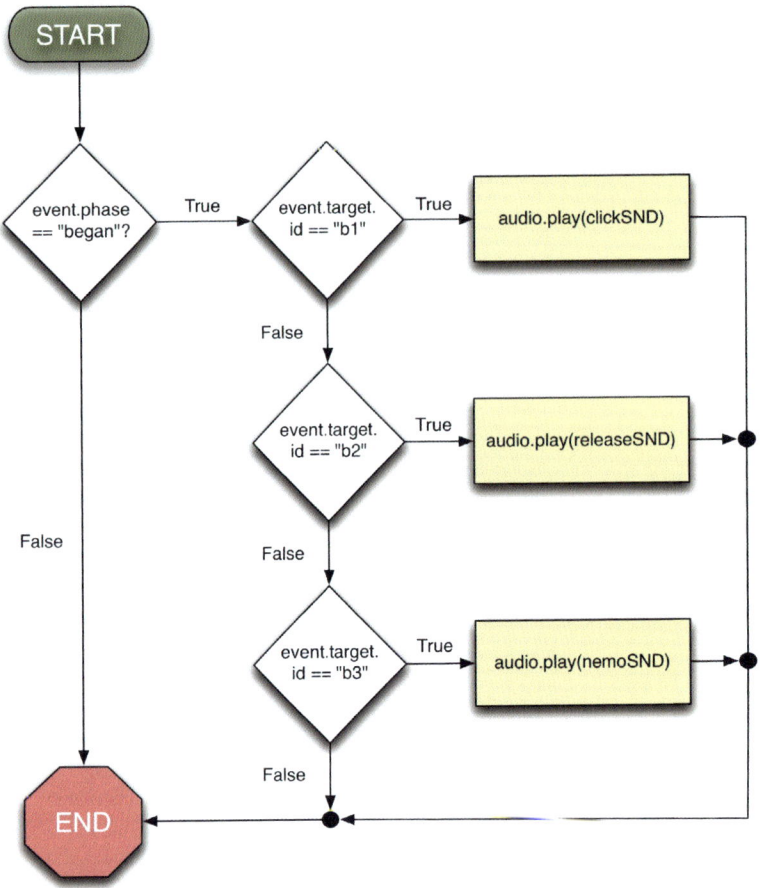

Limit Chunks to Specific Event Phase and Button ID

```
1   function onButtonEvent( event )
2       -- only play sounds once:
3       if event.phase == "began" then
4           -- play sound specific to each button:
5           if event.target.id == "b1" then
8               audio.play(pressedSND)
9           elseif event.target.id == "b2" then
10              audio.play(releasedSND)
11          elseif event.target.id == "b3" then
12              audio.play(nemoSND)
13          end
14      end
15  end
```

logic checks for that phase first, and then checks to see which button was pressed. Then, you can use the event data passed to it to determine the "target" of the event (which is the button that the user pressed). Once you have the target, you can check its "id" attribute to determine its identity.

To access the button data we need, we'll use the "dot dot dot" syntax, moving more deeply into the event table with each "dot" to reach the id (see syntax note below). Once we have the syntax to reach the button's id, we can use it in a sequence of 'if-elseif' tests to play the correct sound.

This example is available in the downloads in the "hand_coded" folder inside of the multiple_buttons example.

In *Drawn2Code*, it is **easier not to do it this way.** Since *Drawn2Code* automatically writes so much code for you, there's no real penalty to using what is given to you. In this example, as you create each button script object, *Drawn2Code* supplies each of the three event-handlers, into which you can put the appropriate sound effect (or other action).

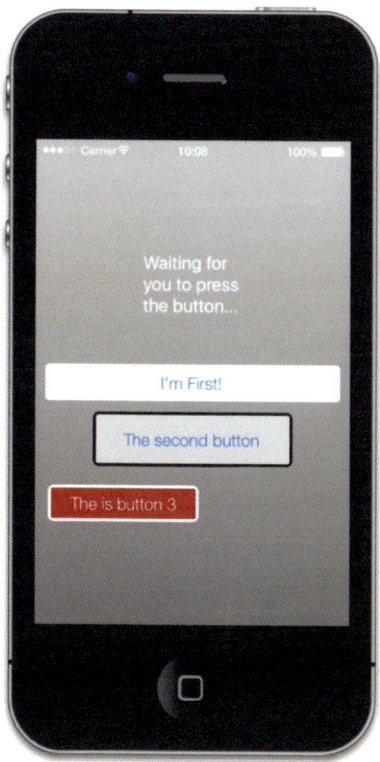

Multiple Shape Buttons

Run this example in the chapter downloads: *multiple-buttons.d2c*.

Syntax note: using "dot dot dot"

In code box #8, the function contains an example of the "object dot attribute" style (e.g., event.phase) but even more with more than one dot. The can be confusing the first time you see it or try to use it in your code. It is an object-oriented syntax that can be read from left to right, with each successive item becoming more specific, until the desired object or property is reached. For example, this is the syntax used to access the id value for the touched object:

```
event.target.id
```

We start at the left, with the event *table*, which contains useful information about the touch event. One piece of information is the object that *generated* the event (i.e., the button that was touched), which is called the "target". So, by adding the ".target" object, you reach the button widget that was touched. If you want to know something about that button (which you do), you can access the desired attribute (id) by added ".id" (see the table "Finding Nemo").

Syntax	Meaning
event	The touch event (a Lua table), named "event", which contains information about the touch.
event.target	The target of the touch event, which is the object that was touched.
event.target.id	The id of the button object that was touched. One of the buttons had the id "nemo".

Finding The ID

Each "dot" you add to the syntax provides more specificity, until you reach the necessary part. As an analogy, let's say you wanted to write the syntax necessary to "find Nemo" (itunes.apple.com/us/movie/finding-nemo/id255295077). You might start in the ocean, then the reef, then the anemone to get to Nemo. The OO syntax for Nemo's address would then be:

```
ocean.reef.anemone.Nemo
```

Easy! Unless he's **missing** (itunes.apple.com/us/movie/jaws/id526768967).

Advanced: A function to make buttons for you

The prior example, in which 3 buttons were created and individually configured, works fine, but it can be a time-consuming, copy-and-paste exercise. That means, of course, that you have an opportunity to **create a function** to make this work easier! It is possible to create a function that will make these buttons for you, customized for your particular UI needs. This only really makes sense, however, if the buttons will all conform to a similar pattern (or "theme"). For example, if you are standardizing on shape buttons, with a particular shape, colors, and font, then a function could be written to create them for you.

This is a somewhat more *advanced* topic, so feel free to skip to the next section if this looks uninteresting.

```
1   function getButton( buttonID, labelText, xPos, yPos, w, h )
2
3       button = widget.newButton {
4           id = buttonID,
5           label = labelText,
6           shape = "roundedRect",
7           x = xPos,
8           y = yPos,
9           width = w,
10          height = h,
11          strokeWidth = 3,
12          strokeColor = {default = {0}, over = {.1}},
13          onEvent = onButtonEvent
14      }
15
16      return button
17
18  end
```

Ideally, you'd be able to create a button **in one step**, something like this:

```
b1 = getButton("btn1", "A button in one step!", cx, cy, 300, 36)
```

This line of code is creating a button with the identifier "b1" by calling a function named "getButton( )" and passing 6 parameters: the id, label text, x location, y location, width, and height. You could customize your function to take any additional parameters you cared to (such as the font or fill color). But we'll just start with the basics. (code box #7):

Once the function is in place, creating a button (or three) become simple matter. For example, in the download you will find an app called "multiple_buttons_function" which creates three buttons similar to the last example (but with a common theme) like this:

```
b1 = getButton("btn1", "Button the First", cx, cy, 200, 36)
b2 = getButton("B2", "The second button", cx, b1.y+b1.height+20, 200, 36)
b3 =
  getButton("nemo", "Don't touch the button!", cx, b2.y+b2.height+20, 200, 36)
```

Obviously, if you needed a different style of button, or wanted to change the theme of your buttons, you could modify the getButton( ) method as you see fit. In addition, after the buttons have been created, you may still modify some attributes. For example, you may change the button's label text and fill color:

```
b1:setLabel("I'm First!") -- can set/revise the button text
b2:setFillColor(.85) -- can set basic fill color (but not 2 color tables)
```

A simple counter

Let's create a fairly simple app that uses buttons to demonstrate how this all comes together. Our app ("Simple Counter") has three image buttons and one large text display object. This app will support users who need to count but are unsure how to do so. What would you count? Perhaps people entering a building, cars entering a parking lot, runners passing a checkpoint, or bottles of root beer on the wall. The possibilities are indeed endless. Although it may seem like such an app is targeted solely at users of diminished cognitive capacity, the need to keep accurate count in stressful or distracting environments may be challenging even for the mentally competent.

What should this app look like? Well, the counter itself -- the number the count is at — should be fairly large and easy to read. The main button that performs a count (i.e., adding 1 to the count) should span the UI to make it easy to press. Other, lesser used buttons should probably be smaller. See "Simple Counter: The User Interface" to see an example.

How would you build this app? Let's start by looking at the user interface (UI). The UI consists of 4 big, easy to read objects. Is "uncount" a word? It is now. It is just "undo" and "count" merged. How will you code such a visual *masterpiece*? Well, one object at a time, top to bottom and left to right.

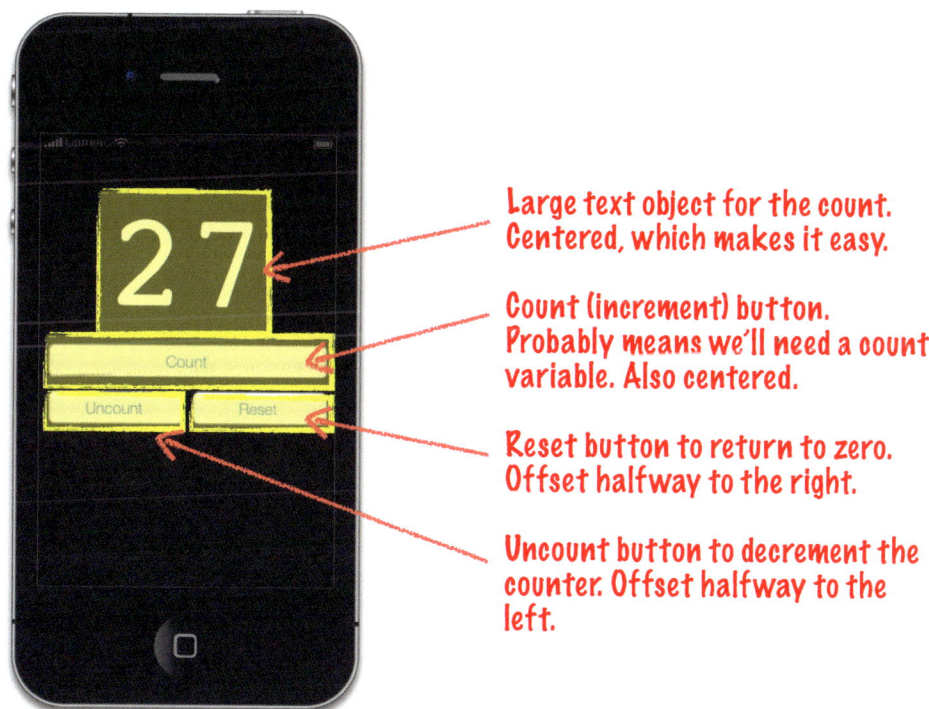

Simple Counter: The User Interface

```
1    -- set up the UI
2    -- large text obj for the count
3    txt_count = display.newText("0",0,0,"Courier",144)
4    txt_count.x = display.contentCenterX
5    txt_count.y = 130
6
7    -- button to increment counter
8    btn_count = widget.newButton
9    {
10       id = "btn_count",
11       label = "Count",
12       x = cx,
13       y = cy,
14       defaultFile = "button.png",
15       overFile = "pressed.png",
16       onEvent = onButtonEvent
17   }
18
19   -- button to remove 1 from count (or "uncount")
20   btn_uncount = widget.newButton
21   {
22       id = "btn_uncount",
23       label = "Uncount",
24       x = cx - .244*w,
25       y = cy,
26       defaultFile = "button-half.png",
27       overFile = "pressed-half.png",
28       onEvent = onButtonEvent
29   }
30
31   -- button to reset counter
32   btn_reset = widget.newButton
33   {
34       id = "btn_reset",
35       label = "Reset",
36       x = cx + .244*w,
37       y = cy,
38       defaultFile = "button-half.png",
39       overFile = "pressed-half.png",
40       onEvent = onButtonEvent
41   }
```

Here's the big counter display at the top (displaying "0" to start)

Here's the "count" button, centered.

Here's the "uncount" button, sized by the png file and offset about 24% of the width to the left.

Here's the "reset" button, same size but offset about 24% to the right.

Simple Counter: Coding the UI

Note that, although the **order of the code mimics the layout of the UI elements**, it doesn't necessarily *have* to. The widgets appear where they are on screen because of the (x,y) coordinates you give them, not because of the order they appear in the code. However, the location of the widgets are often calculated based on the position of prior widgets, so having the order in the code mirror the order on screen **is actually helpful**.

The code to set up this UI is in box #7 on the prior page. While this may look like a lot of code, it is really **just four blocks**, each doing **one thing**. The numbers that position the buttons were finalized using trial and error.

Notice that, for the buttons, you have specified that when a button event occurs ("onEvent") you want the method "onButtonEvent" executed. Now, you have to provide this method to hook those buttons up.

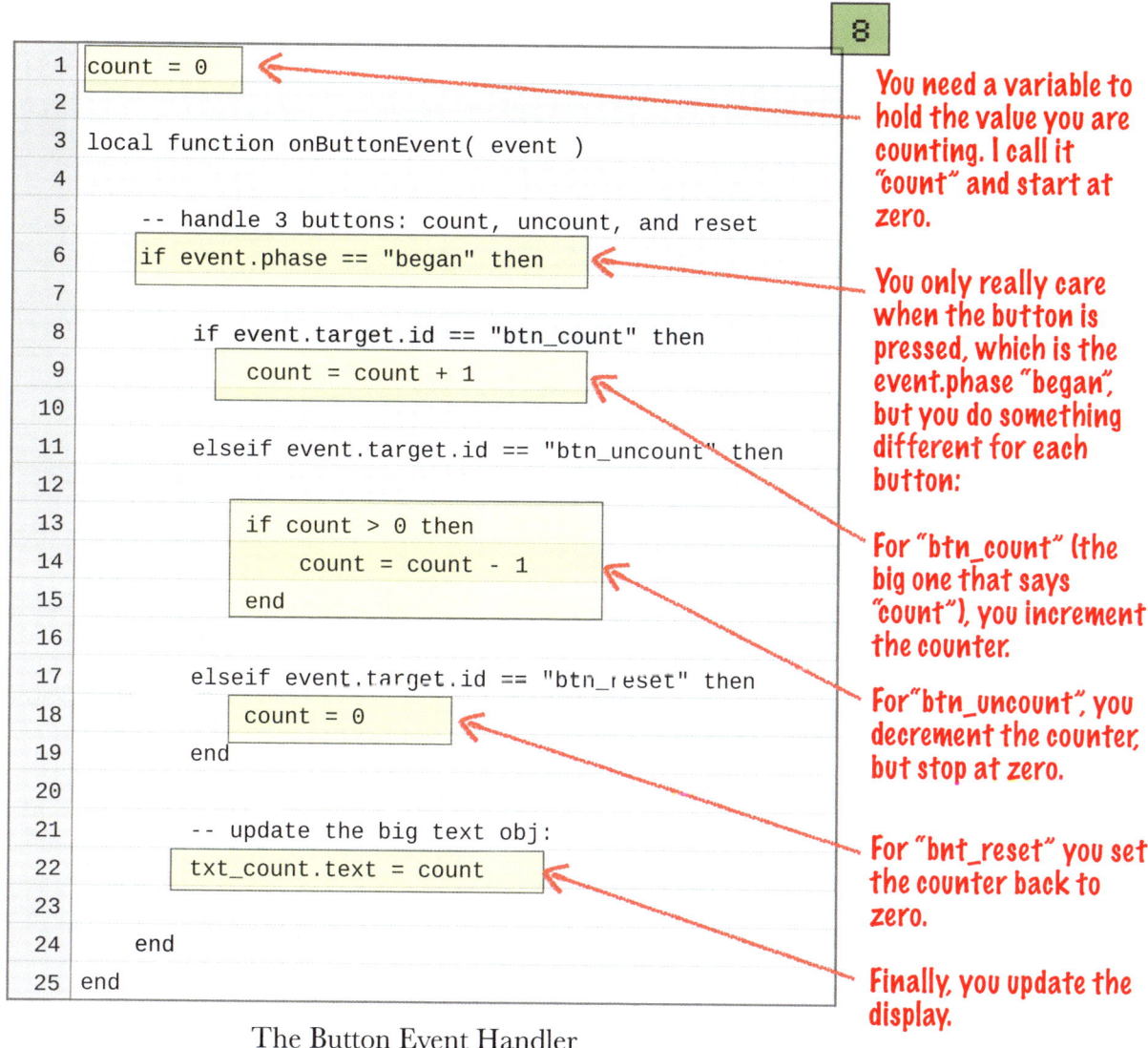

The Button Event Handler

Button event-handler (code box #8)

In the construction code for the buttons (above) you hooked them up to an event listener you called onButtonEvent, which means you **have to provide** a function of that name. It is a single function that will **handle all three of your buttons** ("count", "uncount", and "reset"). Note that the function to handle the button events will usually be placed *above* the UI setup (even though it may make sense to code the UI first). In other words, although the code in the outline could be cut-and-pasted in your IDE, you should **use the downloaded code** instead.

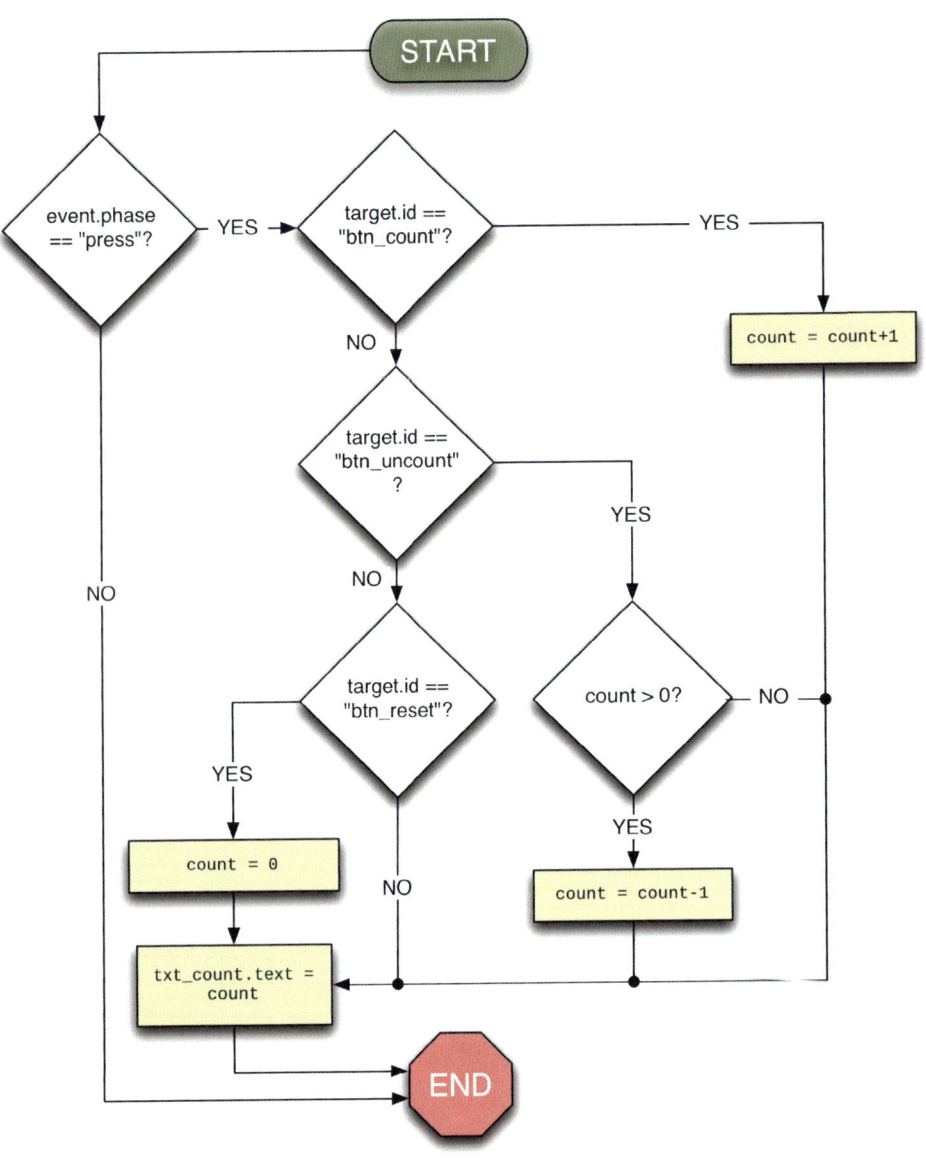

Flowcharting onButtonEvent()

116

This function uses 'if-elseif' logic you used earlier, in addition to simpler 'if-then' logic. There are two examples of 'if-then' logic above: Checking to see if the button was *pressed* (i.e., the event phase was "began") and checking to see if the count is greater than zero. There are three parts to the 'if-elseif' logic, one for each of the buttons.

For "btn_count", you *increment* the counter by adding one. For "btn_uncount" you *decrement* the counter, but not if the count has hit zero. Finally, for "btn_reset", you return the count to zero. After all of the buttons have been processed, you update the on screen display object for the count.

Flowcharting the increment/decrement logic

In this case, you want to make sure the decrement doesn't make the count go negative. If you think about it, there would be at least a couple of ways to handle the decrement task. This is true for many scripting tasks. The logic used in the app only performs the decrement if the counter is greater than zero (see "Flowchart of the Decrement Logic"). However, we could let the decrement occur no matter what, then check *afterwards* to see if the count was less than zero. If it was, you could set it back to zero (see "Alternate Decrement Logic").

Is one of these solutions correct (or "more correct")? No, not really. The original approach is simpler and uses less code, so it might be preferable on those grounds. However, in general, I think the best approach is the one you understand and can document and maintain the best.

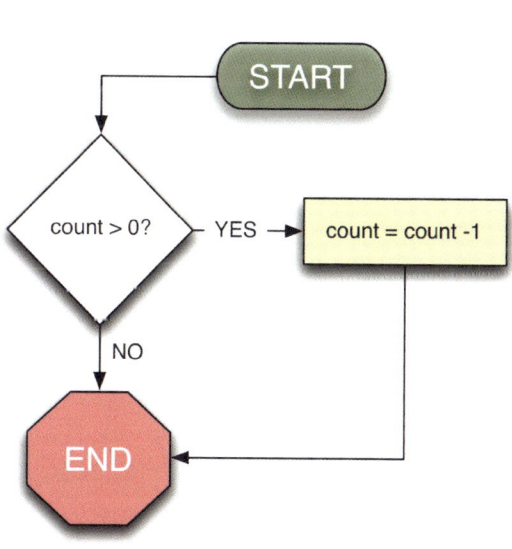

Flowchart of the Decrement Logic

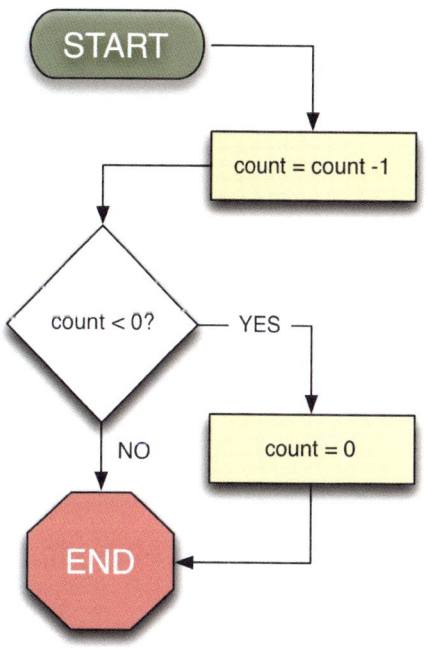

Alternate Decrement Logic

Okay, as a larger example, how about **flowcharting the entire `onButtonEvent()` function**? It is a bit more complex (see the flowchart above), but it allows you to visualize the logic in a way that is hard to do when just staring at the code. Do you see where the decrement logic is in the event handler?

Since your logic doesn't contain a final "else" block, if all three of these questions are false, then none of the blocked code will be executed. That makes sense in this case, since there only are three possible phases, and you are covering each of them (i.e., there is no fourth possibility).

That's an app!

Together, these two chunks of code, setting up the UI and handling the button events, create your fancy counter app. As an event-driven app, the UI is set up and displayed, then the app waits. It will wait forever, or as long as the device is operational, until the user touches a button. In response to the touch, the linked event-handling function is called (or "invoked") and the appropriate code inside it executed, changing the number onscreen accordingly.

Summary

This is a large chapter and contains a number of "firsts" for you. You now know how to create and use the Solar2D *button widget*. Although your tools may make them easy to create and customize, the code you place in the event-handling function can be simple or quite complex (depending on what action(s) you wish to take in response to a button press). Frequently, you will need to create code to implements the logic needed to respond accordingly. Graphical flowcharts can help you visualize and understand the flow of execution created the logic you are using. You also learned more about the *event-cycle* and the 3 phases of the button widget ("began", "moved", and "ended") and used the first and last phases to play different sound effects. You also learned to use the "dot dot dot" syntax to find the `target.id` of the event source to enable you to take more appropriate action. Finally, you learned to create a simple counting app with an attractive UI.

Chapter resources

In the chapter resource download for this book (www.lillipellilabs.com/mobiledev/download/chapter_resources.zip), you'll find the following app in folder "5":

This download includes:

1. text_button (including *your-first-button.d2c, button-with-changing-text.d2c, button-with-resetting-transition.d2c*)
2. shape button (including *shape-button.d2c, shape-button-transition.d2c*)
3. button_enclosed_function (one alternate syntax for button event handlers)
4. image_button (including *image-button.d2c, image-button-transition.d2c*)
5. button_click_sound (playing a sound when pressed)
6. button_click_sounds (playing sounds based on event.phase)
7. multiple_buttons (scripting more than one button)
8. multiple_buttons_function (using the getButton( ) function)
9. widgets_btn_counter (the handy counter app)

End-of-chapter exercises

1. <u>A magical sound</u>. Create an app that:
   a. Loads and plays a magical sound when it runs.
   b. Has a button of your favorite type that plays a magical sound when pressed.
   c. Has 3 buttons, one of each type, that each play a unique magical sound when pressed.

2. <u>Your Wizarding School nickname</u>. Create an app that:
   a. Displays your nickname when it runs.
   b. Has a button of your favorite type of button that displays your nickname when pressed.

c. Has two buttons: The first button uses a transition to fade your nickname *in* and the second button uses a transition to fade it back *out*.

3. Create an app with a multiline text object that displays a **magical rhyme** of at least four lines.

4. Create an app with a button and a text display object.
   a. Starting from zero, count up by one each press.
   b. If the count == 10, change the color of the number to **red**.
   c. Modify (b) so that the number is red when the value is 10, otherwise it is green.
   d. Modify (c) to play a magical sound when the color changes.
   e. Draw a *flowchart* for this app. You can use Visio (on Windows), OmniGraffle (Mac), or a web-based tool like gliffy.com. Or you can use a pencil and some paper.

5. Display your name in a *text display object*.
   a. Add the "tap" listener to this object and switch the text between your name and your **Wizarding School** nickname (i.e., start with your name, then switch to your nickname when tapped. Then, switch back to your name when tapped, and so on).
   b. Modify (a) to play a **magical sound** when your nickname (but not your name) appears.

6. Modify the **magical rhyme** exercise (above) by adding a button to add 1 rhyming line to the multiline text object for each press. So, this would need 4 presses to display the entire rhyme. On the fifth press, start over.

7. Create a simple dice-throwing game: Simulate rolling 1 die (e.g., generate a random number between 1-6) in response to a button press and display the result as a *text display object*. You can generate a "dice roll" using the math.random() function:

```
roll = math.random(1, 6)
```

Use *boolean logic* to assess the result:
- If the user rolls a 6, display text declaring them a "winner".
- If the user rolls a 1, declare them a loser. Be as kind as you wish to be.
- Add sound effects to enhance your game.

Integrate

8. Create an app with your name displayed inside of your favorite shape. Add the tap listener to the shape.
   a. When the shape is tapped, change the fill color to a new random color.
   b. Modify (a) to also change the color of your name to a new random color.
   c. Modify (b) to also play a *magical sound* when tapping the shape.
   d. Modify (c) by adding a counter to display the number of times the shape has been tapped.

9. Add 3 text display objects to exercise #1 (a magical sound)
   a. Display the number of times each button was pressed to the right of each button.
   b. Add a 4th text display object to show the sum of all button counts.
   c. Add a button to reset all counts to zero.

Challenge

10. Create an app with 2 buttons and 2 text display objects. Count the number of presses on each button and display that value in the text display objects.
    a. Set the text color to color for the higher count red. Make sure that the lower color stays (or goes back to) white.
    b. Add one more text display object. If the two counter values are equal, display "equal" in the text object, otherwise display "not equal".

11. Create an app with a *button* that generates a random number between 0 and 100 (integer values) and displays it. Then:
    a. Keep a running total of the generated numbers and display it.
    b. Calculate the average of these numbers and display it.
    c. State whether the current number is odd or even.

12. Create a counting app with a *button widget* and a *text display object*. Start counting at 1 and count up by 1 each time the *button widget* is pressed until the counter reaches 10.
    i. After reaching 10, restart the counter at 1.
    ii. Count backwards by 1 after hitting 10 instead of resetting to 1. When you hit 0, start counting up again.

13. Create your own button style using a `getButton()` function (i.e., based on code box #9). Recode one of the above apps to use this function.

14. Create a better dice-throwing game. Here are the rules: Each time the user throws the dice, generate two random numbers between 1 and 6 (you are throwing 2 dice). If the player rolls a double, you add the squared die value to the score. Otherwise,

you subtract the added score of the dice times 2.

So, scoring is as follows:

Dice Roll	Points
1 & 1	1
2 & 2	4
3 & 3	9
4 & 4	16
5 & 5	25
6 & 6	36
Anything else	Subtract 2*(die1 + die2) from the score

Your interface needs a *button widget* (to "throw" the dice) and 4 *text display objects*: one to display the result for each die, one to show the score for that roll, and the last one to keep a running score.

Text Fields & Loops

Your second widget

Of course, buttons are great, but why stop there? There are several more widgets to learn, each serving a specific need. In future chapters you will learn to use check boxes, radio buttons, sliders, tables, and more. In Chapter 6 the focus is on the text field. Once you master the text field, you can write apps that accept user input.

What is your favorite scripting language? | Lua |

The native library

You get the text field widget from the native library, **not** the widget library. There are other widgets available in the widget library, and Solar2D is revising the widget library all the time. However, as of build 2020.3635, there is no text field *widget*.

Instead, you'll create text fields using the native library. However, these text fields are not part of the same "canvas" Solar2D uses to draw widgets; as a result, text fields will display on top of display objects and any widgets you are using. In addition, these text fields may not respect all display group

Native Warning

actions. Finally, there are issues with the way text appears in text fields, sometimes requiring you to adjust the text field settings based on the font you are using.

Text fields

This UI component, as its name suggests, is a *field* (as in an area onscreen with distinct rules and capabilities) in which *text* can be entered and/or displayed. Text fields are used in an app UI to allow the user to enter textual or numeric data, or to display results of some procedure.

Text *fields* are distinct from text *display objects* (which you have been using) both visually and also in their ability to **allow data input** by the user.

The syntax is slightly different from using regular widgets, but is still quite understandable. A basic text field (see "Native Text Field in the Solar2D Simulator") can be set up with these lines of code (code box #1):

Native Text Field in the Solar2D Simulator

```
1  Obj1 = native.newTextField(ccx, ccy, 80, 30)
2  Obj1.id = "Obj1"
3  Obj1.font = native.newFont(native.systemFont, 18)
4  Obj1.align = "right"
5  Obj1.inputType = "number"
6  Obj1:setTextColor(.2, .2, .2)
7  Obj1:addEventListener("userInput", Obj1UserInputHandler)
```

Basic setup

The setup seems pretty normal, right up until line 3. Setting a font for the text field is slightly more involved than that for widgets from the widget library and it's easy to forget this difference. You should also set the text color as the default color has been invisible in some releases. This text field will align its content to the right, which is the usual alignment if your are expecting the user to type in a **number**. Of course, the user has no idea what you want them to type in this app, because the text field doesn't have a label and there's no instructional text. Not the best UI. You'll fix it in a moment.

In *Drawn2Code*, the text field object can be found in the widgets palette. I know, I just said it wasn't a Solar2D widget. But it is still a "widget". Once added, you can customize it using the script object's settings panel ("Text Field Settings Panel"). This gives you easy control over what the widget looks like and how it behaves.

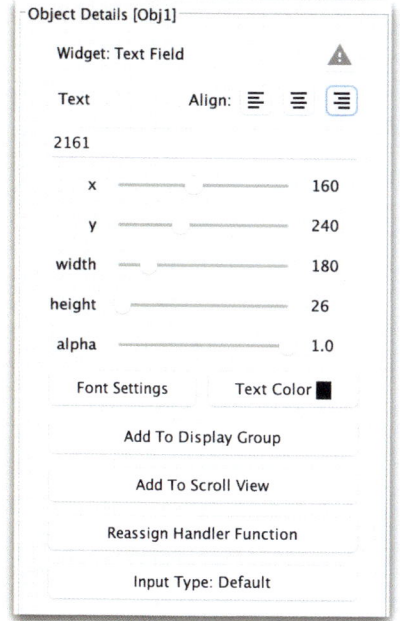

Text Field Settings Panel

The textfield will most likely need to be connected to a listener. If coding by hand, you can see the listener connected on line 7 (box #1). This is accomplished with the `addEventListener()` function. For text fields, you specify that you want to listen for "userInput" and handle it with a function you will write called `fieldHandler()`.

Drawn2Code will automatically hook the text field to its listener and allow you to easily switch the input type using the bottom button on the settings panel ("Text Field Settings Panel"). When hand coding, you can see this setting on line 5 (box #1). The options are: "default" (text), "decimal", "number" (integer), "phone", "url", and "email". This setting will control which keyboard is displayed to the user when they tap inside the text field.

Next, you'll need to supply the event-handler function (i.e., with the name defined in line 7 of box #1). This handler is a bit more complex than what you would typically see working with buttons, but easy to learn. An example function is shown below (code box #2).

In *Drawn2Code*, this function will be written automatically and placed in the stack (above the widget script object). For example, if you start with an empty *Drawn2Code* design and add a text field, your stack will look like "Basic Text Field Stack".

Basic Text Field Stack

In this block of code (box #1) you, the programmer, get to name the *text field object* (called it "Obj1" here) and the *event handler* (called "Obj1UserInputHandler"). When coding by

125

hand, could call these whatever you wish, but should name them something appropriately descriptive. Of course, what goes inside the event-handler function is largely up to you as well.

Text fields produce multiple event phases

One key to understanding text fields is to know that they produce multiple event phases, in the same way that user touches (but not taps) do. For text fields, the event phases are: "began", "editing", "ended", and "submitted". You most likely won't need to respond to all of them. To deal with them, you'll use some simple 'if-then' logic to ensure you are responding appropriately to the event phase. The basic logic is flowcharted in "Basic Text Field Handler Logic". Can you see how the flow of execution is diverted to the appropriate chunk of code (i.e., the yellow boxes)?

Code box #2 shows an implementation of this logic and prints information about the user's interaction to the console.

You can access the text the user has typed into your text field using event.target.text, but most likely want to wait for the "submitted" (or "ended") phase. If they've typed in a number (which is likely, since you specified that as the input type and only the numeric keypad will load on the device), you can get the text and convert it to a number like this:

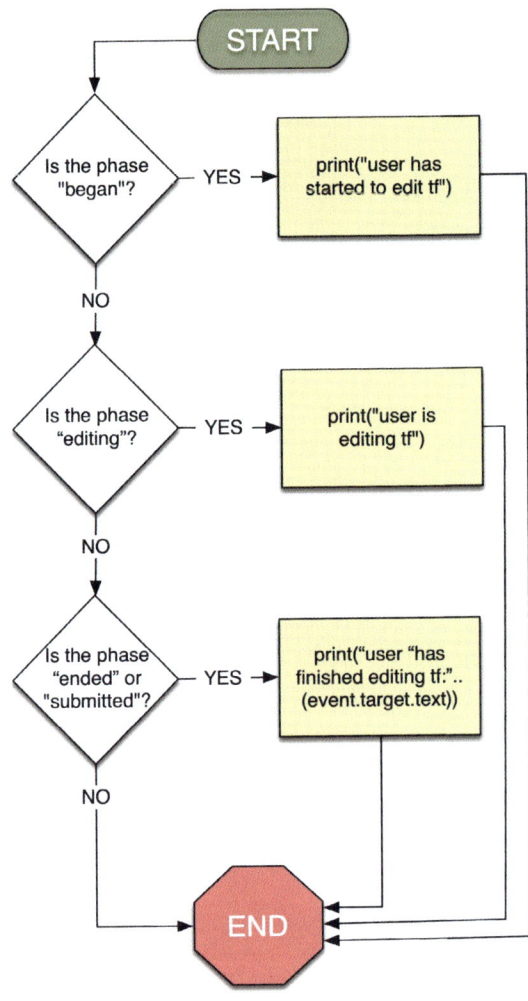

Basic Text Field Handler Logic

```
num = tonumber(event.target.text)
```

You might have noticed as well the somewhat odd line of code doing something with the keyboard (lines 15 and 22, box #2):

```
native.setKeyboardFocus(nil)
```

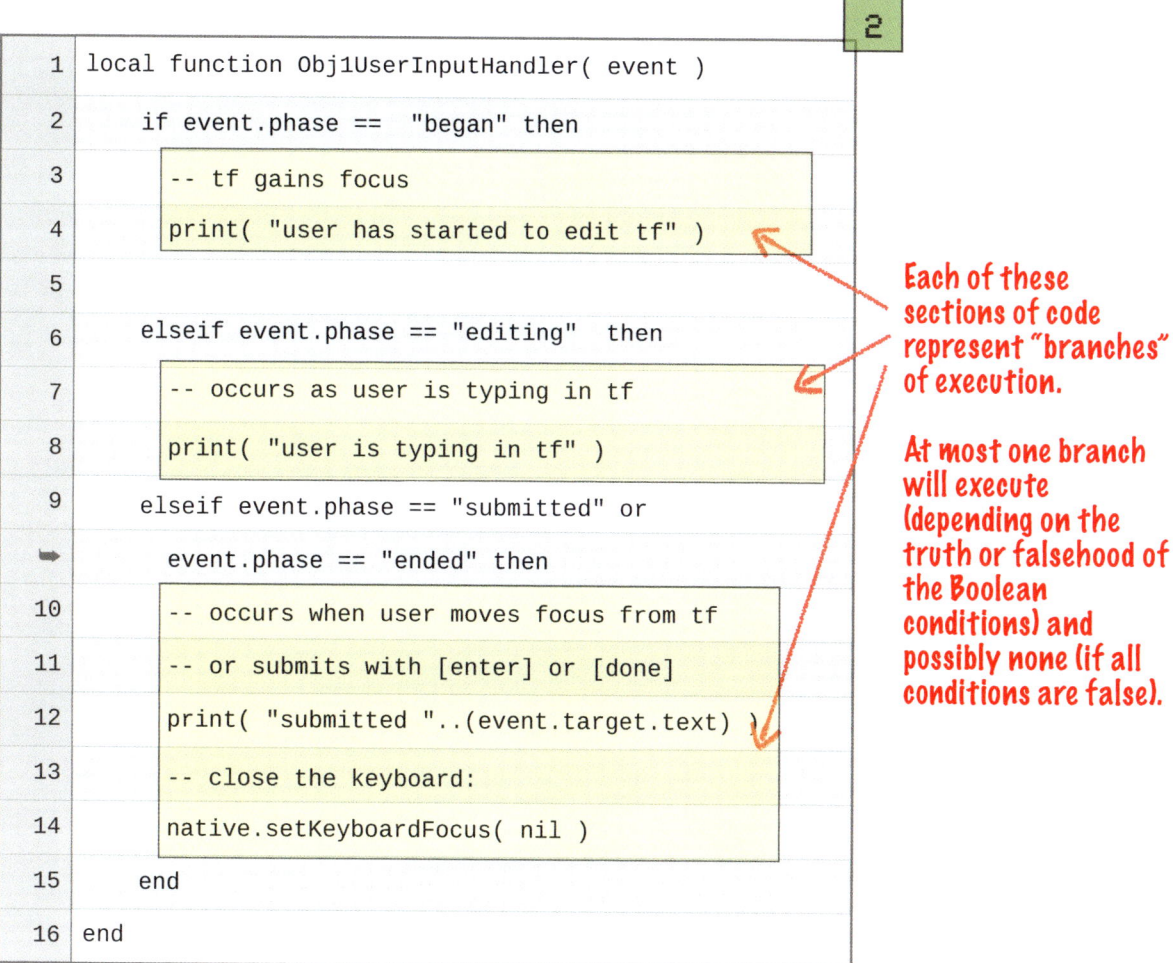

This is the statement that will **dismiss the onscreen keyboard** (i.e., on the device or in the iOS simulator, but not the Solar2D Simulator). This doesn't have anything to do, however, with the keyboard on your computer or laptop. It only dismisses the keyboard or keypad which slides up on the device's screen. Of course, if your app is going to cause a keyboard of some sort to slide onscreen, you will also have to code your app to accommodate it (otherwise, the keyboard will cover the bottom of our app). You'll learn how to handle this below.

Simulator and platform issues

There are some important differences in how the text field works when executed in different environments. If you are having trouble with the text field in the Solar2D Simulator, it may be time to install and configure the **Android Emulator** (covered in Appendix A) and/or the **iOS Simulator** (covered in Appendix B).

However, while the text field works in the Android Emulator, the input text is typically drawn too high. In fact, the top half of the input is often unreadable. This is a longstanding issue on Android (with several potential workarounds).

Gotchas

Another issue is that when a user *submits* the text field by tapping the "enter" button, both a "submitted" and an "ended" event phase are generated (in that order). To some extent, this makes sense, because when submitting the input the user has also completed (or "ended") their data entry. However, since two **separate event phases will be generated**, you (the developer) have to be careful to only take action once by detecting the event phase and controlling the flow of execution using 'if-then' logic (just as you did with button widgets in Chapter 5).

Note that, if you need more than one line of text input, you may use a "text box" rather than a text field. The syntax is the same, except that you use `native.newTextBox()` rather than `native.newTextField()`.

Finally, note that on iOS devices, the numeric keypad doesn't have an "enter" key to submit entered data. This will require you to supply a button onscreen to perform this and dismiss the onscreen keyboard. You'll learn how to do this later in this chapter.

	Case	Example	Recommendation
1	You need to repeat the task a certain, known number of times.	Contact each member on a 4 member list (e.g., to **remind each** about upcoming meeting).	`for`
2	You need to perform some task zero or more times. You don't know how many times, but you can tell when you need to stop.	If **pizza** is needed at the next meeting, contact members on your list until someone volunteers to bring it.	`while`
3	You need to perform some task at least once, and possibly more than once. You don't know how many times, but you can tell when you need to stop.	Since **root beer** is always required, contact members on your list until someone volunteers to bring it to the next meeting.	`repeat until`

Three Cases of Repetition

The logic of loops

In Chapter 5 you learned about controlling the **flow of execution** using 'if-then' statements (along with 'else' and 'elseif'). Another common programming need is to *repeat* some task, or, put another way, to "loop" the flow of execution.

Loops are frequently used in animation, working with structured data (such as the Lua table), various gaming tasks, as well as many types of calculations (such as earned interest). We'll use loops in several apps this semester, starting quite soon.

There are **three classic situations** in which you might need to loop: 1) You need to repeat some action (i.e. chunk of code) a certain, *known number* of times; 2) You need to repeat some chunk zero or more times and, although you don't know how many times, you can *figure out* when you are done; or 3) You need to repeat some chunk one or more times (which is similar to #2, however, you know in advance you must perform the chunk *at least once*).

As an example, let's say you are in charge of making some phone calls to your teammates (see "Three Cases of Repetition"). Here's the three possible cases or situations:

1. You need to call everyone to **remind each** of them about the meeting and confirm their attendance. You have 4 teammates, so you know you'll have to make 4 calls.

2. You are in charge of getting a volunteer to bring **pizza** to the next team meeting if another food item isn't already being supplied. If necessary, call list members until someone volunteers to bring it. If food is already arranged or unneeded, then no call is necessary. So, you'll need to make zero or more calls. If calling, you may have to go through the list multiple times. You can stop calling as soon as you get a volunteer.

3. You are in charge of getting one of your teammates to volunteer to bring **root beer** to the next soiree. Since root beer is always needed, you know you have to place at least 1 call. You still have 4 teammates, but you don't know in advance who will agree to bring the root beer. As with case #2, you don't know how many calls you'll need to make (but it will take at least 1).

As is the case with most modern languages, there are (not entirely coincidentally) **three different kinds of loops in Lua**: the 'for' loop, the 'while' loop, and the 'repeat until' loop. The 'for' loop is used for situation #1 (when you know how many times you need to loop), the 'while' generally used for situation #2 (when you need to loop, but don't know in advance how many times), and the 'repeat until' loop for situation #3 (when you know you need to perform the task one or more times).

The following sections discuss each of the loops in detail, but there's a bit of setup needed for these scenarios. Firstly, this simulation needs a table to store team members in. You can set a team of four (simulated) people up like this:

```
teammates = {"Harry", "Ginny", "Ronald", "Hermione"}
```

So, this table has 4 teammates. But how many times will each loop repeat? Let's create a loop to see.

The 'for' loop (a known number of repetitions)

The syntax of the 'for' loop is reasonably straightforward, at least in comparison to other languages. You have to specify a counter to use, where to start counting, where to finish counting, and what to count by.

```
for variable = beginning, ending, step do
     -- chunk of Lua/Solar2D
end
```

The "chunk" of Lua/Solar2D statements can be any length and can call built-in or user-defined functions. As with the other loops, you may nest other loops inside this and use 'if-then' logic to split the flow of execution inside the loop.

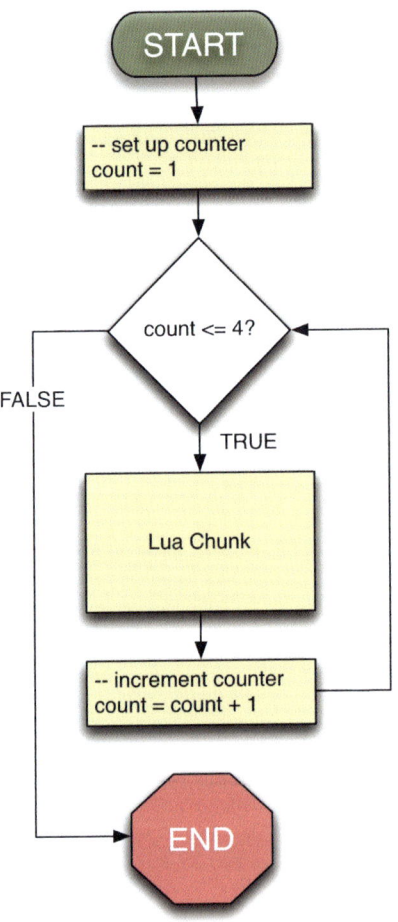

The 'for' Loop

The increment (or "step") is optional and can take on any value (not just integers) and may be negative. If the step is omitted, the 'for loop' will count by 1.

Situation #1

So, to simulate situation #1 (above), in which you must contact each member of your team to convey some information, you might write a 'for' loop as follows:

```
1  print("Reminder: Meeting tonight!")
2  teammates = {"Harry", "Ginny", "Ronald", "Hermione"}
3
4  for callNumber=1, #teammates do
5      print("Call #"..callNumber.." made to "..teammates[callNumber])
6  end
```

Note that the expression "`#teammates`" is a nice bit of Lua syntax that gives you easy access to the number of items in a table. This is generally preferred to, say, using the actual current number in the table (in this case, 4), since that could change. When executed, since there are 4 members of our team, this will output "Reminder: Meeting tonight!" then the list of (4) calls mades to the console, confirming you have called each teammate:

```
CONSOLE
Reminder: Meeting tonight!
Call #1 made to Harry
Call #2 made to Ginny
Call #3 made to Ronald
Call #4 made to Hermione
```

Why does the "reminder" text only display once? Location is everything! Since it isn't in the loop (i.e., between the "do" and the "end"), then it isn't part of the repetition.

131

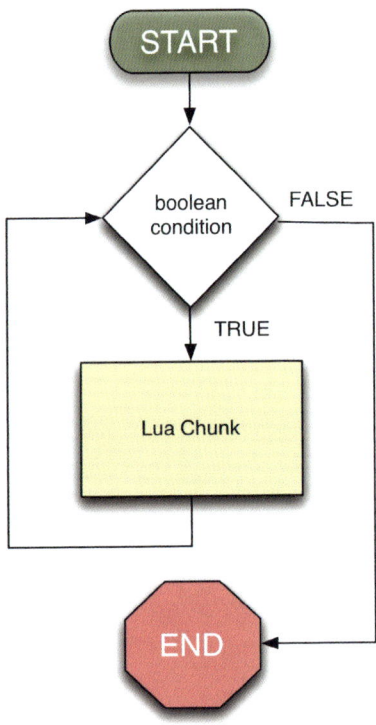

The 'while' Loop

The 'while' loop (repeat zero or more times)

The syntax of the 'while' loop is even easier than the 'for' loop. To use a 'while' loop, you only need to be able to express the Boolean condition that determines whether the loop continues or ends.

```
while condition do
    -- chunk of Lua/Solar2D
end
```

Note that the condition in the 'while' loop is checked first, before executing the chunk. If the condition is initially `false`, the chunk is *skipped* and the loop terminates. While the condition is `true`, the loop will be executed repeatedly.

A 'while' loop that uses a counting index

Before getting to situation #2 as describe above, just consider a simple example that uses a simple counter to move through the `teammates` table:

```
1  teammates = {"Harry", "Ginny", "Ronald",
        "Hermione"}
2  count = 1
3  while count <= #teammates do
4      print( teammates[count])
5      count = count + 1
6  end
```

For this simple loop, we should see the names of your teammates at the console:

```
CONSOLE
Harry
Ginny
Ronald
Hermione
```

Nothing super exciting and hopefully what you see in the console above is exactly what you expected to see.

Situation #2

As a second example, let's look at situation #2 (above), where you know you need get someone to volunteer to bring pizza only if it is needed. It is a **bit more involved** to simulate this at least *somewhat* realistically. First, you need to know whether pizza is required or not. You can simulate that part using `math.random()`, so that each time the app is run, you get a random outcome in which the code in the 'while' loop is possibly skipped. This is an adaptation of the technique discussed above to determine whether a teammate has volunteered or not.

If pizza is required about 50% of the time, you could create a `pizzaNeeded` variable and assign it a `true` or `false` value based on a `math.random()` comparison:

```
pizzaNeeded = math.random() > .5
```

You can use this `pizzaNeeded` variable to partially control the 'while' loop (so that it only executes if `pizzaNeeded` is `true`). You can also use this same basic technique to simulate whether the team member volunteers to bring pizza or not. To do so, you'll create a `volunteer` boolean and make it (randomly) `true` 20% of the time:

```
volunteer = math.random() > .8
```

Successfully simulating this situation also requires **two counters**: one to count the *call number* (just like in the 'for' loop) and one to act as an *index counter* to the table of teammates (it can't be the same counter as the call number because we may have to go through the table *multiple times* before someone volunteers). It might be implemented as shown in code box #5.

Of course, in general, the 'while' and 'repeat until' loops don't intrinsically *need* a counter and, even in this example, the counter doesn't determine whether the loop proceeds or exits (the booleans `pizzaNeeded` and `volunteer` do that).

Notice also that the condition which defines the 'while' loop is evaluated *first*, before the chunk is executed. If the condition is `false`, the chunk is *skipped altogether* (i.e., no code in the body of the loop is executed if the condition is false from the beginning). This is what gives the 'while' loop the capability to loop zero times. You could write a 'for' loop that didn't loop, but it wouldn't make much sense to do so.

What does the *output* of this loop look like? Well, it is different every time you run it (since it is based on a random number). Since there's an 80% chance that each caller will say "no", it could take a while. Here's what one run looked like for me:

```
CONSOLE
We need pizza!
Call #1 to Harry failed.
Call #2 to Ginny failed.
Call #3 to Ronald failed.
Call #4 to Hermione failed
Call #5 to Harry succeeded - we have pizza!
```

Of course, every time you run this loop, you will probably see very different results (due to the use of random numbers in the code). In some cases, the 'while' loop won't loop at all, because the `pizzaNeeded` will start out `false`. In such a case, you'd just see:

```
CONSOLE
Pizza isn't needed at this meeting.
```

```
1   pizzaNeeded = math.random() > .5
2   if not pizzaNeeded then
3       print("Pizza isn't needed for this meeting.")
4   else
5       print("We need pizza!")
6   end
7
8   volunteer = false
9   callNumber = 1
10  teammateNumber = 1
11
12  while pizzaNeeded and not volunteer do
13      volunteer = math.random() > .8
14      if volunteer then
15          print("Call #"..callNumber.." to
16              "..teammates[teammateNumber].." succeeded - we have pizza!")
17      else
18          print("Call #"..callNumber.." to
19              "..teammates[teammateNumber].." failed.")
20          callNumber = callNumber + 1
21          teammateNumber = teammateNumber + 1
22          if teammateNumber > #teammates then teammateNumber = 1; end
23      end
24  end
```

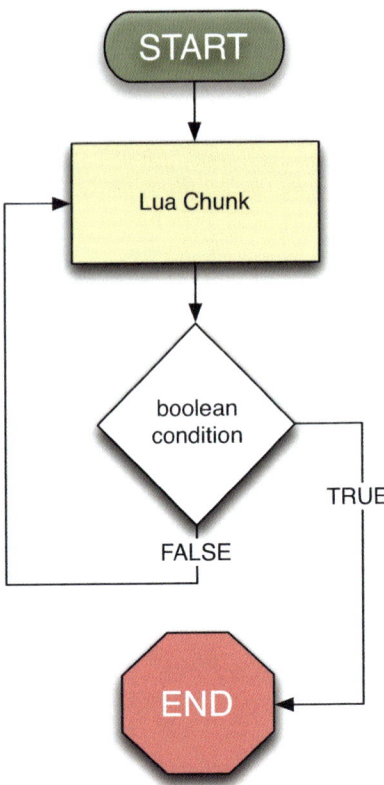

The 'repeat until' Loop

The 'repeat until' loop (repeat one or more times)

The 'repeat until' loop is almost identical to the 'while' loop (and is also called the 'do while' loop), the difference being that the condition is not checked until *after* the Lua chunk (the body of the loop) has executed one time placed at the end (i.e., the last line) of the loop.

```
repeat
    -- chunk of Lua
until condition
```

The "chunk" of Lua/Solar2D statements can be any length and can call built-in or user-defined functions. As with the other loops, you may nest other loops inside this and use 'if-then' logic to split the flow of execution inside the loop.

Two important notes:

1. The loop **repeats as long as the condition is `false`** (i.e., exits when the condition turns `true`). This is the *opposite* of the 'while' loop which exits when the condition is `false`.

2. The loop condition is not checked until *after* the chunk (the body of the loop) has executed *one time*. So, the loop always **executes at least one time**, even if the condition is true before the loop starts.

Attention

As such, you must write this chunk with the understanding that, because it is inside a 'repeat until' loop, it *will* be executed at least one time.

Simple counting with a 'repeat until' loop

Situation #3 isn't quite as complicated as #2, but it isn't a great initial example. So, let's start with a simple example that is just a basic counter. We'll use the counted number to access and display the names of the people in our team, just as you did with the 'while' loop above.

```
1  teammates = {"Harry", "Ginny", "Ronald", "Hermione"}
2  count = 1
3  repeat
4      print( teammates[count] )
5      count = count + 1
6  until count > #teammates
```

The caution with this example is that if the `teammates` table is *empty*, then when line 4 executes the first and only time, you are acting an empty table and will see a "nil" at the console. However, in this case, with the same four names in the table, the output will be identical to the simple 'while' loop above:

```
Harry
Ginny
Ronald
Hermione
```

Situation #3

In situation #3, you need to call the members of your team to solicit a volunteer to bring root beer to the meeting. Since you **always need root beer**, you know you'll need to *make at least one call*, so the 'repeat until' loop is a great choice. You could implement as follows (box #7):

```
1   print("We always need root beer!")
2   teammates = {"Harry", "Ginny", "Ronald", "Hermione"}
3
4   callNumber = 1
5   teammateNumber = 1
6   repeat
7
8       volunteer = math.random() > .8
9       if volunteer then
10          print("Call #"..callNumber.." to "..teammates[teammateNumber]..
                "succeeded - we have root beer! (volunteer = true)")
11      else
12          print("Call #"..callNumber.." to "..teammates[teammateNumber]..
                "failed. (volunteer = false)")
13          callNumber = callNumber + 1
14          teammateNumber = teammateNumber + 1
15          if teammateNumber > #teammates then teammateNumber = 1; end
16      end
17
18  until volunteer
```

Note that we still need two separate counters: the `callNumber` counter to keep track of the number of call made and `teammateNumber` counter to act as an index to the `teammates` table. The `teammateNumber` counter is controlled with an 'if-then' statement (on line 15) to keep it from counting past the last value in the `teammates` table. The loop exits after the `volunteer` variable is true (which only has a 20% chance for each repetition).

As with the 'while' loop simulation above, the output of this 'repeat until' loop will vary depending on the random numbers generated. There will be at least 1 call and, perhaps, many more. So, it could be as quick as:

```
CONSOLE
We always need root beer!
Call #1 to Harry succeeded - we have root beer! (volunteer = true)
```

Or quite a bit more drawn out:

```
CONSOLE
We always need root beer!
Call #1 to Harry failed. (volunteer = false)
Call #2 to Ginny failed. (volunteer = false)
Call #3 to Ronald failed. (volunteer = false)
Call #4 to Hermione failed. (volunteer = false)
Call #5 to Harry failed. (volunteer = false)
Call #6 to Ginny failed. (volunteer = false)
Call #7 to Ronald succeeded - we have root beer! (volunteer = true)
```

Remember that the 'repeat until' loop will always execute the enclosed chunk one time, even if — for example — `volunteer is` initially `true` (i.e., perhaps someone has already volunteered to supply root beer). If this isn't the behavior you want, it can cause unexpected results. In general, the 'for' and 'while' loops are used much more often than 'repeat until'.

Breaking out of a loop

It is possible that, during the execution of any of these loops, you find yourself needing to write an *exit* to "break out" of the loop. That is, you want to end the repetition *immediately*, without waiting for the current chunk to finish executing or for the loop to terminate naturally. This can be done using the `break` keyword, although this is generally discouraged. It is better to write the condition in such a way that the loop will end on its own, without need of a `break`.

A game of dice

With two dice, how many rolls does it take to get a double? Of course, it may be different every time you try. You can use loops to create a simple game that keeps rolling until you get a double. Ahh, but **which loop**?

Since you don't know (in advance) how many rolls it will take to get a double, the 'for' loop would be a poor choice. A 'while' loop will work fine, but we'll need a Boolean variable to control it. Let's call it _double and initialize it to `false`. We'll also keep track of the number of times we've rolled using `rolls` (initialized to `0`).

A 'while' loop works

Here's a 'while' loop to do it:

```
1   _double = false
2   rolls = 0
3
4   while not _double do
5       rolls = rolls + 1
6       d1 = math.random(1,6)
7       d2 = math.random(1,6)
8       print("Roll "..rolls.." is "..d1.."-"..d2)
9       if d1 == d2 then
10          _double = true
11      end
12  end
13
14  print("It took "..rolls.." rolls to get a double")
```

If you run this, you'll get results like:

```
CONSOLE
Roll 1 is 6-3
Roll 2 is 3-6
Roll 3 is 1-3
Roll 4 is 5-3
Roll 5 is 1-1
It took 5 rolls to get a double
```

Even better, since you are using random numbers, it is a new game every time you play!

But a 'repeat until' works better

Interestingly, although the 'while' loop works *fine* in this scenario, a 'repeat until' will work *better*. Since you know that you are going to **have to roll at least once** to get a double, this makes sense. Using 'repeat until' you can eliminate the _double variable and simplify the loop a bit.

Here's what it looks like:

```
rolls = 0

repeat
    rolls = rolls + 1
    d1 = math.random(1,6)
    d2 = math.random(1,6)
    print("Roll "..rolls.." is "..d1.."-"..d2)
until d1 == d2

print("It took "..rolls.." rolls to get a double")
```

Of course, the output from this loop will have the same format as the 'while' loop above, with the results being (quasi) random each time you play.

Now, how about an example that uses a text field and a loop in a way that makes sense?

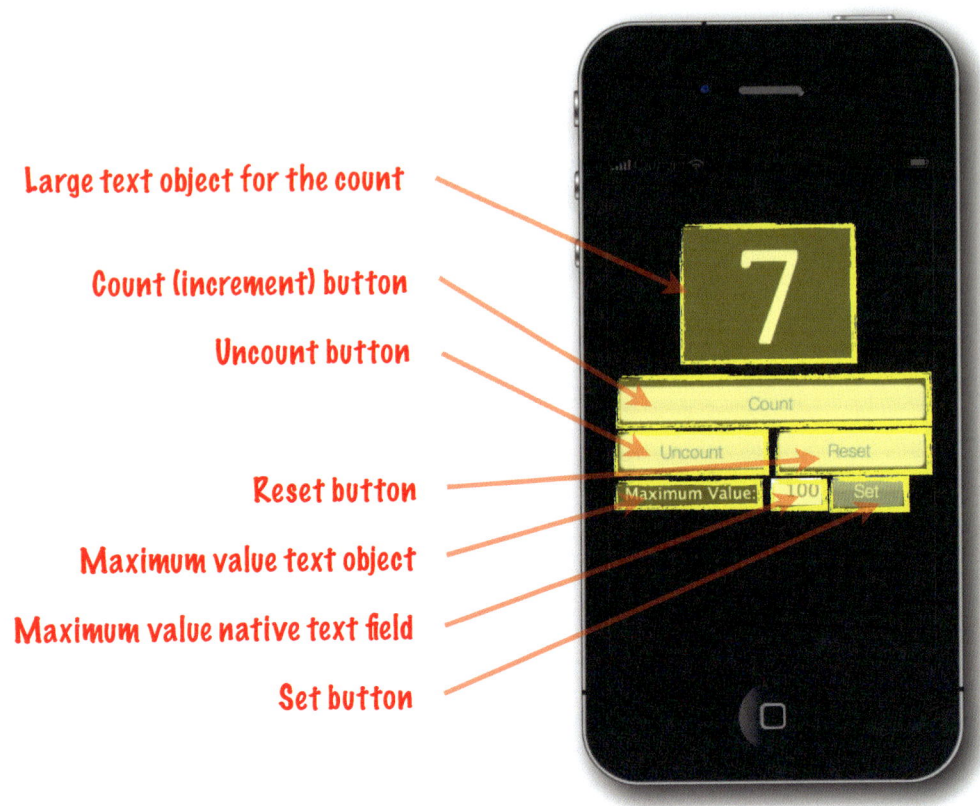

Simple Counter 2: UI Layout

An example with buttons and a text field

Okay, now that you know how to put buttons and text fields in an app, let's add a text field to your very handy counter app that will allow the user to specify a max value to count to. This isn't super-complex, but will create a few issues that you might not have considered, including:

1. You will need to **slide your UI up** when the device keyboard (the numeric keypad in this case) slides up. You might think that that would happen automatically, but it doesn't.

2. You'll need to play around with the animations (transitions) to get the **timing to match the speed of the device keyboard**.

3. You will need to **dismiss the device keyboard and slide your UI back** into place when the user completes editing the text field.

The issue of handling the device keyboard/keypad is somewhat **troublesome**, since the Solar2D simulator doesn't *display* it (i.e., it doesn't simulate the onscreen keyboard; you enter data using the actual physical keyboard on your development machine). You will have to design your UI and then build it (from the Solar2D Simulator) to see it run either on an actual device or the "real" iOS simulator.

Where'd That Keyboard
Come From?

The iOS keyboard is 216 default (320x480) content pixels tall, meaning that the bottom of any content you want visible when the keyboard is up can't go past y = 264 (480 - 216) pixels. Note in the screen shot ("Where'd That Keyboard Come From?" below) how I have shifted up all of the UI elements to allow the user to see the text field that they are editing.

How do you create an app like this? Obviously, I'd recommend using *Drawn2Code* at least to set the UI up. The following code examples were done by hand (to fit on the page), but are consistent with what you'd do in *Drawn2Code*. Also, sometimes seeing everything on one page is helpful.

Let's tackle it in three pieces: setting up the UI, writing the button event handler, and writing the text field event handler.

Cross-Platform Mobile Application Development — Chapter 6

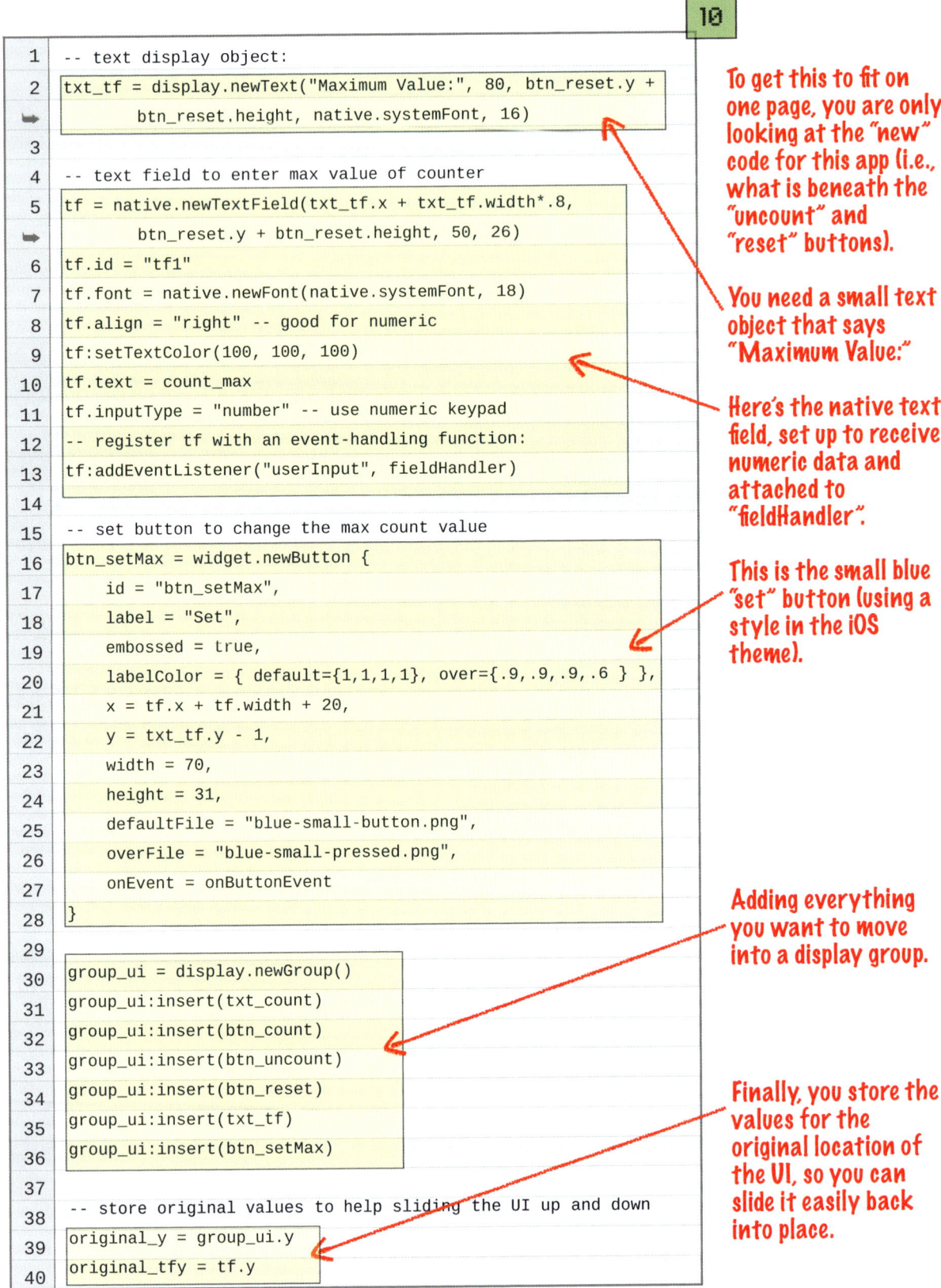

Simple Counter 2: Setting up the UI

1. Setting up the UI

You have 7 objects to set up: 4 buttons, 2 text objects, and 1 text field. Additionally, you create a display group to hold 6 of the objects (all but the text field). This is, obviously, based on the Simple Counter app from Chapter 5. You are adding a "row" of 3 widgets to the UI to allow the user to set the maximum count value using a text field. The discussion is focused primarily on these new elements and their functionality.

As with the Simple Counter app from the previous chapter, the order of the code mimics the layout of the UI elements (for convenience). Remember that, although a native text field can be placed in a display group, it doesn't respond to any statements acting on the group (so there's not really any point inserting there in the first place). The UI setup code omitting the "count", "uncount" and "reset" buttons (which you learned in Chapter 5) is shown in "Simple Counter 2: Setting up the UI".

I know that there are a lot of x's, y's, width's, and height's, especially if you include the code for the prior objects which I've omitted here. However, if you will read the code from the top down, and keep in mind the UI layout in the screen shot above, most of it should make sense. As with the original Simple Counter, the precise pixel values are often the result of some trial-and-error work to get objects into the desired size and position. The small blue button uses image files from "Widgets 1.0" and is included in the download for this chapter.

2. Button event-handler

In the construction code for the buttons you hooked them up to an event listener that was called `onButtonEvent`, which means **you have to provide** a function of that name. It is a single function that will **handle all four buttons** ("count", "uncount", "reset", and "set"). This function is shown in "Function `onButtonEvent()`".

As with the Simple Counter example, your button handler is only responding to "press" events (not "release" or "move"). Note also that the function to handle the button events (i.e., this function) will usually be placed above the UI setup (even though it makes sense to code the UI setup first). In other words, although the code in the outline could be cut-and-pasted in your IDE, you should **use the downloaded code** instead.

Also, remember that **you have to be able to slide the UI objects up and then back down** whenever the device keyboard appears. You should be able to pick out the two `transition.to()` function calls under the "btn_setMax" section. Those are sliding the UI elements back down screen after dismissing the keyboard. To know where to slide them back down to, you have to have the value where they were, hence the need for the "original" variables you created at the end of setting up the UI.

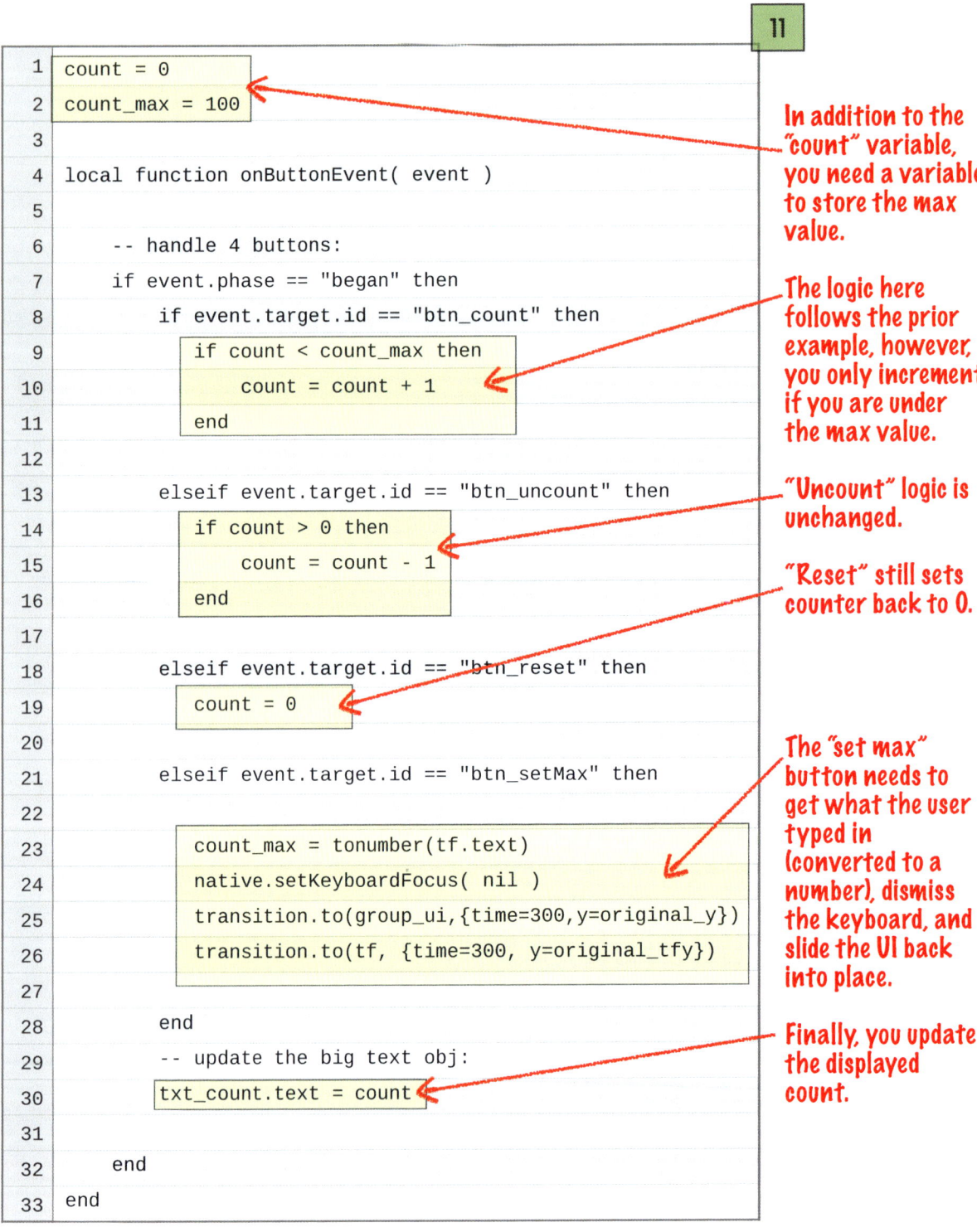

Function `onButtonEvent()` (Flowchart Below)

Why are there **two** `transition.to()` function calls? Because on older Solar2D builds you had to move the display group and the text field *separately*. That was a pain.

Okay, how about flowcharting the whole function? This is a bit more involved, but might be really useful to see. I've put the flowchart at the end of the chapter, as an appendix.

3. Text field event-handler

Finally, you must supply the event handling function for the text field. User interaction with the text field needs to be handled in two ways, First, when they enter the text field, the numeric keypad on the device will automatically slide up. As noted before, you have to slide your UI up as well, which is accomplished with two `transition.to()` function calls in the "began" phase (i.e., when the user enters the text field).

You also slide the UI back down here, when the user submits the text field (i.e., hits the "return" key or "done" button).

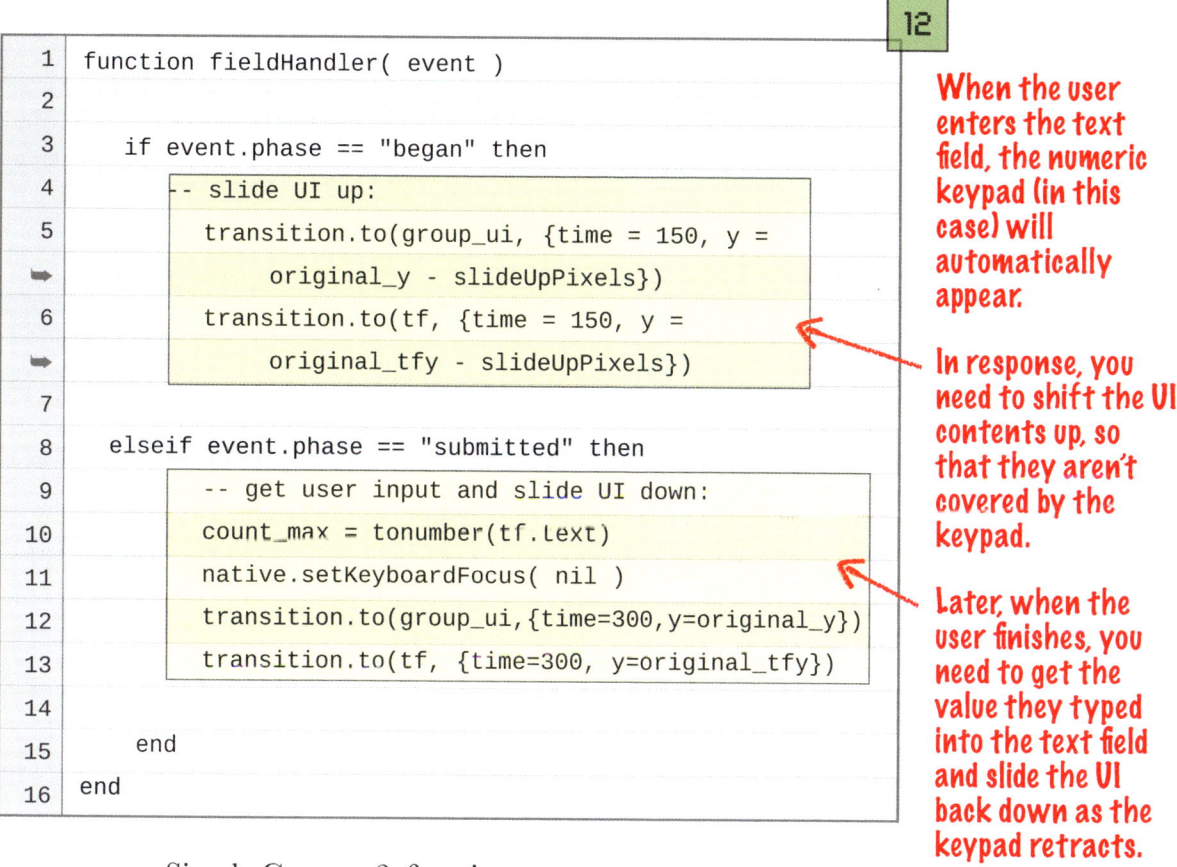

Simple Counter 2: function `fieldHandler()`

That's Simple Counter 2!

Together, these three chunks of code, setting up the UI and handling the button and text field events, create your app. It adds just a bit of functionality beyond the previous chapter's Simple Counter, but the new text field causes the on-screen keyboard to appear, which is problematic. In response, you must shift your UI up and out of the way, otherwise, the user wouldn't be able to see the text field they are typing in! After they finish typing, you must slide the UI back down, as the keyboard retracts.

This is available in both a hand-coded and *Drawn2Code* design (*counter-max-value.d2c*). In addition, there's a bonus version with a countdown effect added (*counter-max-value-countdown.d2c*).

Drawn2Code tip: You can simulate loops by using a timer (see how in the first bonus app).

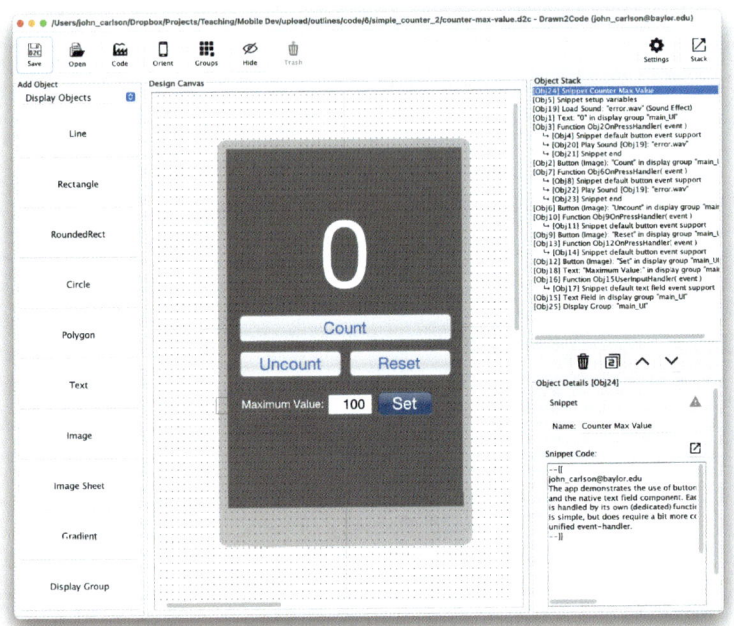

counter-max-value.d2c

Summary

• •

In this chapter you learned to use the text field widget, part of the native library, to accept text input from the user. Apps that use a text field will typically be event driven (as discussed in Chapter 5). You can handle user activity (i.e., entering, editing, and/or submitting) in the text field using the "userInput" listener and a function you supply. You learned how to use this input as both text and numeric data. One special UI requirement of the text field is that it may be necessary to move (transition) a text field being edited up the screen to avoid being covered by the keyboard sliding up from the bottom of the screen.

In addition, you learned to script situations in which you need to repeatedly execute a block of code (zero or more times). Based on the nature of the situation, you can now appropriately select and use the 'while', 'for', and 'repeat until' loops. Finally, using loops you learned to script a simple game of dice.

Chapter resources

In the chapter resource download for this book (www.lillipellilabs.com/mobiledev/download/chapter_resources.zip), you'll find the following 9 apps in folder "6":

1. native_textfield (the native text field demo)
2. for_loop_simple (the 'for' loop listing teammates)
3. for_loop_situation-1 (the 'for' loop example for situation #1)
4. while_loop_simple (the 'while' loop that lists teammates)
5. while_loop_situation-2 (the slightly complex 'while' loop for situation #2)
6. repeat_until_simple (the 'repeat until' loop that lists teammates)
7. repeat_until_situation-2 (the 'repeat-until' loop for situation #3)
8. loops_roll_dice (a game of dice)
9. simple_counter_2 (*counter-max-value.d2c*)
10. **BONUS APPS**: *counter-max-value-countdown.d2c* (a version of Simple Timer 2 with a countdown timer), *two-screens-with-textfield.d2c* (a small app that switches screens).

End-of-chapter exercises

1. Create an app with 1 text field and at least 1 text display object. Prompt the user to enter their **Wizarding School** nickname in the text field and display what they enter in between your first and last names.
2. Create an app that rolls 1 die 10 times and adds up all of the values.
    a. Display the result in a text display object.
    b. Display "Winner" if the total is over 40. Play a winning sound to help the user celebrate.

3. Create app that rolls 2 dice (i.e., generates 2 random numbers, perhaps named "die1" and "die2") 10 times. Display "Winner" if the user rolls a double (i.e., if die1 == die2) at least once. Play a winning sound to mark this important event.

4. Create an app that rolls a die 100 times.

    a. Display the total and the average on screen. The average should be somewhat close to 3.5 (for a 6-sided die).

    b. Add a textfield to control how many loops are run (i.e., instead of the fixed number 100).

5. Create an app that rolls 2 dice 100 times. Count the total number of doubles and display the result on screen.

WARNING

If you find yourself "playing the dice" *just one more time*, you may be experiencing the early stages of gambling addiction (en.wikipedia.org/wiki/Problem_gambling). Other recognized signs include: Yelling "I'm a winner!" at unsuitable moments; inappropriately asking friends to "blow on your dice" for luck; sudden obsession with random numbers and the mathematics of probability; unexplained loans or cash advances; and a recent dependance on root beer to "make it through" frequents runs of bad luck. Additional warning signs can be reviewed here: psychcentral.com/lib/2008/warning-signs-and-risk-factors-for-pathological-gambling/. If you believe that you or someone you love is suffering from gambling addiction, please get help.

6. Create an app with 1 text field, 1 button, and 1 text object. Take whatever the user types into the text field and, when they press the button, add it to a running total and clear the text field. Display the running total in the text object.

7. Add a subtract button to #6. Now, whatever the user types into the text field can be added or subtracted from the running total, depending on which button they press.

8. Draw a flowchart for #9. You can use Visio (on Windows), OmniGraffle (Mac), or a web-based tool like gliffy.com. Or you can use a pencil and some paper.

9. Create an app with 1 text field, 1 button, and 1 text object. Check the text entered into the text field to see if it matches a code you specify in your code. If so, display your Wizarding School nickname.

Challenge

10. A bit more of a challenge: Modify #3 to roll 2 dice 20 times and display "Winner" only if two doubles are rolled in a row. Play a winning sound if you wish.

11. Add a "min value" textfield to the "Simple Counter 2" app from this chapter to allow the user to set a minimum value (in addition to the maximum value) for the counter.

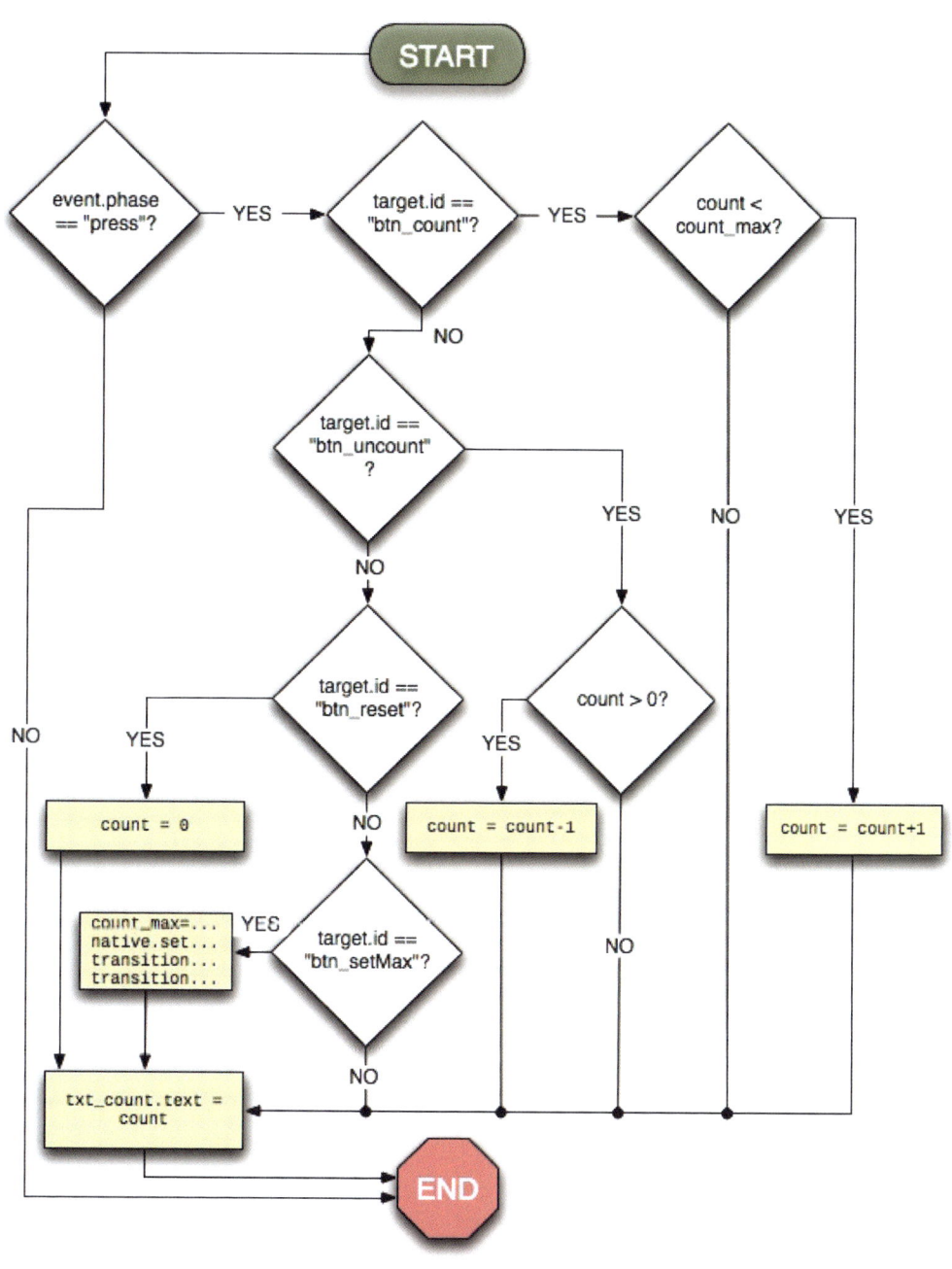

Flowchart of Simple Counter 2 `onButtonEvent()` Function

NOTES

Sliders & Functions

7

Your third widget

The Slider

Now that you have mastered buttons and text fields, the focus in this chapter moves to *sliders*. Sliders are another way to allow the user to input information into your app. Sliders store an *integer number* between 0 and 100 (which can be thought of as a percent) and can be oriented either horizontally (as shown) or vertically, depending on your UI requirement.

As the user moves the slider, the slider's *value* changes in increments of 1. You can use that value to do anything you'd like. You can also use simple algebra to convert the slider value into any range and increment you wish. In fact, you'll find a function in this chapter to help you do just that.

Sliders make sense when you want the user to have control over some value in your app and that value has a defined lower and upper value. This could include a changing financial value (like interest rate), changing an app setting (like the volume of music or effects), setting a range within which some variable is allowed to vary (such as return on investment), or to represent the progress of some variable from a starting value to an ending value (assuming you wanted to give the user *control* over the progress, such as with an audio or video playhead during a song or movie).

Functions

You've been writing and using Lua and Solar2D functions for some time, principally to handle events generated by the widgets you've utilized (i.e., the button and text field). However, functions are useful for more than event-handlers (although that certainly is handy). In this chapter, we'll explore writing functions that calculate a value and *return* that value as a result to the line of code that calls the function.

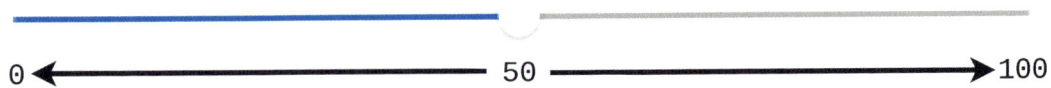

Sliders

Sliders (docs.coronalabs.com/api/library/widget/newSlider.html) are graphical widgets (in the widget library, not the native library — woohoo!) that have a round *knob* that the user can drag along a defined channel, oriented either horizontally or vertically. The default orientation is horizontal, the range is set from 0 to 100, and the default location for the knob is at the midpoint (with a value of 50).

In *Drawn2Code*, just add a slider from the widgets palette, which will add 4 script objects to your stack. If coding by hand, remember to require the widget library toward the opt of your code (this is added automatically by *Drawn2Code*, see Obj4 in the stack to the right).

As with buttons, this widget will also require some script to create it (Obj1) and an event-handler (Obj2) to react to slider movement. A tiny app with just a slider can be set up that easily, but before we work with slider, let's look at some of the syntax that they use.

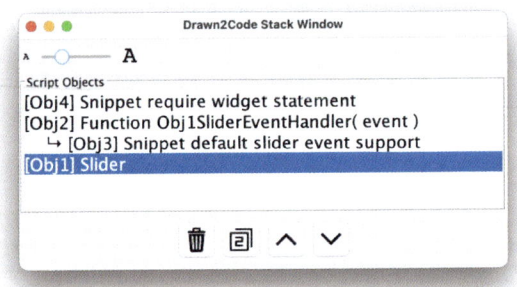

Adding a Slider to Your Stack

Sliders are created with a similar syntax to that of buttons:

```
Obj1 = widget.newSlider
{
    id = "Obj1",
    x = 160,
    y = 240,
    width = 280,
    listener = Obj1SliderEventHandler
}
```

If coding by hand, although you *can* specify a slider without the size and location, it won't be particularly *useful*, since it defaults to location (50, 0) with a width of 100 pixels, which is quite small and behind the status bar. Likewise, you can omit the "id" attribute, but this will make it more difficult later to determine which slider (if you have more than one) was slid.

Drawn2Code will set up a fully-configured slider with a variety of customizable features in the settings panel.

Slider Configuration

Event data

When the user moves the slider, a table of event data is sent to the event-handler (e.g., `Obj1SliderEventHandler()`), including event.value, event.phase, and event.target.id. Like all of the widgets, Solar2D will report on the nature of the current action. The phases of the event can be "began" (when the user just touches the slider), "moved" (when the user slides the slider knob), and "ended" (when the user releases focus from the slider). See "Event Data" for the meaning of these values.

Data	Meaning
event	A table containing data about the slider event
event.value	The current integer value of the slider (0-100)
event.phase	The phase can be "began", "moved", or "ended"
event.target.id	The id of the slider being moved

Event Data

The slider event-handler can be fairly straightforward. The default *Drawn2Code* snippet looks something like this:

```
function Obj1SliderEventHandler( event )
    print("Slider ".. event.target.id .." "..event.phase
        .. " now at "..event.value.."%")
end
```

This is, obviously, a very simple event-handler that only reports one what the user is doing with the slider.

Note that you are using event.value in code box #2 to access the value (number) on the slider, however, you may also use the object identifier itself (e.g., Obj1.value). Using the syntax in code box #2, you should see a very descriptive event notification displayed at the console. It might look something like this:

```
OUTPUT
Slider Obj1 began now at 50%
Slider Obj1 moved now at 50%
Slider Obj1 moved now at 49%
Slider Obj1 moved now at 48%
Slider Obj1 moved now at 48%
Slider Obj1 moved now at 49%
Slider Obj1 moved now at 50%
Slider Obj1 moved now at 51%
Slider Obj1 ended now at 52%
```

This app is available in the chapter downloads as *slider-event.d2c*.

When you try this note that, since the app will report the *value* of the knob as you move it over **each pixel**, you will see a fairly substantial list of events at the console. Notice **three things** in box #3:

1. The slider <u>value</u> starts at 50, which is the default. It is just a number (i.e., it isn't really a percentage, although it can be helpful to think of it as such).

2. The slider <u>value</u> only changes during the "moved" phase.

3. The slider <u>value</u> changes by 1 depending on the *direction* you move the slider and there are **no fractional values**. If you look, you'll see I moved the slider to the left a bit, and then back to the right.

This usually prompts two questions: (1) What if I don't want to **start at 50**? and (2) What if I don't want an integer **number between 0 and 100?** These are both good questions and I'm glad I asked them for you.

Change the starting value

Question #1 is the easier of the two. It is not at all unreasonable to think that you might want the slider to start of at zero, for example. Or some other number that isn't 50. You may set the slider value when you create the slider, by specifying a *value* setting (between 0 and 100), such as "value = 75". Additionally, you may set the value of the slider *at any time* and using the `setValue()` function. Or, can use the settings panel in *Drawn2Code* to adjust this easily using a slider.

Change the range (minimum and maximum values)

You **cannot change** the minimum and maximum values on the slider. Instead, to deal with question #2, you need to use a bit of *algebra* to **convert the slider value** to the range you desire. Algebra is the branch of mathematics dealing with the use of letters and symbols in equations which describe their relationship to some result. With sliders, you often want a number in a defined *range*, with some *minimum value* and *maximum value*.

Attention

So, for example, what if you want the slider to represent the **roll of a dice**? In this case, the slider has to be in a range from 1 to 6, not 0 to 100 (assuming you are using a six-sided die).

157

You can get this using a handful of operations:

1. Divide the slider value by 100 (to make it a percentage from 0% to 100%).

2. Multiply the result of step 1 by the maximum value in the range, minus the starting/minimum value. In this case, (6-1) = 5.

3. Add the starting/minimum value (+1) to the result of step 2.

4. If you want this to be an integer (which you do for dice), you **truncate the number** to remove any decimal component using `math.floor()`.

Dice Value Slider

The complete expression looks something like this:

```
math.floor(1 + 5*event.value/100)
```
(4)

Again, this is just basic algebra and can be implemented in a variety of equally-correct ways.

Displaying and updating the value

Note that the slider does not display its current value; however, you can easily add a text display object to the slider app you are building. If you add this to your design as, say, Obj5, then you can put the "dice value" into it using:

```
dieValue = math.floor(1 + 5*event.value/100)
Obj5.text = dieValue
```
(5)

But <u>where should you put this code</u> (code box #5)? Knowing "where to code" is as important as "what to code".

You would want to place this code <u>inside the event-handler</u> for two reasons:

1. The syntax shown uses the event table, so it needs to be inside of a function that has access to the event table. Typically, this is inside of event-handlers.

2. You want it to update as the slider is moved. The code inside the event-handler for this widget runs each time the slider is touched.

This app is available in the chapter download as *slider-dice-demo.d2c*.

Note

Thinking about box #5 in particular, has the code *changed* the slider in any way? Does the slider work *differently* because of the algebra? **No, not at all.** The slider still "slides" from 0 to 100. You are just using algebra to treat the slider value as a variable in an equation (you might even say a "function") that produces the output you want.

Note

Using a slider as input isn't always appropriate, certainly, but it can be used to easily and visually input values in any continuous range, either as integer or real numbers (using algebra). If that is not the sort of data that your app needs, then the slider wouldn't be the best choice.

Putting the algebra in a function

If this task of converting the slider value into numbers that meet a particular need is a *common* one, which it probably is, it might be nice to put it into a function. That way, when you need to perform this task, you don't have to *remember* the exact algebra. You can just call your function and let it do the math for you.

So, let's make that function step-by-step. First, you need the **basic outline of the function**: The header that contains the name of the function and any parameters it takes and the end statement to finish the function. your function can be called by any valid Lua identifier, but something descriptive is often helpful. Maybe "`getValueInRange()`"?

To get started, you need four components:

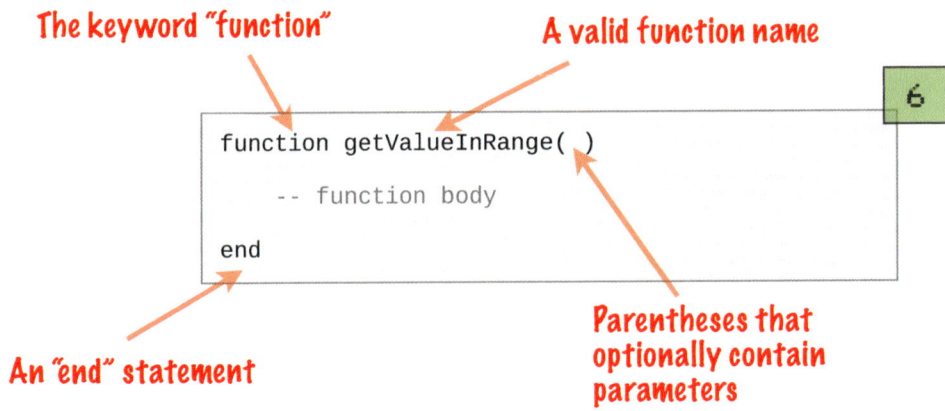

Four requirements of a valid function (code box #9):

1. The keyword "function".

2. A valid function name (a Lua identifier).

3. Parentheses that may either be empty or contain one or more parameters (which we'll discuss next). Multiple parameters are separated by commas.

4. The keyword "end".

The code in box #6 is a *valid* function, although it doesn't *do* anything. For this function to work, you need two more things: (1) to **define the parameters** you need passed to the function, and (2) the body of the function that includes the **expression** (i.e., your equation) that uses these parameters (not just a comment that says "function body"). You'll add these in two steps.

First, the parameters you need are the value to be adjusted along with the minimum and maximum values you want your *output* to have (i.e., the value that is returned). You haven't included the parameters yet, so the parentheses in box #6 are **empty**.

Let's fix that:

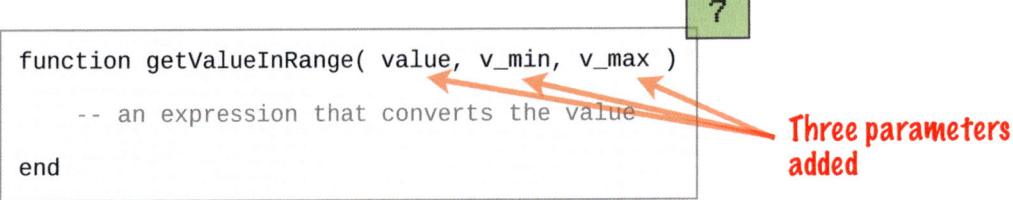

The parameters can be given any valid Lua name, but should be at least minimally descriptive to remind you what to pass to the function. For this function, I've defined **three parameters** to pass:

1. The *value* you need to process (e.g., from a slider), called `value`
2. The *minimum value* of the output range, called `v_min`
3. The *maximum value* of the output range, called `v_max`

When using or "calling" your function, you will need to use its name and pass it the three parameters it is expecting (see box #9 below if you just can't wait to see the syntax).

Second, what goes inside your function? You need an expression that performs the work of shifting the value passed into the range you need to have (see box #4, above). You also need to "return" the result of the expression, so that the converted value is delivered back to the calling statement. Returning is super-easy in Lua, you just use the `return` keyword followed by the value you want returned. Here's what this could look like:

Dice Slider

```
function getValueInRange( value, v_min, v_max )
    newValue = v_min + value*(v_max-v_min)/100
    return math.floor(newValue)
end
```

8 — Processing and returning the result

When you want to *use* this function, perhaps inside an event-handler, you just "call" or "invoke" it using its name and pass it the parameter data it is expecting. In addition, if the function returns some value, the calling statement has to utilize or "consume" that value in some way. For example, this might look like this:

```
dieValue = getValueInRange(slider.value, 1, 6)
```

9

161

This is available in the chapter downloads as *slider-dice-function.d2c*. To try to add something a bit cool to this version, let's also define a table containing the die symbols (characters):

```
die_symbols = {"⚀","⚁","⚂","⚃","⚄","⚅"}
```

Note that these symbols may not work on all computers. These were placed here using the *drag-and-drop from a character palette technique*, which is **kind of flakey**. The current version of *Drawn2Code* will actually "clean" these characters from a snippet if you try to use them, since they aren't typically useable. So, you've got to look at the hand-coded version to have any hope of seeing this in action (look for it in the "slider_dice_symbols" folder). Regrettably, it actually sounds more fun than it is.

Attention

A better function

The function you've created works great. Unless you don't want **integer numbers**. When thinking about dice, or screen coordinates, or the number of customers in line, integers do make sense. But for lots of stuff, like monetary amounts, physical measurements, rates and percentages, and so on, you need decimal ("floating point") numbers. Decimal numbers aren't hard to get, you just need to remove the `math.floor()` call that truncates the results. The "real" question is, *how do you know* when the user wants floating-point numbers and when they want integers?

The most straightforward way might be just to **look at the numbers that the user passes** for `v_min` and `v_max`. If both of these are integers, you could *assume* that the users wants an integer result. If either value is a decimal number, then we'll make the assumption that they want a floating-point number result.

For example:

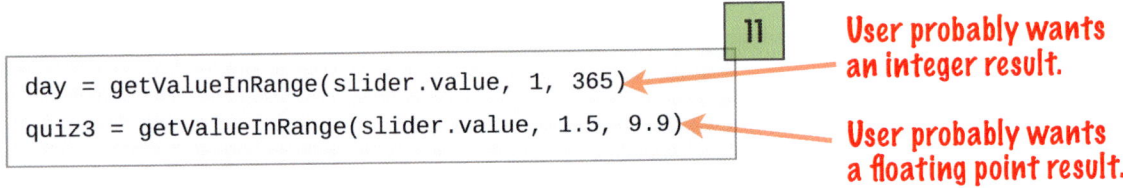

```
day = getValueInRange(slider.value, 1, 365)
quiz3 = getValueInRange(slider.value, 1.5, 9.9)
```

User probably wants an integer result.

User probably wants a floating point result.

In the top statement in code box #11, you might need the day in a year, as a whole number with no decimal component. If you pass your function the values 1 and 365, your function *should* be smart enough to return that kind of result. In the second statement (still in box #11), the user is clearly okay with decimal values, since they are part of the requested range.

While there might be **several good ways** to discern whether a number is an integer or not, the one that seems to work best for me in Lua is to use a string function to find any periods (e.g., ".") in the parameter passed (see code box #12). This is done for both v_min and v_max. If there is any decimal component on either v_min or v_max, even a ".0", this approach will detect it.

```
function getValueInRange( value, v_min, v_max )
    -- assume integers:
    isInteger = true

    -- check for any periods in the v_min and v_max parameters
    -- note: to search for ".", you have to precede it with a "%"
    if string.find(v_min,"%.")~=nil or string.find(v_max,"%.")~=nil then
        isInteger = false
    end

    -- try to convert to numbers (in case strings passed)
    v_min = tonumber(v_min)
    v_max = tonumber(v_max)
    newValue = tonumber(value)

    -- check that these are all valid numbers (needed for arithmetic)
    if v_min ~= nil and v_max ~= nil and value ~= nil then
        newValue = v_min + value*(v_max-v_min)/100
        -- convert to integer if needed:
        if isInteger then newValue = math.floor(newValue); end
        return newValue
    else
        return nil
    end
end
```

12

A few notes on this function:

1. Number values ended in ".0" should be entered as strings (e.g., `"1.0"` instead of `1.0`).

2. The function in box #12 can be used with **any value** passed to it, not just the value on a slider. The function doesn't "know" *where* the value came from, nor does it matter to the operations inside the function. You could be processing a value the user entered in a text field, a value you read from a database, or a value that was the result of some other calculation or process.

3. The function does **basic error-checking** on the values passed. If any aren't numbers or can't be converted to numbers, the function returns nil.

4. The function is **not an event-handler** (like most of your previous functions). It does something else. It "handles" the programmer's need to process a piece of data, rather than handling a user event.

5. Our function **returns a result** (the value converted into the desired range). This is easy to do, using the `return` keyword followed by the result you want to return. The returned result is sent back to the calling statement and is "plugged into" the expression where the function was called.

   - Note that **functions do not have to return** a result and there is no special set up required to return results. The value returned can be of any type that can be used in the expression that calls the function.

Most of the examples of functions you find in Solar2D documentation will declare them to be `local`, which restricts their use to the Lua code in the current chunk, beneath the function declaration. There isn't yet a compelling reason to use `local`, but if you do want to (or paste a function that is local into your code) be aware that you will need to place it above (i.e., prior to) any call to that function.

Slider playground

Okay, let's make use of this fancy new function! Here's an app that uses it to convert the slider value on a single slider to various ranges that are more useful. In other words, it takes the one 0-100 slider values, and uses it to change several onscreen elements at once.

Specifically, the app takes the single slider value and converts it to:

1. Two screen display values to locate a horizontal and vertical lines that move with the slider.

2. RGB colors to set the fill color on the stack of three colored dice.

3. Values for the colored blocks/dice (the bottom one is a magic 20-sided die).

The current value on the slider, as well as these calculated conversions are updated live (as the user moves the slider). The magic happens in the slider event-handler.

For example, here's the code to get the value for the fill color of the red block (named `rect_red` in the script):

13

```
-- set the red fill color:
colorValue = getValueInRange(value, "0.0", "1.0")
-- enclose .0 numbers in quotes
rect_red:setFillColor(colorValue, 0, 0)
```

Slider Playground

Here's the code to update the three colored dice:

14

```
-- set dice (colored blocks) values:
rect_red_txt.text   = getValueInRange(value,  1, 6)
rect_green_txt.text = getValueInRange(value, 6, 1)
rect_blue_txt.text  = getValueInRange(value, 1, 20)
```

Yes, that second die is reversed. The numbers were just put on *backwards* at the factory!

This is available in the chapter downloads as *slider-playground.d2c*.

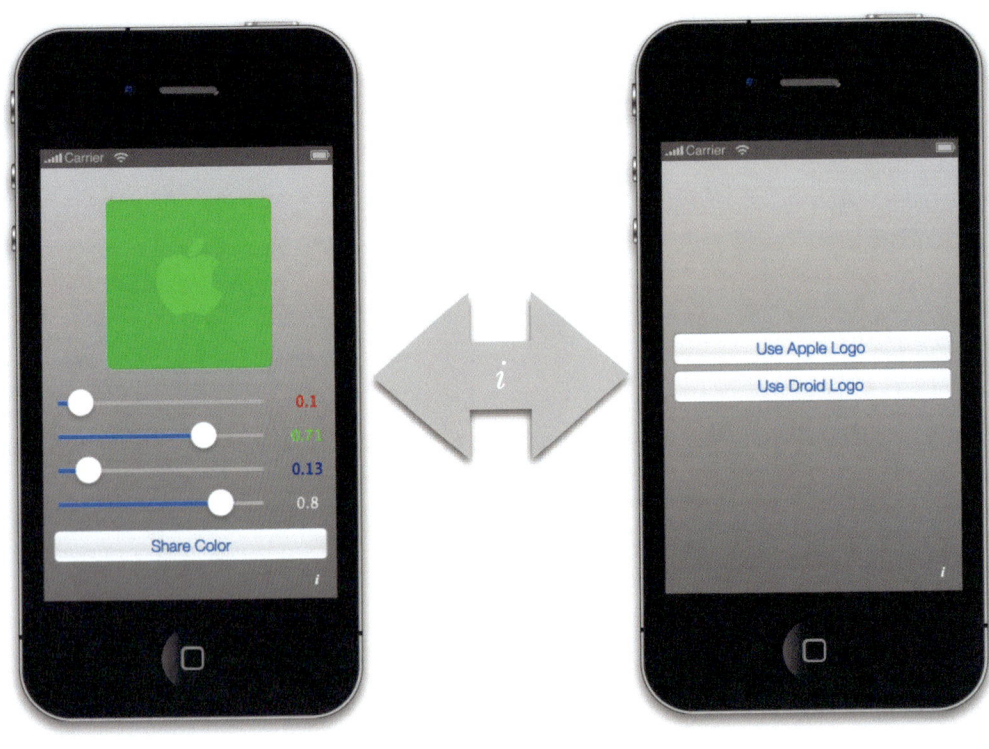

RGB Sliders   Settings Screen

An app with a bit of actual utility? Egads!

How would you like to finish with an app that might actually be "useful"? While basic colors can be easily created using RGB values, it becomes much harder to get specific shades of color, especially when you don't even know what a color you have in mind would be named. Wouldn't it be nice to have an app that allowed you to mix your own color by using sliders to change each component of the color? That would be cool.

You have **all of the tools** you need to make such an app, so it is just a matter of putting it together. At a minimum, you need separate sliders each for red, green, blue, and alpha (transparency), along with a filled shape to display the color that has been created with the sliders.

Multiple sliders

Handling multiple sliders is much like handling multiple buttons. You could give each slider its own (individual) event handler, which would make sense if the sliders did substantially different things. However, these sliders are actually quite similar in function, meaning that we might be better off using a single event handler. If you give each slider its own "id" attribute, you can figure out which slider was *slid* using the syntax "event.target.id". However, in this case, there's no real need to do that either. We can just get the current values on all 4 sliders at once in a single, fairly simple event handler.

Here's what it looks like:

```
function sliderHandler( event )
    red_val = getValueInRange(slider_red.value, "0.0", "1.0")
    txt_red.text = red_val

    green_val = getValueInRange(slider_green.value, "0.0", "1.0")
    txt_green.text = green_val

    blue_val = getValueInRange(slider_blue.value, "0.0", "1.0")
    txt_blue.text = blue_val

    alpha_val = getValueInRange(slider_alpha.value, "0.0", "1.0")
    txt_alpha.text = alpha_val
    txt_alpha:setFillColor(1, 1, 1, tonumber(txt_alpha.text))

    -- update the large filled rectangle:
    rect_bigColor:setFillColor(red_val, green_val, blue_val, alpha_val)

end
```

The value of the slider that is being moved is available as "event.value", which you pass to the "getValueInRange" function (previously discussed) to convert it to a decimal value between 0.0 and 1.0. The result is used to set the text next of the touched slider and to update the fill color on the large rounded rectangle.

A settings screen

You might have noticed that there's a white logo *underneath* the filled rounded rectangle. The white helps you see the color you've made better than the gray gradient. And it's cool. You might have also noted the small "*i*" at the bottom of the app, which leads to a settings screen

167

allowing you to customize the logo (see "Settings Screen"). When you press the "*i*", the main screen slides up (using a `transition.to()` and the settings screen slides into its place (again, using a `transition.to()`).

Sharing your awesome color

Finally, to add something **above and beyond**, what if you could also email (or SMS) your *awesome color* to a friend or other color aficionado? The would be really cool. That's the purpose of the "Share Color" button and it is easy to do in Solar2D with just a bit of code (coronalabs.com/blog/2012/01/03/composing-email-and-sms-in-corona/; see code box #16).

```
local options =
    {
        to = {john_carlson@baylor.edu, someone_else@somewhere.com},
        isBodyHTML = false,
        subject = "My Awesome Color",
        body = ("My awesome RGBA color is "..txt_red.text..",
                "..txt_green.text..", "..txt_blue.text..",
                "..txt_alpha.text)
    }
native.showPopup("mail", options)
```

16

Your app doesn't send the email *itself*, but it sends the data necessary to make an email (or SMS) to the native app on the device. This is probably for the best, as the mechanics of sending email (or SMS) messages is complex and certainly doesn't need to be duplicated in every app that needs that function.

All you need to do is populate a table with data that includes information about the message you want to send (box #16, lines 2-9). Any items that you omit will simply be blank (and up to the user to enter) in the resulting message.

Native Warning

Regrettably, as you can see, this technique does use the **native library**, which has a history of causing a bit of trouble. The caveat here is that **none of the simulators** will actually *send* an email or SMS message, or even simulate doing so. The only way to test sharing is by installing the app on an actual device.

This is available in the chapter downloads as *color-calculator-simple.d2c*. If you happen to have an Android device handy, the "RGB Sliders" app can be downloaded here: lillipellilabs.com/mobiledev/download/apk/widget_sliders_rgb.apk

Apart from the obvious legal troubles this app is asking for, it should be ready to upload to the app stores and make a fortune.

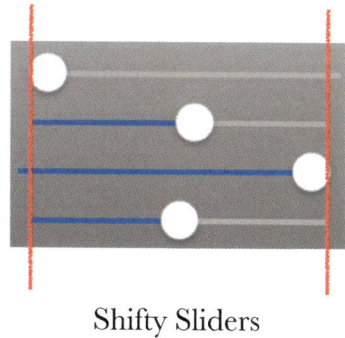

Shifty Sliders

Slider misalignment ("shifty sliders")

There is one significant "gotcha" when using sliders: The *position* of the slider on iOS devices **changes depending on the position of the knob**. This issue can be seen in the `widget_sliders_rgb` app above. For example, when the knob is very close to either the right or left side of a horizontal slider channel, the horizontal position of that slider is changed to *shift the channel away from the knob a bit* (up to about 9 pixels). Looking at the figure "Shifty Sliders", you can see the shift in the first (on the right edge) and third (on the left edge) sliders.

This happens when you position any of the slider knobs close to the left edge (e.g., at a value of 4 or less) or the right edge (e.g., at a value of 96 or more). However, this change is only apparent when the slider is **added to the screen** or **returns to the screen after being moved** offscreen (e.g., via a transition).

Moreover, even while they can be **clearly misaligned**, the slider will still report that it is in the *same location* (i.e., it doesn't see that it has been moved). Note that simply moving from an (x, y) position to a "(top, left)" position doesn't solve the problem.

Fixing the shift

To "fix" this, you'll need to detect the position of the knob (i.e., the slider's value) and compensate for the shift by adding or subtracting an amount equal to the shift. To do this, the position of each slider is updated both when they are each initially placed onscreen and when they transition back onto the screen (after the user accesses the settings).

Advanced

To accomplish this, a smaller function has been included called "`fixSliderXPosition( slider )`". It takes a slider as a parameter and performs the correction by changing the slider's x value. This is slightly **complicated** by the fact that the actual shift is based on the knob's *distance* from the edge, with the slider shifting less and less as the knob moves away from the edge. So, the function uses a bit of algebra to calculate the needed amount to keep the slider in place (see code box #17).

The caveats for this fix are that it **only works with sliders sized similarly** to those in the app and **only works with horizontal sliders**. A more general fix will require some additional work or a Solar2D update.

The "fixed" version of this app is in the chapter downloads as *color-calculator-fix.d2c*.

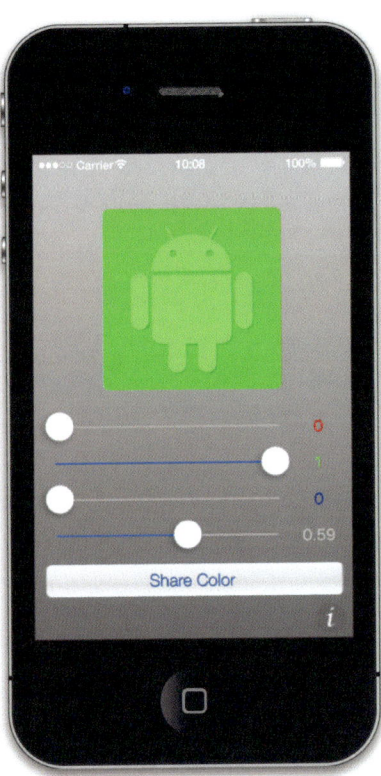

Correctly Aligned Sliders

17

```
1   function fixSliderXPosition( slider )
2       -- Note that this only fixes default horizontal sliders!
3       -- Here's the adjustment:
4       if slider.value > 93   then
5           slider.x = sliderX + slider.value - 91
6
7       elseif slider.value < 7 then
8           slider.x = sliderX + slider.value - 9
9
10      else
11          slider.x = sliderX
12      end
13
14  end
```

Summary

In this chapter you learned to use Solar2D slider widgets. Sliders store an integer number between 0 and 100, allowing the user to slide on onscreen knob to adjust the slider's value. Like other widgets, sliders have multiple phases which you can respond to programmatically. These phases are: "began", "moved", and "ended". You can code your script to respond to any or all of these to take appropriate action at a specific time. You also learned more about creating your own functions and using custom functions (i.e., those that aren't included in Solar2D).

Chapter resources

In the chapter resource download for this book (www.lillipellilabs.com/mobiledev/download/chapter_resources.zip), you'll find the following fantastic apps in folder "7":

1. slider_events (*slider-events.d2c*)
2. slider_events_full (*slider-events-full.d2c*)
3. slider_dice_demo (*slider-dice-demo.d2c*)
4. slider_dice_function (*slider-dice-function.d2c*)
5. slider_dice_symbols (coded by hand)
6. slider_playground (*slider-playground.d2c*)
7. color_calculator (*color-calculator.d2c*)
8. color_calculator-ios-fix (*color-calculator-fix.d2c*))

End-of-chapter exercises

1. Create an app with two sliders.

   a. Display the sum of the slider values in a text display object.

   b. Display the result of subtracting the second slider value from the first in a second text display object.

2. Create an app with two sliders.

   a. Make the sliders act like 12-sided dice. Display the value of each die in a text display object.

   b. Add a third display object that states whether the values match.

   c. Add a fourth display object that states whether the sum is over 20.

3. Create an app with three sliders with text display objects for each value. Use the `getValueInRange( )` function to: .

   - Make slider 1 act like a 6-sided die.
   - Make slider 2 act like a 12-sided die.
   - Make slider 3 act like a 20-sided die.

4. Create an app with 1 slider and 1 text display object. Start the value at 0 and display that in the text display object. As usual, update the slider value as the user moves the slider. However,

   a. **Change the color** of the value based on the value:
      0-25 White
      26-50 Red
      51-75 Green
      76-100 Gold

   b. Play an appropriate **sound** when the color changes.

   c. Add a button to **reset** the value back to 0.

5. Create an app with 1 sliders and 1 **display shape** of your choice. Use the slider to adjust the **grayscale** (color) of the shape, from white to black.

Integrate

6. Create an app with 2 sliders and 1 **display shape** of your choice. Use the sliders to locate the **(x, y) location** of the shape and move it as the sliders are adjusted.

7. Create an app with 2 sliders with text display objects for each value.

    a. Update the values as the sliders are moved and **draw a star** (i.e., a polygon display object) adjacent to the larger value.

    b. Play an appropriate sound when the star shifts location.

8. Create an app with 3 sliders with a text display object to display each value. You'll <u>create 2 custom functions</u> that use these 3 values to do each of the following:

    a. Create a function to find the **maximum slider value** and display it in a text display object (which will change as the sliders are adjusted).

    b. Create a function to calculate the **average slider value** and display it in a text display object.

Challenge

9. Create an app with four sliders, one button, and one text display object. When the button is pressed, run a function you've created to sort the values on the sliders and display the sorted results in the text object (e.g., something like "22, 50, 61, 100").

10. Create an app with a slider and a button. When the button is pressed, play one of your collection of *Wizarding School* sounds. Use the slider to control the volume. You can use the `audio.setVolume()` method to do this, passing it a value between 0.0 and 1.0. For example, `audio.setVolume(.25)` will turn the sound level to 25%.

NOTES

Coding & Debugging

Debugging is a critical skill and simply means *removing all bugs from a program*. Debugging is an integral part of programming. No programmer, however experienced, can sit down and write bug-free code of any real sophistication without testing and debugging their work.

Bugs

From Wikipedia (en.wikipedia.org/wiki/Software_bug):

> *A software bug is an error, flaw, mistake, failure, or fault in a computer program or system that produces an incorrect or unexpected result, or causes it to behave in unintended ways.*

That is, a "bug" is an error of about any sort that produces bad results of almost any kind. Bugs do *not* include sloppy, poorly designed, and/or inefficient code. Such code may **attract bugs**, but in and of itself does not constitute buggy code.

The idea of a software "bug" (en.wikipedia.org/wiki/Software_bug#Etymology) goes all the way back to 1843, but the first use of the term "bug" to describe a technological glitch is thought to have originated in hardware engineering since, as many books point out, early electromechanical devices could malfunction due to actual bugs crawling into the mechanisms and disrupting relays and such.

Bugs can include*:

- **Syntax errors** (e.g., that cause the app not to run/compile or to crash at a particular point).

- **Logic errors** (e.g., code runs, but produce unexpected results due to incorrect Boolean conditions controlling the flow of execution).

- **Arithmetic errors** (e.g., divide by zero or overflow errors).

- **Misuse** or misunderstanding of concepts, language, or tools used (e.g., Solar2D), for example in mistakenly expecting a certain function to do something a certain way. Or, perhaps, using a coding approach or technique that is unsuitable.

- **Platform (Solar2D and/or Lua) bugs** that need to be worked around.

- Finally, some writers contend that the misinterpretations and/or **misspecification** of end-user needs should be considered a bug.

Also, while the topic of bugs may seem quite remote from that of hacking and computer virii, coders of malware and other ne'er-do-wells rely on bugs in widely installed software to create exploits to gain illegal access. So, bugs may open the door to criminals, in addition to causing damage due to the failures they cause in systems that rely on the buggy code.

Keep these in mind while coding (the "three laws of debugging"):

1. **Ease**: It is much easier to create bugs than to find and fix them. In fact, creating bugs often take no effort at all.

2. **Evade**: Given #1, it is typically easier to work to avoid bugs than to find and fix them after the fact; likewise, it is typically better to find and fix bugs early in the process, rather than letting them fester in your code.

3. **Educate**: The only good news is that finding and fixing a bug does provide the opportunity to learn how to avoid ever creating that bug again.

---

* en.wikipedia.org/wiki/Software_bug#Common_types_of_computer_bugs

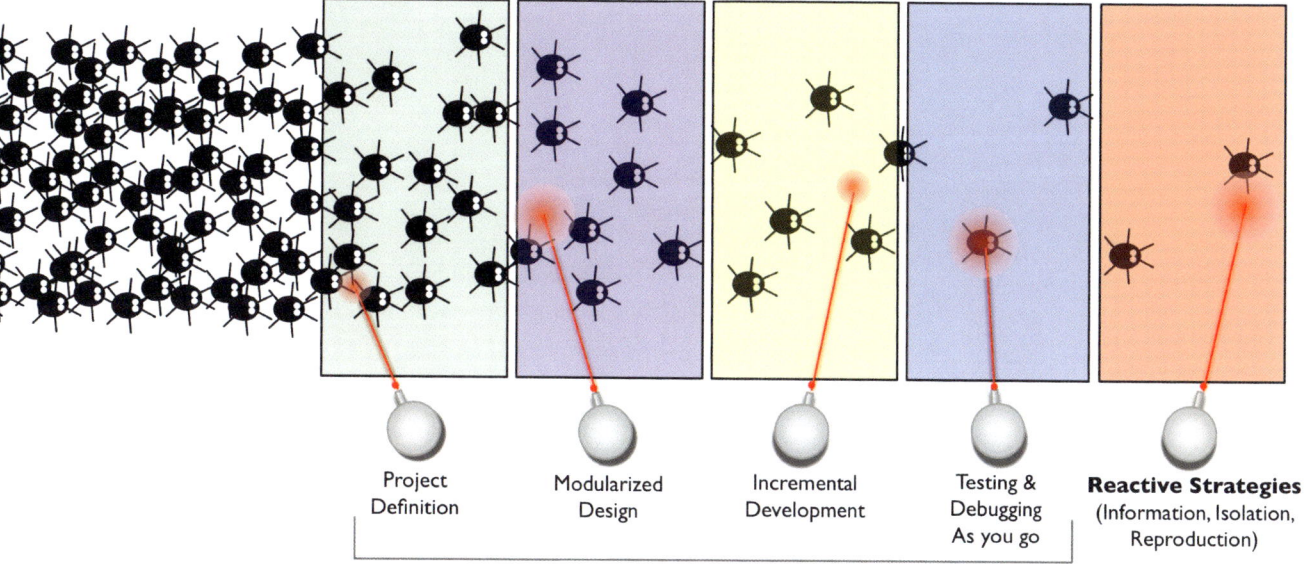

Debugging Strategies

In general, we can divide our bug-fighting strategies as *proactive* (put in place to avoid or minimize bugs from the start of development) and *reactive* (dealing with bugs that weren't avoided). These are complementary approaches that work together to reduce or eliminate software bugs (see "Debugging Strategies").

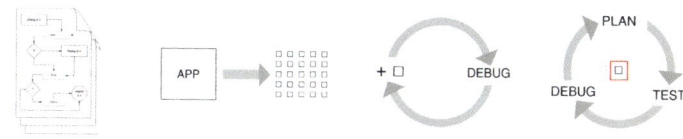

Proactive strategies

It is important to recognize that "testing and debugging" isn't simply a later phase in waterfall development (en.wikipedia.org/wiki/Waterfall_model). A smart developer will **work proactively to avoid bugs** early (and throughout) the development process. A bug that is found and fixed early in the process usually takes less time than later in the process. A bug that is avoided (or "e-voided", I guess), takes no time to find and fix. **Saving time saves money**.

There are *four key strategies* to embrace: Define the project, modularize the project, incrementally build the project, and test and debug as you go.

1. Define

Define the project's purpose and scope: having a clear understanding of what you are coding and what functionality it needs to include is crucial to a project's success. *Scope creep* (continually finding yourself adding features that you and/or the end-user sees as needed) is the result of an inadequate definition at this stage and a frequent cause of subsequent problems. Define the user interface (UI) clearly (having a clear idea of what screens will look like in advance will leave you with screen space where you need it so that widgets sizes and locations don't have to be continually tweaked).

Define

2. Modularize

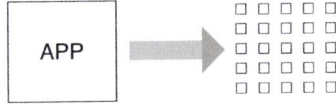

Modularize

Modularize your project by decomposing it into smaller "sub projects". If possible, split the user interface (UI) from the underlying logic and processes using, for example, "model-view-controller" compartmentalization (en.wikipedia.org/wiki/Model–view–controller). Define each module to the extent possible. Within each module, attempt to break the task into subtasks that can be developed separately.

3. Incremental build

Incrementally build your app. The goal is to enter *very little code* (i.e., an "increment" of code) before running and testing the app. This will help you identify problems *right away*, making it easier to identify the code that is causing the problem. Don't wait until you have entered 200 lines of new code to run it!

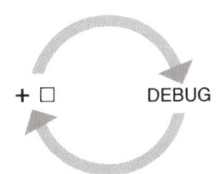

Incremental Build

One weird trick to bug-free code

As a flowchart, incremental development looks something like the flowchart labelled "Incremental Development". Try to train yourself in the habit of working in this "code —> run —> debug —> fix" loop and to avoid ever adding very large increments of code.

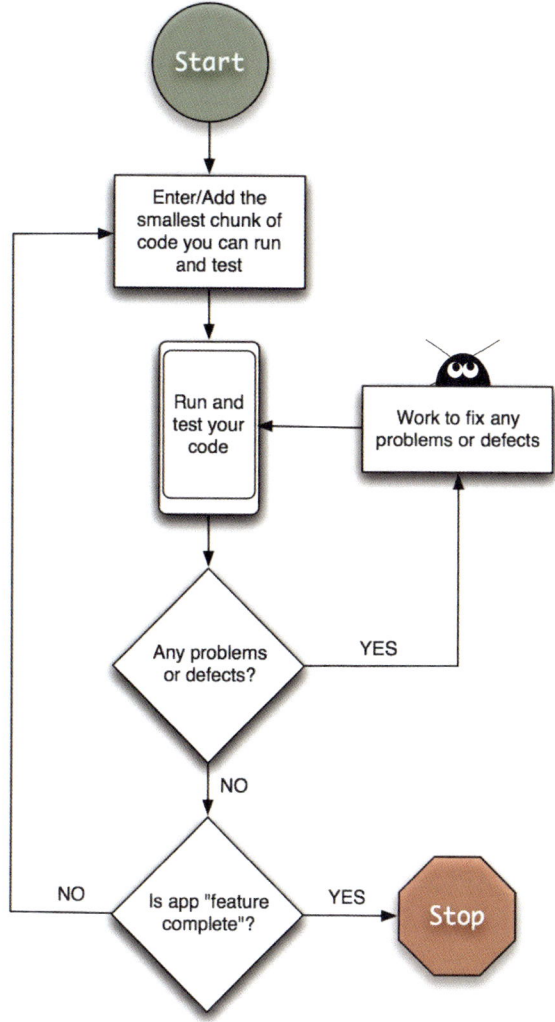

Incremental Development

4. Test & debug as you go

Test and debug as you go: Testing and debugging go together hand-in-hand like, well, two hands. Testing includes the continuous validation of your app as you go during incremental development. That means testing the interface layout and functionality, as well as the validity of all operations, functions, calculations and so on. Such testing requires planning as you code to allow for functions and modules to be easily validated.

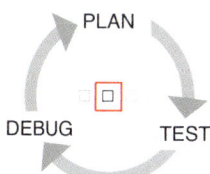

Validation Cycle

For example, many business apps will work with money and perform calculations on monetary amounts; getting the correct result is generally considered to be desirable. Get into the habit of planning how to test each part of your app and working to support and conduct such testing in a continuous and ongoing manner.

Debugging: Reactive Strategies

Reactive strategies

Even using proactive strategies to the fullest, bugs will still creep through. Finding bugs later in the development process is a bit like being a detective. Bugs can be easy to find or very difficult. Next, we discuss three basic techniques at our disposal: (1) look for clues; (2) isolate the error; and (3) reproduce the error.

1. Look for clues

Look for clues in the information you already have or can create. You have several potential sources for information: (a) warnings in the IDE, (b) Lua console messages, (c) the device screen, and (d) logging more information.

```
1  cx = display.contentCenterX
2  cy = display.contentCenterY
3  cw = display.contentWidth
4
5  slider = widget.newSlider {
6      x = cx,
7      y = cy,
8      width = 0.9*cw,
9      listener = sliderListener
10 }
```
[1]

a. Look for **warnings from the IDE** (e.g., LuaGlider). For example, if you type the code above (code box #1) into LuaGlider, you might see this (notice the <mark>yellow</mark> warning symbol and underlining on line 5):

```
⚠  slider = widget.newSlider
```

If you "hover" your mouse over the warning, you will see a message describing the issue (in this case, `widget` is "possibly not initialized"). Although ZBS won't show you the error in this manner, as soon as you try to run the code you'll see a message in the console (discussed below) stating that on line 5 there was an "attempt to index global 'widget' (a nil value)". Note that your code may still work fine with certain warnings present. In other cases, the warnings will presage errors that will produce bugs during testing.

The "possibly not initialized" and "nil value" warnings are pretty common, and simply mean that you haven't created or defined the item you are trying to use (`widget`, in this case). Remember, before making any widgets, we have to **require** the widget library:

```
widget = require "widget"
```
[2]

Once this statement is placed in your code, above the spot where you use `widget` (perhaps on line 4 of box #1), the warning will go away.

Emors involving "M"

Many of the warnings you see will be due one of the following "M" errors:

- **M**issing statements (like box #1)
- **M**isplaced code (e.g., code that is placed either above or below where it needs to be)
- **M**istyped code (e.g., `prnit("Hello World")`).

- **M**is-capitalized code or filename(s) (especially where filenames are case-sensitive).
- **M**is-scoped code (e.g., using `local` inappropriately).
- **M**issing resources in project folder (e.g., forgetting to put an image in the project).
- **M**issing code elements (such as unbalanced parentheses, missing quotation marks, absent 'end' statements, etc.).
- **M**ultiple variables and/or functions sharing the same name. Each entity should get a unique identifier.

b. Look at the **Lua console** (the text output at the bottom of your IDE or open console window) for messages from Solar2D. If you have *multiple* errors listed, look at the *topmost one first*. Here's the console output you would see trying to run box #1, which might look like a bit of a mess (box #3).

```
OUTPUT                                                                    3

Copyright (C) 2009-2017  C o r o n a   L a b s    I n c .
Feb 20 17:00:18.596 Corona Simulator[1896:507]       Version: 3.0.0
Feb 20 16 17:00:18.596 Corona Simulator[1896:507]    Build: 2017.3184
Feb 20 16 17:00:18.727 Corona Simulator[1896:507] Runtime error
...Projects/Teaching/Mobile Dev/outlines/ch-08/main.lua:5: attempt to index global 'widget'
 (a nil value) stack traceback:
        [C]: ?
        ...Projects/Teaching/Mobile Dev/outlines/ch-08/main.lua:5: in main chunk
```

However, the console output contains **vital clues** about what the nature of the bug is. The key lines have been colored red (by me) and translate something like this:

"on line 5 of the main.lua script, you have used the term 'widget', which hasn't been defined (i.e., its value 'nil')"

Again, this is the same error we might see in the IDE and is caused by the missing require statement in code box #2.

Once you fix your **topmost error** and save the file, either all of the problems are gone, or Solar2D will identify additional problems that need your attention (again, start by trying to solve the topmost error listed -- the one with the *lowest line number*).

c. **Observe what appears** (and what does not appear) **on the screen**. This can be fairly obvious (like a button appearing in the wrong location) or more difficult (like an image being placed behind another image and therefore not visible). Once we learn to work with physics bodies, there will be many more opportunities to look closely at what is (or isn't) occurring on screen.

That doesn't look right, or is it *too right?*

For example, in the screenshot to the right, you'll notice that the button appears to be partly off screen. That's not good; it might fall off.

```
 1  local widget = require "widget"
 2  cx = display.contentCenterX
 3  cy = display.contentCenterY
 4  cw = display.contentWidth
 5
 6  button = widget.newButton {
 7      id = "btn1",
 8      x = cw,
 9      y = cy,
10      width = 300,
11      height = 36,
12      fontSize = 20,
13      label = "hello",
14      emboss = true,
15      defaultFile = "button.png",
16      overFile = "pressed.png",
17      listener = buttonHandler
18  }
```

4

183

What would cause such a glitch? Well, here's the code that was used to set up the button up (see code box #4).So, if the button is too far to the right, that would indicate that the x value of the button is too high, so we should double-check the line of code which sets it (box #4, line 8). You can see that I "accidentally" set the x value to cw, which is the content *width*, rather than to the content *center* (cx). That mistake will shift the button precisely half of the display width to the right, which is the error we are observing.

d. **Get more information**: There are also techniques that can be used to create information by exposing data that already exists (but is not in view) or by adding new data within the program (i.e., by adding new, perhaps temporary, variables). The "key" technique is *logging* (or "outputting" — creating a text description of some occurrence) the current state of program variables and/or flow of execution to the console. In Lua, we use the `print()` function to do basic logging.

For example, if I was still struggling with the *mystery of the misplaced button*, I would probably want to confirm the x location that Lua sees for that button.

To do so, I need to know the value of `button.x`, which could be logged in this way:

```
print("button.x = "..button.x)
```
5

Box #5 displays a brief description of what variable we are looking at concatenated with the variable itself. If we did this for the `button` widget shown just above, we might see output that looks something like box #6, which is showing the x position of our button to be 320.

```
OUTPUT
Copyright (C) 2009-2018   C o r o n a   L a b s   I n c .
Feb 20 16 17:00:18.596 Corona Simulator[1896:507]    Version: 3.0.0
Feb 20 16 17:00:18.596 Corona Simulator[1896:507]    Build: 2018.3326
button.x = 320
```
6

Remember, this x is at the horizontal center of the button, not the top-left corner. The value 320 happens to be the `display.contentWidth` for the default iPhone that Solar2D uses (e.g., an iPhone 3), which tells us again that I used the wrong `display` property when locating the button.

Likewise, if your app isn't responding to an event (such as a button press), then the first thing to check would be if the event-handler is being called:

```
function buttonHandler( event )
    -- log text to confirm event-handler called:
    print( "a button event has occurred" )

    -- code to handle button event, perhaps:
    count = count + 1 -- and so on...
end
```

By adding this print statement we are creating observable evidence of whether the button is properly connected to the event handler. When I press the button, I would expect to see something like this at the console:

```
OUTPUT

Copyright (C) 2009-2018   C o r o n a    L a b s    I n c .
Feb 20 16 17:00:18.596 Corona Simulator[1896:507]    Version: 3.0.0
Feb 20 16 17:00:18.596 Corona Simulator[1896:507]    Build: 2018.3326
a button event has occurred
a button event has occurred
```

If I don't see that text (at the bottom of box #8), then I know that I need to look more closely at my button setup, looking for typos in the configuration table. And also, hmm, why does the text display *twice?*

2. Isolate the error

If you find yourself in the unenviable situation of having a bug in your app and no clue where the "bad" code is, you need to try to identify the line (or lines) of code causing the bug. This can sometimes be done by *commenting out* lines that you think may have something to do with the bug or, conversely, *commenting out* parts of the app that you think are working fine. In addition, you can comment out code that you believe to be wrong and paste in *known good code* (i.e., if a button isn't working, replace the suspect code with button code from an app you know to work).

- The goal of these approaches is the same: To find the line (or lines) of code that contain the error.

- If the error disappears after you comment out a particular line, guess what? You just found the problem.

3. Reproduce the error

It may be the case that you simply *can't* isolate the error. You might run into this if there actually isn't a "bad" line of code. Some errors stem from missing lines of code, for example, in which case there's *nothing to isolate*.

- In this situation, try to create a simple app with only the functionality that is giving you trouble. This is sometimes called a **test case**.

- Copy & paste or type from scratch the relevant code from the app containing the bug, but only enough to perform the **one specific task** you are having trouble with.

- When you do so, either your test case will work fine, indicating that the problem is elsewhere in your code (so you've just ruled out a chunk of code), or it will reproduce the some error you are seeing in your full app (indicating that the code that was tested is, in fact, the source of the error).

- For example, if an image isn't displaying, create an app that *just displays that image*, without any other extraneous code. That will help you start to figure out where the mistake lies.

Summary

Finding and fixing software bugs are a part of every developer's life. The way you approach your work can have a real impact on the nature and amount of **bug problems** that you will have to deal with. Following the proactive strategies discussed (*project definition, modularized design, incremental development,* and *testing & debugging as you go*) can reduce this number and help you find bugs more quickly (when they are, hopefully, somewhat easier to tackle). For bugs that slip through your proactive measures, you may utilize any combination of reactive strategies (*information, isolation,* and *reproduction*) to finish them off.

Although bugs are frequently a frustrating aspect of coding, try to focus on what you can take away by finding and fixing bugs. Sometimes, the harder the problem is to debug, the more you can learn via the process.

Chapter resources

In the chapter resource download for this book (www.lillipellilabs.com/mobiledev/download/chapter_resources.zip), you'll find 3 troubled apps to debug in folder "6":

1. Debug This
2. Debug This Too
3. Debug This Three

End-of-chapter exercises

Download the three apps (above) that desperately need your **debugging expertise** and get them working! You'll find versions for ZBS and *Drawn2Code* users. But why pick? Do them all.

NOTES

Dragging & Collisions

This chapter will build your skills to encompass *dragging* onscreen objects and detecting whether they have *collided* with another object or the screen edges. You will also learn about timers and delve more deeply into the Lua table. These skills, along with the ability to display and transition images, and to play sounds, will enable the creation of **simple games** (without the use of the physics engine) or **rich business apps**.

Tapping, images & sounds

As a reminder, here is the Solar2D syntax for creating images and sounds as well as listening for (and responding to) user taps (originally covered in Chapter 4). For images (preferably png) you use `display.newImage()` which takes 3 parameters: The image *file name* and the (x,y) values to use in placing the image by its *center*. For example, here's the code used to set up and scale the "momoney" image used in Chapter 4:

```
1  momoney = display.newImageRect("mobdev.png", 64, 100)
2  momoney.x = display.contentCenterX
3  momoney.y = display.contentCenterY
```

To play a sound (Solar2D supports several sound formats, however, not all are compatible across platforms — see note below) when the image is touched, you need to create the sound object using `audio.loadSound()`, attach an event listener to the image object, and provide an event-handling function to receive the tap events:

```
1  chaching = audio.loadSound("chaching.mp3")
2
3  function tapHandler( event )
4      audio.play(chaching)
5  end
6  momoney:addEventListener("tap", tapHandler)
```

In *Drawn2Code*, you would create an image display object and a load sound action object. Then, add the tap listener to the image and create a play sound action in the event-handler. And your done.

Remember, to run this app as coded you need to have the image and sound file in the **same project folder** (i.e., together with your "main.lua" and "config.lua" files). If everything is in place, when you tap the image, you should hear the "cash register" sound.

Playing "background" music

The ability to play brief "sound effects" such as "chaching" is obviously appropriate in games and also helpful in rich, *gamified* apps. In addition to these short sound effects, you can play longer sounds such as background or ambient music. To play sounds of long duration, you will typically need to access larger sound files. Typical sound effects could be a few KB to 100 or more KB, while longer, several minute sound files can easily be over 1MB. These larger files need to be handled differently.

Instead of loading the entire audio at once and holding it in memory, your app will need to treat it as a file *stream*, which continuously reads just as much data as is needed to keep playing the sound continuously (reducing the memory "footprint").

To demonstrate, I've downloaded some free background music from JewelBeat:

```
happy_music = audio.loadStream("JewelBeat - Happy Moments.wav")
audio.play(happy_music, {loops = -1, fadein = 3000})
```

This sound file is 2.8MB and is 16 seconds long. The code in box #4 tells the app to load the sound as an audio *stream*, then to play it with two settings: "`loops = -1`" tells it to loop as long as the app is running, while "`fadein = 3000`" tells the app to fade the sound in gradually, reaching full volume over a period of 3 seconds (3000 milliseconds).

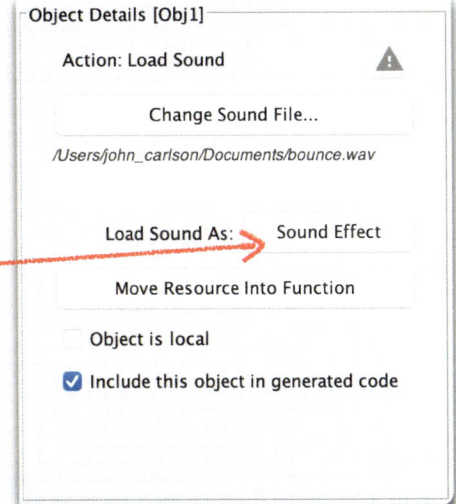

To load background music in *Drawn2Code*, just switch the type of sound in the load sound script object (in the settings panel). For example, if you load a sound called "bounce.wav" to your stack as Obj1, then you'll see the "Load Sound As" button right in the middle of the settings panel. If you press the button, you can toggle the sound between a "sound effect" and "background music".

A note on sound file formats

Solar2D supports several sound file formats, however, only .wav (16-bit) and .mp3 are cross-platform. In addition, iOS supports .caf, .aac, and .m4a, but not .m4p (which is Fair-Play encrypted audio purchased from iTunes), while Android also supports the .ogg format. The .aac and .m4a formats both use the advanced audio codec and are basically the same. Note, however, that the Solar2D Simulator running on Windows does *not* currently support .ogg (although Android devices do). See the table "Sound File Formats" for a summary of compatibility.

Gotcha

	wav	mp3	aac/m4a	ogg	caf
iOS	✓	✓	✓		✓
Android	✓	✓		✓	

Sound File Formats

As with fonts, when testing your app remember that certain sound files may play within the Solar2D Simulator, but fail to play once installed on a real device.

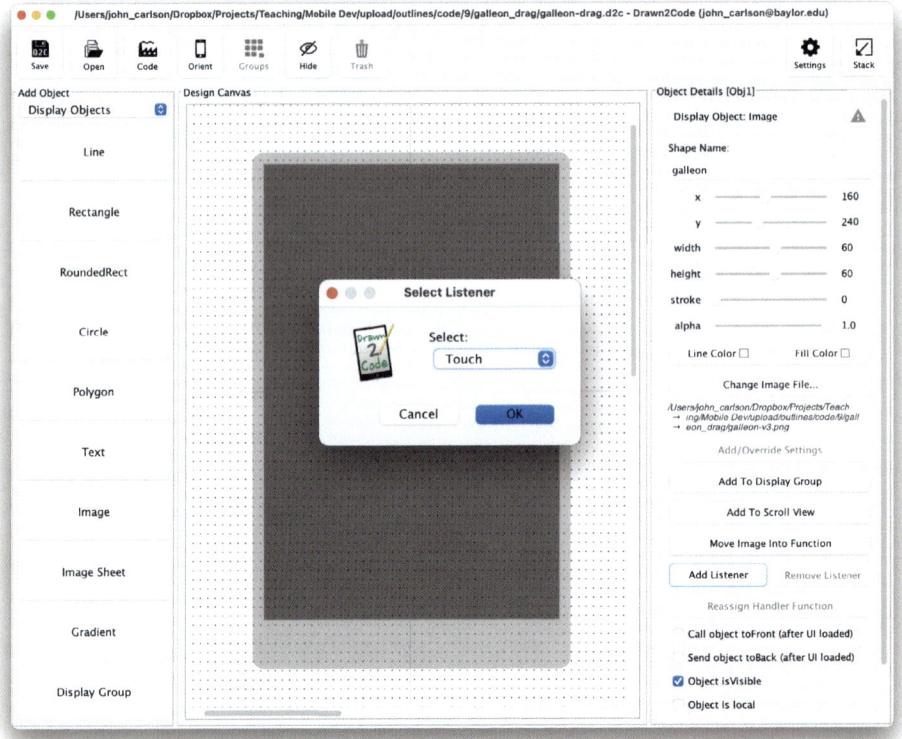

Adding the Touch Listener to Handle Drags

Listening for and handling a drag

You've already learned about tapping and touching images and buttons, but there's more! So far, we've skipped doing anything for the "moved" phase, which is what we need to handle to do something when the user *drags* an object. We'll focus on dragging the "momoney" image here. You simply add the event listener to listen for "touch" events (covered in Chapter 4):

```
momoney:addEventListener("touch", simpleDrag)
```

In *Drawn2Code*, just hit the "Add Listener" button in the settings panel of the display object you want to be able to drag (see "Adding the Touch Listener to Handle Drags").

Next, let's look at the required event-handling method (called "simpleDrag" in this first example). In this minimalist function you just need to move the object along with the user's finger (i.e., the touch point):

```
1   function simpleDrag ( event )
2
3       t = event.target
4       phase = event.phase;
5
6       -- move event target with user's finger:
7       if (phase == "moved") then
8           t.x = event.x
9           t.y = event.y
10      end
11
12      return true  -- req'd to tell Solar2D you've handled event
13
14  end
```

[5]

Although this function is pretty simple (box #5), it does provide an initial technique for dragging. You are doing two key things here: Limiting your actions to the "moved" phase (which means that the flow of execution only reaches lines 8 & 9 when the user is moving their finger on the screen) and, when appropriate, moving the display object along the path defined by the user's moving finger. To do this, you set the position of the target of the event (the momoney display object at t.x, t.y) to the location of the user's finger (which is event.x and event.y) on lines 8 & 9.

Finally, you return true on line 12 to tell Solar2D that the move has been *handled*. A false or nil response would tell Solar2D that the user wasn't touching the correct object, or that the function *failed to handle* the touch, and no action would be taken under the "moved" phase. The false or nil response will pass the touch down to any objects underneath the touched object, so under certain circumstances this makes sense. Also, a true response does <u>not</u> mean the function only works once. The event handler is called *continually*, as the user moves the touch point, to keep the object under the user's finger, pixel by pixel.

If you are planning to copy and paste any of these code boxes to test, be sure to put the event-handler (box #5) *prior* to the event registration (box #5). This app is available in the chapter download as the drag_simple project. While this function will get the job done, it has a few flaws and omissions that you need to address. The key to doing so will be for you to understand the difference between the "touch point" and the "target point".

Of course, if you are using *Drawn2Code*, then the event-handler has already been added to your stack and contains a better version of the dragging code. More on that next.

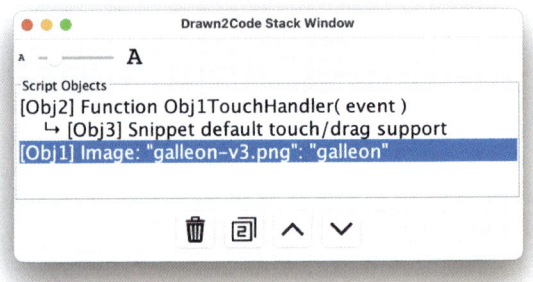

Stack with Default Touch/Drag Support

More sophisticated drag handling

If you took the time to run the above project, you might have noticed an issue. When you start your drag, the image **jumps** to center itself on your finger (or mouse pointer in the simulators). This isn't ideal, especially for a gaming situation where such a jump might put the object in harm's way. The reason it does this is because **you told it to** on lines 8 and 9 (box #5): event.x and event.y are the location where the user touched the object. So, unless the user touched at the *exact center*, the object will jump slightly so that it is now centered at the point of the touch. See "Touch Point versus Target Point" for an illustration.

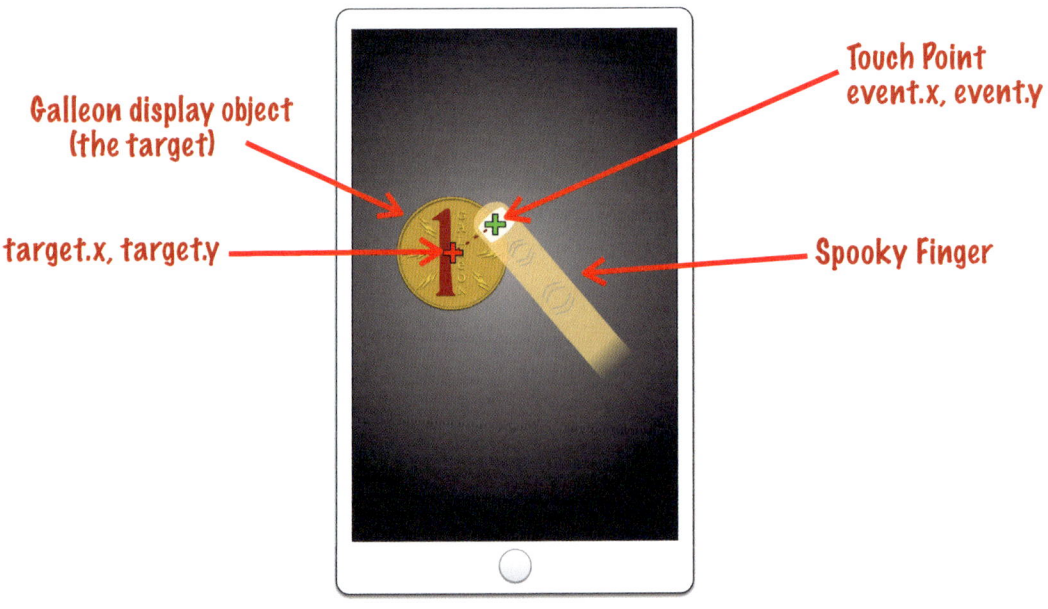

Touch Point versus Target Point

Of course, as the user drags the object, it will remain centered on the finger (or mouse pointer) and won't continue to jump. However, if the user releases the object and then re-touches it, the jump will occur again. Anytime there's a gap between the red "x" and the green "x", you'll see such a jump. You will want to fix this. A more complete drag handler will need to respond correctly based on the touch phase and will need to set the focus for the drag listener at the start of the drag (i.e., the "began" phase) and release the focus at the end (i.e., at "ended" and/or "cancelled").

While this may sound like a great deal to do, it is actually fairly straightforward and (even better) this improved function can be used to handle drags in most situations (i.e., it is *reusable*). This is also the default drag support for *Drawn2Code*.

The app demo that uses this is `drag_demo`, however, it isn't very interesting. You can still drag the `galleon` image around (without the jump), but *nothing happens!* You need to be able to **collide** with something and generate some *reaction* to the collision.

Basic collisions

If you put something else onscreen (i.e., another display object in addition to your precious galleon, you can detect whether your dragged object "hits" or "collides" with it, since you know (programmatically) the size and location of both objects. But, what should you hit? That is, what should you put onscreen to collide with? Since we are dragging a coin, let's add a bank to deposit it in.

Your first collision app will allow the user to drag the galleon image into your bank account. We'll add counters and sound effects as well, to make it more fun. You have all of the pieces you need to do this, it is just a matter of putting them together (correctly) in an app.

Requirements

1. Display the galleon image
2. Display the bank image
3. Add the touch listener to the galleon script object to allow it to be dragged
4. Detect whether the galleon has collided with the back
5. If a collision has occurred, play a sound ("chaching") and remove the galleon from the screen.

Galleon   Bank

Take a minute and think: Can you **visualize** what the design will look like? Apart from #4, you know how to do each of these things. Let's tackle this step-by-step:

1. Start by getting the resources you need together and putting them into a new folder for this design. You need: galleon.png, bank.png, and chaching.wav. These are all available in the chapter download.

2. Start a new *Drawn2Code* design and add both of the images and load the sound file. Set the project folder to the folder that your resources are in.

3. Add the "touch" listener to the galleon script object.

4. Save your design and test it. .Can you drag the galleon around?

5. Add the "Overlap Detection" function to your stack and move the supplied overlaps( ) function up toward the top.

6. Edit the default touch/drag support snippet inside the touch event-handler to check for overlap. You're going to add some code to do that, right after the lines where t.x and t.y are updated as the galleon is moved. Your going to call the overlaps( ) function and pass it the object id's for your galleon and your bank. In *my* stack, the galleon is Obj1 and the bank is Obj4. So, I've added the call like this (code box #6):

Putting Your Coin in the Bank

```
1    -- move the target:
2    t.x = event.x - t.x0
3    t.y = event.y - t.y0
4
5    -- you can check for collisions here:
6    if overlaps(Obj1, Obj4) then
7        print( "overlap!" )
8    end
```

Just type those three lines in your snippet and use the correct object id's in your stack.

7. Save your design and test it. Do you see "overlap!" at the console when you drag the galleon over the bank? If so, you've just detected your first simple collision!

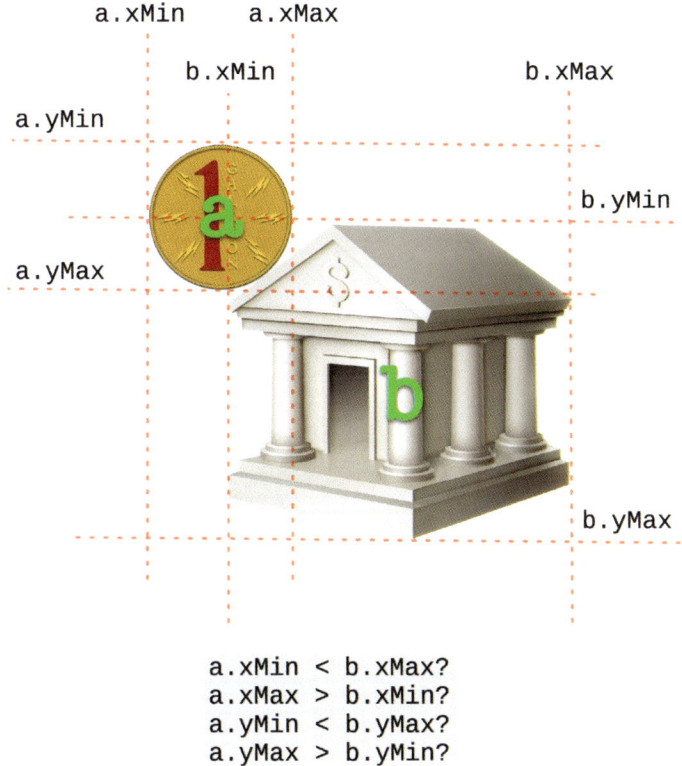

Visualizing Overlap Detection Math

Detecting overlap

There's more to do when the overlap occurs, but let's stop and look at how this overlap detection works. The overlap detection (box #7) works by checking the edges of each object (a and b) to determine whether there is overlap both *horizontally* (x-axis) and *vertically* (y-axis). The function also verifies that both objects *exist* (i.e., are not nil) before performing the check.

```
function overlaps(a, b)
    if a ~= nil and b ~= nil then
        return a.contentBounds.xMin < b.contentBounds.xMax
        and a.contentBounds.xMax > b.contentBounds.xMin
        and a.contentBounds.yMin < b.contentBounds.yMax
        and a.contentBounds.yMax > b.contentBounds.yMin
    else
        return false
    end
end
```

If either object is `nil`, or either axis doesn't overlap, the function returns `false`. If there is overlap on both axes, then the function returns `true`. The order of objects you pass this function doesn't matter (i.e., I could have called "overlaps(Obj4, Obj1)" and gotten the same results.

Do you think we need to edit the overlaps(a, b) method? Looking at code box #7 (or at the code in your stack), it appears to be checking for overlap between two program entities called "a" and "b". But we don't have an "a" and "b" in our stack.

Answer: There's no need to edit the overlaps(a , b) function at all. The two parameters (a, b) are simply proxies to use inside the body of the function. Whatever you pass to the function when you call is (e.g., line 6 in box #6) will be referred to as "a" and "b" inside the function, but the function will actually check the two objects that you pass.

There's more you'd probably like to do when the overlap occurs. Let's add a sound effect first.

Sound effect

There is a bit of a trick to get the sound effect to work well, which you might not have expected. After all, you already know how to load and play a sound! In fact, if you've followed the step-by-step instruction above, you already loaded the sound. So, it is ready to play! I'll bet you even have an idea where to put the code to play the sound (hint: it is where you've got the print("overlap!") statement.

The complications
There are two complications to getting this working correctly:
1. There's no place to put the play sound script object, since it needs to be inserted into the middle of an existing snippet.
2. The code inside of the overlap check will get executed as the galleon is moved, pixel-by-pixel. So, when the overlap starts, you'll hear a wall of sound rather than one nice sound effect.

Let's tackle problem 1 first. Start by adding a "Play Sound" script object to your stack. It will appear at the bottom of the stack, but the location isn't important now. You stack might look something like mine (see "Adding the Sound Effect"). Set the audio channel (in the settings panel) to 1. With the sound effect still selected, put down the "Edit' menu and select "Copy The Script Object's Code to the Clipboard". This will, you might have guessed, copy the code generated by the script object to the clipboard. This will let us paste it in the existing snippet, right where we need it to go.

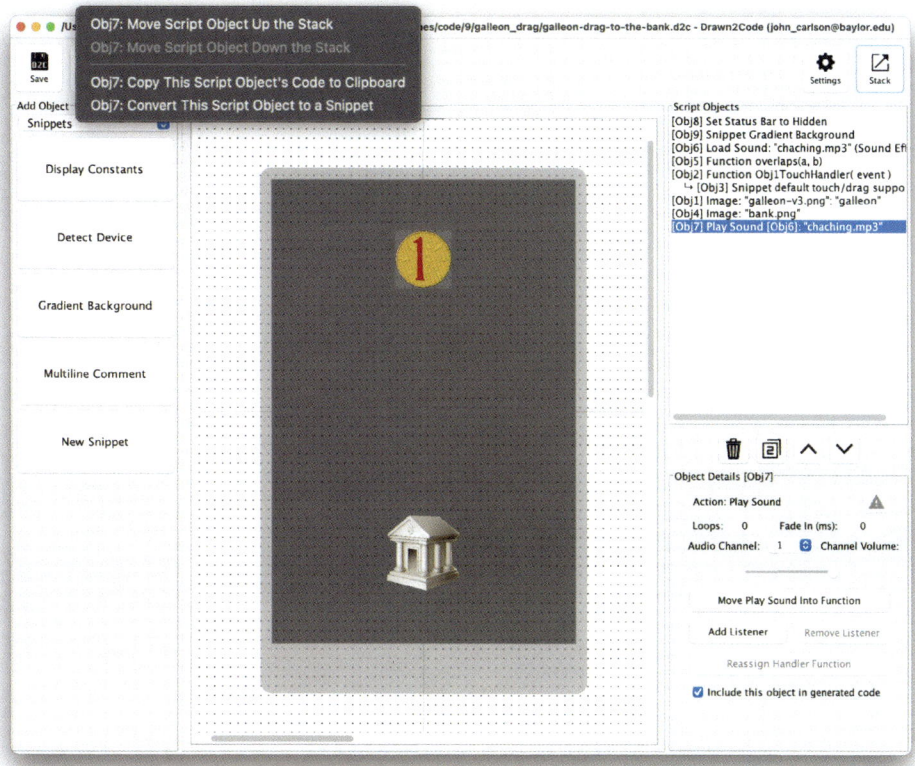

Adding the Sound Effect

You'll paste it right here:

```
 1  -- move the target:
 2  t.x = event.x - t.x0
 3  t.y = event.y - t.y0
 4
 5  -- you can check for collisions here:
 6  if overlaps(Obj1, Obj4) then
 7      -- play audio on channel 1-32 (select channel 0 for the default):
 8      -- https://docs.coronalabs.com/api/library/audio/play.html
 9      --(see pages 85-86, 105-107, 192, 296 of CPMAD textbook for usage)
10      Obj7 = audio.play( Obj6, { channel = 1, })
11  end
```

Next, either delete the play sound object (for me, Obj7) or remove it from the generated code. Then, save your design and test it. You should hear sort of a screeching sound when you drag the galleon over the bank. That's the sound playing on top of itself, over and over.

To solve the second problem, you're going to check to see if the audio is playing before trying to play it again (to make sure it is only playing one time per "collision"). This is actually easy, since there's a function built-into Solar2D to do this: isAudioChannelPlaying( ). You're going to edit the 'if-then' statement (i.e., line 6 in box #7) that does the over lap check to also call this method:

```
if overlaps( Obj1, Obj4 ) and not audio.isChannelPlaying(1) then
```

With this modification, you should hear a normal "cha ching" sound when the "collision" occurs. This app is available in the chapter download as *galleon-drag-to-the-bank.d2c*.

Timers

While dragging your coins to the bank is definitely fun to play (at least the first time), it could certainly stand some improvements. What if the bank jumped around on its own? What if new coins appeared in random locations? What if there was a time limit counting down? A key technology you'll use to get ideas like these to work is called a timer.

Timers offer a capability similar to loops, enabling you to specify code to be executed repeatedly, with some interval measured in milliseconds. The syntax involves three parameters: The delay/interval (in milliseconds), the function you want to run, and the number of repetitions (with 0 meaning "infinite"). The initial performance of your function will occur after the specified delay and, if you have more than one repetition, each will be separated by the delay value.

Timers are implemented in the timer object, which contains four functions: `cancel()`, `pause()`, `performWithDelay()`, and `resume()`. A timer is started by calling `timer.performWithDelay()` and passing the three required parameters (see line 7 in box #12): The interval in milliseconds, the function to execute, and the total number of times the timer should run the function. Note that the first run of the identified function occurs *after* the first interval, so the interval also works as a delay (note that there is no "perform" or "performWithoutDelay" function).

As a simple example, code box #8 creates a timer that will run the "doBug()" function 5 times:

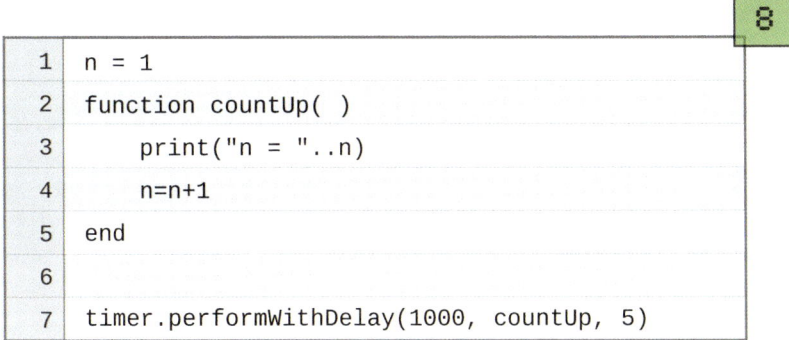

```
1  n = 1
2  function countUp( )
3      print("n = "..n)
4      n=n+1
5  end
6
7  timer.performWithDelay(1000, countUp, 5)
```

So, this timer(box #8) will call the `doBug()` function after 1 second, then call it 4 more times at the same 1 second interval. The output will look something like this:

```
OUTPUT
n = 1
n = 2
n = 3
n = 4
n = 5
```

Timed galleons

While one galleon is nice, lots of galleons is nicer. And a galleon that jumps around the screen? Awesome! So, let's use a timer to make these ideas work.

Ten galleon timer

First up: We'll load up with galleons! Let's do it step-by-step:

1. Create a project folder with the galleon.png image in it.

2. In a new *Drawn2Code* design, add the galleon image and a timer script object (in the "Actions" palette). Set the timer to 10 receptions (or more, if you are feeling bold).

3. Move the galleon image script object into the timer event-handler (by hitting "Move Resource Into Function" in the objects settings panel).

201

4. Add a new snippet and move it into the event-handler as well.

5. Type this into the new snippet to randomize the location of the image object that was just created:
   ```
   Obj1.x = math.random(20, 300)
   Obj1.y = math.random(20, 460)
   ```

6. That's it! Save your design and test it. You should see 10 (or more) galleons appear, a new one each second.

You should see something like "Ten Galleon Timer" after the 11 seconds has elapsed (including the initial 1 second delay). It is much less fun as a screenshot. Find this in the chapter downloads as *ten-galleon-timer.d2c*.

Galleon jump

How about a version with one galleon that **jumps around the screen**? That's a pretty easy modification. Let's tackle it step-by-step as well:

Ten Galleon Timer

1. Create a project folder with the galleon.png image in it.

2. In a new *Drawn2Code* design, add the galleon image as Obj1 and a timer script as Obj2 (in the "Actions" palette). Set the timer to 10 receptions (or more, for more jumping).

3. Create a transition object for the galleon image and select the "x" and "y" checkboxes. The values on the sliders don't matter, because you'll be typing over those with math.random( ) expressions in a moment.

4. With the transition script object selected, use the "Edit" menu to convert it into a snippet. You'll need to confirm you want to do that (since the snippet will replace the script object). Once converted, move the new snippet into the timer's event-handler.

5. Finally, edit the snippet you just moved to replace the literal x and y values with expressions matching those in step 5 (above):
   ```
   Obj5 = transition.to( Obj1,
       { time=1000, x=math.random(20, 300),
         y=math.random(20, 460) } )
   ```

6. That's it! Your design might look like "Galleon Jump Design" (although, obviously, your object id's may be different).

A Beginner's Guide Using Solar2D

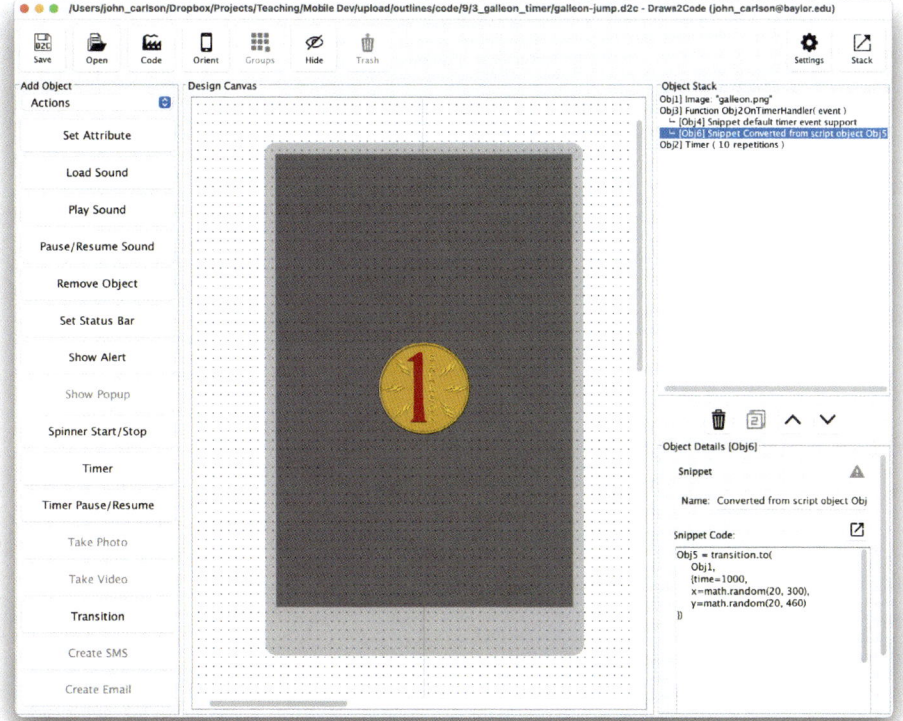

Galleon Jump Design

You should see one galleon jump around the screen, transition to a new location every second. Not really something a screenshot can capture. But, you can find it in the downloads as *galleon-jump.d2c*.

Extending a display object with additional attributes

If you wanted to make the *dragging to the bank* design a bit more interesting, you could count the number of coins that have been "deposited".

Since, at least conceivably, there could be multiple banks to use, it would be best if the bank itself maintained the count. The most elegant way to do that is to add an *attribute* to the bank display object itself. Luckily, this is a very easy to do in Lua/Solar2D. There's no special syntax or setup. Rather, you just add the attribute and set it to some value. For example, if your bank display object is Obj4 like mine, then you could add a coin count attribute like this:

```
Obj4.coinCount.= 0
```

Okay, let's code this!

203

Start with the existing *galleon-drag-to-the-bank.d2c*. If you are following along, you should **duplicate the design file** and name it something unique (I've called it *galleon-drag-to-the-bank-count.d2c*, which isn't very creative).

Once you are ready, let's do it step-by-step:

1. In the duplicated design, add a snippet to your stack with the above code in it. If your bank display object isn't Obj4, then use your correct object id.

2. Add a text display object positioned at the bottom of the screen for the deposit display (mine is Obj11).

3. Next, open the snippet with the touch/drag support and prepare to do a bit of editing. After playing the audio (on my line 73), you're going to *increment the counter*, *update the deposit display* at the bottom of the screen, then *remove the deposited coin*, and finally *create a new coin* for the user to deposit.

Galleon Deposit

Here's what the edits look like in place:

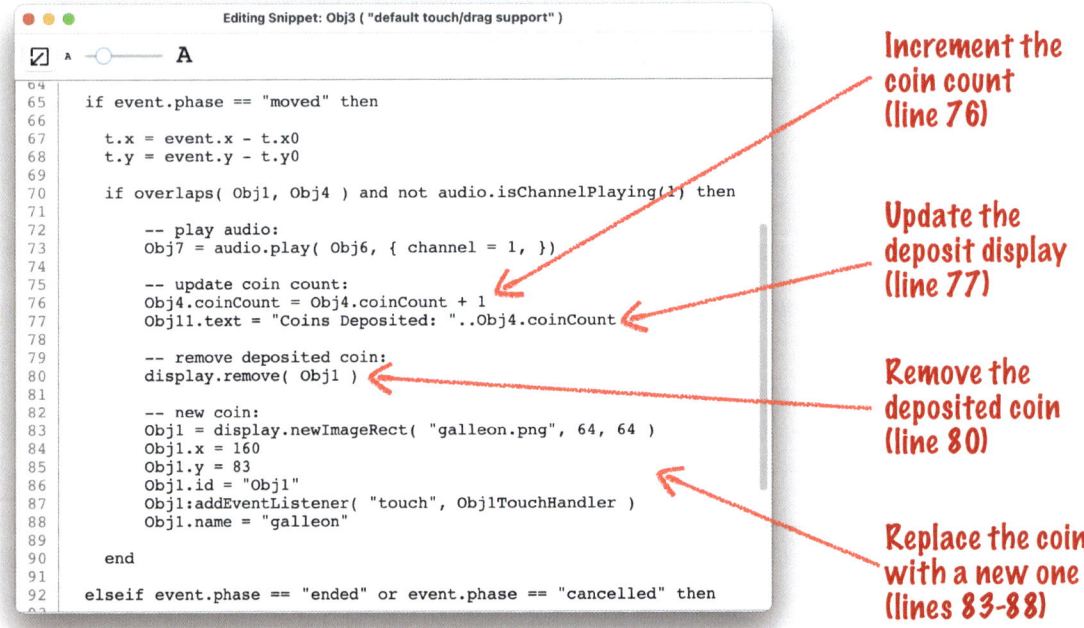

Depositing a Coin

That's it! In the version in the chapter downloads, I've also added a bit of eye-candy in the form of a nice gradient background and a healthy lawn for the bank to sit on. As noted earlier, it is available in the downloads as *galleon-drag-to-the-bank-count.d2c*.

Notes

This is **cool** because "coinCount" isn't an *existing attribute* of display objects. However, we can **add new attributes** to a display object simply by defining the addition and initializing it to some value (0, in our case). This adds the attribute to *that specific object* (i.e., just that bank and not all banks or any other display objects).

Also, by removing the coin when it is "deposited", you no longer need to check if the audio is playing (as the coin will be removed as soon as it overlaps the bank).

Tables

• •

I've avoided focusing very deeply on Lua tables up until this point (or, at least talking about what I did with tables explicitly). Of course, you've *used* them everywhere. Tables were introduced in Chapter 1 and you **can't avoid** using them all the time (whether you fully realize it or not). Anytime you pass data inside curly braces "{" and "}", you are using a table. So, when you add widgets to the screen, call `transition.to()`, create colors or gradients, used `native.showPopup()`, and so on, you are using a table to pass structured data. See "A Table of Tables" for examples.

In many cases, you define the table "in-line", so that the key-value pairs are entered continuously, with no line breaks. In other cases, it makes sense to insert a line break after some (or all) key-value pairs, to make reading large tables easier. However, these line breaks are merely a code formatting decision as they play no part in how the table is read by Solar2D.

Tables of your own

In addition to using tables as parameters to pass data to Solar2D functions, you can also use them to store structured data **for your own use**. Structured data is just a set of information with an organizing system for access and retrieval. Many languages have arrays, along with several other typical structured data types. In Lua (and thus Solar2D), you have just one structured data type: The table.

Use	Example
| **Creating widgets** | ```
btn = widget.newButton {
    label = "Start",
    id = "btn_start",
    onEvent = startButton
}
``` |
| **Defining transitions** | `transition.to(btn, {time = 1000, x = newX})` |
| **Configuring a gradient** | ```
gradient = {
    type = "gradient",
    color1 = {.8, .8, .8},
    color2 = {.3, .3, .3},
    onEvent = onButtonEvent
}
``` |
| **Vertices on a polygon** | `vertices = {50,50, 75,100, 25,100}`
`triangle = display.newPolygon(cx, cy, vertices)` |
| **Sending e-mail** | `native.showPopup("mail", {subject = "hi", to = "john_carlson@baylor.edu"})` |

A Table of Tables

A table is simply a place to put stuff. You can think of it as an actual, physical table (like, for example, a **kitchen table**). Each item you add to the table must have a unique name (the "key") and a value (the data item). The key can be of any type, but not nil. You can store anything you'd like to in a table and you can have as many tables as you need.

The key-value system used in tables is a way to organize or "structure" your data. Back to the kitchen table analogy: After "storing" items on the kitchen table, you can "retrieve" an item by asking, for it. However, you have to use syntax that people at the table will understand. For example, if you want the salt, you could say "please pass the salt". You could try just saying "kitchen table dot salt", but that only works if your kitchen table supports Lua

Structured data is immensely helpful for managing data in your apps. As an example, if you had an app that needed to keep track of customers, you might create a "customer" table to store data about each customer, such as their name, address, and so on. That would make it easy to work with customers, enabling us to access information about a customer by asking for, for example, the customer's "Name" or "Email", and so on (see "A Customer Table: Structured Data").

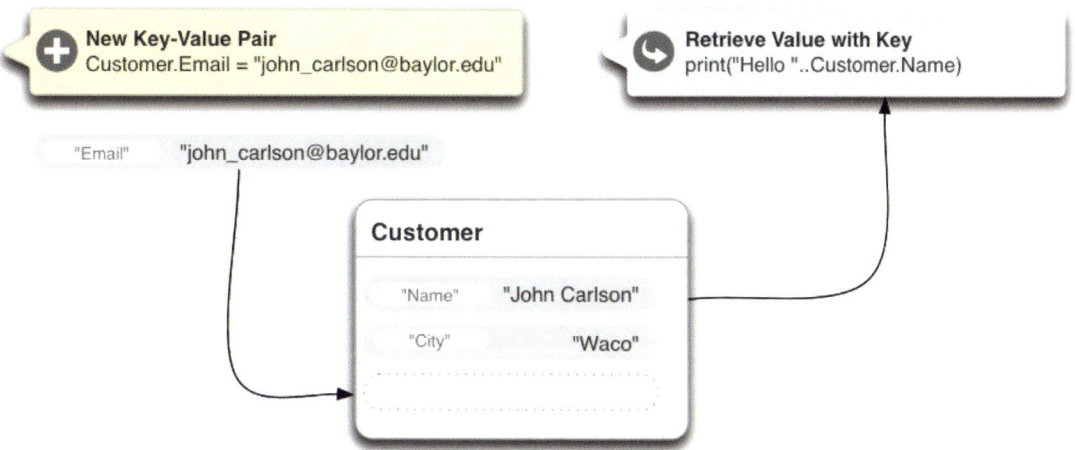

A Customer Table: Structured Data

Datasets

As a second example, what if you wanted an app with *more than one* galleon (or anything else)? Maybe dozens? Or a random number? Well, you could just create a bunch of independent galleon image objects, but it would be very hard to write efficient code that did anything with them. What if you want to randomly move or hide them? Or address a subset of them? What if you want to detect collisions on randomly located galleons? You'd need an **individual identifier for each one**. Here's how you'd create 2 galleon game objects (**not using a table**):

```
1   -- image "galleon.png"
2   Obj1 = display.newImageRect( "galleon.png", 64, 64 )
3   Obj1.x = 160
4   Obj1.y = 240
5   Obj1.id = "Obj1"
6
7   -- image "galleon.png"
8   Obj2 = display.newImageRect( "galleon.png", 64, 64 )
9   Obj2.x = 185
10  Obj2.y = 265
11  Obj2.id = "Obj2"
```

If you wanted *even more* of these objects, you'd repeat and adapt these lines of code (e.g., lines 1-5 in box #10 would be repeated and adapted *over and over*). While you *could* write such code, it is much easier to do if you create and store your objects in a table.

For example, to create 10 randomly located **bugs galleons in a table**, you could do this:

11

```
1  coins = {}
2
3  for n = 1, 10, 1 do
4      local coin = display.newImageRect("galleon.png", 64, 64)
5      coin.x = math.random(0, display.contentWidth)
6      coin.y = math.random(0, display.contentHeight)
7      coin.id = "coin"..n
8      coins[n] = coin
9  end
```

The code in box #11 creates an empty table called coins (on line 1), then uses a 'for' loop to create 10 display objects based on the coin image ("galleon.png"). They are randomly placed on the device screen. The table of galleons is called "coins" (notice the "s") and it holds 10 galleon display objects.

Table advantages

But how does that make things *easier*? For starters, you just created 10 galleon display objects with 9 lines of code (box #12), whereas the previous approach took 12 lines (box #16) for just 2. A bit of simple math will tell you that the "table approach" requires **fewer lines of code** when creating multiple coins. Even better, with your game objects in a table, you can **work with them together as a set**. For example, let's say you wanted to *move* all of the coins to new, random locations. Since they're in a table, you can loop through them again to change their positions:

12

```
1  --* relocate and animate all coins:
2  for n = 1, #coins, 1 do
3      newX = math.random(0, display.contentWidth)
4      newY = math.random(0, display.contentHeight)
5      transition.to(coins[n], {delay=1000, time=2000, x=newX, y=newY})
6  end
```

No need to write individual lines of code to deal with each of the 10 bugs. You can treat your bugs as a set, allowing us to do things with the set almost as easily as doing something to an individual member of the set. But wait — there's more! Even though this is pretty convenient, imagine how much more so it would be if you had 100 coins — or 1,000! The code in box #12 would **work unmodified**. You would not have to change a line of code for it to be able to handle differently sized tables. It will just loop as many times as it needs to.

Not just coins

Of course, you can put anything you'd like to into a table, if it makes sense to do so. Not just coins. For example, here's a table of random numbers:

```
1  math.randomseed(os.time())
2  randomNumbers = {}
3
4  for i=1, 100, 1 do
5      randomNumbers[i] = math.random()
6  end
```
13

Now that they are in a table, it makes it easy to do some arithmetic on them as a set (i.e., a table). Do you want to know the sum? The average? Easy. Just loop through the table:

```
1  sum = 0
2  for j=1, #randomNumbers, 1 do
3      sum = sum + randomNumbers[j]
4  end
5  avg = sum / #randomNumbers
6
7  print("n = "..#randomNumbers)
8  print("sum = "..sum)
9  print("avg = "..avg)
```
14

If you run this (the code in boxes #13 and #14), you'll see something like this output:

```
OUTPUT
n = 100
sum = 51.307362834135
avg = 0.51307362834135
```
15

209

Of course, since you are working with random numbers, the output will vary (perhaps more than you might expect).

Imagine what you could do with background music, collisions, timers, random numbers, and tables...

Thirty Taps

Okay, stop imagining.

Let's say you want ten galleons randomly added and located on screen, shifting locations every second for 30 seconds. The goal is to tap each coin 3 times, to move it to your bank (the row of empty circles at the bottom of the screen). Each time you tap a coin it will be shaded darker, which will help you figure out how many more taps it needs.

The challenge is that you only get 30 taps.

That's a lot of functionality. How many lines of code do you think you'll need? 300? 500? 1,000 or more? What if I told you you could do it in under 200 lines? Less than 30 script objects! Would you be interested in that? Of course you would.

This app creates a table of 10 coins that are randomly positioned (and rotated for effect). Background music is started right away and a 30 second timer is started.

Thirty Taps

The game ends when

1. You win by filling your bank at the bottom of the screen
2. When you run out of taps
3. When the timer ends

Basic setup starts the same as *ten-galleon-timer.d2c*, but extra attributes are added to each coin: a tap counter (to tap the number of successful taps on that coin) and a boolean variable called `isSaved` to easily keep track of coins that have been successfully saved in your bank.

You can see the entire design to the right ("Thirty Taps Design"). It is only composed of the script objects you see in the stack, and many of those could be consolidated.

You can see the attributes added to new galleon coins on lines 15 and 16 of code box #16. Both the ten galleons and the ten empty circles for the bank are created using 'for' loops.

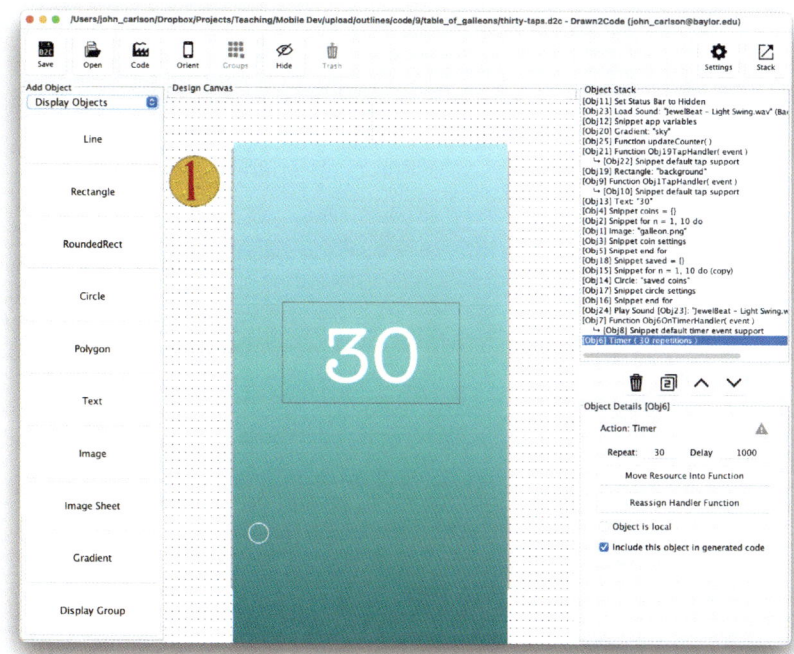

Thirty Taps Design

```
1   -- image "galleon.png"
2   Obj1 = display.newImageRect( "galleon.png", 64, 64 )
3   Obj1.x = -57
4   Obj1.y = 34
5   Obj1.id = "Obj1"
6   Obj1:addEventListener( "tap", Obj1TapHandler )
7
8   -- coin settings:
9   Obj1.x = math.random( 20, 300 )
10  Obj1.y = math.random( 20, 460 )
11  Obj1.rotation = math.random(360)
12  Obj1.id = "Coin "..n
13
14  -- extra attributes for thirty taps:
15  Obj1.tapCount = 0
16  Obj1.isSaved = false
```

211

Making loop that contain script objects

In many cases, you'll just use a snippet to enter your 'for' loop in its entirety. However, things get a little tricker if you want to place existing script objects inside the loop. In that case, there are two easy options:

1. Copy the script object code to the clipboard and paste it into the 'for' loop you are making.
2. Surround the script object(s) you wish to be in your loop with separate snippets that start and end your loop.

Since you've already used the "copy script object code to the clipboard" technique in this chapter, let's look at examples of the "surround with snippets" approach. Both the coins and the "bank" circles are done this way.

Take a look at a portion of the stack for this design (see "Two Loops in Thirty Taps").

The loop to create the 10 galleon coins start at Obj2 and goes to Obj5. Objects 2, 3, and 5 are all snippets that surround Obj1 (the galleon display image script object). Since Obj1 is inside of the loop, 10 Obj1's will be created and added to the table. This can be a little confusing, but you won't use the Obj1 identifier again outside of this loop. Instead, you'll access the coins using `event.target` syntax inside the tap handlers and by looping through the coins table, where each coin can be accessed using an index number .

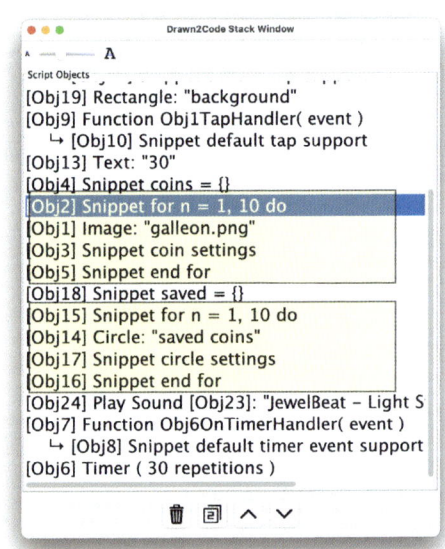

Two Loops in Thirty Taps

Likewise, the loop to create the 10 circles for the "bank" at the bottom of the screen starts at Obj15. You can see that Obj14 (the circle display object) is surrounded by snippets to make it part of the loop (so that 10 circles will be created).

Note that for loops that don't need to contain one or more script objects, simply entering them in a single snippet (or as part of an existing snippet in the right location) is perfectly fine. There wouldn't be any need to breaking the lines of code up into multiple snippets, unless that helped you organize your code.

When a galleon coin is successfully tapped, the tap-handler adds 1 to that coins tapCount variable:

```
event.target.tapCount = event.target.tapCount + 1
```

If this coin has been tapped 3 times, then it is marked as "saved" and removed from the screen (so as not to interfere with tapping).

```
1  event.target.tapCount >= 3 then
2      event.target.isSaved = true
3      display.remove( event.target )
4  end
```

17

Finally, in the timer handler (see "Game Timer Handler"), the game countdown from 30 is decremented (lines 171-174), the coins are sent to random locations (lines 182-183), and the number of "saved" coins is counted (lines 185-187).

The number of saved coins is then used in a loop (lines 192-194) to fill circles in the "bank" to show how many coins have been saved.

I do also slide the background rectangle (with the gradient) up every second, which has the effect of darkening the screen as the time is running out.

The app is available in the chapter downloads as *thirty-taps.d2c*.

```
168
169  countDownFrom30 = countDownFrom30 - 1
170  print( countDownFrom30 )
171  if countDownFrom30 < 1 then
172      gameOver = true
173      audio.pause( Obj23 )
174  end
175
176  saveCount = 0
177
178  if not gameOver then
179      -- randomize the coins
180      for n = 1, #coins do
181          if coins[n] ~= nil then
182              coins[n].x = math.random( 20, 300 )
183              coins[n].y = math.random( 20, 460 )
184
185              if coins[n].isSaved then
186                  saveCount = saveCount + 1
187              end
188          end
189      end
190
191      -- update the score circles:
192      for m = 1, saveCount do
193          saved[m]:setFillColor(1)
194      end
195
196      -- slide background up:
197      Obj19.y = Obj19.y - 12
198
199  end
200
```

Game Timer Handler

Summary

In this chapter you learned how to make display objects draggable by adding the touch listener. You learned how to use the touch event handler to make the dragging smooth and keep objects onscreen (if you so desire). You also learned how to detect collisions between 2 objects during a drag. Draggable objects add a new level of interactivity to your apps. You also added background music to give your apps an appropriate atmosphere. Finally, you learned to use timers to conduct receptive actions and give your games a "heart beat".

Chapter resources

In the chapter resource download for this book (www.lillipellilabs.com/mobiledev/download/chapter_resources.zip), look for folder "9".

This folder includes:

1. galleon_drag (simple drag example)
2. galleon_drag_to_the_bank (dragging the galleon to a target)
3. galleon_timer (*galleon-jump.d2c* and *ten-galleon-timer.d2c*)
4. galleon_drag_to_the_bank_count (dragging galleons to the bank and keeping count)
5. table_of_galleons (using a loop to place 10 galleons in a table)
6. thirty_taps (exhilarating game requiring the quickest of reflexes)
7. **BONUS**: Eight bonus apps including Clover Tap! Just in time for St. Patrick's Day, Clover Tap! is a rollicking game which involves you tapping moving clovers to win.

End-of-chapter exercises

1. Create an app with your two favorite display objects (shapes). Make one of them draggable.
   a. Check for overlap and report the result at the console.

b. Change the color of the "target" shape (i.e., the one that isn't draggable) to red when the collision occurs and back to white (or another default color) when the overlap ends.

2. Create an app with your two favorite display objects (shapes). Make them both draggable. Watch for overlap and:

    a. Report the result at the console.

    b. Randomize the fill colors of both shapes when you detect it.

    c. Play a sound when you detect it. Make sure the sound is only played once per collision (i.e., not continuously as the shapes remain overlapped).

3. Create an app with your favorite display object (shape).

    a. Use a timer to make the shape jump around randomly 20 times.

    b. Play some appropriate background music while the shape is jumping.

4. Create an app that loads a table with 1000 random numbers between 1 and 10. Display the sum and average in a text display object.

5. Create an app with two display objects (shapes) and make one of them draggable.

    a. Count the number of overlaps 1 time per "collision" (making sure not to count continuously while the shapes are overlapping).

    b. Change the color of the "target" shape 1 time per "collision" (also making sure not to continuously change colors while the shapes are overlapping).

6. Create an app that fills a table with 1000 random numbers between 1 and 100.

    a. Display the sum and average.

    b. Display the minimum and maximum values in the table.

    c. Modify this app so that the number of items in the table is based on the value of a slider (between 100 and 1000). Add the slider and a button to trigger the calculations.

7. Create an app the plays some relaxing background music. Maybe something **magical**?

    a. Add a button toto allow the user to pause/play the music.

    b. Add a slider to control the volume.

8. Rework #1 using a timer so that the previously stationary target shape moves randomly on its own.
9. Rework #1 using a timer so that the previously draggable shape now moves on its own.

10. Create an app that fills a table with a random number of coins or other image objects (up to a couple of dozen) and displays them.
    a. Display them randomly located.
    b. Make it so that the bugs are initially not visible (i.e., they are transparent) and only *appear 1 at a time*, every 500ms (using a timer).
    c. Make it so that the bugs *disappear* in the same manner after a delay.
11. Create an app with a random number of coins onscreen and a bank (or other target) in the middle. Allow the user to drag the coins into the box to make them disappear.
12. Create an app with a slider and two buttons. When the "show" button is pressed, display the number of coins indicated by the slider in random locations. When the reset button is pressed, remove all of the bugs.

Switches & Segments 10

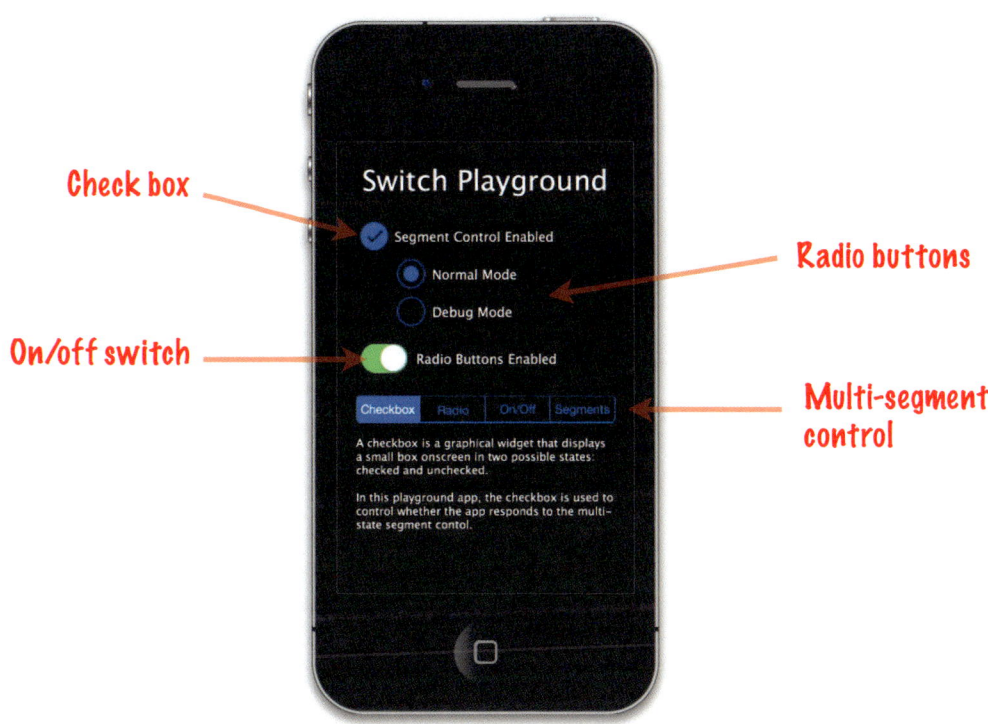

Switches & Segments

New widgets

This chapter examines a variety of switches, covering a total of 4 somewhat-related widgets. Solar2D bundles 3 widgets together under the general name "switches" (docs.coronalabs.com /api/library/widget/newSwitch.html) while the segmented control (docs.coronalabs.com/ api/library/widget/newSegmentedControl.html) allows you to create a "multi-segment" button that acts something like a row of radio buttons (i.e., only one segment can be selected at a time). See the table "Comparison of Switching Widgets" for a quick summary of their similarities and difference.

	Checkbox	Radio Buttons	On/Off Slide (Toggle)	Segmented Control
Widget	Switch (style ="checkbox")	Switch (style = "radio")	Switch (style = "onOff")	SegmentedControl
Integral Text Label?	No	No	In some themes there may be "on" and "off" labels	Yes, each segment has a label
Listener	onPress or onRelease	onPress or onRelease	**onRelease**	onPress or onRelease
Event Handler Goes…	Above	Above	Above	Above
States	On/Off	On/Off	On/Off	Numeric state for each segment (1..n)
iOS8+ theme				
Android theme				

Comparison of Switching Widgets

Platform differences

All of these are built into the widget library, so you will gain access to them by requiring the library (as in box #1). As with prior widgets, these will automatically use the correct visual theme, based on the device they are running on. The current iOS8 theme can be seen in the figure "Switches & Segments", while a comparison to the Android theme can be found in the table above.

```
local widget = require "widget"
```

Note, however, that the **correct theme will not necessarily load** in the Solar2D Simulator. This can be *inconvenient* (to say the least) when testing an app design across platforms. As such, you may end up seeing an Apple device with Android-themed widgets, or vice versa. Beyond the mild entertainment value of seeing this, such an incongruous display may give the sense that you are temporarily inhabiting a bizarre, alternate reality.

To fix this, you need to know more about the *platform* that your app is running on.

Basic platform detection

For most complex apps (and even some simple ones), you may find that you need to detect the platform your app is running on. In this chapter, that includes knowing whether the app is running on the *simulator* to enable you to programmatically set the theme if that is the case. Fortunately, this is relatively easy to do in Solar2D with the system.getInfo( ) function. You can use system.getInfo("model") to access the device's (real or simulated) model name, while system.getInfo("environment") will let you determine whether or not you are running on the simulator.

For example, the code in box #2 will set four boolean variables (isApple, isAndroid, isWindows and isSimulator), based on these function calls and a bit of 'if-then' logic.

```
model = system.getInfo("model")
isApple = false
isAndroid = false
isSimulator = false
isWindows = false
if system.getInfo("environment") == "simulator" then
    isSimulator = true
end

if string.sub(model, 1, 2) == "iP" then
    isApple = true
elseif model == "WindowsPhone" then
    isWindows = true
else
    isAndroid = true
    -- needed to see correct widgets in simulator:
    if isSimulator then widget.setTheme("widget_theme_android"); end
end
```

The only thing that is at all "tricky" here is the way you determine if it is an Apple or Android device: You look at the first 2 letters of the model name for the string "iP", which if present means it is an Apple device. If not, it is an Android device. This is quicker than testing for the various Apple product names (e.g., iPad, iPhone, iPod). More complete device

219

detection is discussed on a [coronalabs blog](). Of course, when the *iWatch* comes out, this may no longer work.

For convenience, a more complete detection snippet is available to add to your *Drawn2Code* app design (in the snippets palette).

What up, switches?

Switches are graphical widgets (in the widget library) that have two states: on (true) and off (false). In *Drawn2Code*, you can add a "Switch" via the widgets palette. There are **three versions** of the switch: The radio button, the checkbox, and the on/off slider.

In *Drawn2Code*, you can select the type of switch using the button below "Font Settings". Let's look at each type in turn.

Switch Settings Panel

Checkboxes

A checkbox is a widget that typically displays a small box or circle onscreen in one of two possible states: checked (i.e., with a check-mark) and unchecked, which correspond to being either "on" or "off". An interface may have multiple checkboxes, any number of which may be checked. Starting in iOS7, the checkbox is now a *circle*, while the current Android theme displays a dark grey surrounding shape that is almost invisible on a black screen.

The Checkbox (or Checkcircle?)

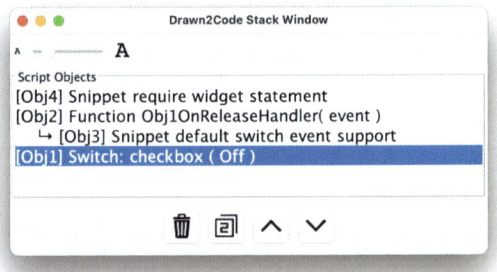

Stack with New Switch

The checkbox is the default type created in *Drawn2Code*. Creating one will add four script objects to your stack (see "Stack with New Switch").

220

The syntax create a checkbox is quite like the button widget:

```
Obj1 = widget.newSwitch
{
    style = "checkbox",
    id = "Obj1",
    x = 30,
    y = 100,
    initialSwitchState = false,
    onRelease = Obj1OnReleaseHandler
}
```
3

Which just puts a checkbox on screen, without any text or label (which isn't built-into the checkbox).

Adding a text label

If you want to label the checkboxes with some text, which you **generally do**, you'll need to add it yourself. You can call it anything we'd like, but it might make the most sense just to call it "label" and make it an *attribute* of our switch. For example:

```
checkbox.label = display.newText("I lost my check! Have you seen it?",
        checkbox.x + checkbox.width + 100,
        checkbox.y, native.systemFont, 14)
```
4

Which produces a checkbox that looks something like this:

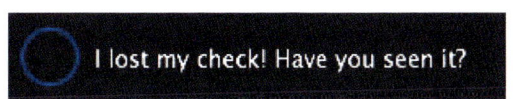

Where oh where has my little check gone?

Of course, checking the box doesn't **do** anything (yet). Notice in box #3 that you have hooked the checkbox up to a listener called "Obj1OnReleaseHandler". So, that's what you have to provide (shown in box #5). This function doesn't do anything particularly useful, but it does demonstrate the syntax for using checkboxes and detecting their state.

```
1   function Obj1OnReleaseHandler( event )
2
3       s = event.target
4
5       if s.isOn then
6           checkbox.label.text = "I found it! Thank you!"
7       else
8           checkbox.label.text = "I lost my check! Have you seen it?"
9       end
10  end
```

Adding this function (code box #5) *above* the checkbox creation code changes the checkbox text when the user taps it and looks like this:

I found it! But why did it **move away**?

Issue: Centered text

Which, regrettably, probably **doesn't look quite right** to you. You might have noticed that the text object that you are using to describe what checking the checkbox will do has *shifted* quite a bit to the right, almost as if it doesn't *like* the check all that much. What is going on?

Gotchas

Well, because the new text "(I found it! Thank you!") is *shorter* than the old text ("I lost my check! Have you seen it?"), it appears to be shifting to the right (but it really isn't). **The center hasn't moved.** Whatever it is doing, it looks bad. Moreover, this will be an issue for radio buttons and the on-off slider as well, so you need to fix it.

The *easy* fix is just to left-justify the text. If coding by hand, you can add a key-value pair to the text object's settings table (e.g., align = "left"). In *Drawn2Code*, just hit the alignment button in the text display script object's settings panel.

For example, if the text display object is Obj5, the settings panel would look as shown to the right (see "Aligning the Text"). Just hit that left-justify button and you're done.

After selecting the checkbox, you should see:

Back together again

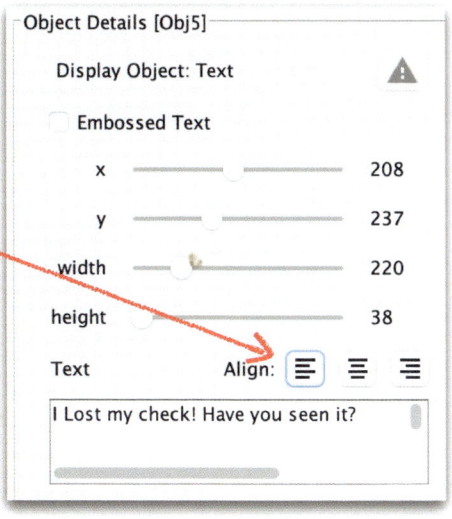

Aligning the Text

Note that this may require you to move the text location a bit as well to keep the distance you want to see between the checkbox and the text.

Of course, if you think about it, this would be an issue for *any text* that you wish to "stay put" in regard to its left or right alignment while the content changes (like a score, a count-down timer, a numeric result you want to line up with other results). If you want the text constantly re-centered, which is how Solar2D is designed to do it, then there's no trouble at all. However, if you want it to remain justified to the right or left, you may have to use this approach.

Issue: Tappable text label

A second issue that you might discover while playing with this simple app is that the checkbox text isn't "tappable". That is, in most apps the user can tap the switch itself or it's associated text label to "switch" the switch. This is a nice feature because it gives the user more on-screen area to target with their clumsy fingers.

To make this happen in Solar2D, we'll need to add the "tap" listener to the text display object (covered in way back in Chapter 4). In *Drawn2Code*, just select the text display script object and hit the "Add Listener" button, then select "Tap".

Inside the new event-handler (for the text display object), you want to detect the current state of the checkbox using its `isOn` attribute, then "toggle" it using the boolean operator "not". Finally, you want to run the checkbox's event-handler to replicate actually tapping the checkbox itself.

This may sound a bit complex, but the code to actually do it is quite short (code box #6):

```
1  function Obj5TapHandler( event )
2    Obj1:setState({isOn = not Obj1.isOn, onComplete = Obj1OnReleaseHandler})
3  end
```

Either function works equally well, so the choice of syntax is personal. While they say that brevity is the soul of wit, you should remember that it isn't your goal to write funny code.

A complete example

In addition to making the checkbox label "live", you also need to test how our checkbox appears on other platforms you wish to support, such as Android. While it is easy to switch the hardware device in the Solar2D Simulator, the widget theme does not necessarily change with it, as discussed above. This complete example **handles both issues** and can serve as a reference for your future checkbox endeavors.

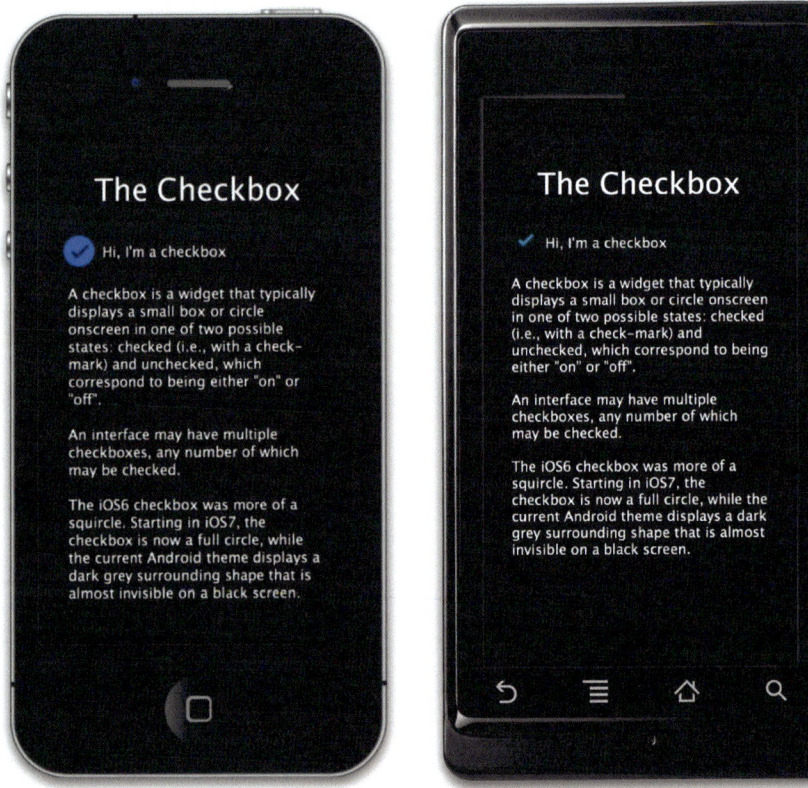

The Checkbox: iOS and Android Themes

Looking at the Android checkbox, notice how, if you bring your eye up *very close* to the picture and *squint*, you can just make out the square outline? Notice how dumb you look doing this? Themes shouldn't make you look dumb.

Radio buttons

Radio Buttons (On and Off)

A radio button is a graphical widget that is typically used in groups of two or more. Although these groups are typically arranged vertically, that is not a requirement. The radio button displays a circle with two possible states: on (with a filled circle) and off (empty circle).

In other words, it is quite similar to the checkbox. However, unlike checkboxes, only one radio button in a group can be selected at a time. The previously selected radio button will automatically de-select (i.e., switch off) when a new radio button is selected (i.e., switched on). While it is possible to start your app with more than one radio button selected, or without one selected (as with this app), this is probably not the best design choice.

Setting up a radio button is almost identical to checkboxes as well, except that the style parameter in the settings table is set to "radio" instead of "checkbox". As with checkboxes, the radio buttons don't include a text label, so you must place one manually. The complete set up is shown in code box #7.

```
1  --* button 1:
2  radio1 = widget.newSwitch
3  {
4      style = "radio",
5      id = "rdio1",
6      x = 80,
7      y = 80,
8      initialSwitchState = true,
9      onRelease = onRadio
10 }
11 --* text label:
12 radio1.label = display.newText("Radio Button 1", 0, radio1.y, f, 14)
13 radio1.label.anchorX = 0
14 radio1.label.x = radio1.x + radio1.width/2 + 6
```

If you enter and run the code it will look something like this:

Radio button (selected)

Note that this button appears selected (or "filled") with a small dot inside. This was done programmatically on line 8 (box #9). The default is "false" or unselected, which can be overridden by setting the `initialSwitchState` to "true".

A single radio button sitting by itself should look **a bit odd**, since radio buttons are designed to be displayed in groups of 2 or more. Adding a second radio button will take the same form at code box #9 (but you'll need to name it something else — maybe "radio2" — and give it a unique id and location). Now that you have 2 radio buttons, you need to put them in a group.

Defining a radio button group

This is the easiest part! To make your radio buttons behave like a group (or "set"), so that only one can be selected and the prior selection is automatically de-selected, you just insert them in a display group. For example:

```
1  radioButtonSet = display.newGroup()
2  radioButtonSet:insert( radio1 )
3  radioButtonSet:insert( radio2 )
```

However, this is actually only required if you want to have **multiple radio button groups**. If you just have a single group, you can **leave off this step** (box #8).

Radio button event handler

Of course, these buttons won't do anything at all unless you provide the event-handler, which has been specified (e.g., on line 9 of box #7) as "onRadio" and must be **placed above the radio button setup code**. A basic radio button event-handler could look like that shown below (box #9).

A simple example is provided in `radio_buttons_little`. Running it on both Apple and Android platforms will reveal a **formatting glitch** we'll need to address (to see it in the

Solar2D Simulator you'll need to include the theme switching code from code box #2), which we'll do next.

```
function onRadio( event )

    if radio1.isOn then
        print("radio button 1 selected")
    else
        print("radio button 2 selected")
    end

end
```

A complete example

Radio buttons that work well across platforms will need do address any formatting or layout issues as well as making the text labels "live" and setting their anchor values appropriately. All of that is done in this example (in the same way it was done with the checkbox example).

However, Solar2D radio buttons have two additional visual glitches (see "Radio Button Visual Glitches").

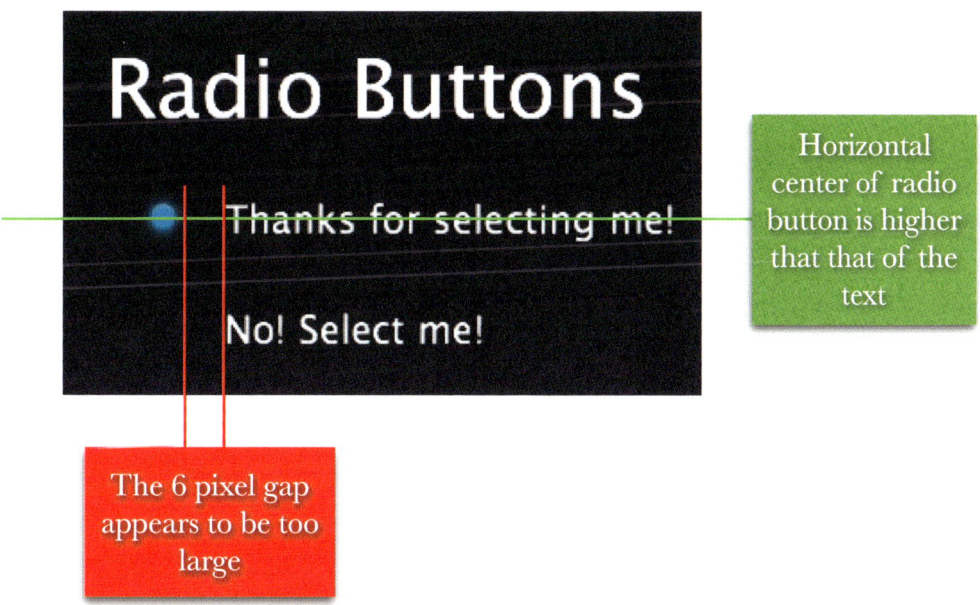

Radio Button Visual Glitches (Android Theme)

227

Issues

If you are really picky about your UI (like me), then the radio buttons are rendered with some minor, but frustrating, inconsistency. Notice:

Gotchas

1. First, the 6 pixel gap used to separate the radio button (and checkboxes) from the text label isn't needed in the Android theme. In fact, if you leave the 6 pixels in, the gap between the radio button and the text will look *huge* on Android. Okay, maybe "huge" is an exaggeration, but the gap looks too large.

2. Second, the text label appears slightly too low, like it has sunken down screen just a bit.

The fix: So how do you solve these **vexing** problems? Well, you already have the information you need to determine which platform you are on (i.e., `isApple` and `isAndroid`), you just have to *use* it. You also have to figure out just how many pixels are needed to fix the appearance of the Android theme. (To make this fix, you'll need to detect the platform your app is running on using the code discussed above in box #2).

Since the problems are associated with the text labels, the fixes are placed there as well (box #10).

```
1  --* text label:
2  radio1.label = display.newText("Pick Me!", 0,
          radio1.y - (isAndroid and 1 or 0), f, 14)
3  radio1.label.anchorX = 0
4  radio1.label.x = radio1.x + radio1.width/2 + (isApple and 6 or 0)
```

The first fix subtracts 1 pixels to the y value of radio1.label (to move it up the device screen 1 pixel), but *only on Android*. The second fix adds the 6 pixel horizontal gap on the x value of radio1.label, but *only on Apple devices*. These values can be adapted based on the current theme supplied by Solar2D or custom, image-sheet based widgets of your own design.

How well do these fixes work? Here's a screenshot of them in action (widgets_radio_buttons):

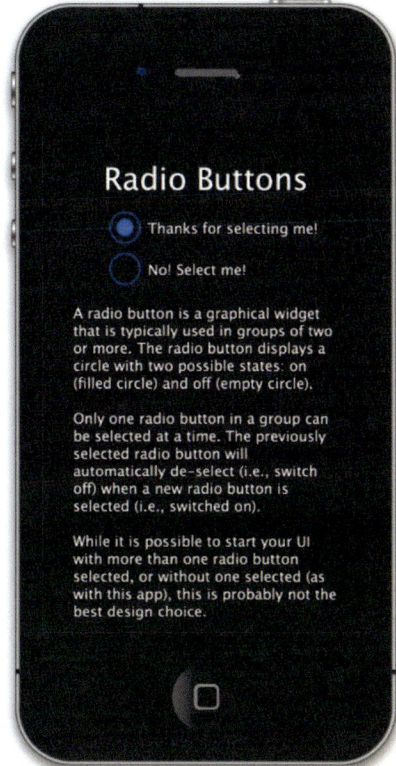 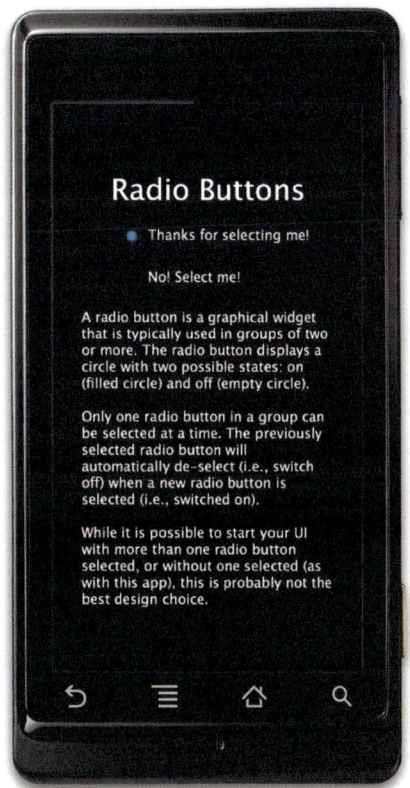

Radio Buttons: iOS and Android Themes

On/off slide (toggle) switch

An on/off slide is a graphical widget that toggles visually between on and off states. The toggle effect is animated when the user taps the switch (there is no need for the user to try to manually slide the knob).

Visually, the on/off slide may include a word or symbol to indicate whether it is "on" or "off", in addition to a change in color or appearance. For example, the current iOS9 theme uses only color to indicate the on/off status, while the Android theme (which is very similar to the iOS6 theme) uses both color and text. This widget works in much the same way as the previous switches and also do not come with a text label.

The On/Off Sliding Toggle

Here's a complete setup of a simple one (box #11):

```
1   toggle = widget.newSwitch
2   {
3       style = "onOff",
4       id = "toggle",
5       x = 80,
6       y = 80,
7       initialSwitchState = true,
8       onRelease = onToggle
9   }
10  toggle.label = display.newText("The slide is open!", 0, 0, f, 14)
11  toggle.label.anchorX = 0
12  toggle.label.x = toggle.x + toggle.width/2 + 5
13  toggle.label.y = toggle.y
```

Which will look something like this:

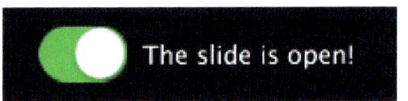

Everybody into the pool!

Once again, the switch won't **do** anything without the event-handler (called "onToggle" here). A simple version of that looks like (box #12) below. This fill app is available in the download as on-off_slide_little.

```
1   function onToggle( event )
2       s = event.target
3       if s.isOn then
4           toggle.label.text = "The slide is open!"
5       else
6           toggle.label.text = "Sorry, the slide is closed."
7       end
8   end
```

Issues

Gotchas

For onOff sliding switches note that, although you can listen to the `onPress` event, the switch doesn't actually toggle until `onRelease`. As such, actions you wish to take that are based on the new (switched) value of the switch need to be done in response to `onRelease`.

There is also a small theme issue we'll need to deal with: The Apple on/off slide is much narrower that the Android one, so you will have to compensate for that when setting the x location. In addition, the x location of the switch in the Android theme is on the knob, rather then centered in the switch, which is a bit of a puzzle. That pushes the text label over way to far to the right, which is easy to fix. Which we'll do next.

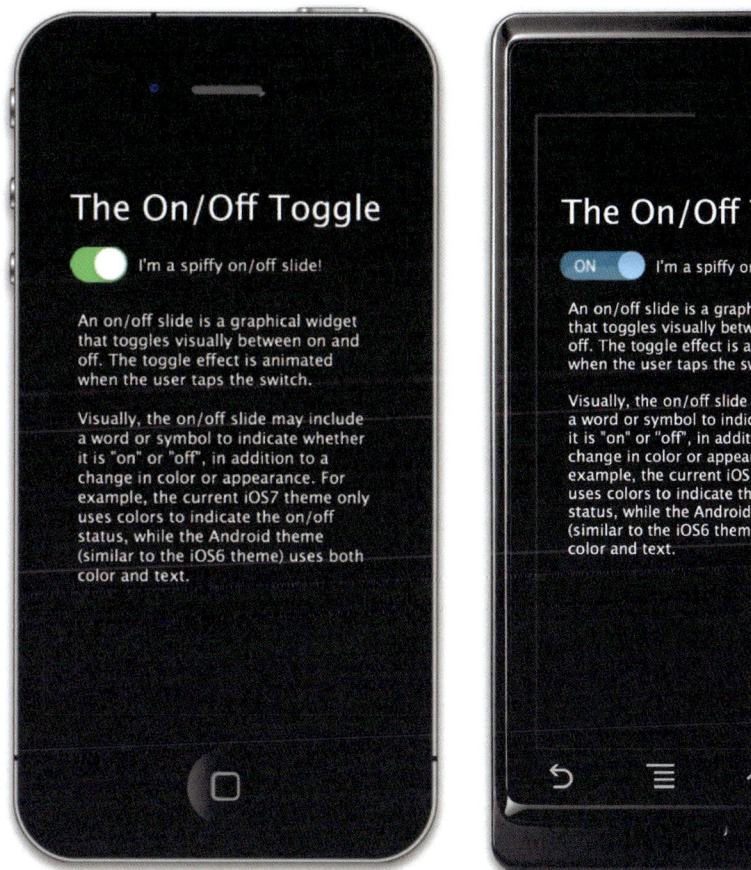

The On/Off Slide: iOS and Android Themes

A complete example

A usable on/off slide will need to have a "live" text label and be formatted and positioned carefully to look and work correctly across platforms, as with the prior switches. However, in this case, the fixes need to occur both in setting up the slide and also positioning the text label. The code to create a "correct" on/off slide is in box #13.

13

```
1  toggle = widget.newSwitch
2  {
3      style = "onOff",
4      id = "toggle",
5      x = (isApple and 50 or 86),
6      y = txt_title.y + 50,
7      initialSwitchState = true,
8      onRelease = onToggle
9  }
10 toggle.label = display.newText("I'm a spiffy on/off slide!", 0, 0,
       f, 14)
11 toggle.label.anchorX = 0
12 toggle.label.x = toggle.x + toggle.width/2 + (isApple and 5 or -60)
13 toggle.label.y = toggle.y
```

The two fixes can be found on lines 5 and 12. On line 5, I set the x location of the switch to 50 on Apple devices and 86 on Android, resulting in an equivalent position. On line 12, I shift the Android switch label to the left, to compensate for the differences in the widget. With these fixes in place, the switch and label look correct on both tested platforms (see "The On/Off Slide: iOS and Android Themes").

Segmented control

This widget looks a bit like a wide, segmented button with multiple, selectable sections (or, perhaps "tabs", since this looks quite a bit like a "tab bar"). Only one segment can be selected at a time, so when the user makes a selection, the previous selection is unselected. This widget doesn't need a separate text label, since each segment gets its own text label, defined in the constructor.

Here's an example:

```
 1  tabs = {"Selected", "Unselected"}
 2  segmentedSwitch = widget.newSegmentedControl
 3  {
 4      x = cx,
 5      y = 60,
 6      segments = tabs,
 7      segmentWidth = 0.86*cw/(#segmentList),
 8      defaultSegment = 1,
 9      onRelease = onSelectSegment
10  }
```

Here's what it looks like in the iOS8 theme:

Segmented control: Very blue

Visually, the selected segment is filled with blue and the text label is white. The unselected segment is filled in black, with the blue used to color the label text. I find the result kind of **hard to read**, especially on some background colors. The Android theme, which is very close to the (old) iOS6 theme, looks better to me:

Android theme: Only blue when selected

If using *Drawn2Code*, add the segmented control from the widgets palette and then hit the "Edit Segments" button to customize it (see "Segment Label Editor"). Just type as many segments as you wish, keeping in mind with width of your supported devices. The number of labels you type will determine the number of segments in the widget.

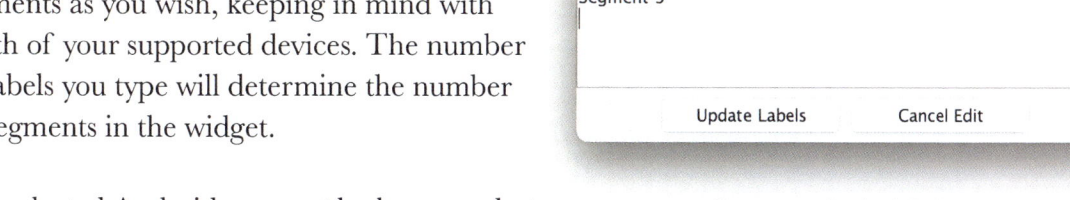

Segment Label Editor

The selected Android segment looks somewhat

depressed, but the iOS segment is truly blue. I guess, no matter the platform, the segmented control is a **sad** widget. It also doesn't do much. The multi-segment control reports the index number of the selected segment (which starts with 1) as well as the text label of the selection. Everything else is up to you. You can find the number of the segment using the `segmentNumber` attribute and the text (or label) of the segment using the `segmentLabel` attribute. So, in this case, you can access these data like this:

```
print(segmentedSwitch.segmentNumber)
print(segmentedSwitch.segmentLabel)
```

But we'll need to put this code inside an event-handler named "onSegmentSelect" (per line 9 of box #15). Here's what that could look like (box #16):

```
function onSelectSegment( event )
        s = event.target
        print(s.segmentNumber)
        print(s.segmentLabel)
end
```

And you should expect to see this output if you tap the "Unselected" tab:

```
OUTPUT
2
Unselected
```

The code for this simple app is included in the download as `segmented_control_little`.

The good news is that, except for the somewhat difficult to read iOS8 theme, there are **no glitches or issues** with this widget. One the other hand, this widget doesn't do anything beyond reporting the tab that was selected by the user. If you want to change the screen content, for example, based on the selection of the segment control, you will need to do that yourself. This can be done, for example, by creating separate display groups — one for each segment — and setting the alpha to 0 for all groups except the selected one.

The next example will do just that.

A complete example

This app will create a UI with a segmented control containing three "tabs": "Description", "Differences", and "Fixes". These tabs will allow the user to switch between text pertaining to each of these three topics. Finally, a checkbox at the bottom of the screen will allow the user to enable a background gradient "fix" to the iOS8 widget. Here's what it looks like:

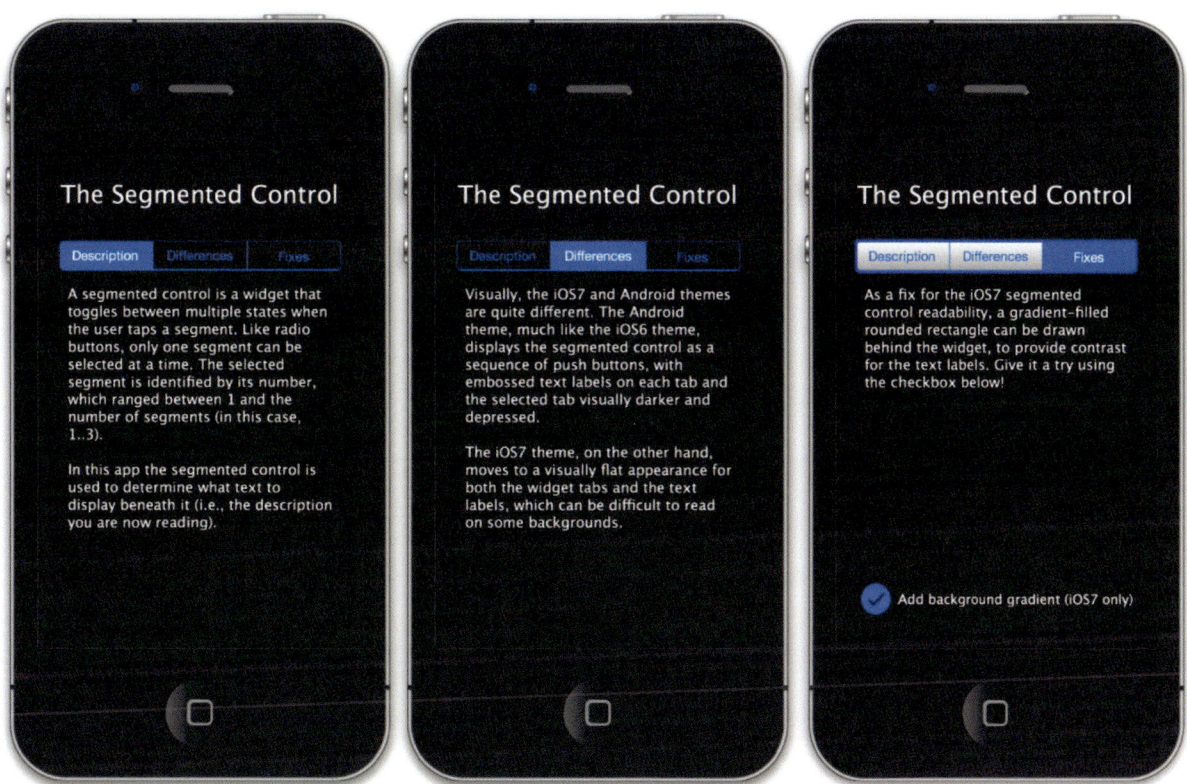

The Segmented Control and Gradient Fix

Notice in the screenshot above ("The Segmented Control and Gradient Fix"), the background gradient checkbox has been checked and the gradient is drawn behind the segmented control widget to make it easier to read. Nice, but it may not be needed with the latest version of iOS.

The text switches when the user makes a new selection on the segmented control, however, as noted previously, this switch has to be done *programmatically* (i.e., by you, the programmer). Perhaps the easiest way to do it is by creating three separate text display objects and then setting the alpha values so that only the desired (selected) text object is visible. We'll call these `text_description`, `text_differences`, and `text_fixes`.

In addition, to make the checkbox and its associated label also show and hide appropriately (i.e., to only be visible on the "fixes" tab), we'll put those in a display group called `cbx1` and set its alpha value as well.

All of this will be handled inside the event-handler for the segmented control using an 'if-elseif' structure (code box #18):

```
function onSelectSegment( event )

    s = event.target

    if s.segmentNumber == 1 then
        text_description.alpha = 1
        text_differences.alpha = 0
        text_fixes.alpha = 0
        cbx1.alpha = 0

    elseif s.segmentNumber == 2 then
        text_description.alpha = 0
        text_differences.alpha = 1
        text_fixes.alpha = 0
        cbx1.alpha = 0

    elseif s.segmentNumber == 3 then
        text_description.alpha = 0
        text_differences.alpha = 0
        text_fixes.alpha = 1
        cbx1.alpha = 1

    end

end
```

Note that this could be shortened significantly, if you were into that kind of thing.

The rounded-rectangle and gradient, named "seg_bg", are set up like this:

```
1   if isApple then
2       seg_bg = display.newRoundedRect(segSwitch.x, segSwitch.y,
            segSwitch.width, segSwitch.height, 2)
3       seg_bg_gradient = {type = "gradient", color1 = {1, 1, 1},
            color2 = {0.7, 0.7, 0.7}, direction = "down"}
4       seg_bg:setStrokeColor(0.05, 0.4, 1)
5       seg_bg.strokeWidth = 3
6       seg_bg:setFillColor(seg_bg_gradient)
7       seg_bg:toBack()
8       seg_bg.alpha = 0
9   end
```

Looking at box #19, notice that these are only created on Apple devices and the gradient is quite subtle (line 4), the rounded rectangle is sized and located using the segmented switch's size and location (line 2), has a blue stroke (lines 6 & 7), and is initially hidden (line 8). Feel free to play around with these settings to achieve the look you desire.

The checkbox (which is **only visible on Apple devices**) event-handling function is only responsible for transitioning the gradient's alpha from 0 to 1 and then back again, as appropriate (code box #20).

```
1   function onCheckbox( event )
2
3       s = event.target
4       if s.isOn then
5           if isApple then
6               transition.to(seg_bg, {time = 500, alpha = 1})
7           end
8       else
9           if seg_bg.alpha > 0 then
10              transition.to(seg_bg, {time = 500, alpha = 0})
11          end
12      end
13
14  end
```

Switch playground

Finally, the switch playground app pulls all of these widgets together in a working example. It also includes a (kind of crude) capability to disable widgets (the radio buttons, in this case), which is sometimes useful to be able to do, as well as the ability to display a native pop-up information dialog.

Enabling and disabling widgets

You already have the capability to *hide* a widget, either by making it invisible or by moving it off-screen. However, in some UI scenarios it is possible that you might want the user to *see* a particular component (such as a checkbox, radio buttons, etc.), but not be able to *use* it. That is usually accomplished by disabling a widget, however, as noted above, there's no quick way to do that.

One way to work around this limitation is to create a semi-transparent rectangle to "cover" the widget(s) when I want them "disabled". Then, we'll hook the rectangle up to an event listener called `doNothing()`, which *does nothing* (except to intercept any taps that might make their way to the covered widget(s).

In the playground app, you are going to disable the radio buttons using this technique. Here's the code that sets up this "disabling" rectangle (actually, rounded rectangle, which looks a bit better):

```
1  function doNothing( event)
2      return true
3  end
4
5  disabler = display.newRoundedRect(0.44*cw, 0.335*ch, 180, 80, 6)
6  disabler:setFillColor(0.8)
7  disabler:addEventListener("tap", doNothing)
8  disabler:addEventListener("touch", doNothing)
9  disabler.alpha = 0
```

So, when this rectangle (called the `disabler` — that almost sounds like a **super-villain!**) is visible (`alpha > 0`), it *intercepts* the user's attempt to operate the radio buttons, calling the function `doNothing()` which simply returns `true` (telling Solar2D that the user event has been *handled* and not to pass it down to other listening widgets, but otherwise doing nothing).

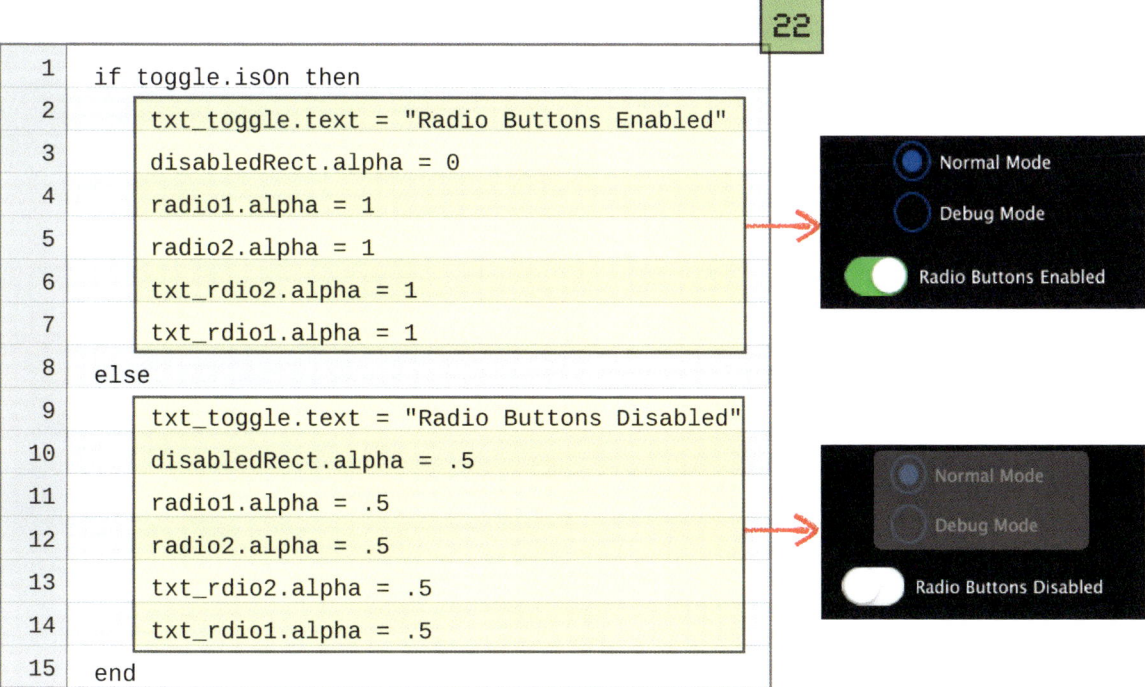

```
1   if toggle.isOn then
2       txt_toggle.text = "Radio Buttons Enabled"
3       disabledRect.alpha = 0
4       radio1.alpha = 1
5       radio2.alpha = 1
6       txt_rdio2.alpha = 1
7       txt_rdio1.alpha = 1
8   else
9       txt_toggle.text = "Radio Buttons Disabled"
10      disabledRect.alpha = .5
11      radio1.alpha = .5
12      radio2.alpha = .5
13      txt_rdio2.alpha = .5
14      txt_rdio1.alpha = .5
15  end
```

The app is also visually "greying out" the radio buttons to provide a clue to the user that the widgets are disabled and won't respond to their touch. This is done in code box #24, by setting the alpha of the visible components to 0.5 (lines 10-14).

For the covering box (the `disabler`), any positive alpha value will cause it to receive the user events and effectively block the radio buttons underneath. Re-enabling the radio buttons is done in lines 3-7 (box #22), by making the covering box invisible and the radio buttons and text labels 100% visible.

Of course, this technique could be used to "disable" any onscreen widgets, not just radio buttons.

Alert dialog pop-up

One final technique you might have noticed in the switch playground is the alert dialog. Alert dialogs pop-up in front of the screen content,

native

presenting information of some sort to the user along with one or more buttons which provide user-response options. In this app, I use the alert dialog to confirm that you've disabled the radio buttons.

The alert dialog is a `native` component, which means you might get interesting and perhaps *inconsistent* results in the Solar2D Device simulator versus actual devices (do you remember the horror that is the native textfield?).

The function you call in the native class is `showAlert()`, which takes several parameters (box #23): The alert title, the alert message, and optionally a table containing the buttons to display (at the bottom of the alert) and a listener to handle a button press.

```
native.showAlert("Attention", "Radio buttons are disabled!", {"Dismiss"})
```

In this case, the device simulator shows an odd dialog box that doesn't look anything like a real alert pop-up (see screenshot below on the left), but does let you test and debug your functionality. The actual popup that appears on the device looks more correct (below in the middle is the iOS Device Simulator and on the right is the Android Emulator).

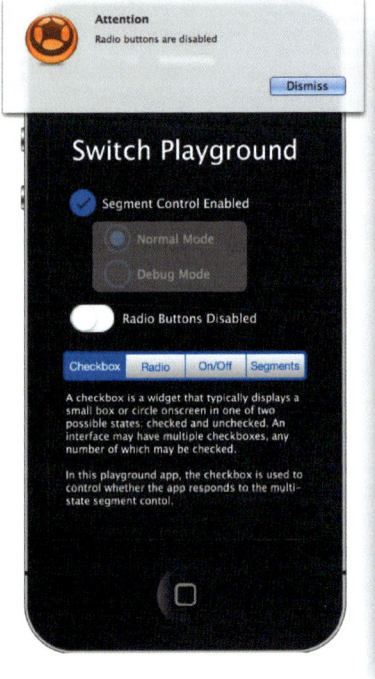
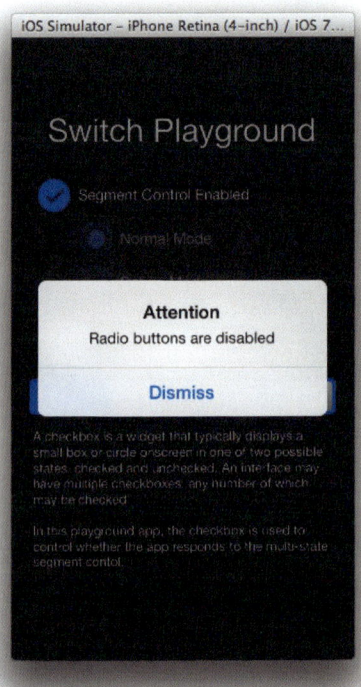
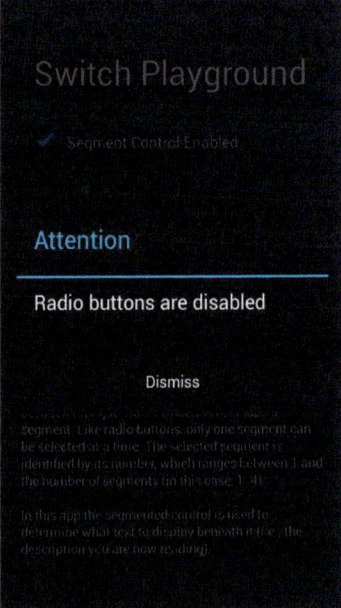

Solar2D Simulator   iOS Device Simulator   Android Emulator

Note that, although the button(s) parameter is "optional", if you don't include it, it **won't work** in the iOS Simulator (or device, most likely). Be sure to include at least an "okay" or "dismiss" button or else the user won't have any good way to dismiss the alert dialog. If you simply want to provide a way for the user to get rid of the alert dialog, there is no need to hook the "okay" or "dismiss" button up to a listener. However, if you have multiple buttons and need to provide functionality when the user presses one, a listener is required.

In *Drawn2Code*, you may add an alert dialog from the "Actions" palette and then customize it with the settings panel. By default, the event-handler is supplied with a helpful default snippet. For an alert dialog script object identified as Obj11, the settings panel would look like this (see "Alert Dialog Settings Panel"). Note.that *Drawn2Code* doesn't simulate what the dialog will look like, so you'll want to test your settings in the simulator.

Alert Dialog Settings Panel

Summary

In this chapter you have been introduced to Solar2D switches, including the checkbox (or "checkcircle"), radio button, on-off ("toggle") slider switch, and segmented control. Each of these is useful in distinct scenarios to create the UI you want. Each also has minor issues to work with to achieve the result you want. Some of these work-arounds require you to know about the device that your app is running on, made possible by the basic platform detection discussed. All of these features are available in the current version of *Drawn2Code*.

Although these widgets aren't able to be individually enabled and disabled, you learned a technique (using the "disabler") to achieve this effect. Finally, you learned to get the user's attention with a pop-up dialog box.

Chapter resources

In the chapter resource download for this book (www.lillipellilabs.com/mobiledev/download/chapter_resources.zip), look for folder "10".

This folder includes these fantastic apps:

1. checkbox_little
2. on-off_slide_little
3. radio_buttons_little
4. segmented_control_little
5. widget_checkbox
6. widget_on-off_slide
7. widget_radio_buttons
8. widget_segmented_control
9. the_disabler
10. widget_switch_playground

End-of-chapter exercises

1. Create an app with three checkboxes (no labels needed for these). Count the number of checkboxes checked and display that number in a label on screen.

2. Modify #1 with text display objects next to each checkbox. Put a random number between 0-100 in each text objects when the app starts. In a fourth text display object, display the sum of the selected numbers.

3. Create an app with a checkbox and the name of your favorite **Wizarding School** character in a text display object.

   a. Reveal the name only when the check box is checked.

   b. Include an image of your favorite **Wizarding School** character.

   c. Use an on/off slide switch instead of a check box.

4. Create an app with a multi-segment control to display your *three most favorite* **Wizarding School** images. Give each image a short name and use those names in your three segments. Display the correct picture (only) as the user switches the control.

5. Create an alternate version of #3b or 3c with a checkbox that adds a *tint* to your character image to simulate the eating of a **Jolly Bear's Multiflavor Jellies** gummy bear. When the check box is checked, use `setFillColor()` to tint the image a random color. When the check box is unchecked, remove the tint (i.e., using `setFillColor(1)`).

6. Create an app with a picture of your favorite **Wizarding School** character and a group of radio buttons to allow the user to pick the flavor of **Jolly Bear's Multiflavor Jellies** consumed from 3-4 options you provide.

   a. For each choice, give an appropriate tint to your **Wizarding School** character.

   b. Add an alert dialog to one of the radio button selections that lets the user know that this flavors may produce tints with visually disagreeable results.

7. Create a version of #2 that:

   a. Displays the average of the selected numbers in a fifth text display object.

   b. Add a button to re-randomize the numbers.

8. Modify #6 by adding a check box or on/off slider to enable/disable the tinting radio buttons.

9. Create an app that fills a table with 100 random values between 0 - 1000.

   a. Use 4 radio buttons to control the calculation conducted and result displayed: sum, average, min, and max.

   b. Add a button to re-randomize the values in the table.

NOTES

Tabs & Tables

Tab Bar with Four Icons

This chapter focuses on the Solar2D *tab bar* (which is somewhat similar to the segmented control discussed in Chapter 10) and the *table view widget* (which has nothing at all to do with the Lua table). You will also investigate the scroll view and spinner widgets, to round out your widget-based app development skill set. Let's get going!

Tab bar

One final "switching" widget at your disposal is the tab bar, (docs.coronalabs.com/api/library/widget/newTabBar.html)which is a row of icon buttons that run (typically) across the bottom of the device screen and is used to toggle content, similarly to the multi-segment control. In most UI designs, the tab bar will generally remain "on top of" any other content (which it does by default), although it is possible in some designs to transition on and off screen as needed. For example, the screenshot above shows a tab bar with 4 icons: "To Do", "Class Dates", "Documents", and "Teams". An app using such a tab bar would toggle content based on the user's selection in the tab bar (again, just as you did in Chapter 10 using the segmented control).

Tab bar versus segmented control

Okay, so why would you use a tab bar instead of a segmented control? Three key reasons: First, although they perform essentially the same UI task (switching content), they are **visually distinct**: The segmented control uses *text labels*, while the tab bar uses *icons with optional text labels*. Second, the **placement** of the segmented control is much more flexible as it can go anywhere on the screen and make sense to the user; the tab bar is typically restricted to an edge of the screen (although this isn't a requirement). Third, the user's **expectations** regarding their behavior is distinct: a segmented control switches a *content area* on a given screen, while the tab bar switches the *entire screen* to another content screen. Of course, these widgets aren't really competing with each other and could both be used in the same app to carry out their distinct roles.

Syntax and requirements

The tab bar is created using the **widget library** (so you'll need to require that) and the `newTabBar()` constructor. Within the constructor, each tab is defined in a separate settings table. For example, the first tab ("To Do") is defined in code box #1.

```
1  {
2      label="To Do",
3      id = 1,
4      size = 11,
5      defaultFile = "check-grey.png",
6      overFile = "check-blue.png",
7      width = 36,
8      height = 36,
9      onPress = onBtnPress,
10     selected = true
11 }
```

Note that there are **no default icons**, so you need to have a set of icons *ready to use*. They default in size to 32x32 pixels, but larger images will be automatically scaled to fit and will look fine (assuming they are close to square). As with all of your mobile app graphics, images will need to be created in several sizes and named systematically (i.e., as discussed in Chapter 4) in order to look good when deployed on devices of different size.

There are online resources for you to use, include Google's free icon pack (github.com/google/material-design-icons/releases/tag/1.0.0) and the diverse collection at flaticon.com.

> Download Google's free icon pack on Github.

In addition, each image needs to have **two forms**: The unselected or "default" image and the pressed or "over" image. The look and feel of these is entirely up to you as the designer. One typical look is for the default icon to be a flat grey shade and the "selected" icon to be colored using some theme that is consistent with your app.

Looking at lines 5 and 6 (code box #1), you can see the "default" (*unselected*) and "over" (*pressed*) image files specified. These need to be in the same folder as the "main.lua" file (although you can specify a different base or resource directory to help organize large projects; see Appendix C for details).

So, for an app with 4 tabs you need a total of 8 images (two for each tab: One "default" and one "over" image). That means that the syntax shown above (box #1) will need to be repeated three more times to define all of the tabs (if you peek at the source code, you'll see I've done that in a table called "tabs").

The 8 images I created for this tab bar demo are shown in the table "Table of Tab Bar Images". Obviously, I've used shades of grey as the default (unselected) image and a blue candy-ish theme for the colored "over" (*selected*) icons. The particular style you use should be driven by the overall design theme of the app. If the four tabs are defined in a table called `tabs`, then the constructor for the button bar will look like this (code box #2). Notice on line 6 (box #2), you are identifying the settings table created describing the tabs (also called "tabs", a part of which was shown in box #1).

Image	Filename
	check-grey.png
	check-blue.png
	calendar-grey.png
	calendar-blue.png
	docs-grey.png
	docs-blue.png
	teams-grey.png
	teams-blue.png

Table of Tab Bar Images

```
1    tabbar = widget.newTabBar{
2        left = 0,
3        top = ch-barH,
4        width = cw,
5        height = barH,
6        buttons = tabs
7    }
```

The final piece of the puzzle is the event handler function, which is referred to (box #1) as onBtnPress (as always, you can call it whatever you would like to). Notice also that, since the listener is hooked up in the tab definition, it is possible to use a separate event handling function for each tab.

```
1    local function onBtnPress( event )
2        id = event.target.id
3        if id == 1 then
4            page_txt.text = "To Do"
5        elseif id == 2 then
6            page_txt.text = "Class Dates"
7        elseif id == 3 then
8            page_txt.text = "Documents"
9        elseif id == 4 then
10           page_txt.text = "Teams"
11       end
12   end
```

In *Drawn2Code*, you may add a tab bar widget and configure it via its settings panel (see "Tab Bar Settings"). You can edit the number and order of the tabs (see "Tab Editor") and select the background image. Note that, if you use a background image, you also need to supply the icon highlight images (in three "slices"). More on this below.

For this first example app, I am simply changing the text on screen, in a text display object called page_txt, to the

Tab Bar Settings

name of the page (box #3). It isn't terribly exciting, but it does demonstrate the use of the Solar2D tab bar with all images set up.

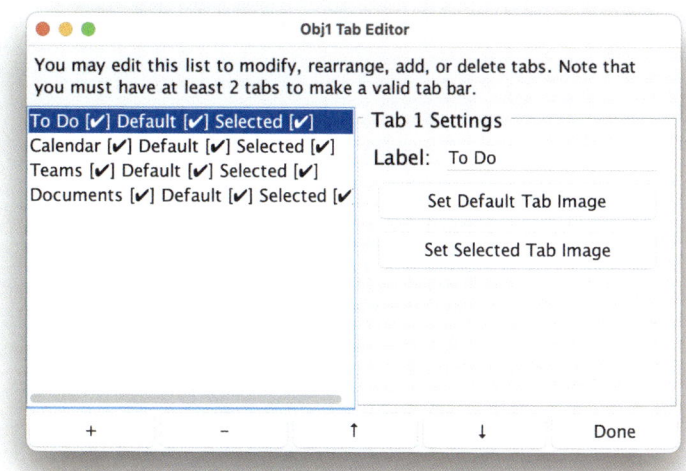

Looking at the Tab Editor, each tab needs a name (text) and two icon images (one for the default and another for the selected state). As you make these selections, the checks will appear to confirm them. Once complete, hit "Done" to close the editor.

Tab Editor

Tab Bar with Background and Highlight Images

This app is available in the download as *tab-bar-little.d2c*.

Notes and glitches

As noted above, there's just one text display object essentially shared by all of the tabs. Another way to do this would be to have four different text display objects (i.e., one for each

249

content area). Then, you set their visibility (i.e., alpha level or isVisible attribute) after the user makes a selection on the tab bar. You'll see this approach in action in this chapter.

Note that the default tab bar has a **white background** (or, perhaps closer to ecru?), which can't be set to a different color. To get the look in the screenshots above, I've created a background image. Unfortunately, you can't *simply* set a background image. You are *also* required to configure the "selected" highlight effect (i.e., the light grey rounded rectangle) using three additional images. Since the icons could have varying widths, these slices allow the center to be stretched without distorting the ends. The slices represent the left (" ["), center (" ☐ "), and right ("] ") images:

Tab Background and Three Slides

Gotcha

However, when you specify the background and selected images, the tab bar also **repositions the icons** down several pixels.

Compare the two tab bar screenshots below. The one on the left is the default tab bar (without background or highlight images), while the one on the right has the customized settings used in the first demo app.

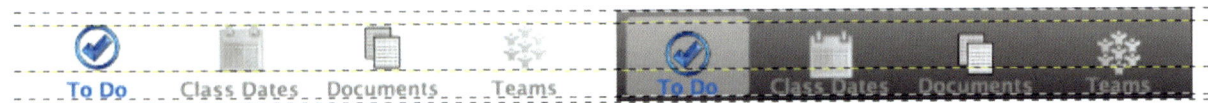

Basic Tab Bar (No Background Image)   With Background & Selection Images

Do you see how the icons in the right-hand version have **shifted down** by about 5 pixels? Ugh, that doesn't look good. The calendar icon looks like it is now touching the top of the text label. Initially, I thought that the shift was centering the icon inside the highlight image, but it isn't. Worse, while you can adjust the x and y offsets for the label (e.g., the "To Do" text), you can't adjust the icon offset. The only quick "fix" is to make the label text *smaller* when using the custom background, which does help but, obviously, makes the text a bit harder to read. The better fix would be to **redo the icon files to include the text** in them, sized and placed as you desire, then not use tab bar labels at all. The rest of the apps in this chapter will stick to the default tab bar.

Table view widget

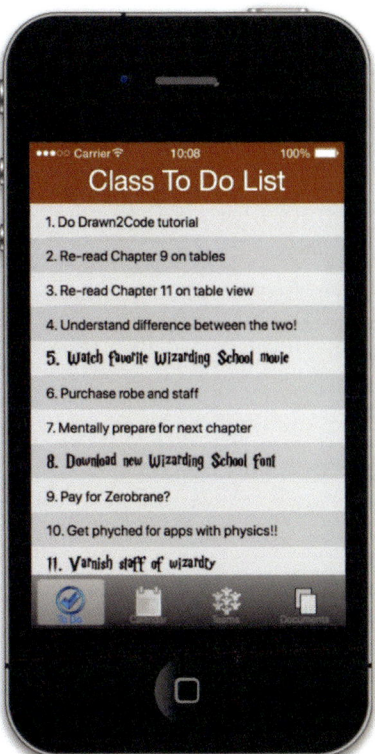

Let's add a feature to your tab bar app: A list of to do items in the form of a "table view widget". The Solar2D table view widget (docs.coronalabs.com/api/library/widget/newTableView.html) is distinct from the Lua "table", which is a data structure and not a widget. You use Lua tables all of the time (and did so in several places above). We'll use *both* a table and table view widget to extend your app.

Distinguishing these two concepts is important. We've been using tables for quite a while to put stuff in (like the collection of bugs you were trying to debug in Chapter 9), to organize settings (like the tab bar or `transition.to()` settings), and so on.

These tables store code and data in memory for you to access and use. The Lua table itself has no visual component. When you wanted to show and hide a `bug` in

Gosh there's a lot to do!

the `bugs` table, for example, you had to do it ourselves. The table simply held your bug display objects in memory.

The Lua syntax is pretty flexible, but a typical data table could be set up as follows:

```
1  todoData = {}
2  todoData[1] = "Do Drawn2Code tutorial"
3  todoData[2] = "Re-read Chapter 9 on Lua tables"
4  todoData[3] = "Re-read Chapter 11 on table view widget"
5  todoData[4] = "Watch favorite Wizarding School movie"
6  todoData[5] = "Purchase robe and staff"
7  --* etc.
```

This code (box #4) will create a Lua table called `todoData` and add 5 items to it (I add more items in the downloadable code and in the screenshot). However, as noted, it **won't display anything** on the screen. These items only exist in memory.

If you want to *see* the items in your table `todoData`, you *could* create text display objects for each of them and stack them vertically on screen. That would work fine. However, what if there were more than 5 items in the list? What if there were 15? Or 50? More than a dozen or so won't fit on smaller device screens, unless you make the font pretty small, so this would be tough to do (for the time being, at least).

Using a *table view widget* is one solution. The *table view widget* is an easy way to display a scrolling list of items. You can put as many items as you wish in it, and the user can scroll the list to bring offscreen items into view. The list can include your text "todo" items, but also any other display objects you care to use. By default, the widget will take up the **entire screen**, but it can be resized and repositioned easily. To create such a list requires a couple of steps. First, you construct it (box #5):

```
1  todoTableView = widget.newTableView {
2      left = 0,
3      top = todo_bkg.y + todo_bkg.height*.5,
4      height = ch - display.statusBarHeight - tabbar.height,
5      width = cw,
6      onRowRender = onRowRender,
7      onRowTouch = onRowTouch,
8      listener = scrollListener
9  }
```

The table view is positioned with its top directly under the brown "todo_bkg" rectangle with the title text (line 3). However, if you read over the configuration in box #5, you'll notice that nowhere are the table view contents provided. So, `todoTableView` is **initially empty**. If you want your to do list to display a numbered list of your to do items (i.e., those stored in the table `todoData`), we'll need to use a 'for' loop to create each row one at a time, by calling a function I'll call `onRowRender` and hooking the row up to an event handler I'll call `onRowTouch`.

To add a row to the *table view widget*, you use the `insertRow` function (inside the loop) as follows (box #6):

```
1  for i = 1, #todoData do
2      todoTableView:insertRow {
3          rowHeight = 34,
4          rowColor = {default={.8}},
5      }
6  end
```

These settings are fairly self-explanatory. You have control over these attributes individually, for each row. So, should you need to, you *could* make each row a **different color and height** (among other settings). However, in this example, you are sizing each row the same 32 pixels tall. Although, if you look at the screenshot carefully, you may note that the running version alternates the row color and uses the "Harry P" font when appropriate; these modifications are in the downloadable code.

For the code in boxes #5 & 6 to work, you need two supply these two functions (box #7). The event handler doesn't do anything in this app (it just displays the user's selection at the console). The real action is in onRowRender().

```
1   function onRowTouch(e)
2       print("You pressed row "..e.index..": "..todoList[e.index])
3   end
4
5   function onRowRender(e)
6       local row = e.row
7       local rowGroup = e.view
8       local text
9       item = tostring(todoData[e.index])
10      text = display.newText(row, row.index..". "..item, 0, 0, f, 14)
11      text.anchorX = 0
12      text.x = 16
13      text.y = row.height*0.5
14      text:setFillColor(0)
15
16  end
```

The syntax is somewhat convoluted, but much of it can be used without significant modification in any table view widget you might need to create. I've colorized some of the key items to help you keep them straight (see "Making Sense of the Table View").

Note that, as of version 1.57, *Drawn2Code* does not yet support the table view widget. This app is available in the chapter download as *tab-bar-with-tableview.d2c*.

253

Item	Description
todoData	The table data structure (like an array) that holds the text "to do" items.
todoTableView	The table view widget that appears on screen and contains rows with formatted "to do" items pulled from the todoData.
onRowTouch	The event handler (function) called when a user touches a row of todoTableView (which isn't doing anything in this app).
onRowRender	The function that pulls items from the todoData and formats each row for placement in the table view widget (todoTableView).

Making Sense of the Table View

Scroll view widget

Now that you have your *table view widget* working, you need some **content** for the other three tabs, right? So, let's learn a couple more widgets! So far, you have been adding content to your device screen all over the place, but had no ability to **scroll** to see content that couldn't fit on the screen. Fortunately, Solar2D has a widget for you (the *scroll view widget*) which you can place content on. Then, you put the *scroll view widget* on your screen somewhere. As long as the content is larger than the screen (or the scroll widget), the user can push up or pull down to scroll and see more content.

You can create a simple (empty) *scroll view widget* like this (box #8):

```
1  scroller = widget.newScrollView {
2    --* required setting:
3    listener = onScrollEvent
4  }
```

There are several optional settings that could be added to box #8 and, although you can make the *scroll view widget* less than full screen, it requires an additional step that isn't covered here. You are going to add two *scroll view widgets* to this app to allow you to scroll around a calendar and a block of text.

Scrollable image: Calendar

Let's say you have *largish* (yes, that is a word) image of a calendar, with months arrayed in a grid (because you do). Let's call it `cal_img`. It is **too big to fit** on the device screen, at least without scaling it down so far as to be unreadable. So, to add "scrollability", you have to add it to your `scroller` object:

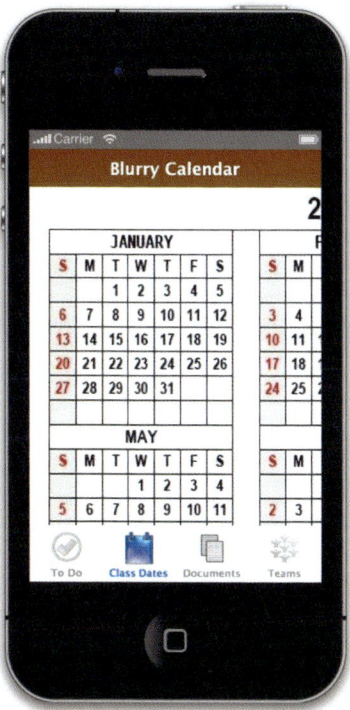

```
scroller:insert(cal_img)
calGroup:insert(scroller)
```

It may be blurry, but it scrolls.

Finally, you will add the `scroller` object to the appropriate display group (`calGroup`, in this case).

The result? When you select the "class dates" tab you should now see a (blurry) calendar, which is way too big to fit onscreen, but which you can scroll around because you put it in a *scroll view widget*.

Scrollable text: Team information

Of course, you can "scroll" more than images. You can put any display object on a ScrollView widget. For example, if you had a large block of text to display, you could place that on one to make it scrollable. Since the actual text contents aren't important to demonstrate a scrollable text object, I have just created it using on online "lorem" text generator. But, I've made it pretty long. I start by creating the team_txt object empty then add the gibberish in a second step (not shown here):

```
teams_txt = display.newText("", 0, 0, 500, 1000, f, 16)
```

You can see that the text object is sized to be wider than the screen (at 500 pixels) and 1500 pixels tall. Way too tall to fit on screen at full size, so scrolling is a requirement. The set up for this new scroller is shown next (box #11):

```
1   teams_scroller = widget.newScrollView {
2       width = 320,
3       height = ch - teams_title_bkg.height,
4       scrollWidth = teams_txt.width,
5       scrollHeight = teams_txt.height,
6       listener = onScrollEvent
7   }
8   teams_scroller.x = 0
9   teams_scroller.y = teams_scroller.y + 60
10  teams_scroller:insert(teams_txt)
```

You can see that I am setting the size and location of the scroll view widget before inserting the text object. Although the display object is sized larger than the default display size, it could be *restricted* to fit in either the available horizontal or vertical space (in this case, by specifying the width at 320 or less and the height at 380 or less), if that was what the UI design needs. Obviously, if you fit it *entirely* in the available space, there would be no need for the scroll view.

Finally, I insert the title bar objects and the scroll view object into a display object called `teamGroup` (box #12):

```
1   teamGroup:insert(teams_scroller)
2   teamGroup:insert(teams_title_bkg)
3   teamGroup:insert(teams_title_txt)
4   teamGroup.alpha = 0
```

The result is show in the screenshot "Scrolling Text" and the working version is in the chapter download as *tab-bar-two-scrollers.d2c*.

Scrolling Text

Scroll view notes

There are a few things to keep in mind when using the scroll view:

1. The scroll view can't handle very **large images**. Images over 2048x2048 may not behave consistently.

2. The default background color is **white**, which means any text you put on it will need to have its **color changed** (since the default text color is also white and will be unreadable).

3. Alternatively, you may with to change the background color of the widget, which you may do in the construction using the `bgColor` attribute.

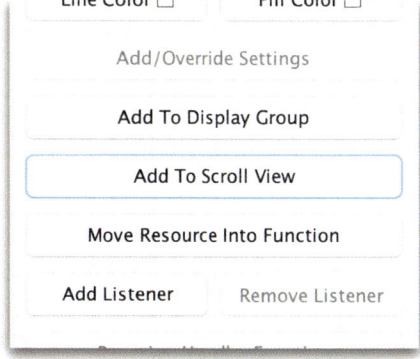

Add To Scroll View

Drawn2Code does support scroll view widgets. You can add one from the widgets palette, as you might expect. Display objects and widgets may be added to it via the "Add To Scroll View" button in their individual settings panels. A simple example is available in *scroll-view-little.d2c*.

But wait — I hear you cry — you still have **one empty content area!** Luckily, I have one last widget for you...

Spinner widget

spinner.png

The *spinner widget* is a widget that spins (docs.coronalabs.com/api/library/widget/newSpinner.html). That's its job. To spin. This is an "activity wheel", with the job of letting the user know that your app is **working on something**. It may be waiting on a response from a web service, a database, the execution of a complex function, and so on. The spinner reassurcs the user that your app hasn't crashed and is making progress toward eventually not having to display the spinner.

Note that this widget **does not communicate the "progress" of a task**, just that the task is ongoing. Of course, the amount of the task that is completed could be shown as a percentage in the center (for example), if it was appropriate to share that information.

There are countless different spinner designs; unfortunately, Solar2D doesn't include a default version. It is unlikely that you'll want to use the image of an arrow that Solar2D uses to demonstrate the widget. Instead of finding a free image to use on the web, I created a simple one ("spinner.png"). This "spinner" is just a **regular png image** (not an animated image). Solar2D will do the spinning for us. It does take a couple of steps, however.

Image sheet

First, you need to set up the image as an "image sheet" for use as a spinner (box #13):

```
1  options = {
2      width = 128,
3      height = 128,
4      numFrames = 1
5  }
6  spinnerSingleSheet = graphics.newImageSheet( "spinner.png", options )
```

Image sheets allow you to create animations out of a collection of individual images. An image sheet contains each of frame of the animation as individual images which are laid out next to each other. However, in this case, the sheet is just one image that will be rotated. The width and on code box #13 here refer to the actual size (in pixels) of the spinner image (or of each spinner image in a sheet of images). After running box #13, your app is ready to use the "spinnerSingleSheet" object (which you could call whatever you'd like). You do this in box #14, setting up the widget:

```
1   spinner = widget.newSpinner
2   {
3       x = cx,
4       y = cy,
5       width = 128,
6       height = 128,
7       sheet = spinnerSingleSheet,
8       startFrame = 1,
9       deltaAngle = 10,
10      incrementEvery = 20
11  }
12  -- loading text:
13  loading_txt = display.newText("Loading", cx, cy, "HarryP", 24)
```

The width and height in code box #14 refer to the size you wish to display the spinner in (in pixels). On the last line (box #14), I've placed the text "Loading" in the center of the spinner. It isn't part of the spinner image since, if it were, it would spin as well!

It looks like the screenshot "The spinner in action". Of course, it isn't in action, since it is just a screenshot. This is quite a disappointment. However, if you blink *really fast* while slapping your face, this will start to **look like it actually is spinning**. Not working yet? Keep trying.

As mentions above, image sheets may contain a sequence of images (i.e., instead of the single image used here). In image sheets containing multiple images, be sure to arrange the images in the **desired sequence** to produce the animation you want to see. Finally, note the image sheets are based in the Solar2D "graphics" table, not the "widgets" table (even though the spinner is a widget). Why? Other Solar2D objects (that aren't widgets) can also use image sheets.

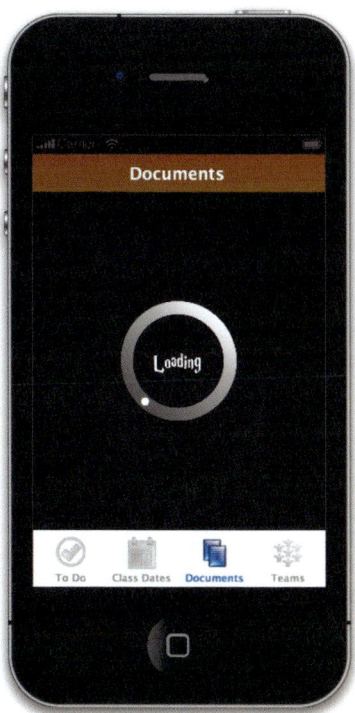

The spinner in action!

In *Drawn2Code*, you'll be prompted to create an image sheet when you add a spinner widget. The image sheet display object is found in the "Display Objects" palette and will prompt you for a filename. This could be a single image (as in this example), or a sequence of images for Solar2D to animate.

To view a working spinner, you'll end up with four script objects in your stack.

Note that the spinner widget isn't really a "widget". It is more of an animated image. As such, there is no default listener attached (or event-handler supplied).

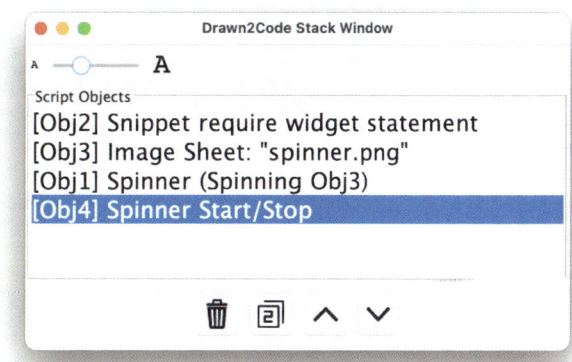

A Spinner in Four Script Objects

After seeing your spinner, you may be disappointed to see that it doesn't spin. To start it spinning, you'll need a "Spinner Start/Stop" action (in the "Actions" palette). This is Obj4 in the stack shown. Obviously, the order of these objects is important. The image sheet has to be loaded before the spinner object is created. That means, Obj3 has to be above Obj1 (in the stack shown) for the app to actually run. Likewise, you can't start/stop a spinner (Obj4) before the spinner exists (Obj1). So, Obj4 needs to be after/below Obj1 in this simple stack (*spinner-little.d2c*).

One more thing

Although the tab bar has been staying put to allow the user to navigate the UI, it doesn't always have to be *visible*. For example, as the user is scrolling the calendar or the fascinating teams text, you could make the tab bar slide off screen to allow an unrestricted view of the content. Then, when the user stops scrolling, you could slide the tab bar back on screen. How? Just using your awesome `transition.to()` skills to move the y location!

The feature has been added to the final example for the chapter:
`widget_tab_bar_full_version`.

Summary

In this chapter you have learned the ins and outs of two of Solar2D's most complex widgets: the tab bar and the table. These both have several options which change their appearance significantly. The tab bar has similarities with the segmented control widget (covered in Chapter 10), but is typically used to switch an entire screen of content rather than a subpart of the screen. The Solar2D table widget can be used to display a scrolling list of information and is vastly configurable.

 The current release of *Drawn2Code* supports the tab bar widget (with widget background and 3-part tab highlight images) the scroll view widget, and the spinner widget. However, the table view widget is not (yet) supported.

Chapter resources

In the chapter resource download for this book (www.lillipellilabs.com/mobiledev/download/chapter_resources.zip), look for folder "11".

This folder includes these fantastic apps as well as the award-worthy tab and spinner graphics:

1. tab_bar_little
2. table_view_little
3. scroll_view_little
4. spinner_little
5. tab_bar_tableview
6. tab_bar_two_scrollers
7. tab_bar_full_version
8. spinner.png
9. tab bar images for todo, calendar, documents, and teams.
10. tab bar background image and 3-part selected highlight images.
11. Bonus: Icons for tab bars styled like movie film. Maybe to help with an exercise below.

End-of-chapter exercises

1. Create an app with a *tab bar widget* with three tabs along with three text display objects.

    a. Use the tabs to switch between text descriptions of your three favorite movies.

    b. Make it so that at least one of the movie descriptions is too long to fit on screen. Use a *scroll view widget* to let the user see it all.

2. Create an app with a Lua table (the data structure) containing a list of your favorite **Wizarding School** characters, quotes, spells, or locations. Then display that onscreen using a *table view widget*.

3. Create an app with the image of your favorite **Wizarding School** student on a *scroll view widget*. Add content to the scroll view that is just off screen (i.e., above the top, below the bottom, to the left of the left edge, and to the right of the right edge). Allow the user to scroll the image to view the bonus content.

4. Create an app using a *spinner widget*. Add a button to allow the user to start and stop the spinner.

5. Create a version of #1 that displays movie posters (images) in addition to the text descriptions for these three movies. Make one or more of the movie posters too big to fit on the device screen and use a *scroll view widget* to allow the user to view it.

6. Create a version of #2 that customizes the font on particular list items that contain a key word or phrase of your choice.

7. Create a version of #2 that hides the tab bar when the user is scrolling the content (and to make it reappear when the user stops scrolling). Use whatever kind of transition you like to perform the "hiding" and "showing" effects.

8. Create an app with two *spinner widgets*. Add a button to alternate between running one spinner or the other. Add unique background music to each spinner that only plays when it is spinning.

Physics I

It's built in

Solar2D includes a built-in "physics engine" (based on the open-source Box 2D engine) that enables you to create apps with objects that respond the way actual objects would in a real, physical environment (docs.coronalabs.com/api/library/physics/index.html). You can add gravity to a scene and watch your display object fall off the screen! Even better, the objects will interact (if that is what you want) by bouncing off of each other, or sliding down a surface with a level of friction you specify. Collisions can be easily detected and responded to. You get all of this — and more — by requiring the physics library and "starting" the engine:

```
1  local physics = require "physics"
2  physics.start()
```

To create a display object that you wish to apply physics to, you need to add it to the physics engine. To do this, the physics table includes a function called "addBody".

Wow, *physics*.

For example, to create a ball (okay, it's just a *circle*) and add it to the engine, you just do this:

```
1  ball = display.newCircle(180, 50, 20)
2  physics.addBody(ball)
```

Although the code in box #2 does omit some details, it will run without trouble. If you do run it, you'll need to be quick to see the ball dropping! It will start falling **right away**, accelerating at a pace dictated by a simulated gravity. If you missed it, just hit command-r (Mac) or control-r (Windows) to reload it.

Drawn2Code gives you access to many of the basic physics features (via the "Physics" palette). The "Add Body" script object is the key to creating and configuring physics bodies. This first app, with a ball dropping off screen uses only three script objects (*ball-drop-no-floor.d2c*). The physics body can be adjusted via the settings panel for Obj3.

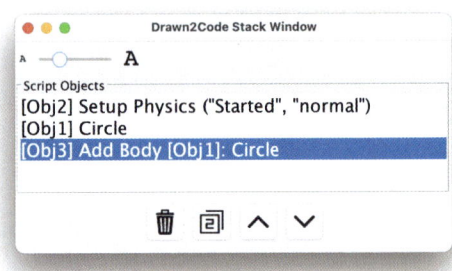

Dropping the Ball

If you are wondering *why* the ball doesn't bounce, the answer is simply that there's nothing for it to bounce *off* of. The edges of the display don't represent physics bodies or boundaries. Indeed, unless you stopped the simulator, the ball is still falling. Watch out below!

A bouncing ball

To make the ball bounce, you will need to add a "ground" (or "floor", but `floor`, although not listed as such, is a reserved word, so don't use it as an identifier!) to the app. Assuming the usual constants have been set, a ground can just be a rectangle placed at the bottom of the display:

```
1  ground = display.newRect(cx, ch, cw, 0)
2  physics.addBody(ground)
```

In this case, I've made the ground "0" pixels tall, although, that specific value isn't important to the physics. It could be 1 pixel or 100 pixels tall and work the same. The difference is that the zero height won't be visible onscreen, so the ball will appear to bounce on the display edge. Play around with different values and see what happens!

If you add this code (box #3) to your app and run it, you'll see the ball bounce... oh... no, wait a moment. It doesn't bounce does it? What's going on? Well, since you didn't say otherwise, your "ground" rectangle **is also falling**, along with the ball, although you don't see it since it starts at the bottom of the screen. How do you fix that? You'll need to learn about the different types of physics bodies.

Types of physics bodies

To tell an object like the "ground" **not to fall**, you need to set the *type* of physics body it is. You have three choices:

1. "dynamic" (the default) bodies will react to gravity and collisions.
2. "static" bodies don't move or react to gravity or collisions.
3. "kinematic" bodies are not effected by gravity, but are affected by other forces (such as collisions).

Since you didn't specify otherwise, the ball and the ground are both "dynamic", which means that gravity operates on both of them and therefore both start falling as soon as the app starts. How do you fix that? If you want the ground to be stay put, you need to make the ground "static". You can do that by changing the `addBody()` function call above (in box #3) to include the keyword "static"(in quotes) or by changing its `bodyType` attribute (box #4):

```
1  ground.bodyType = "static"
2  -- or
3  physics.addBody(ground, "static")
```

A Bouncing Ball

And so, after making one of the changes suggested in box #4, you should see the white ball drop down to the brown ground and bounce a few times before coming to rest.

It would probably be preferable to *see* the ground, so let's move it up a bit and fill it with an appropriately "groundish" color:

```
1  ground = display.newRect(cx, ch, cw, 10)
2  ground:setFillColor(0.65, 0.3, 0.18)
```

Ah, that looks better. Now that the height of the ground is 10 pixels, you see the top 5 pixels on the device screen (the other 5 pixels are drawn below the bottom edge, since the rectangle is vertically centered there).

The screenshot to the right ("Bouncing Ball") shows what this looks like mid-bounce. You might be wondering why the ball bounces to the height that it does (or, perhaps, why it doesn't bounce higher). These are good questions. A physics body's bounce is partly determined by its "bounciness".

Bounciness

While the ball above does bounce, it is a bit on the flat side. What if you want it to be more *bouncy*? Easy, there's a setting precisely for that, but you'll need to amend your `addBody()` function call:

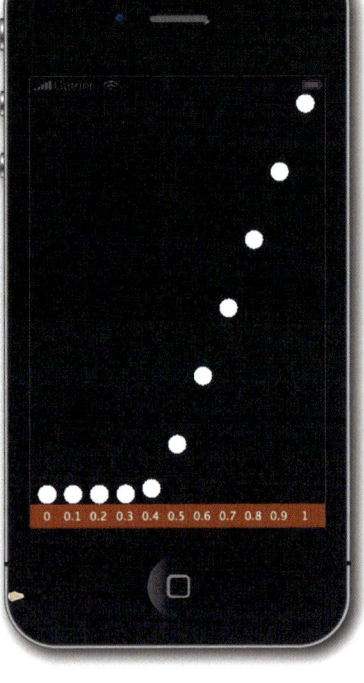

Bounce Values: 0.0 - 1.0

```
1  physics.addBody(ball, {bounce = .7})
```

The "bounce" of the body can be set using the `bounce` attribute, which goes from 0.0 to 1.0 (representing no bounce at all to perfectly bouncy). The default value is 0.3, which is somewhat bouncy. To make it even bouncier, you can set the precise value you want (shown in box #6).

Playing with the bounce

Try entering a value of 1.0 for `bounce`. What happens? The ball bounces *forever*. Okay, now try entering a `bounce` value of 0.0. What happens? Huh? The ball still bounces?! How

Type of Ball	bounce **value?**
Golf ball	
Soccer ball	
Quaffle ball	
Bowling ball	
Meatball (no sauce)	
Play-Doh™ ball	

Relative Bounciness

can that be? You haven't eliminated all of the bounce because the **ground still has the default bounce** of 0.3. If you change it to 0.0 as well — try it — the ball won't bounce at all. It is like landing in tar.

The screenshot at the right (`11_bouncing_balls`) shows 11 balls, dropped from the top of the screen, with bounce values incrementing from 0.0 to 1.0 by 0.1. The screenshot really doesn't communicate nearly as much as watching these actually bounce, so go ahead and download it and give it a try! On some devices, the rightmost ball eventually falls off of the screen. If this happens to you, make sure your monitor isn't *tilted* slightly.

In this app the ground adds no bounce at all (i.e., bounce is set to 0). Thinking about these different levels of bounce, see if you can figure out good values for the balls listed in the table "Relative Bounciness".

You'll learn about **irregular shapes** (like a football) later, since that adds some complexity!

Other attributes

In addition to `bounce`, you can also set: `density`, `friction`, `radius` or `shape`, and `filter`. These are defined as (docs.coronalabs.com/api/library/physics/addBody.html):

1. The `density` of a body represents the degree to which the matter that it is composed of is compacted. The mass of the body can be determined by multiplying the density by the area. The default value is 1.0, representing water. Less dense materials, such as wood, should be given values less than 1.0, while denser materials, such as iron should be given larger values.

2. The `friction` of a body represents the resistance the surface of the body provides to other surfaces it moves (slides) against. The value 0.0 means no friction, while 1.0 represents strong friction. The default value is 0.3.

3. The `radius` of a body represents the circular shape that defines its outer bounds. If the shape is rectangular (or close to it), then don't set this. If the shape is circular (or close to it) setting the radius is recommended.

4. The `shape` of an irregular body represents its outer bounds. This is provided in a table of {x,y} values and **must be given in clock-wise order**. The shape defaults to the bounding rectangle, so it is unnecessary to set the shape (or radius) for simple rectangles (or circles).

5. The `filter` of a body allows advanced customization of collision detection settings.

For your ball, it would make sense to define the radius (since it isn't a simple rectangle). The radius can easily be set via the body's settings panel (see "Physics Body Settings").

How do I know that the radius is 20? Well, if you look way back at box #2, you'll see the radius as the third parameter in the construction of the ball display object. For the smaller balls used in the "10 balls" example, the radius would be 10. More on these various options below.

What happens if you set the radius incorrectly? That's actually an interesting question! If you set it too large, say 30, then the ball won't ever hit the ground. It will almost appear as if the ball has a **force field** around it, protecting it. On the other hand, if you set the radius too small, say 10, then the ball will appear to sink into the ground, as if it were landing in mud. Give it a try!

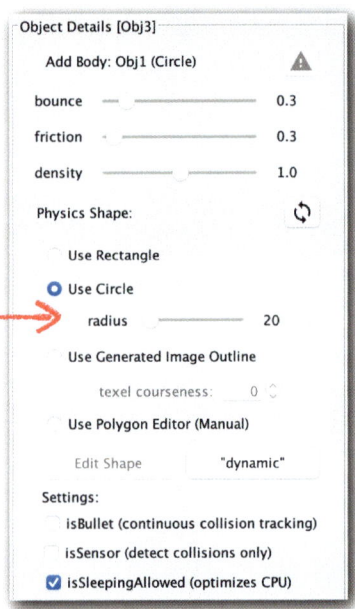

Physics Body Settings

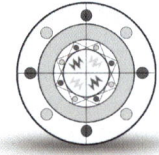

Magic Ball

Using images rather than basic shapes

What if **you don't want a ball that is just a white circle?** That's okay. Let's display an **image of a magical ball**, rather than the plain circle. This is easy to do, although you do have to acquire a graphics file you want to use. For this demo, you'll just use the "Magic Ball" above (find "magic-ball.png" in the resource download), which happens to be circular.

```
1  ball = display.newImageRect("magic-ball.png", 40, 40)
2  ball.x = cx
3  ball.y = 0
4  physics.addBody(ball, {bounce = 0.7, radius = 20})
```
7

If you make this change to your code (i.e., in code box #2), you should see the magic ball drop magically in place of the white circle. Note that the radius is correctly set to 20, so that the magic ball is seen as a circle by the physics engine.

270

Having multiple physics bodies

How can you **add another physics body** to your app? Easy, just create it and add it as another physics body. There's no limit to the number of separate bodies you can use. The introductory tutorial on physics objects on the Solar2D site is a square wooden "crate" (developer.coronalabs.com/content/game-edition-box2d-physics-engine); you'll use the iron lockbox instead (to make this work, you'll need to copy "iron-box.png" into your project folder). If you add this code (box #8) to the app, you'll see both the lockbox and the ball fall at roughly the same time.

```
1  box = display.newImageRect("iron-box.png", 50, 50)
2  box.x = cx
3  box.y = 0
4  physics.addBody(box, {density = .5, bounce = .2})
```

Important

Note (again) the use of the function `newImageRect()` here (rather than `newImage()`) on line 1 of code box #8, which is **preferred when creating new, rectangular physics bodies**. This is the default in *Drawn2Code*. This function takes the name of the image file along with the width and height desired. This allows the object to be sized at the time of creation (avoiding the use of `xScale` and `yScale`, which are **ignored** by the physics engine).

However, `newImageRect()` does not accept x and y values (somewhat oddly), which must be set after the object's creation (e.g., see lines 2 and 3 in code box #8).

When you run this, you'll see something like the screenshot "A Ball and a Box". Both the iron box and the ball will initially drop and hit the ground. This app is available in the chapter download as "`ball_and_box`".

When you run it, if you watch closely, you'll see the iron box

A Ball and a Box

271

bounce up and hit the magic ball while it is still dropping, making the ball bounce much higher than it otherwise would. Try playing around with the initial location of the box and see how it changes the interaction with the ball. What happens if you start the box out at box.y = 300, for example?

In any case, **rectangular bodies are easy**, since their shape matches the shape used for physics (i.e., the rectangle that bounds the rectangular shape). For other shapes, there's more work to do.

Irregular shapes

What if I don't want a circle or a square? One common "alternate" shape is a *triangle* which can be used, for example, as a ramp or wedge. For this, you can use a Polygon display object with three vertices (see Chapter 4). To make a simple ramp constructed of faux iron, you can use these settings:

```
ramp_vertices = {
    160, 240,
    230, 320,
    90, 320,
}
ramp = display.newPolygon(74, 331,
    ramp_vertices)
ramp.id = "ramp"
ramp:setStrokeColor(0.4, 0.4, 0.4, 1.0)
ramp:setFillColor(0.6, 0.6, 0.6, 1.0)
ramp.strokeWidth = 6
physics.addBody( ramp )
```

If you add this "ramp" as a new display object (box #9) and position it to the left, you can drop the magic ball on it so it will knock the ball back over to the right (and into the lockbox).

However, if you code this by hand, you'll notice that this really **doesn't work correctly** (*Drawn2Code* is smart enough to handle this issue automatically).

What actually happens will depend on where you position the ramp and where you drop the ball from. I've positioned them onscreen in the demo in such a way that the ball will end up as shown in "The Ball at Rest". As you can see, the ball appears to be levitating in mid-air. A screen shot just won't do it justice. You'll need to run it to fully experience the *oddness*. It is available in the chapter downloads as `triangle_ramp`.

What's going on?

Hybrid draw mode

Well, let's try to **see what's happening** by starting a *debugging mode* called `"hybrid"`, which is typically set before you turn physics on (i.e., in the code shown in box #1).

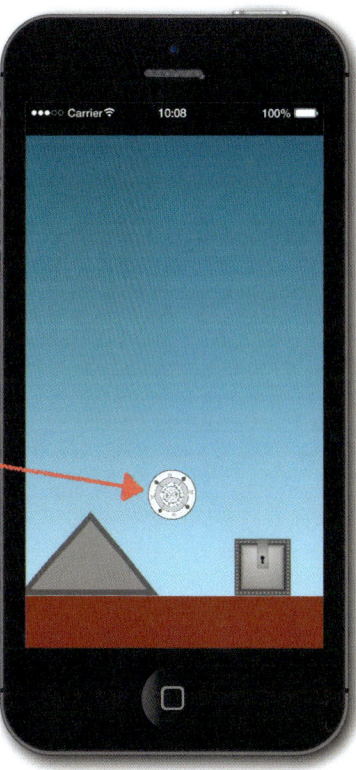

The Ball at Rest

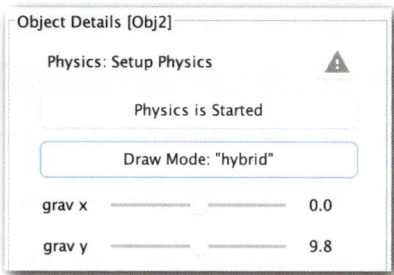

Hybrid Mode

You can do this in *Drawn2Code* by accessing the "Setup Physics" settings panel and hitting the "Draw Mode" button until it says "hybrid").

This mode will show your display objects while also **overlaying the shape the physics engine sees**.

What you see will look something like the screenshot "Boxing a Triangle".

Do you notice how the shape outlines for the ball and the lockbox are exactly the same size as their respective display objects? But look at the ramp (triangle). Its physics shape is a *rectangle*. It is as closely fitted to the triangle as possible, but it still is clearly wrong. However, this rectangle is the shape Solar2D is using to drive the physics on it, not the triangular shape in the image.

Obviously, that isn't what you want.

Boxing a Triangle

273

The solution

You want the ramp object to **act like a triangle**, not a rectangle. To do that, you have to add the `shape` attribute to the `physics.addBody()` function call. The shape of the triangle is the three corners, starting at the top and going around clock-wise. Each corner (or "vertice") needs an x, y coordinate value. These can be fixed pixel values or formula that calculate these values. Here's one way to write the code by hand:

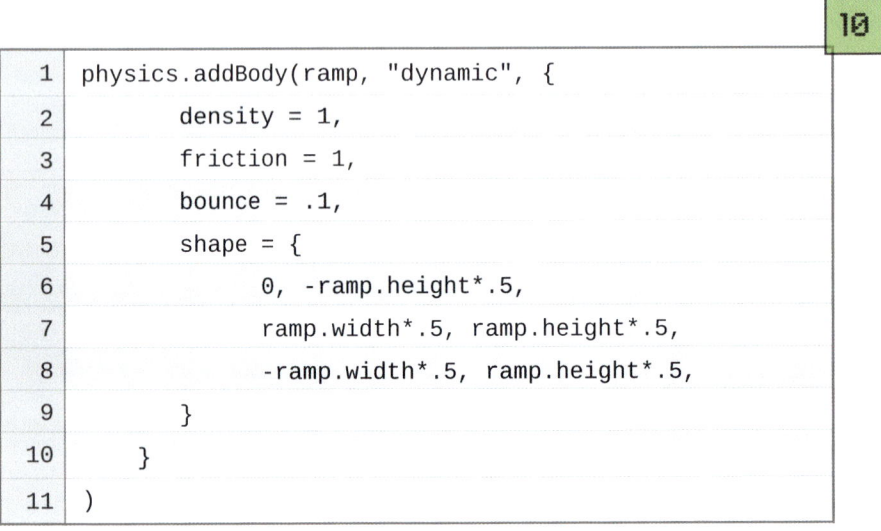

```
physics.addBody(ramp, "dynamic", {
        density = 1,
        friction = 1,
        bounce = .1,
        shape = {
                0, -ramp.height*.5,
                ramp.width*.5, ramp.height*.5,
                -ramp.width*.5, ramp.height*.5,
        }
    }
)
```

If you make this change (replacing the `physics.addBody(ramp)` statement in box #9 with this revised version in box #10) you will see a big difference. Each of the three vertices is calculated using a bit of algebra based on the size of the image (specifically, its width and height). Once the shape is defined, the ramp can be moved or rotated as needed with the shape intact.

There are two key body shape "gotchas" to keep in mind:

1. The (0,0) point is in the **center of the body** (regardless of the shape).
2. Only **convex shapes** are allowed.

Gotchas

Finding the points

So, to identify the 3 (x,y) points that define your triangular ramp, you need to start at the (0,0) point, which is in the center (not the top-left corner as some documents say). Then, you'll need to move 1/2 the distance of the width and height of the ramp (called W and H in the figure to the below) to get to the vertices (see "Three Vertices" for an illustration of these points).

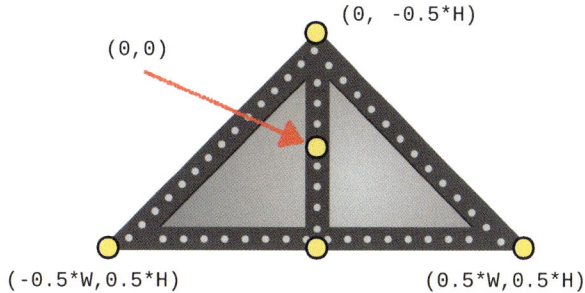

Three Vertices

If you are planning to have a number of complex, irregularly-shaped bodies in your app, you might benefit from using a 3rd party tool like Physics Editor www.codeandweb.com/physicseditor) to automate the creation of the shape data.

Since our "ramp" polygon is 140 pixels wide and 80 pixels tall, the "physics points" we need are (based on the calculations above): (0,-40), (70, 40), -70, 40). In *Drawn2Code*, switch the physics shape to "Use Polygon Editor (Manual)" and enter the points listed above (see "Entering Shape Manually").

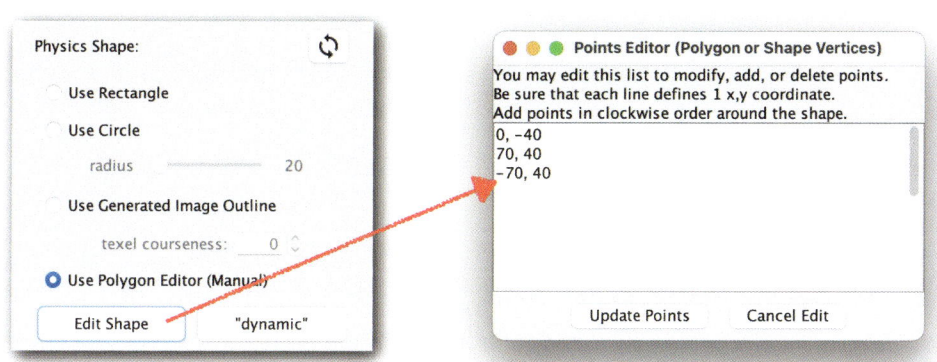

Entering Shape Manually

Potentially an easier way

This can be a bit of a pain, especially with more complex polygons. However, in most cases, you'll be **using an image** rather than a simple shape. In this case, rather than calculating the vertices yourself, you can ask Solar2D to do it. With relatively simple irregular shapes Solar2D can figure out the outline for you using the newOutline() function (in the graphics table).

To access this feature in *Drawn2Code*, select "Use Generated Image Outline" and enter the telex courseness of the shape (see "Automatic Outline").

Notice that you aren't required to specify any point coordinates at all. The `newOutline()` function analyzed the image and recognizes the outline shape for you, with some limitations. Depending on the complexity of the shape, the `newOutline()` function may not create an accurate or usable outline. You may use the "hybrid" draw mode to example the generated outline and see if it matches your expectation. If it doesn't, you can adjust the "texel courseness", which defines how closely you want the outline to follow the precise contours of the shape. A courser setting may allow for a smoother and potentially more useful outline.

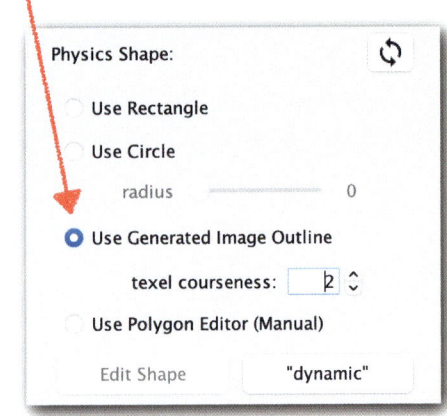

Automatic Outline

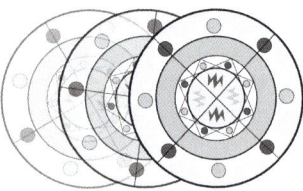

Rolling Instead of Sliding

Making the ball *roll*

Depending on how closely you've adapted the code in these examples, you may notice that the ball **doesn't appear to "roll"**. That is, instead of *rotating* as it moves, it just moves (or maybe "slides"). **It looks strange**. Why does it do this? Well, you need to give the ground and the ball some additional *friction*.

Friction and sliding

As with "real" friction, friction in Solar2D impedes the ability of two surfaces to slide against each other. With friction set to 0, the surfaces will move freely against each other. A value of 1 represents "fairly strong" friction (according to Solar2D). If the friction on the bodies are set too low, the ball won't rotate as it moves.

Getting the onscreen behavior you want may take some **trial and error**.

In *Drawn2Code*, you can easily adjust friction for a specific physics body using the slider in that bodies "Add Body" settings panel (see "Adjusting Friction"). In this way, each physics body can have a unique friction (just as in the real world).

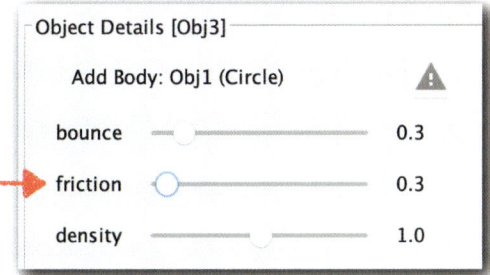

Adjusting Friction

Explore the settings

Open `triangle_magic-ball` (in the chapter download) and experiment a bit with these values.

Set Friction	What happens?
Set ground to 0 and the other bodies to some positive value	
Set the ground to 1, but the ball, lockbox, and ramp to 0	
Change the ramp to 1	
Change the lockbox to 0.5	
Change the ball to 0.5	

Friction and Object Behavior

Try the suggestions in the table "Friction and Object Behavior". Do you notice that, depending on the settings, **completely different** things happen onscreen? In certain cases the ball doesn't *roll*, it *slides*. Setting the friction differently can make the ground seem like ice, mud, concrete, grass, tar, etc.

277

A Stack of Boxes

Fun with loops and timers

Well, there's no denying that dropping stuff and seeing what happens can be fun. But, what if you want *more than just one* of some particular physics body? Maybe you want to stack *several* lockboxes on top of each other? Maybe you want *lots of balls* to drop? That is where loops and timers can be helpful.

You've already used loops in the second demo app in this chapter (`10_bouncing_balls`) to drop 10 balls of increasing bounciness. In this example, you are going to use a 'for' loop to drop objects on top of each other, while carefully adjusting the settings so that you create a stack (rather than a mess). It is a bit harder than you might think.

Let's start with a stack of lockboxes (see the screenshot "A Stack of Boxes"). Instead of just creating one individual lockbox, you'll use a 'for' loop to do it (code box #11).

```
1  for i = 1, 6 do
2      lockbox = display.newImageRect("lockbox.png", 43, 43)
3      lockbox.x = cx + 100
4      lockbox.y = 60*i - 100
5      physics.addBody(lockbox, {density = .6,
6                                bounce = 0,
7                                friction = .5}
8                     )
9  end
```

This will, as you can probably tell, create not 1 but 6 lockboxes. You don't want to put them at the same (x,y) location, because the 2D physics engine will shove objects out of the way of new objects being added with any overlap. This can cause some odd results, so it is better to put them onscreen with no overlap at all.

Play around with the settings and see what happens! You can adjust the density of the lockboxes on line 5, the bounce of the lockboxes on line 6, and the friction of the lockboxes on line 7. If you make the lockboxes just a bit too bouncy, they won't end up stacked, since they'll bounce off each other. If you set your friction too low, the lockboxes won't stack either (they slide off each other as if they were coated in teflon). Finally, fiddle with the density of the ball. If you make it dense enough, compared to the lockboxes, it will knock them over rather than bouncing off of them. To illustrate this, the next section will drop a series of balls of increasing density.

Using timers in place of loops

You can also execute a repetitive task using timers, while also control how quickly (slowly) each repetition occurs. As an example, have a look at the *Drawn2Code* version of the chapter example that drops 10 balls. It does this using a timer that calls a timer handler function every second. Inside the handler function is the code to create and add 1 magic ball to the physics engine (i.e., dropping it).

For example, if you have a function to drop a ball named `dropBall()`, you could drop 10 balls, 1 per second like this:

```
1  timer.performWithDelay(1000, dropBall, 10)
```

The downloadable *Drawn2Code* design for dropping 10 magic balls uses this technique.

Game basics: Runtime and enterFrame

You already know how to use a timer to create ongoing game activity (you did that in Chapter 9 with the fun Buggy apps). However, Solar2D provides another way to achieve this behavior that has some advantages. Solar2D updates your physics-based game at a fixed speed which is, by default, 30 times per second. This is called the "frame rate" of the game and is measured in "frames per second" (or "FPS"). So, the **default frame rate is 30 FPS**. This is essentially a timer that is **already running** that you can tap into to run code of your own.

You can tell Solar2D to **execute a function** of your choosing at the start of every frame (i.e., 30 times per second) by attaching an event listener to the global `Runtime` object. `Runtime` listeners are not attached to any widget, display object, group, etc., and run continuously no matter what is or is not onscreen or what the user is doing. The syntax to attach such a listener is simply:

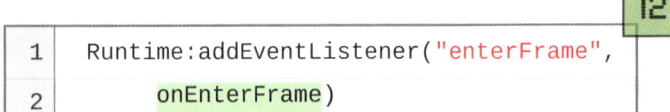

Knocking Down the Crates

The result of executing code box #12 will be that a function named `onEnterFrame()` will be called 30 times per second. As such, you want to be **extra careful** about what you do *inside* that function, since Solar2D will attempt to do whatever you put there 30 times each second.

A Runtime object can be added to your *Drawn2Code* stack via the "Physics" palette. It has a very simple settings panel that allows you to add and remove listeners (the Runtime can listen for multiple types of events simultaneously) such as "enterFrame". For example, if the Runtime object is Obj8, its settings panel would look like "Runtime Settings".

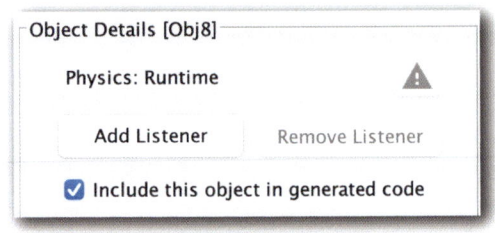

Runtime Settings

The ball drop (stacked_boxes_vs_10_balls)

Let's start with something kind of simple: You're going to use the Runtime listener to drop a ball on to the ramp **every 2 seconds** (see code box #13).

```
1   dropTime = 0
2   ballCount = 0
3
4   function onEnterFrame(e)
5       if e.time - dropTime > 2000 and ballCount < 10 then
6           ball = display.newImageRect("magic-ball.png", 40, 40)
7           ball.x = display.contentCenterX - 120
8           ball.y = -400
9           physics.addBody(ball, {density = ballCount*0.1, bounce
            = .7, friction = 0.5, radius = ball.width*0.45})
11          dropTime = e.time
12          ballCount = ballCount + 1
13      end
14  end
```

As you can see, the ball creation chunk has been **moved inside** the onEnterFrame() function and coded to only execute every 2000 milliseconds (i.e., every 2 seconds). You could slow the FPS down instead (i.e., so that onEnterFrame() was only called every 2 seconds), but that would mess with the physics of the game. So this millisecond-based algebra is the preferred approach.

Additional considerations

First, you are keeping count of the balls created using the variable ballCount, and stopping after 10 *angry* balls (if you don't, it will keep dropping balls until the app is exited). You could add additional frame-based code inside onEnterFrame() (box #13) as well, such as testing to see if something has happened onscreen or to take some action if certain conditions are met. For example, you could also stop the ball drop if the **lockbox tower has been knocked over**. How could you tell that? Well, the y value of the top box will have increased from its landing location.

Second, you are also basing the density of each ball on ballCount (line 10, box #13), so that the density of the balls *increases* with each new one created (this isn't a requirement, obviously, it is just done to make this a bit more interesting). You can play around with these settings on line 10 to get very different results. If you make the balls less dense, they won't knock over the lockboxes and will accumulate in the valley between the ramp and the lockboxes. If you make the first ball dense enough, it will knock the lockboxes right over. You can also start the balls higher up in the air (i.e., by making their y values negative), so that they arrive *later* and are moving *faster* (unless they've reached terminal velocity) when they hit the lockboxes.

One final consideration when using the Runtime event listener is that you should **remove the listener** if and when you are done with it. Otherwise, even after all of your balls have dropped, for example, the function is still being called and the boolean condition is still being evaluated 30 times per second, which is super inefficient (and would waste the user's battery on a mobile device).

Don't Forget

The necessary "removal" code is very similar to the code in box #12, except that you are *removing* the listener instead of *adding* it in code box #14:

```
1  Runtime:removeEventListener("enterFrame", onEnterFrame)
```
14

The removal statement could be called, for example, after the 10 ball limited had been reached, by using code like this at the of end the onEnterFrame() function (i.e., from box #15):

```
1  if ballCount == 10 then
2       Runtime:removeEventListener("enterFrame", onEnterFrame)
3  end
```
15

Note: In *Drawn2Code*, there isn't currently (1.571) a way to do this via a script object, so you'd need to create a snippet with code such as this.

Game basics: Runtime and Touch

Although you've been making apps that respond to user touch since Chapter 4, there's a new approach you can use now that you have access to the Runtime object. Previously, you've needed to attach your "touch" or "tap" listener to **particular widgets or display objects**; however, using Runtime you can **listen to the entire screen**. This makes it possible to add new features that would have been difficult before, such as allowing the user to drop a ball from any location on the screen by simply tapping or touching *there* (either listener works fine, but "tap" is easier).

Step-by-step

Let's do that in *Drawn2Code*, step-by-step:

1. Create a new *Drawn2Code* design and save it to a new folder for this project.
2. Add the "Setup Physics" script object.
3. Add the "magic ball" image to your stack and let *Drawn2Code* copy it to the project folder if needed. Resize it however you would like. The location on screen isn't critical, since we'll be editing that via a snippet in a moment, but place it just above your screen on the design canvas.
4. Add the magic ball display object as a physics body. Although this is an image, it is also a circle, so you are better off using the *circle physics shape*.

    Set the physics shape to the circle with the radio button, then hit the "refresh" button to update the radius automatically.

5. Add the Runtime object and add the "Tap" listener to it. Note that this adds three script objects: The Runtime object, a handler function named "onTap", and a default snippet inside the new function.
6. Move the image and add body script objects into this new "onTap" function.
7. **Save it and test!** If you've followed these steps correctly, you should be looking at an empty simulator screen. But, if you'll tap it, you should see

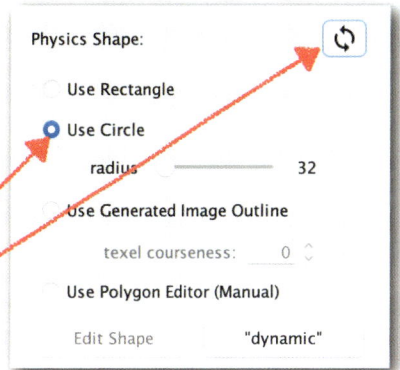

283

magic balls dropping down the screen (or wherever you placed the ball image in step 2).

8. Add a new snippet and type this into it to relocate the ball to the tap locations:

   ```
   Obj1.x = event.x
   Obj1.y = event.y
   ```

9. Move this snippet snippet into the onTap( ) function and shift it up one step in the stack (so that it is below the magic ball image and above the "Add Body" script object. Your stack should look quite a bit like "Tap to Drop Design Stack".

10. **Save it and test!** Now, you should see a magic ball being dropped from wherever you tap! This app will go on forever, just waiting for another tap.

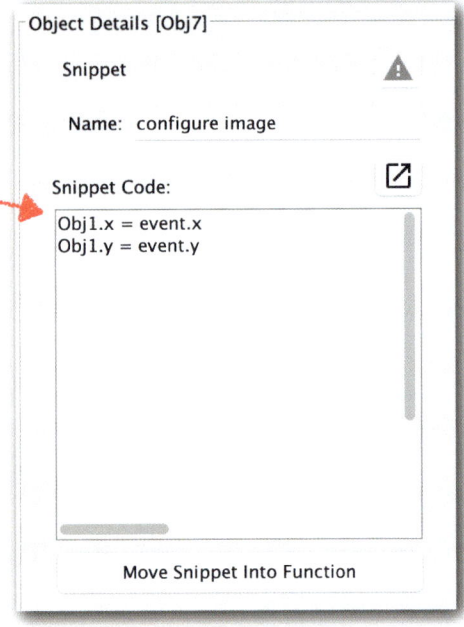

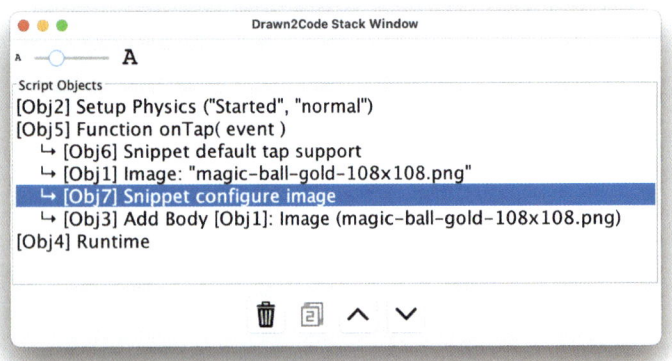

Tap to Drop Design Stack

That's it!

The "tap" generates an (x, y) coordinate you can refer to as "event.x" and "event.y" in the onTap( ) function. That's what we do in the snippet (Obj7), which locates the magic ball Obj1 at the tap location prior to adding it as a physics body. As such, the ball drops directly from the tap location. You can find this in the download as *tap-to-drop_step_by_step.d2c*.

Don't Forget

Note: If you are using "touch" instead of "tap" be sure to drop the ball only if the *touch phase* is "began". If you don't limit the code you execute in this way, it will run two or three times for each touch (since there are three separate touch phases: "began", "moved", and "ended"). Remember, each touch generates both the "began" and "ended" phases and may *also* generate a "moved" phase, if the user moves their finger during the touch. Using "tap" avoids this issue but may not be appropriate for your app.

284

This modification has also been made to the more complete version from the previous section, so that you can drop the magic balls from different heights to get different ricochets from the ramp (*tap-to-drop-stacked-boxes.d2c*).

Using both together

How about an example using both enterFrame and tap? We could create a game with moving platforms by adjusting the position or rotation of a display object inside of onEnterFrame( ). Let's start by creating a small shelf which moves back-and-forth, horizontally across the width of the screen.

Bouncing Platform

1. Create a new *Drawn2Code* design and save it to a new folder for this project.
2. Add a small rectangle as Obj1. I've colored it red.
3. Add the Runtime object and add the "enterFrame" listener to it.
4. Create an app level variable (e.g., in a snippet toward the top of your stack) like this:

   ```
   delta = 2
   ```

5. Inside onEnterFrame( ), perhaps at the end of the default snippet (or a new snipped), add this code to move and switch direction when Obj1 hits the edges of the screen:

   ```
   if Obj1.x + Obj1.width/2 > 320 then
       delta = -delta
    elseif Obj1.x - Obj1.width/2 < 0 then
       delta = -delta
    end
    Obj1.x = Obj1.x + delta
   ```

6. **Save it and test!**

You should see a simple app with a platform bouncing left and right. I've added a magic ball drop as part of *moving-platform.d2c*.

Everything moves

What if you want more platforms? Do you need separate onEnterFrame( ) functions? No! Just add the code for all moving platforms in the same spot. You can create multiple "delta" variables or multiple a fixed delta to scale the speed to what you need.

As a crazy example, I've put together a design with 7 moving objects. In addition to the moving shelf, there are objects rotating (and counter-rotating), rising and falling, and stepping. There's a lot going on and the screenshot doesn't do it justice (see "Everything Moves"). All of this is done in the single snippet inside of onEnterFrame( ). Have a look at *movements.d2c*.

Everything Moves

Summary

Now you are a master of physics! At your command are the key elements that cause and sustain motion in a 2-D world, including gravity, mass, friction, bounce, and density. You know how to create objects and add them as physics bodies so that they will be animated by the physics engine. In addition, you've learned about the Runtime object and how to use it to add touch sensitivity to the entire screen (i.e., not just to an individual display object or physics body).

Up next: collisions, damage, and sound effects (Chapter 13)!

Chapter resources

In the chapter resource download for this book (www.lillipellilabs.com/mobiledev/download/chapter_resources.zip), look for folder "12".

This folder includes these fantastic apps:

1. ball_drop_no_floor
2. bouncing_ball
3. bouncing_magic-ball
4. 11_bouncing_balls
5. triangle_ramp
6. triangle_magic-ball
7. ball_and_box
8. stacked_boxes_vs_1_ball
9. stacked_boxes_vs_10_balls
10. 10_balls_increasing_density
11. stacked_boxes_vs_tap_to_drop
12. tap_to_drop_step_by_step
13. moving_platform
14. everything_moves
15. **BONUS:** Soon to be a classic tap to drop game: *tap-to-drop-domino-knock.d2c*

End-of-chapter exercises

1. Using lockboxes for walls and the triangle ramp for a roof, build a house and then drop 1 **magic ball** on it.
   a. Make sure to confirm that the ball deflects off of the roof correctly (i.e., that the roof is acting as a triangle).
   b. Modify this so that a ball is dropped only when the user taps the screen.
   c. Modify it so that the ball is dropped from the location where the user taps.

2. Create a version of #1 that:

   a. Drops 10 (or more) **magic balls** on it using a timer or a loop.

   b. Make it so that the 10 balls aren't dropped until the use taps the screen.

3. Play around with the density, friction, and bounce values for #1 or #2. Create two apps to demonstrate:

   a. Conditions under which the "house" *impervious to damage*.

   b. Conditions under which it is *easily destroyed*.

4. Modify one of the above apps so that a "drop sound" is played when the user taps the screen.

5. What's your favorite sport that uses a ball? Ping pong? Keep thinking. Find an image of the ball used in your sport and modify one of the above apps to use that kind of ball.

6. Modify #2 so that a drop sound is played for each ball drop.

7. Using loops, can you create a pyramid of lockboxes more than 5 lockboxes tall? Can you land a **magic ball** on the top and have it stay there?

8. Design an app with a series of moving platforms (at least 3) that can carry a dropped **magic ball** from a starting point to an ending point.

9. Using lockboxes and triangles, create a castle that looks at least something like a fictional grand **Wizarding School**.

   a. Add the ability to drop **Wizarding School** "tormentors" onto the school you designed in #8. Yes, "tormentors" can look a lot like **magic balls** (if you can't find or make something better).

< MOB DEV

NOTES

Physics II: Collisions   13

Collisions: Already happening

You might have noticed that in the examples in the prior chapter (Chapter 12) the ball "collided" with the ramp and bounced off of it. The ball also "collided" with the lockboxes and knocked them down (if you played with the settings enough). So, once you start the physics engine, collisions with physics bodies are handled *automatically* by the engine to produce realistic results. So, what are you going to learn in Chapter 13? You are going to **listen for the collisions and then take some additional action** when they occur, such as playing a sound, changing a color, calculating damage, and so on.

Solar2D has some demo apps to help you understand collisions (docs.coronalabs.com/guide/physics/collisionDetection) which use a small wooden crate (a "Corona Crate"). These are nice, but in this chapter you'll learn to work with **vastly superior** steel lockboxes and the magic ball (adapted from Chapter 12).

A Corona Crate

Adding the listener

You can attach a listener to either a *display object* (like a ball or lockbox) or to the *Runtime* object. Note that the listener is not added to the physics body. What you attach it to will determine the **type of information** you can get from the collision event. Let's start by simply adding the listener to your magic ball and dropping it onto a ground, like you did in Chapter 12. Here's the setup for the ball (code box #1):

Steel Lockbox   Magic Ball

```
1  ball = display.newImageRect("magic-ball.png", 40, 40)
2  ball.x = cx
3  ball.y = 0
4  physics.addBody(ball)
5
6  --* add the listener:
7  ball:addEventListener("collision", onBallCollision)
```

Notice on line 7 (box #1) that you are listening for collisions by adding the "collision" (no "s"!) listener and naming your event-handler "onBallCollision". So, you need to provide the function of that name (code box #2):

```
1  local function onBallCollision( event )
2      if e.phase == "began" then
3          --* do something
4          print(event.other)
5      end
6  end
```

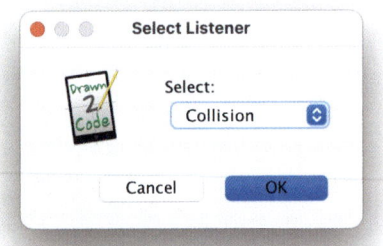

Using *Drawn2Code*, listeners can be added to any display object via the "Add Listener" button in the script object's settings panel. Select "Collision" from the list of options (see "Add Listener Dialog"). As usual, *Drawn2Code* will provide a default event handler named using the object id (e.g., Obj1CollisionHandler) with a default snippet the displays collision data.

Add Listener Dialog

The collision event

The event information (named "event" on line 1 of box #2) that is received by your function (sometimes called "event" — you can use whatever identifier you wish to) is a table describing the collision event.

It includes two key pieces of data:

1. The *identity* of the object that the ball collided with (conveniently named other).
2. The *phase* of the collision (either "began" or "ended"): Each collision has distinct starting and stopping points that allow you to take action at either or both points.

Information about the collision

Notice that collision events, like touch events, have **distinct phases** (in the case of collisions, just "began" and "ended"). So, every collision will fire **both** of these events, just like every user touch does. If you don't want your code to run twice for each collision, you need to limit your response to either the "began" or "ended" phase. In box #2, you can see that you are limiting your action to the moment the collision starts (i.e., its "began" phase).

Just bouncing, that's all

What exactly are you doing in box #2 when the ball hits something? Just trying to write some information about the event out to the console. Unfortunately, if you run this and look at the console, it **isn't super helpful** (output box #3):

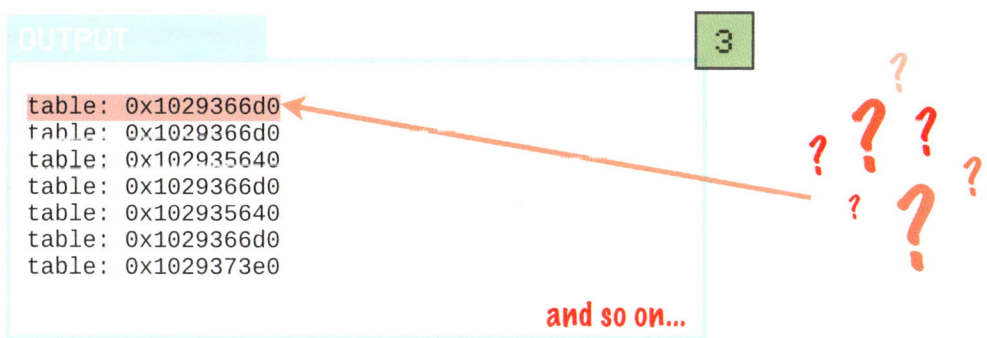

These lines of output (box #3) are giving you the **hexadecimal address** of the "other" object in each collision, which isn't very useful. For example, what is "table: 0x1029366d0"?

Is it the ground? The ball? A lockbox? The ramp? Okay, in this simple app you know what it is, right? It can only be the ground. But for more complex apps, if you are planning on *doing something* with this information, we'll need to find a way to *supply more useful information*.

One easy way to do that is to set the ".id" attribute (or a ".name" attribute) for each of your bodies. For example, you might do that for the ground like this (box #4):

```
ground.id = "The Ground"
```

Then, you can *amend* the print statement in box #2 to look something like this (box #5):

```
print( "The Magic Ball is hitting "..e.other.id )
```

That way, every time a collision occurs, we'll see much **more descriptive** information about it:

```
OUTPUT
The Magic Ball is hitting The Ground
The Magic Ball is hitting The Ground
The Magic Ball is hitting The Ground
The Magic Ball is hitting The Ground
The Magic Ball is hitting The Ground
The Magic Ball is hitting The Ground
```

If you've used the default settings, the ball should bounce about 6 times, reporting that it hit "The Ground" each time (i.e., as shown in output box #6).

Note that, as you might expect, the *Drawn2Code* collision snippet is already set up this way (so you won't see the dreaded HEX addresses). If there is either an id or name attributes set, it will be displayed at the console (see "Default Collision Snippet").

```
-- information about the collision:
if event.phase == "began" then
    if event.other ~= nil then
        if event.other.name ~= nil then
            print("Obj1 colliding with "..event.other.name )
        elseif event.other.id ~= nil then
            print("Obj1 colliding with "..event.other.id )
        end
    end
end
```

Default Collision Snippet

Adding the listener to the Runtime object

Perhaps you want more data about the collision event, such as the names of both objects involved in the collision. Although it is implicit in the previous app (it can only be the ball and the ground), in more complex apps it might not be. This is accomplished by adding the listener to the Runtime object instead of just to a specific UI object, however, the syntax will need another few small tweaks. To start, we'll add the listener:

```
Runtime:addEventListener( "collision", onCollision )
```
₇

The code in box #7 will cause your app to call a function we've identified as "onCollision", so as usual, you must supply that function (code box #8):

```
1  local function onCollision( event )
2      if e.phase == "began" then
3          print (event.object1.name.." hit "..event.object2.name)
4      end
5  end
```
₈

When using the Runtime object, the collisions are reported using the syntax "object1" and "object2" (not "other"). Incorporating these changes into the code (collisions_0_runtime) will yield output something like this at your console:

```
OUTPUT
The Ground hit Magic Ball
The Ground hit Magic Ball
The Ground hit Magic Ball
The Ground hit Magic Ball
The Ground hit Magic Ball
The Ground hit Magic Ball
```
₉

Of course, what happens on screen is identical. The key difference is that you are seeing the actual name attributes of both objects involved in the collisions reported to the console. This additional information may or may not be useful to you, depending on your purpose.

Note the Difference

293

More Collisions To Report

Comparing the two approaches

However, these first examples are meant to be simple. The difference between these approaches might be more apparent if you had more objects on screen, such as your ramp and stack of lockboxes.

Let's compare the output for these two approaches. On the top, you see the output when the event listener is added to the ball (code box #10), while the bottom is the output when the listener is added to the `Runtime` object(code box #11.

In this app, you drop a set of lockboxes (named "Lockbox 1" through "Lockbox 6"), "The Ramp", and "The Magic Ball". See the screenshot "More Collisions To Report" to see what this looks like or, better yet, run the two apps (`collisions_1_ball` and `collisions_1_runtime`).

Again, **what happens on the device screen is identical**, but the information you have available to use in your app is different. Notice also *how* different the information is. It isn't just providing more detail about the same collisions, the bottom output (listening to the Runtime) is reporting **far more collisions**.

In code box #10, you can see the collisions that are occurring with the ball: It hits the ramp first, then lockbox 5 and lockbox 4, before ricocheting back to the ramp. After that, it bounces back to the lockboxes, striking lockbox 6. This is exactly what you should see, if you watch the app run and focus on the ball.

If you are interested in *all* of the collisions, not just those involving the ball, then look at code box #11. As you can see, "Lockbox 6" (the bottom-most lockbox created) hits the ground first, as you would expect. It is the lowest lockbox in the column of lockboxes you create, all falling at the same speed toward the ground and, as such, it hits the ground first. Then, "Lockbox 5" lands on top of "Lockbox 6", and so on.

The collision results reported at the console are understandable as you watch the process unfold on screen and remember what you are listening to (i.e., the ball or `Runtime`, in this case). When testing this, make sure to set your workspace up so that you can see the simulator running and watch the event information showing up simultaneously in the console.

	Add Event Listener to: display object	Add Event Listener to: Runtime object
Available Listeners	collision, preCollision, postCollision	collision, preCollision, postCollision
Event Name of Object(s)	other	object1, object2
Function Placement	above	above
Collisions Information	targeted on display object	covering all possible objects

Listening for Collisions: Where to Add the Listener

These approaches have more similarities than differences. One approach isn't better than another, it depends on your needs. However, there are slight differences in syntax, depending on what you attach the listener to. See the table "Listening for Collisions: Where to Add the Listener" for a summary of some of the key syntax and requirements of these approaches.

```
56  -- information about the collision:
57  if event.phase == "began" then
58    if event.object1 ~= nil and event.object2 ~= nil then
59      if event.object1.name ~= nil and event.object2.name ~= nil then
60        print( event.object1.name.." colliding with "..event.object2.name )
61      elseif event.object1.id ~= nil and event.object2.id ~= nil then
62        print( event.object1.id.." colliding with "..event.object2.id )
63      else
64        print( "colliding object1: "..event.object1 )
65        print( "colliding object2: "..event.object2 )
66      end
67    end
68  end
```

Default Snippet for Runtime Collisions

Note that the *Drawn2Code* default snippet for listening to Runtime collisions provides another example of the appropriate syntax (see "Default Snippet for Runtime Collisions").

Eye on the ball

Let's focus on just the ball and what it collides with. From this vantage point, you'll use the collision data to play a "bounce" **sound** and to visually show which lockbox is being hit (which you'll do by **tinting** the lockbox red). You can start with the basic code from the first example in the prior section (`collisions_1_ball`), which already is focused on the ball. However, you need to add some code to the event-handler ("onBallCollision") to: Play a sound, tint the lockbox that is hit, and un-tint it after the collision is done. You also need a sound effect.

Making your own sound effects

Obviously, to have a sound effect in your app, you will need to have a **sound file** to play. A variety of sound effects are available online, including "free" (as in no cost whatsoever to download or use) and "royalty free" (fee to download, but free to use in commercial projects). Sources include freesound.org (completely free), soundbible.com (free and royalty free), prosoundeffects.com (single and multi-user licenses, royalty free), or even the iTunes Music Store (search for "sound effects library").

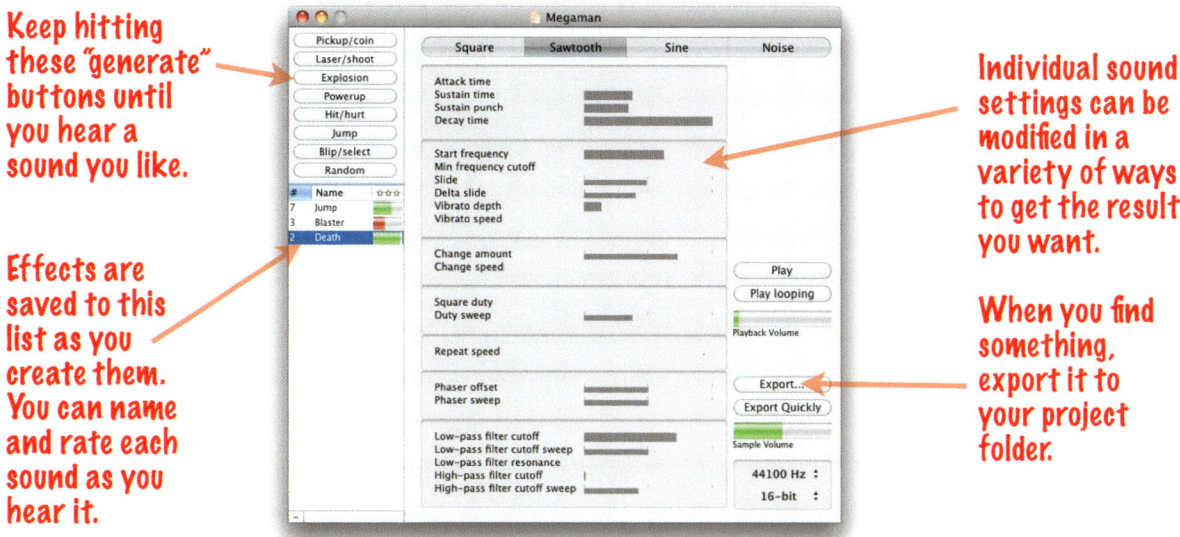

bfxr (Mac) at https://www.bfxr.net

bfxr

In addition, there are a variety of apps that will allow you to **create your own sound effects**, unencumbered by any licensing restrictions. One such app is called "bfxr" and has both Mac and Windows versions. More importantly, it is **completely free**. It is easy to use: start by deciding a "category" for the sound you want from the list at the top, left (see the screenshot "bfxr (Mac)". Then, hit the button for the category you picked to generate a random sound of that type. Keep hitting the button until you hear one that you like, then export that sound to a file to use in Solar2D.

I used bfxr to create a sound effect named "hitSound" to be used when the ball collides with anything ("low-bump.wav", in the chapter download).

You'll load it using the `audio.loadSound()` syntax covered in Chapter 4. This should probably be done *outside* of any function and toward the top of the code, so that it is only loaded once, when the app initially starts. You can then play the sound anytime it is appropriate, using the syntax on line 3 of the event-handler (box #12).

Adding a tint

Inside the event-handler function (box #12), you have access to the object that the ball hit via the syntax `e.other`. So, one way to figure out whether the ball has hit a lockbox is to look at

297

the name (via e.other.name) of the object struck to see if the word "Lockbox" is in it. You do this in line 6 (box #12) with an 'if' statement and the built-in string find() function.

```lua
local function onBallCollision( e )

    audio.play(hitSound)

    -- tint the lockbox that was hit and untint afterwards:
    if tostring(e.other.name):find("Lockbox") ~= nil then
        if (e.phase == "began") then
            e.other:setFillColor(.8, 0, 0)
        elseif (e.phase == "ended") then
            e.other:setFillColor(1)
        end
    end

end
```

The result

With these modifications, the revised app (collisions_2) should be ready to test. The only visual change is that when the ball hits a lockbox (or lockboxes, as the case may be), the lockbox(s) will be **tinted red**. The ball can (somewhat obviously given the screenshot) touch more than one lockbox at a time. As soon as the collision is over, the tinting is removed, so you have to watch closely for it (it was actually tough to get a good screenshot for it — see "Hitting the Lockboxes!").

Finally, you should **hear** the sound playing every time the ball hits something (but not, given how we've coded this, for *other* collisions, such as the ramp hitting the ground or the lockboxes hitting each other, etc.).

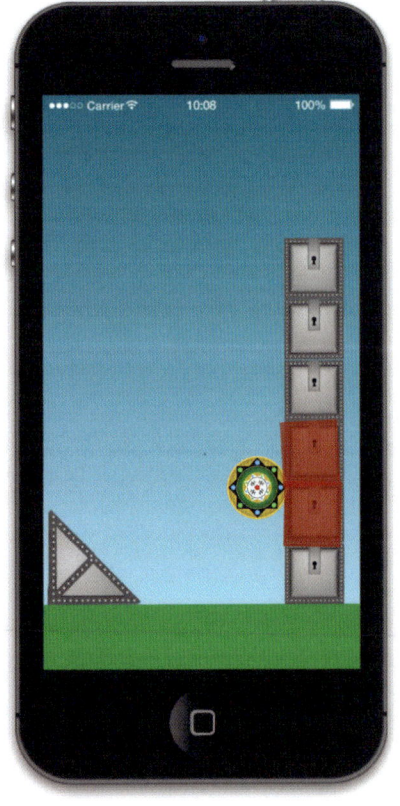

Hitting the Lockboxes!

Damaging the lockboxes

You've hit these lockboxes so many times, it seems unlikely that they wouldn't have suffered any damage at all! And yet, they haven't. To do "damage" to a game object, you'll need a **health or damage attribute** to keep track of how the object is doing. This is easy to do in Solar2D, for example, to add a `damage` attribute the lockbox, it might be as simple as:

```
1  lockbox.damage = 0
2  -- or --
3  lockbox.health = 100
```
13

However, it would also be helpful to have the lockboxes in a Lua table (like an array of lockboxes), so that you can treat them as a group and individually address them. As such, the actual syntax will be slightly different from box #13 (we'll see it in an example below). In addition, wouldn't it be nice to have a way to visually see the "health" or "damaged" state of each lockbox? Yes, it would. This is often done via a "health bar", which gets smaller as damage is taken.

To show this, I've added a green health bar on the right side and a red damage bar on the left of each lockbox:

Healthy Lockbox

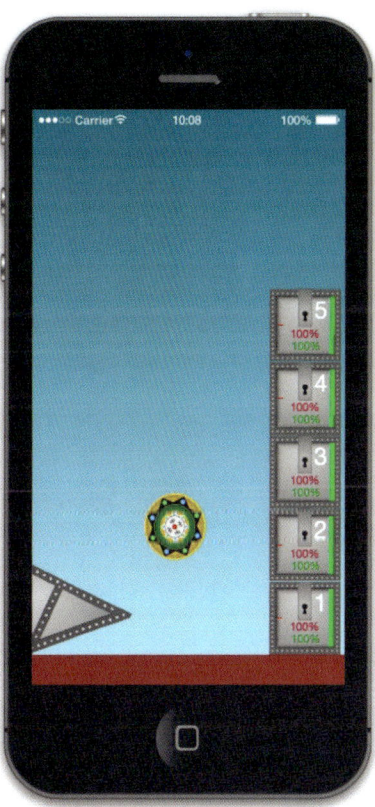

A Stack of Healthy Lockboxes
(About to be Hit)

How is this **magic** accomplished? The status bars are just standard (filled) rectangles, drawn on top of the lockbox image. Both the lockbox image and the status bars are put into a *display group* stored in a table called "lockbox".

See box #14 for the relevant code.

299

```
1  lockbox = {} -- table of lockboxes
2  b = {} -- lockbox images
3  h = {} -- lockbox health bars
4  d = {} -- lockbox damage bars
5  for i = 1, 6 do
6     b[i] = display.newImageRect("lockbox.png", 43, 43)
7     barHeight = b[i].height*.8
8     h[i] = display.newRect(0.33*b[i].width, barHeight*0.5, 3, barHeight)
9     h[i]:setFillColor(0,1,0)
10    h[i].anchorY = 1 -- anchor health bar at the bottom
11    d[i] = display.newRect(-0.33*b[i].width, barHeight*0.5, 3, barHeight)
12    d[i]:setFillColor(1,0,0)
13    d[i].anchorY = 1 -- anchor damage bar at the bottom
14    d[i].scaleY = 0.05 -- start damage near zero (small but visible)
15    lockbox[i] = display.newGroup()
16    lockbox[i]:insert(b[i])
17    lockbox[i]:insert(h[i])
18    lockbox[i]:insert(d[i])
19    lockbox[i].x = cx + 100
20    lockbox[i].y = 60*i - 100
21    lockbox[i].name = "Lockbox "..i
22    lockbox[i].damage = 0
23    lockbox[i].number = i
24    physics.addBody(lockbox[i], {density = .6, bounce = 0, friction = .5})
25 end
```

The lockbox as a display group

There's a lot going on here. For each lockbox, three tables, b, h, and d are stored in a **display group**, which is stored in the table lockbox. The lockbox images and the health/damage indicators, are stored in tables (b, h, and d) to give you easy access to change them later in the code. This is the only real trick and allows each lockbox (display group) to have unique, individually modifiable components. You will need this capability next to change the **tint on the image** (to indicate it is taking damage) and to **adjust the size** (height) of the health indicator bar to reflect this damage.

Setting the status bars

The location of the two status bars are based on the center of the lockbox being (0,0). In addition, you want the **health bar to have its anchor at its bottom** rather than its center, so that as it decreases the user can visually see it dropping. So, you set the anchorY value to 1 (lines 9 and 11, code box #14).

The (x,y) location of the status bars are based on the size of the lockbox and the desired size of the status bar. If you size the status bar at 80% of the height of the lockbox (line 7), you'll get a bar that looks good on the lockbox image. The bars are located to the left (line 10) and right (line 8) of the center of the lockbox image and are 3 pixels wide. The fill color is set as usual, red for the damage bar (line 12) and green for the health bar (line 9).

Tinting and untinting the correct lockbox(es) take II

This does seem needlessly complicated, which I deeply regret. To change the *tint* of the lockbox that is struck and also adjust the status bars, you need to address the specific image and status bars involved in the collision. Although they are part of the display group stored in the lockbox table, they are not easily addressable via this table. However, you have stored them in their own tables (b, h, and d), which *are* addressable if you know the **index number** of the lockbox display group they belong to. So, by storing this index in line 23 (code box #14), you can access it when you need it by using the .number attribute of the group (line 7, code box #15), giving you the ability to change the associated image tint and vertical scale of the indicator bars. It seems a bit kludgy to me, but it works when used in the onBallCollision() event handler (box #15).

15

```
1   local function onBallCollision( e )
2
3       --* play sound on every ball hit:
4       audio.play(hitSound)
5
6       --* index of lockbox that was hit:
7       local i = e.other.number
8
9       --* tint/untint lockbox that ball hit:
10      if tostring(e.other.name):find("lockbox") ~= nil
11          and lockbox[i].damage < 100 then
12          if (e.phase == "began") then
13              c[i]:setFillColor(.8, 0, 0)  -- red tint
14          elseif (e.phase == "ended") then
15              c[i]:setFillColor(1)  -- white removes any tint
16          end
17      end
18  end
```

Notice on line 7 (box #15) that you are getting the index number of the lockbox that was struck and storing it as "i". Then, on line 11, you test to see if the lockbox is still "active" by checking whether the accumulated damage is under 100 and, if so, you apply the red tint (line 13) or remove it (line 15) as appropriate.

Calculating damages

Important

How do you calculate damage and update the health of a lockbox? That is also a bit of a trick. If you want to **base the damage on the force of the collision**, which you do (because that is more realistic for this app), you have to wait until **after the collision has completed**. You do this by using the "postCollision" listener. This is a separate listener from the "collision" listener that you are already using.

Actually, there are three distinct collision listeners:

1. "collision": Tells you when two bodies have collided and gives you the "began" and "ended" phases to work with.

2. "preCollision": Tells you in advance of the collision of two bodies. Solar2D calls this listener "very noisy".

3. "postCollision": Tells you when all collision-related calculations have completed.

To use the "postCollision" listener, you need to do the same two things you just did for the "collision" listener: Attach the listener to the physics body (in your case, the ball) and provide the event-handling function with the name you just specified. I have called the function "onPostCollision", but you may name it whatever you wish. Here's how to hook it up (code box #16):

```
ball:addEventListener( "postCollision", onPostCollision )
```

Remember, this line of code (box #16) needs to be placed after (below) your definition of the attached function ("onPostCollision"). Here's what the function looks like (code box #17):

```lua
--* calculate and update damage on the lockbox that was hit:
local function onPostCollision( e )

    if tostring(e.other.name):find("lockbox") ~= nil then

        -- add damage (adjust 20 to get the damage you want):
        box.damage = box.damage + event.force/20

        -- in general, don't let it go to zero or negative:
        local scaleHealthBar = math.max(1 - box.damage, 0.05)
        -- make sure damage doesn't go over 1 (100%):
        local scaleDamageBar = math.min(1 - scaleHealthBar, 1)

        -- scale the vertical size of the status bars:
        h[box.number].yScale = scaleHealthBar
        d[box.number].yScale = scaleDamageBar

        --* do something with badly damaged lockboxes:
        if h[box.number].yScale < 0.01 then
            print("lockbox["..box.number.."] goes *boom*")
            c[box.number]:setFillColor(.4) -- darken lockbox
        end
    end

end
```

Once again, you are limited in your interest to the collisions between the ball and lockboxes, so you use the same 'if-then' logic to test for this condition (line 4, box #17). You can access the lockbox that was hit using the e.other syntax, with e.other.name getting the name (e.g., "Lockbox 3"). The 'if' statement simply checks to make sure that the word "Lockbox" is present in the object that was hit.

You can access the **force** of the collision with the syntax e.force (which is **only available** via the "postCollision" listener. In this case, I am adding e.force/20 to the accumulated damage of the lockbox that was hit (line 7, box #17). Why do I divide the force by 20? There's no fancy physics involved here! Dividing by 20 provided a "realistic" damage and resulted in the behavior I wanted to see on screen. There's no universal formula that will produce correct results in all circumstances. Just play with the numbers to get the results you are looking for.

In addition, you need to **resize the height of the status bars** using a percentage between 0-100%. So, first you need to know what the percentage is (i.e., how healthy is the lockbox?). A simple formula to do that is `1-box.damage`. Then you rescale both the health status bar (line 15, code box #17) to shrink the bar as health declines and the damage status bar (line 16, code box #17) to grow as damage accumulates..

Finally, lockboxes that are grievously injured are darkened to visually indicate their very poor health (line 22, box #17). We'll cover how to make them **explode** in the next chapter. This app is available in the resources download in folder "13" as "collisions_3_status_bars".

Adjustable damage

For one final example, I've provided a Drawn2Code design which allows you to adjust the density of the magic ball and the amount of damage it inflicts. Both of these can be set using the sliders at the bottom of the app. The damage is live and applies to the **next collision**, while the density applies to the **next ball** you drop (tap to drop a new magic ball).

To make this work, the density is read from the left slider and used in the `addBody()` statement for the magic ball using the `slideDamage` variable (code box #18):

```
slideDamage = round( event.value/10, 0 )
```

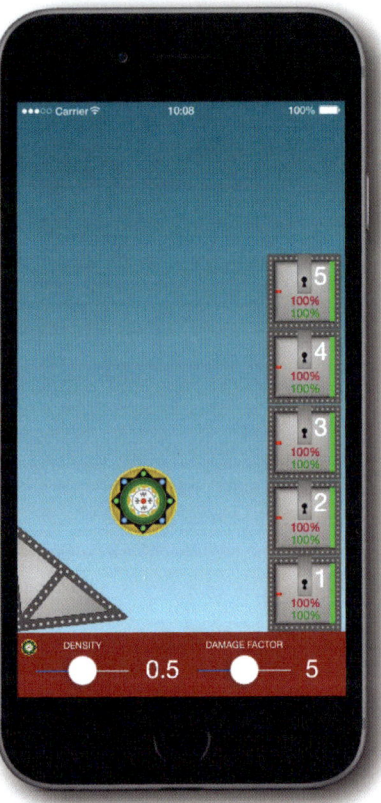

Adjustable Damage!

The slide damage variable is allowed to vary between 0 and 10, using the a `round()` function added to the script stack (since Lua doesn't have a built-in function for this). The slideDamage variable is used in the calculation of damages like this:

```
damageFactor = event.force*(slideDamage/800)
event.other.damage = event.other.damage + damageFactor
```

Note that, since the magic ball is the source of the collision, the lockbox being hit is referenced using the "other" keyword (i.e., event.other). Looking at box #19, you may be wondering where the '800' came from. As with the prior damage calculations, the value is based on getting the results on screen that I wanted (and not due to any complex physics equation).

Since Drawn2Code doesn't (yet) support variables in the addBody() function, the script object with addBody() (Obj41) has been converted to a *snippet* so that it can be edited directly (Obj49). You can see where slideDensity has been inserted in code box #20:

```
physics.addBody( Obj40, "dynamic", { bounce = 0.9,
    friction = 0.2, density = slideDensity, radius = 33 })
```

Note that, in this script stack, Obj40 is the identifier for the magic ball (image) being added to the physics engine.

Summary

In this chapter you have learned the ins and outs (or "crashes and bangs"?) of the collision between two physics bodies. You can listen for collisions in multiple ways, choosing to pay attention to those events that you need to perform some relevant scripting task (such as playing a sound or running a transition). You've learned about the three different collision listeners: preCollision, collision, and postCollision. In general, you will use "collision" to perform tasks that coincide with the immediate collision and "postCollision" to gather information about the impact (or force) of the collision. You learned one technique to create you own, free sound effects using bfxr. Finally, you learned how to implement a "health" bar (or, conversely, a "damage" bar) to physics bodies and adjust this value based on the force of collisions that take place.

 The current release of *Drawn2Code* supports listening to all three collision events and attaching them either to individual physics objects or to a Runtime object. Appropriate default snippets are added in each case.

Chapter resources

In the chapter resource download for this book (www.lillipellilabs.com/mobiledev/download/chapter_resources.zip), look for folder "13".

This folder includes several fantastic apps:

1. collisions_0_ball (just the bouncing ball)
2. collisions_0_runtime
3. collisions_1_ball (ball, ramp, stack of lockboxes)
4. collisions_1_runtime
5. collisions_2_tint_and_sound
6. collisions_3_status_bars (including multiple designs building up to the app with adjustable damage and density)
7. collisions_3_health_bar_alt_syntax (2 variations)
8. **BONUS**: game9 (a thrilling *Drawn2Code* design with moving pieces and a difficult to hit target!). Play until you achieve a score of 5 or more! You start with 9 **magic balls** in the queue. Drop a ball by tapping the queue. You want to get it onto the pink target inside the green pyramid.

End-of-chapter exercises

1. Create a physics app with two "grounds" that a dropping **magic ball** can hit.
    a. Let the user tap-to-drop wherever they want to be able to hear two different collision sounds (i.e., unique for each ground).
    b. Make your own sound effects for each of these collisions.
    c. During each collision, tint the **magic ball** a unique color.

2. Create an app which lets the user tap-to-drop a **magic ball**. Don't provide a "ground" to hit, but play a sound when the ball leaves the screen.

3. Create an app which includes one or more lockboxes, iron-wedges, and **magic balls**. Allow the user to tap to drop a new ball and play different sound effects depending on what the ball hits.

4. Create an app that allows the user to drop a very bouncy **magic ball** on the ground. Keep track and display the number of times the ball bounces.

    a. Play a different sound depending on whether the collision count is *even* or *odd*. You'll need 2 different sounds to make this work.

    b. Add a reset button to set both of the counts back to 0.

5. Extend #3 to count the number of **magic ball** collisions.

    a. Count the number of hits on the the ground and display that number on screen.

    b. Count the number of hits on lockbox(es) and display that number on screen as well.

    c. Count the number of hits on iron-wedge(s) and display that number on screen.

    d. Play different sound effects for each type of collision (i.e., a, b, or c).

6. Modify the `collisions_3_health_bar` app to play an appropriate sound when a lockbox's health is gone.

7. Create an app with a magic ball and a ground. Let the magic ball take damage from the collision.

    a. Tint the ball red during the collisions.

    b. Tint it dark gray and play an appropriate sound when the damage has overcome it.

8. Create a small game with a single ramp (iron wedge) and lockbox. Allow the user to tap to drop a new magic ball. Using a timer, keep track of the x and/or y-value of the lockbox. When it falls off the edge of the ground or is pushed beyond the edge of the screen, drop a new lockbox to replace it.

9. Allow the lockboxes to fight back! Give the magic ball a health or damage attribute and display the damage caused by collisions with lockboxes using a status bar overlaying the ball image.

307

NOTES

Physics III: Explosions

14

Object about to explode
For example, our basic iron lock box, which has taken far too much damage.

Object breaking apart image
Optionally, the original object may be briefly replaced with an image of the object in the process of being destroyed.

Explosion image
Can be cartoonish or realistic and can be layered to create the desired effect.

Explosion sound effect
Like the image, this can be a simple sound (e.g., generated in s/cfxr) or a highly realistic one.

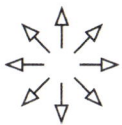

Explosion force
Finally, any objects that are in range of the explosion will need a force (vector) applied to them.

An Explosion in Five Steps

Now that you are a **master of collisions** and understand how to simulate an object taking damage, the final step is to make objects **explode**. So, how do you make stuff go "boom"? Explosions typically involve multiple and overlapping steps the create the effect of blowing something up (see "An Explosion in Five Steps").

To make this happen in your apps, you'll need to:

1. **Remove the object** (i.e., a physics body like the iron lock box) that has been destroyed. Optionally, you could transition it to an image of the object, say, breaking apart, before removing it completely. Objects can be removed using the `display.remove()` function or simply made transparent.

2. Display an **explosion image** of some kind. Explosion images can be *cartoonish* (and quite simple) or *photo-realistic*, depending on your game. In addition, the explosion image may be animated using transitions and/or displayed in multiple stages to improve the effect. For example, images may be randomly sized and rotated (so that they appear somewhat different each time), transparency can be adjusted (to provide a sense of depth), and you may use `transition.to()` to animate any of these image characteristics.

   In any case, for most explosions you will probably want to use a png file with a transparent background. There are a variety of sources online for free "explosion" graphics, however, somewhat cartoonish ones can be easily designed using tools like Photoshop, Pixelmator, and other drawing and editing programs. The simple version used in this chapter was created in about 10 minutes using OmniGraffle.

3. Play a suitably **explosive sound**. As with the explosion image, you have several options when picking a sound. For example, the sound can be a simple sound generated by a tool like bfxr (as is the one you will use in this chapter), a recorded sound, or a sound downloaded (and perhaps purchased) from an online sound effects web site. Like the images, sounds can also be played in multiple channels, to allow for overlapping sounds that may be tied to the appearance of individual explosion images.

4. Finally, you may also wish to apply an **explosive force** to objects in the vicinity of the blast, propelling such objects away from the exploding object and potentially **causing damage** based on their nearness to the blast. This is, perhaps, the most complex step as it involves a bit of algebra and a basic understanding of geometry and trigonometry.

Although this may sound somewhat difficult, it is actually fairly easy. Let's start with a simple example.

An exploding iron box

For your first app you will produce an iron lock box that will **explode** when tapped. That's all. No need for any fancy physics or collision detection. So, you'll need a basic box image placed randomly onscreen. Since this will be done repeatedly (after the box is destroyed), you should put it in a function (box #1):

```
1  function dropIronBox()
2      box = display.newImageRect("iron_box.png", 43, 43)
3      box.x = cx + math.random(-cw*0.45, cw*0.45)
4      box.y = cy + math.random(-ch*0.45, ch*0.45)
5      box:addEventListener("tap", onBoxTapGoBoom)
6  end
```

You are using the basic "iron_box.png" image (line 2) you've used in prior chapters, that you are randomly locating it (lines 3-4), and adding the "tap" listener connected to a function named "onBoxTapGoBoom" (line 5). Now, you need to write this tap event handler (box #2). There are a couple of things in this function (box #2) that need a bit of explanation. First, you need to handle *multiple taps*, since you just want to detonate the iron box once. A second or third tap during the animated explosion will cause some odd behavior onscreen, which you'd like to avoid. So, you **only blow the box up one time**, when it is fully visible (i.e., its alpha is 1) and on the first tap (this logic is found on line 4).

Second, since the box is being removed (lines 11-12), the values for box.x and box.y won't be available afterwards. However, all of the other images need to be centered on that point, so you'll save the box's location in a table called "boom" (lines 7-8) before removing it. After that, you can use boom.x and boom.y to locate the explosion effects.

And what are the "explosion effects"? Well, there are two shown here (box #2): The cartoonish explosion image (`boom_img`) and an image of the iron box breaking up (`iron_box_breakup`). These are both displayed and animated using `transition.to()`. The exact values for the settings (i.e., the animation delays and times) are the result of trial and error and can be adjusted to meet your own requirements.

Finally, you use a timer on line 34 to drop a new iron box (to replace the exploding one) after 1 second. This app is available in the chapter download as `explosions_0`.

```lua
function onBoxTapGoBoom( e )
    --* need to filter out multiple taps or taps during animation:
    if e.numTaps == 1 and box.alpha == 1 then

        --* store box location:
        boom.x = box.x
        boom.y = box.y

        --* remove box image:
        box:removeSelf()
        box = nil

        --* play sound:
        audio.play(boom_snd)

        --* fade in and out the explosion image:
        boom_img = display.newImageRect("explosion.png", 160, 160)
        boom_img.x = boom.x
        boom_img.y = boom.y
        boom_img.alpha = 1
        boom_img.xScale = 0.2
        boom_img.yScale = 0.2
        transition.to(boom_img, {time = 50, xScale = 1, yScale = 1})
        transition.to(boom_img, {delay = 800, time = 1000, alpha = 0})

        --* optional break iron box up:
        box_breakup =display.newImageRect("box-breakup.png",100,100)
        box_breakup.x = boom.x
        box_breakup.y = boom.y
        transition.to(box_breakup, {time = 1800, alpha = 0})

        --* drop a new box so the fun can continue:
        timer.performWithDelay(1000, dropCrate)
        return true
    end
end
```

Dropping a bomb

Now it's the *bomb*

In this second example you'll let the user drop a magic bomb on an iron box. How is a magic bomb different from a magic ball? Well, it isn't really, but when it hits an iron box you will make the box *explode* (collisions_1).

So, you need a basic physics app with sound effects, a ground (onto which you'll drop a randomly-located iron box). You'll put the iron box-dropping code into a function, which will enable us to drop additional boxes as the player destroys them (box #3).

```
1  local physics = require "physics"
2  physics.start()
3
4  local bounce_snd = audio.loadSound("low-bump.wav")
5  local boom_snd = audio.loadSound("boomSound.wav")
6
7  ground = display.newRect(cx, ch, cw, 10)
8  physics.addBody(ground, "static", {friction = 0.5})
9
10 box = {}
11 local function dropIronBox()
12     box = display.newImageRect("iron_box.png", 60, 60)
13     box.x = cx + math.random(-cw*.45, cw*.45)
14     box.y = 100
15     box.name = "Box"
16     physics.addBody(box, {density=.5, bounce=.2, friction=.5})
17
18 end
19 dropIronBox()
```

Next, you'll set it up so that a bomb is dropped from the point where the user/player touches the screen (i.e., {e.x, e.y}).

313

To do this, you'll need to add the "touch" listener to `Runtime` and link it to a function that will execute in response to the touch (box #4):

```lua
local function dropMagicBomb(e)
    --* setup and drop the ball:
    if e.phase == "began" and bomb == nil then
        bomb = display.newImageRect("magic-ball.png", 32, 32)
        bomb.x = e.x
        bomb.y = e.y
        bomb.name = "MagicBomb"

        physics.addBody(bomb, {density = .1,
            bounce = .6, friction = 0.5,
            radius = bomb.width*0.45})

        --* track the ball:
        bomb:addEventListener("collision", onMagicBombCollision)
    end
end

Runtime:addEventListener("touch", dropMagicBomb)
```

Note that controlling for the *touch* phase (i.e., line 3 in box #4) isn't needed if using the *tap* listener. However, if dragging this object is part of your game design, you'll need to remember to do this. Notice also on line 14 that you are identifying the function you want to run when something collides with the bomb (i.e., when the bomb *hits* something). You are calling this function `onMagicBombCollision` (box #5).

Box #5 is performing a simplified version of the explosion animation (note that there's no box break-up included here), but it has to do it for both the bomb itself and — if it hits the box — the box as well. So, code box #5 has three main tasks:

1. Blowing up the bomb (lines 4 - 10).
2. If the bomb hit the iron box, blow it up too (lines 15 - 21).
3. Dropping a new iron box after a 2 second (2000 millisecond) delay (line 24).

As such, depending on whether your player hits the iron box or not, the results will be slightly different. If the "bomb" hits the ground, it explodes by itself. If, however, your player has practiced, they might be able to hit the box. Actually, since the box isn't moving, it's pretty easy. If they do happen to hit the box, it will explode as well (i.e., there will be 2 explosions).

```
local function onMagicbombCollision( e )

    --* blow up the bomb:
    audio.play(boom_snd)
    boom_img = display.newImageRect("explosion.png", 120, 120)
    boom_img.x = bomb.x
    boom_img.y = bomb.y
    transition.to(boom_img, {time = 1000, alpha = 0})
    bomb:removeSelf()
    bomb = nil

    --* if bomb hit the iron box:
    if tostring(e.other.name):find("Box") ~= nil then
        --* blow it up too:
        audio.play(boom_snd)
        boom_img = display.newImageRect("explosion.png",120,120)
        boom_img.x = box.x
        boom_img.y = box.y
        transition.to(boom_img, {time = 1000, alpha = 0})
        box:removeSelf()
        Box = nil

        --* drop a new iron box so the fun can continue:
        timer.performWithDelay(2000, dropIronBox)
    end
end
```

See what it looks like falling and hitting the box (`explosions_1`) in the "Yes...YES...YESSS!" screenshots.

Yes...YES...YESSS!

An iron box that takes proximity damage

Next, let's adapt the example from Chapter 13 that had the health/damage bar added to the iron box. This is a bit more involved, but offers a more realistic game object destruction. This app will involve making 2 key modifications to `explosions_1` (the new example is, as you might have guessed, called `explosions_2`):

1. Change the iron box body to a display object that contains the image and the health bar. Add an attribute to the box for damage (i.e., add ".damage").

2. Add a "blast radius" (which is a circle display object) to the bomb and calculate the damage done to the box by its distance from the center of the blast radius. Use that damage calculation to update the health bar and determine when to explode the iron box.

Blast Radius

The blast radius circle could be invisible (i.e., `alpha = 0`), however, I prefer to *see* it — at the very least for **debugging** purposes. But, it can actually make the blast look a bit more realistic if it has the right color and transparency. Either way, the first step is to update the `dropCrate()` function (box #6).

The `box` is now a display group that includes the box image (`box_img`) and the health bar rectangle (`health_bar`). The `box` also includes the damage attribute (added on line 21), initially set to 0.

```
1   box = {}
2   c_img = {} -- iron_box img
3   health_bar = {} -- box health/damage bar
4
5   local function dropIronBox()
6
7       --* a box is an image and a damage bar:
8       c_img = display.newImageRect("iron_box.png", 60, 60)
9
10      barHeight = c_img.height*.8
11      health_bar = display.newRect(0.33*c_img.width, barHeight*0.5, 3,
12                      barHeight)
13      health_bar.anchorY = 1
14
15      --* assemble the box:
16      box = display.newGroup()
17      box:insert(c_img)
18      box:insert(health_bar)
19      box.x = cx + math.random(-cw*.4, cw*.4)
20      box.y = 100
21      box.damage = 0
22      box.name = "Box"
23
24      physics.addBody(box, {density = .5, bounce = .4, friction = .5})
25
26  end
```

The dropMagicBomb() function is unchanged from the previous example, however, the onBombCollision() function has been changed significantly (box #7). You still start by blowing the bomb up when it hits something (box #7, lines 4-8), but you add the new blast radius circle (lines 11-13).

Once you have that circle, you can use it in a couple of ways. Right now, you are just using it to visually indicate the radius of damage the blast causes (in other words, for this example, the blast radius circle isn't required). You'll use it as a sensor body in your last example of the chapter.

317

```lua
local function onBombCollision(self, e)

    --* blow up the bomb:
    audio.play( boom_snd )
    boom_img = display.newImageRect("explosion.png", 120, 120)
    boom_img.x = bomb.x
    boom_img.y = bomb.y
    transition.to(boom_img, {delay = 100, time = 1000, alpha = 0})

    --* calculate damage (if any) using a blast radius:
    blast_radius = display.newCircle(bomb.x, bomb.y, boom_image.width)
    blast_radius:setFillColor(.8, 0, 0, .5)
    transition.to(blast_radius, {delay = 100, time = 1000, alpha = 0})

    --* calculate distance using a^2 + b^2 = c^2:
    distance = ((bomb.x - box.x)^2 + (bomb.y - box.y)^2)^0.5

    --* close enough to cause damage?
    if distance < 150 then
        damage = 150-distance
        box.damage = box.damage + damage
        if box.damage > 100 then box.damage = 100; end
        --* update health/damage bar:
        scaleDamage = 1-box.damage/100
        health_bar:scale(1, scaleDamage)
    end

    --* done with bomb:
    display.remove( bomb )
    bomb = nil

    --* blow box up too?
    if health_bar.yScale < .02 then
        --* yes!
        audio.play( boom_snd )
        boom_img = display.newImageRect("explosion.png", 180, 180)
        boom_img.x = box.x
        boom_img.y = box.y
        transition.to(boom_img, {delay = 100, time = 2000, alpha = 0})

        --* done with box:
        display.remove( box )
        box = nil

        --* drop a new box so the fun can continue:
        timer.performWithDelay(2000, dropIronBox)
    end
end
```

The box's `damage` is calculated such that it decreases the farther the box is from the explosion. Past 150 pixels, there's no damage at all. The health/damage bar is adjusted accordingly (lines 24-25). Okay, so where did 150 come from?

Geometry

WARNING: This the following discussion may cause a **flashback** to grade-school geometry that, for some, could be uncomfortable. You might remember asking your parents "when will I EVER use this?". Well, today's the day.

Theoretically, with a circle of radius 120 and a square box of width 60, the maximum distance between the center of the box and the center of the circle would be at least 150 pixels. Why? Remember that the reference point for each body is at its center, so the distance from the center of your blast circle to its edge is 120. If the side of the box was just touching the edge of the circle, the distance away would be at least half the width of the box, or 60/2 (which is 30). That's how you get to 150. See the figure "Max Distance that Still Causes Damage is 150".

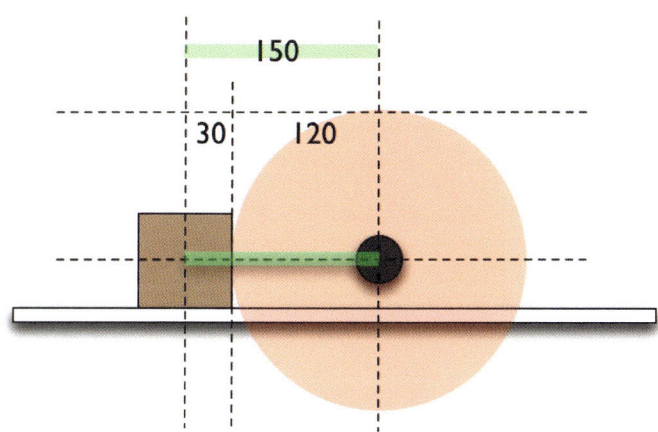

Max Distance that Still Causes Damage is 150

However, the **distance could be greater**. If the bomb exploded at the point were the edge of the blast circle touched the a corner of the box (instead of orthogonally, at the one side), the distance between the center of the circle and the center of the box would be more (just over 150). Of course, in this app, although there's no way for the bomb to explode in mid-air, it will explode when it hits the top of the box. In any case, for these purposes 150 works fine. Note that, in the downloadable examples, these literal values have been replaced with variables representing the width of the box and such, to make the apps easier to modify.

Although it isn't needed for your app, let's briefly consider the closest distance that the bomb and iron box can reach. Although you might guess that it is zero, it isn't (and stop guessing!). Since the distance is measured between the centers of the two objects, the closest the bomb and the box can come is half the width of the box plus the radius of the bomb, or 46 pixels. See the figure "Min Distance is Max Damage". This distance will represent the highest damage your bomb can inflict (unless you put it inside the box!).

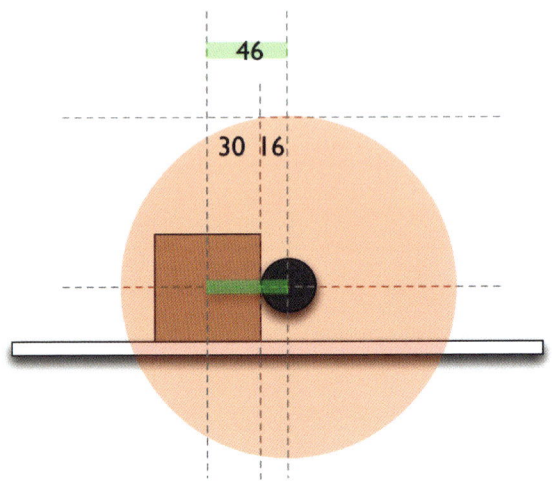

Min Distance is Max Damage

Finally, when the health/damage bar is too small to see, the iron box is exploded as well (box #6, lines 35-39), the box display group is removed from memory (42-43), and — after a 2 second delay — a new iron box is dropped in a random location (46). This app is available in the chapter downloads as `explosions_2` (for both ZBS and *Drawn2Code* users).

Applying a blast force

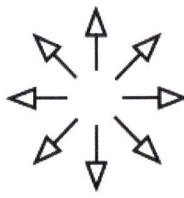

What if you don't want the blast to *destroy* the iron box? What if you want the box (or other object) to be *pushed away* by the "force" of the blast? That is also pretty easy to do, although the mechanics of getting a realistic force are a bit involved. Since your objects aren't moving when they collide (i.e., the blast radius circle and the iron box), there's no *force of impact* calculated by the physics engine. Instead, you need to calculate the blast force manually, based (again) on the distance between the center of the iron box and the center of the blast radius (which is the center of the bomb at impact).

Most of the calculations are done in a new function named `explode()`. This function figures out the distance between the bomb and the box as well as the horizontal and vertical distances (`dx` and `dy`). If the distance is greater than the value discussed above (150), then a blast force is applied to the iron box (which is what you are focusing on) via a function named `blast_force()` (box #8), which is a local function inside of `explode()`.

```
local dx = (bomb.x-box.x)
local dy = (bomb.y-box.y)
distance = math.sqrt(dx*dx+dy*dy)

local function blast_force(e)

    signX = dx/math.abs(dx)
    signY = dy/math.abs(dy)

    power = 11000
    fx = -power*dx/distance^2
    fy = -power*dy/distance^2

    b = {}
    b.x = box.x+signX*math.min(box.width*.5,math.abs(dx))
    b.y = box.y+signY*math.min(box.height*.5,math.abs(dy))

    box:applyForce(fx, fy, b.x, b.y)

end
```

This is somewhat more convoluted than I had hoped for. Frankly, there might be a simpler way to do this while still getting "realistic" results. The key line of code is line 18 (box #8), which applies the "blast" force to the box.

The function `applyForce()` is built-in to Solar2D, but you have to supply the 4 parameters:

1. The amount of force to apply along the x-axis
2. The amount of force to apply along with y-axis
3. The x location of the point at which you want to apply the force (`b.x`)
4. The y location of the point at which you want to apply the force (`b.y`)

Without going into detail on the algebra, you can see that the force applied is based on the relative positions of the iron box and the bomb and a calculation of the distance between the centers of the two objects. Much beyond that, the calculations don't make a great deal of sense, but they do produce seemingly good results.

Where to apply the force?

The location `{b.x, b.y}` is calculated to be the roughly location where the line of force from the bomb blast would hit the iron box. This may seem like an odd detail to include. **Why not just apply the blast force to the center of the iron box?** Well, although you *can* do that, the results *aren't completely satisfying*. If you apply the force to the center of the box, the **box won't "roll" or "tumble"** away from the blast as you would expect. Rather, it stays perfectly "upright" while moving sideways along its arc of motion. That looks kind of peculiar.

One solution is to move the location at which the force is applied, which produces the sought after tumbling effect.

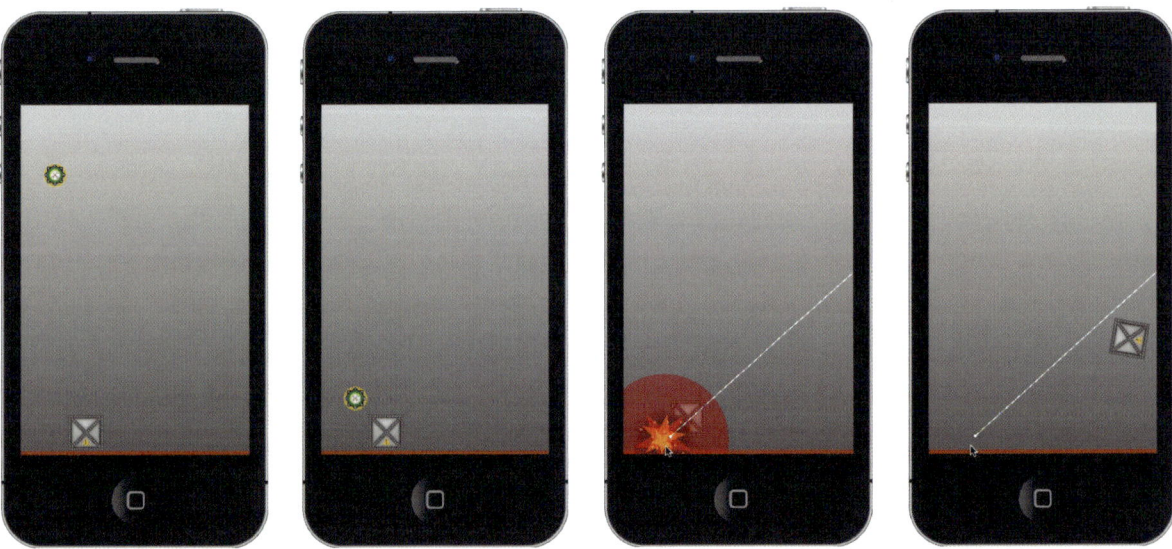

On a Roll: Applying a Force to the Crate

Lines of force

This app (`explosions_3`) also includes code to optionally display the "line of force" that the calculations produce. This is the vector which is applied as force to the iron box to push it away from the blast. This is interesting to see, and really helpful for debugging. The tiny circle on the visible end of the line of force is the location on the edge of the box {b.x, b.y} that you are applying the force to (for example, see the figure above). The length of the line represents the amount of force being applied. In this case, since the bomb exploded right next to the box, a **large force** is applied.

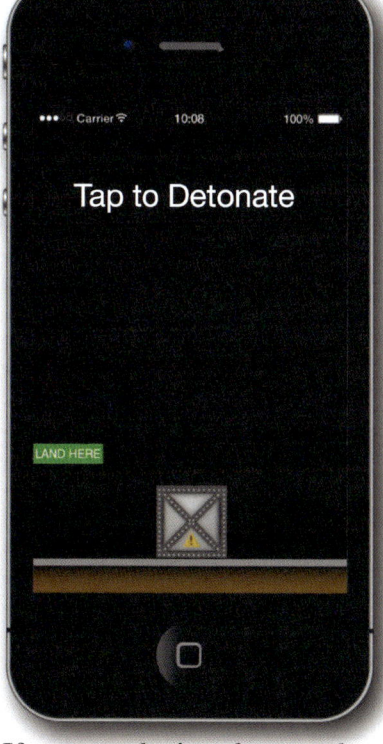

If you get the iron box on the shelf with just one explosion, you get 100!

Drawn2Code: More of a game

The *Drawn2Code* versions of this app are slightly different. The initial version (explosions_3a) starts more simply, without need a bomb to drop. Instead, the force "explodes" from wherever you tap. The closer you tap to the center of the iron box, the stronger the force applied. In addition, there is a small, green shelf. Can you get the box to land on the shelf? The next two versions add a bit more to the gaming aspect of this app. Visual explosions are added to version "b", along with a score-keeping system and code necessary to end the game by detecting when the iron box is successfully moved to the shelf.

Game Ending

Version "c" adds a second level by moving the shelf to a new location and powering up the blast force by 33%. Finally, version "d" moves the blast force calculations and application to a function `blastForce( source, target )`. In the app, when the screen is tapped, I call `blastForce( event, Obj1 )`, which passes the location of the blast (in the event table) and the target of the force (in this case, the iron box: `Obj1`).

You should be able to reuse the `blastForce()` function in your own physics-based games (i.e., that require a force reaction to an event like an explosion). Have fun!

Keeping your eye on the iron box

Both the coded-by-hand and *Drawn2Code* examples need to keep track of the location of the iron box for some of the features to work. In the *Drawn2Code* example (game), the app needs to detect when a box has landed on a shelf, while the by-hand example needs to know when to drop a new iron box. Both examples work similarly, using a Runtime "enterFrame" listener to check the location of the box to determine whether it has settings at a particular y value (i.e., it is sitting on a shelf) or has been blown offscreen (requiring a new box to be dropped).

In the *Drawn2Code* apps (specifically version "d"), I check the box location every second and compare it's current location to the previous location (i.e., 1 second ago). If the location has settled on a preset value (the location of the shelf), then I know the box has **landed there successfully**. The basic logic looks like this (code box #9, *Drawn2Code* Obj32):

```lua
if event.time - lastTime > 1000 then

   lastTime = event.time
   currentY = math.floor(Obj1.y)
   shelf1Y = 296
   shelf2Y = 246

   if not gameOver then
     --* check if iron box has landed on the shelf:
     if gameLevel == 1 and lastY == currentY and currentY == shelf1Y then
       --* won level 1!
       --* move shelf to level 2
     elseif gameLevel == 2 and lastY == currentY and currentY == shelf2Y then
       gameOver = true
     else
       --* update previous y:
       lastY = currentY
     end
   else
     --* game is over
     --* remove listeners
     Runtime:removeEventListener( "tap", onTap )
     Runtime:removeEventListener( "enterFrame", onEnterFrame )
   end
end
```

Refer to *Drawn2Code* design "exposions_3d.d2c" for the details omitted from code box #9.

The coded-by-hand example drops a new iron box if the current box has been blown off screen. In this app I use a timer to check the location of the box 4 seconds after a blast by calling a function `needNewIronBoxCheck()` (line 13, box #10). This function checks to see whether the box has fallen **past the bottom of the screen** or is **off screen to the left or right** (and still falling!). If so, I call the `getNewBox() function` to drop a new box.

```
1   local function needNewIronBoxCheck(e)
2       if box then
3           if box.y > display.contentHeight
4               or box.x < 0
5               or box.x > display.contentWidth then
6
7                   getNewIronBox()
8
9           end
10      end
11  end
12
13  timer.performWithDelay(4000, needNewIronBoxCheck)
```

Why every 4 seconds instead of every second? That's just the amount of time it takes to drop a bomb and blow a box off screen. If you check too early, then the box is still on screen. Since this approach only runs the timer once, the delay has to be long enough to ensure that it will not perform the check **too soon**.

Alternate approaches

Of course, as an alternative, you could repeat the timer and then cancel it when you create a new iron box (which would allow us to check more often and drop a new box more quickly). Or, you could also use the Runtime approach used in the *Drawn2Code* example above. Although it requires a bit more syntax, it does not require that you stop the timer (since there wouldn't be a timer; you would, however, want to remove the Runtime "enterFrame" listener). So, there are different approaches to performing this same task. The "right one" is the one you get working!

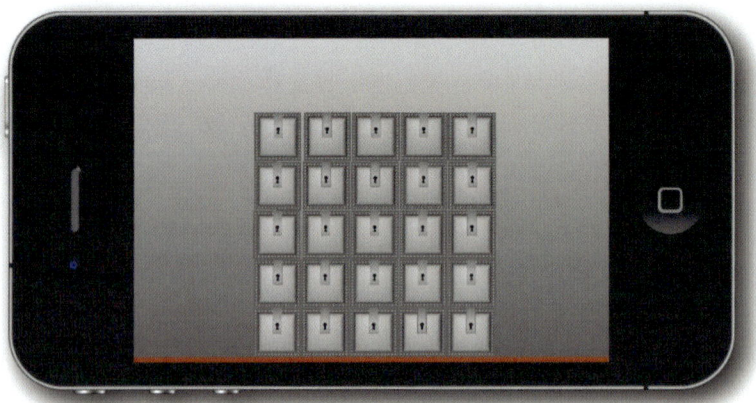

A Palette of Iron Boxes

A pallet of boxes

As one final example, let us consider the situation in which there are many objects onscreen you wish to effect via an explosion. In this case, that means a pallet of iron boxes (see "A Palette of Iron Boxes"). The technique is **very similar** to what we've been doing. However, to allow us to place a bomb (or bombs) inside the pallet (or wherever you want), instead of detonating immediately on contact, the bombs go off after a short delay. This actually simplifies things a bit, since you don't have to keep track of the bomb colliding with anything.

Also, since the boxes end up hitting each other, they will start rolling and tumbling without needing to do anything very special, which simplifies the calculations a bit. You can apply your force **directly to the center of the box**, instead of needing to calculate a good place on each individual box to apply the force.

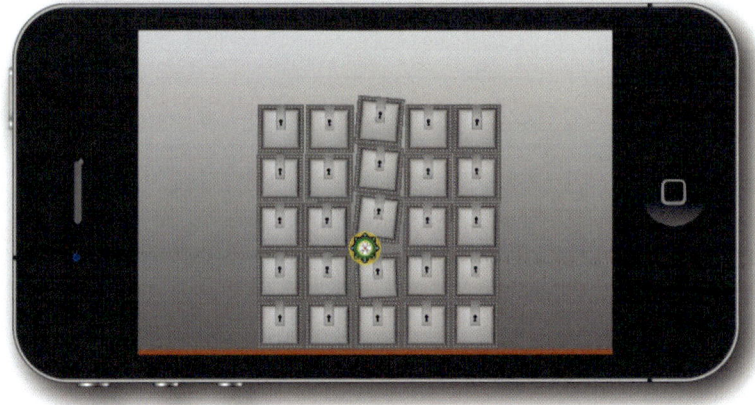

You May Place the Bomb Anywhere

Blast Radius and Application of Force

Using the blast radius

That said, you do need to **apply a force to each box** caught in the explosion. You could loop through a table containing the boxes, however, the approach used here a bit more clever. The code attaches a **collision listener to the blast_radius** (i.e., the circle display object in red you see above), then applies the force to any boxes it collides with. While the blast radius may not reach every single box, the applied forces push even untouched boxes away (much like an actual explosive force).

But, how do you make your app run sideways?

A landscape app

You might have noticed that this app is running in landscape mode (i.e., sideways). However, there's nothing in the code for the app that does this (if you've already peeked). You might suspect that this setting can be found in the "config.lua" file, but it isn't. The settings for the supported device orientations for your app are in the file "build.settings" and can be seen in code box #11.

```
1  settings = {
2      orientation = {
3          default = "landscapeRight",
4          supported = {"landscapeLeft", "landscapeRight"}
5      }
6  }
```

11

In the absence of a `build.settings` file in your project folder, the app will default to "portrait" mode and will allow the user to rotate the device through the four possible modes:

1. "portrait"
2. "portraitUpsideDown"
3. "landscapeLeft"
4. "landscapeRight"

In many apps you will want to limit the device to either modes 1 & 2 or 3 & 4, depending on your UI design. The device (but not the simulator, oddly) will be limited to whichever modes are listed as "supported" in the `build.settings` file.

In *Drawn2Code*, switching to a landscape app is easy. In the toolbar, simply toggle the orientation of the app using the "Orient" button:

If this is a new project, one which hasn't been saved already, a correct "build.settings" file will be created for you when you save the design (and generated code). However, if you are switching the orientation on a current project (i.e., one that has already been saved), you'll need to manually delete the "build.settings" file from the project folder and then save the design again. If so, you'll see the warning message below ("Orientation Warning").

A Beginner's Guide Using Solar2D

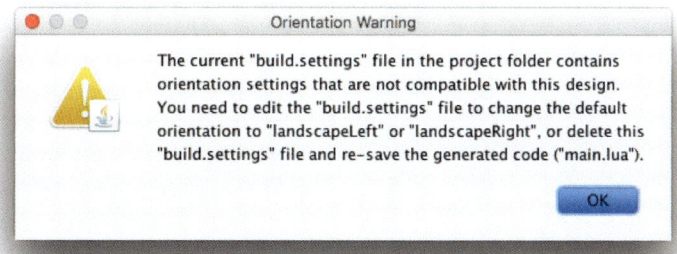

Orientation Warning

By default, *Drawn2Code* won't delete or overwrite an existing "build.settings" file (or "config.lua" file), so you need to trash the correct file yourself. You can do this within *Drawn2Code* if you wish, using the button on File settings panel (see "File Settings Panel").

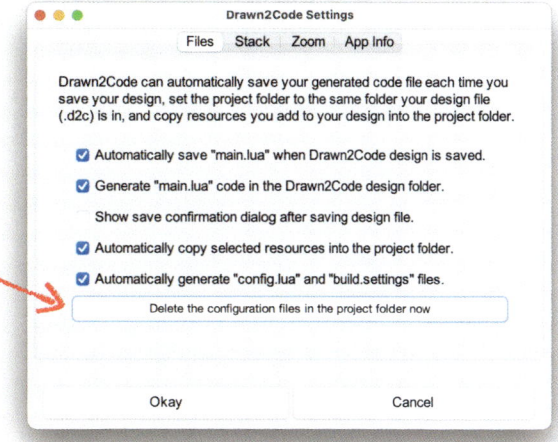

This app is available in the download archive as explosions_pallet. As you play around with it, remember you can place multiple bombs.

File Settings Panel

Summary

In this chapter you have learned how to make a display object "explode" by carefully weaving together transitions, sound effects, and forces pushing outward from the detonation. Together, these provide an effective onscreen simulation of an explosion. Depending on your goals, the explosion can be more cartoonish or more photo-realistic, and sound effects can be likewise tailored as appropriate.

The current release of *Drawn2Code* supports transitions, sound effects, and the physics required to calculate blast forces and apply them to surrounding objects, although the math behind this will need to be adapted to the design of your app. In addition, when adding display groups as physics bodies, *Drawn2Code* will (optionally) insert code to re-center the group at (0,0) so that the physics body will match the actual location of the group.

329

Chapter resources

In the chapter resource download for this book (www.lillipellilabs.com/mobiledev/download/chapter_resources.zip), look for folder "14".

This folder includes these fantastic apps:

1. explosions_0 (tap the box to explode)
2. explosions_0_alt (add the breaking up effect)
3. explosions_1 (tap to drop a magic bomb)
4. explosions_2 (blast radius and proximity damage)
5. explosions_3 (including version a-d as *Drawn2Code* designs)
6. explosions_pallet (landscape app with pallet of boxes)

Resources mentioned:

Adobe Photoshop: https://www.adobe.com/products/photoshop.html

Pixelmator: https://www.pixelmator.com/pro/

OmniGraffle: https://www.omnigroup.com/omnigraffle/

End-of-chapter exercises

Confirm

1. Display your **Wizarding School** nickname (or any word) and make it "explode" when *tapped* (using both an explosion image and sound effect).

2. Modify #1 so that the text only explodes when a **magic bomb** is *dropped on it*.

3. Modify #1 so that each letter of your name can be detonated independently when *tapped* (hint: you can do this by displaying the text in individual characters, each as its own named text display object).

4. Create an app that drops **magic balls** when tapped. Cause an explosion only when two **magic balls** collide.

5. Modify one of the above apps to make it a *landscape app*.

Integrate

6. Create your own "explosion" sound and use it in one of your apps.

7. Create an app with both size iron boxes. Create two new explosion sounds and use them when exploding each box via *tap* (i.e., so that each type of box has a unique explosion sound).

8. Create a *tap-to-drop* game that randomly drops either a *colorful* or *grayscale* **magic ball** to explode when it hits the ground. Use a unique explosion sound for each type of ball.

9. Create an app that drops the alphabet, one letter for each tap. So, on the first tap you drop "A", the second "B", and so one. Make each letter explode when it hits the ground.

10. Create a small game that allows the **magic ball** to be dropped, to bounce off one or more ramps or platforms, then hit a target to make it explode.

Challenge

11. Add a **third level** to the "d" version of the *Drawn2Code* game in explosions_3d.d2c.

12. Modify #2 so that your name (i.e., a display object) is effected by the blast force from a dropped bomb. The force should move your name away from the bomb blast and destroy it only in the case of a direct hit.

13. Modify your choice of app #1-#3 so that the text "breaks apart" as part of the explosion effect.

NOTES

 # Android Build & Test

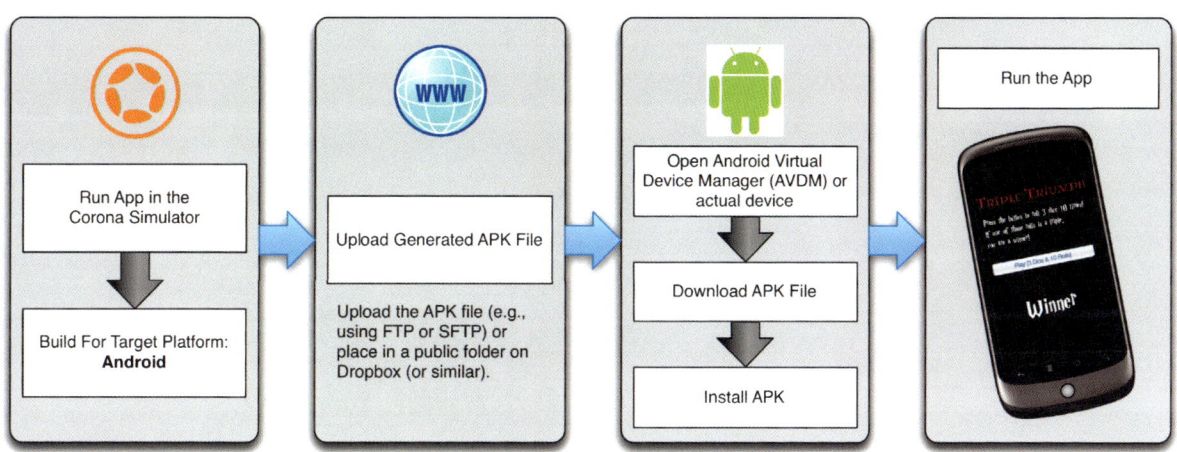

Process Overview

As the development of your app progresses you will, at some point, want to test it *outside* of the Corona Simulator. Why? Well, recall the **text field issues** discussed in Chapter 6 (among other things, the Corona Simulator doesn't display the popup keyboard, making it tough to test the amount and speed of your transitions). If you want to see a text field and test it on a Windows machine, you've got to build it for Android and/or acquire a Mac to test it on. However, text fields are **just one** (albeit glaring) example of differences in appearance and function you will see in apps running on difference platforms and devices. There are **other potential issues** to work through before you app is ready to distribute (for example, each of the various widgets will appear and operate *somewhat differently* depending on the device OS and screen characteristics).

It is generally easiest to test it first in the Android Emulator or the iOS Simulator (Appendix B) before installing it on actual devices. Setting up the Android Studio is a first step. While this is relatively easy to do, it will take some additional setup.

Building for Android

Before you can test your app in the Android Emulator or on an actual (physical) device, you'll need to use Corona to **build your app** for Android. Run your app as you normally would in the Corona Simulator. After it loads, pull down the "File" menu and select "Build > Android".

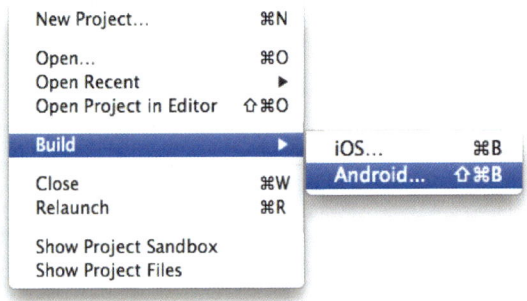

Corona Simulator File> Build > Android

You'll then be presented with a dialog that looks a bit like the screenshot "Corona SDK: Build for Android". Some of these fields will be filled in for you, but others **you will need to enter or choose**. Specifically, you will need to specify a **package name** (which you can make up), and select the "androiddebugkey" as the "**Key Alias**".

Then click the "Build" button at the bottom. Note that the "Build" button won't be *enabled* until you've made the required selections in the dialog box. Also, the building process can take several seconds, during which a Corona advertisement is conveniently presented.

A Beginner's Guide Using the Corona SDK

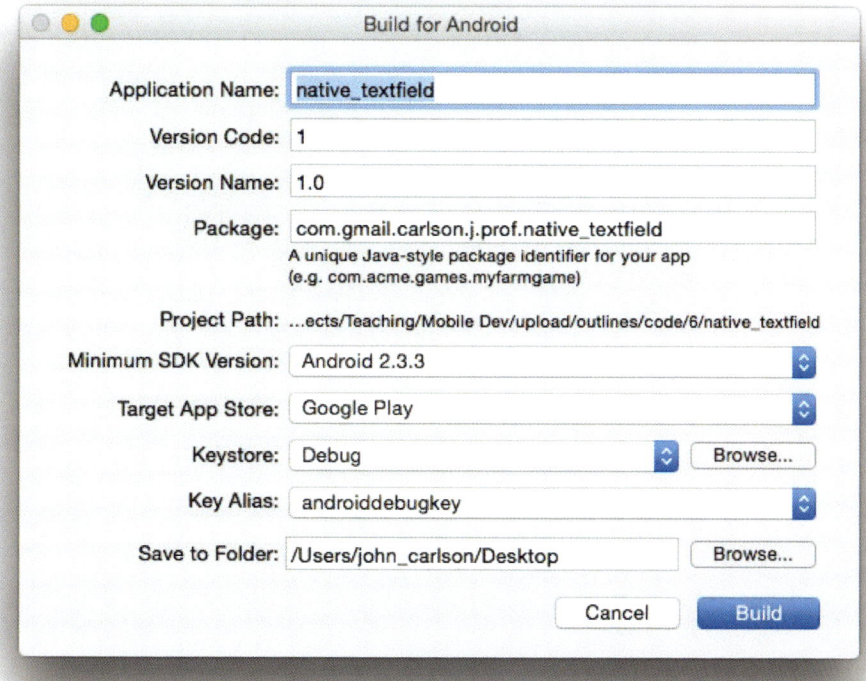

Corona SDK: Build for Android

Upload the APK file

Once the app is built, you will have an Android package ("apk") file saved on your system in your "Save to Folder" location. You'll need to **upload this file** to somewhere accessible on the web (e.g., a dropbox folder, personal webserver, etc.). Note: for convenience, I put the text field app (the troublesome one from Chapter 6) online here: lillipellilabs.com/mobiledev/download/apk/native_textfield.apk.

 Download & set up the Android Studio

To use the Android Emulator you need to download and set up the **Android Studio**. Here's the step-by-step steps:

1. If you haven't already done so, download the Android Studio (formerly called the "Android SDK") for your platform from

   http://developer.android.com/sdk/index.html

2. Install the Android Studio. This places a customized version of the IntelliJ IDE on your machine.

3. Launch Android Studio IDE. It will download several required packages after you capitulate to the license agreements. This process can take a few minutes.

4. After the IDE loads the first time, create a new default app in the startup wizard to load the IDE's main screen (if you don't already see it). You aren't going to actually create an Android app in the IDE, but we need to get the main screen to load to access the tools. The "Android Emulator" is also called an Android Virtual Device (an "AVD"), which we need to configure. Open the AVD Manager (the "AVDM") from the "Tools > Android" menu of the IDE.

5. There is a default AVD already present (but you may also create new AVD's for a specific device and configuration as well). Let's just use the default AVD to get going. However, the default AVD is configured in such a way that it **will not install or run Corona SDK apps!** So, hit **the edit (pencil) icon** in the "Actions" column to get to the virtual device configuration screen.

Attention

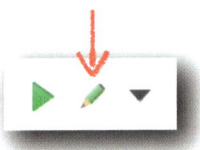

Notice that the default device is set to use Google x86 API's. That won't work

336

for us, because the Corona SDK only supports the ARM family of microprocessors. So, c**lick the "Change…" button** to the right of that:

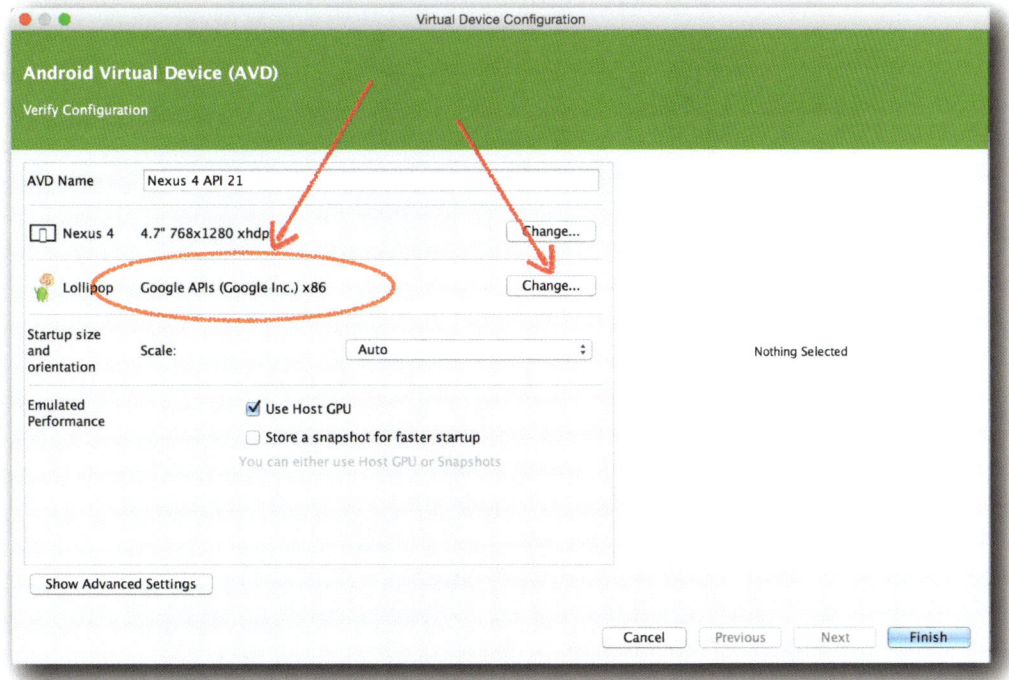

Virtual Device Configuration

This will load a screen where you can choose the API for the AVD to use. You should select the latest (highest numbered) ARM (not x86) option:

Select The Highest Level "ARM" Option

6. After selecting this option in the list, click the "Next" button at the bottom of the screen and then the "Finish" button. This will reconfigure the default AVD to be able to run apps built by Corona SDK (which can take a few minutes). You may leave the AVD Manager open for the next phase.

After that step is complete, you are **ready to use** the Android Emulator. Let's use it to run the "native-textfield.apk" app.

Using the Android Emulator

Before you can *run* your app in the Android emulator, you must download and install it. There are a couple of different ways to do this, but the following technique actually works for both the Android Emulator and real (physical) Android devices.

Start your virtual Android device and download the app

You are finally ready to boot up your virtual Android phone and then install and run a Corona SDK app. These are the steps to take:

1. From the Android Studio IDE, select your new AVD in the AVDM (if the AVDM isn't running, start it from the "Tools > Android" menu).

   Press the green "play" button in the actions column to start your AVD (i.e., the Android Emulator). If you have multiple AVDs set up, be sure to select one that is based on the ARM microprocessor.

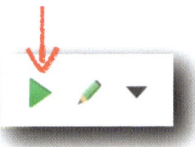

2. Starting the AVD may take a bit of time, sometimes several minutes. After your virtual device loads, use the mouse to "swipe up" to unlock the screen then go to the apps screen and **open the device's web browser:**

A Beginner's Guide Using the Corona SDK

Swipe Up With Mouse   Open App View   Open Web Browser

3. After the browser loads, open the URL for the "apk" file (that you created and uploaded). Or, to test this process, you can download the native text field app here:

   lillipellilabs.com/mobiledev/download/apk/native_textfield.apk

4. After the apk file finished downloading (when the status bar icon has stopped animating), open the download list. You can get to the download list by going back to the App View and selecting the "Downloads" app or use the mouse to pull down on the download icon in the status bar:

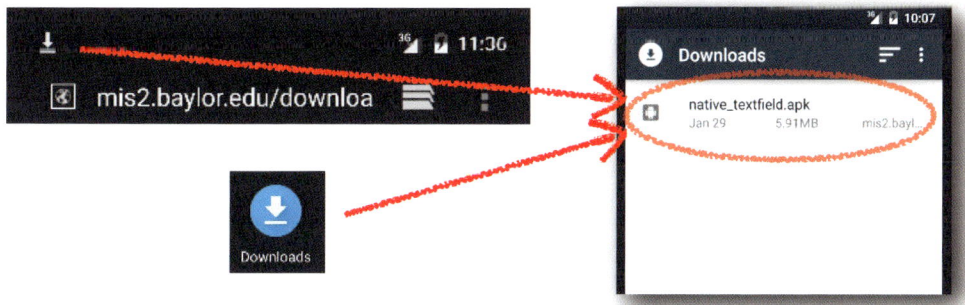

Open The Download List on Emulator

339

5. Select the apk file from the download list and choose "Install". This can take a few minutes as well.

6. After it is installed, you should have the option to "open" it, which should run it. This can also take a bit of time, so be patient. Eventually, you should see an emulator window like the screenshot "The Android Emulator".

The Android Emulator

Congratulations! Now that this is set up, using the Android Emulator **won't be as hard next time**. You will still have to build the app you want to run in the emulator, upload it, then download and install it in the AVD for testing, but you'll have everything in place to do so.

As noted in Chapter 6, this *particular* app demonstrates the Android text field bug, but you can follow this process to build and run any of your apps for testing. Obviously, the app shown here should reinforce the need for such testing.

Real Android devices

As noted above, once you have your app (in the form of an apk file), you can install it on a real Android device in **exactly the same way**: download the file using the web browser on the phone or tablet, then select it to start the installation. Each Android device will be somewhat unique, so adequate testing is crucial.

NOTES

iOS Build & Test

As noted in Appendix A, as the development of your app progresses you will, at some point, want to **test it** *outside* of the Corona Simulator. Why would you want to do this? Well, the iOS Simulator offers a **more realistic** facsimile of an *actual* iOS device than the Corona Simulator does. So, it's a great way to preview the state your app is in and what changes need to be addressed prior to actually sending your app to an app store. There are a variety of **potential issues** to work through before you app is ready to distribute. As an example, each of the various widgets will appear and operate *somewhat differently* depending on the device OS and screen characteristics (i.e., your app may or may not look or behave the way it does in the Corona Simulator)

It is generally easiest to test your app first in the iOS Simulator or the Android Emulator (Appendix A) before installing it for testing on actual devices. For iOS testing, installing Xcode is the first step. Unlike the other tools we've used, such as Corona and Android Studio, Xcode **requires a Mac**.

Attention

 ## Install Xcode

Although Xcode isn't used in this book to write code per se, installing it also installs the **iOS Simulator** (which you do want) and provides the capability to test your app on **actual devices**. If you haven't already done so, <u>install Xcode from the Mac App store</u>. The is a big download (around 2.5GB), so plan on this taking at least a few minutes.

Building for iOS

To test your app in the iOS Simulator (rather than the Corona Simulator), on an iOS device, or to upload it to the Apple App Store you will need to build the app for iOS in Corona. Again, this must be done **on a Mac** with Xcode installed. From the Corona Simulator menu, select "File > Build > iOS" (or hit ⌘B):

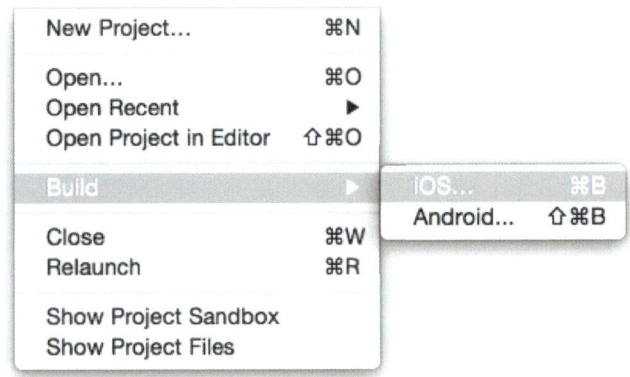

Corona Simulator File> Build > iOS

After doing so, you will see "Build for iOS" dialog (screenshot below).

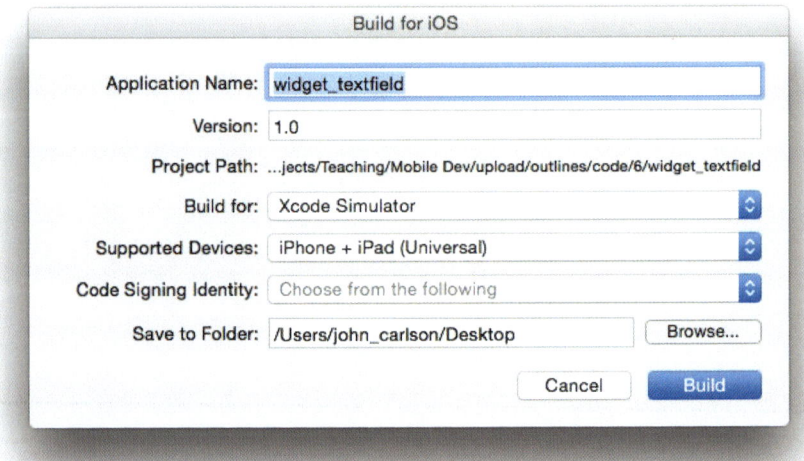

Corona Simulator: Build for iOS Dialog

You need to **select "Xcode Simulator"** in the "Build for" drop list. Once again, there will be a delay as Corona builds the app (and advertises the many upgrade paths), after which the iOS Simulator should open. Depending on the speed of your Mac, this will generally happen either *slowly*, or *very slowly*.

Note that the simulator *may* load with your app on the second "page" of the simulated device. If so, just click the bottom navigation dot to move to the right).

Attention

As an example, if you build the "native_textfield" app, it should appear something like the screenshot "Native Textfield in iOS Simulator".

Native Textfield in iOS Simulator

If you take a moment to compare this to the Corona Simulator (Chapter 6) and the Android Emulator (Appendix A), you'll see that the Corona Simulator is pretty faithful to the iOS Simulator, more so than the Android Emulator. In fact, if anything, this app looks the best on the iOS Simulator.

The iOS Simulator also utilizes (optionally) an onscreen, **virtual keyboard** that mimics the keyboard seen on actual devices (press ⌘K to toggle it on and off). This is essential for testing how your app needs to manage the onscreen keyboard sliding on and off the device screen.

Installing on an iOS device for testing

The next step in development is to test your app on the actual iOS devices you plan to support. Although the iOS device simulator is more faithful than the Corona Simulator, the ultimate arbiter of your app's appearance and functionality is an actual iOS device.

This process is somewhat more difficult than you might expect. The most up-to-date process is covered in detail on the Corona website here: docs.coronalabs.com/guide/distribution/iOSBuild/index.html. The basic process involves four steps:

1. **Create digital certificates** for testing and deploying your app (note: these are 2 different certificates). These are linked to your Apple ID.
2. For testing locally (e.g., on your own device, not downloaded via the app store), you'll need to **register your device in Xcode**.
3. **Create an "App ID"** for your app on Apple's developer website. Each app needs its own ID.
4. **Create "provisioning profiles"** for your app on Apple's developer website. You'll need 2 profiles, one for testing and one for deploying to the App Store. You must link the development (testing) provisioning profile to one registered testing device (e.g., the device you just registered above).

In general, these steps should be done in order. For testing, you can focus just on getting the Development certificate and provisioning profile set up.

NOTES

NOTES

Corona Project Management

In this book's sample code, I have always put all of the Lua/Corona source code into a **single file** called "main.lua". While Lua (and thus Corona) requires the use of "main.lua", it is only special in that it is **executed first**. We can create and use additional Lua files with different names by linking to them inside "main.lua".

Beyond main.lua

Let's start with a simple "proof-of-concept" example. This technique involves using the `require` statement to "import" code contained in separate source files (i.e., code that you are not including in the "main.lua" file). **I created two files** that contain a collection of constants (in "constants.lua") and functions (in "functions.lua"). In the "main.lua" file, we will `require` them (box #1):

Lua Must Be Able to Find These

```
1  require "constants"
2  require "functions"
```

Obviously, Lua **must be able to find these two files**, so you should place them inside your project folder. The names are not particularly important, however, you shouldn't use reserved Lua or Corona terms (like "display" or "table"). Also, the name does not in any way restrict what we can put in the file (for example, if we wished to, we could put a function in "constants.lua" or a constant in "functions.lua". These names are arbitrary and their meaning is up to us. Okay, so, what is *in* these files?

Constants

This first one just has a few business-related "constants" (in this case, these are variables with their values initialized)[1]. These will be used to calculate the price of an order of *something*, measured in dozens. Maybe eggs, but it could be anything. The following are included (box #2):

```
1  dozen = 12
2  priceEach = .29
3  discount = .10
4  couponCode = "AABC"
5  taxRate = 0.075
```

We'll use the pink constants momentarily, after we set up some functions.

Functions

The second file is somewhat longer, but just contains a few functions that might come in handy in our app. Mainly these two:

1. A function to average (missing entirely), called average(). The code for this function is shown in box #3. (Source: http://lua-users.org/wiki/SimpleStats).

2. A function to round called roundTo() (there is now a math.round() function built-in, but it rounds to the nearest integer, which isn't always what you need).

---

[1] Lua doesn't actually support constants, but there is a common workaround that typically involves placing the variables in a table (e.g., http://andrejs-cainikovs.blogspot.com/2009/05/lua-constants.html). That would be covered best in another appendix.

The code for each of these functions was found online and there are links to the respective sources inside the file. Both functions are reasonably straightforward, but they have been coded to deal with cases of bad input, which makes them more resilient when handling real data and users, but does make them somewhat longer than you might expect.

```lua
function average( t )
    local sum = 0
    local count= 0

    for k,v in pairs(t) do
        if type(v) == 'number' then
            sum = sum + v
            count = count + 1
        end
    end

    return (sum / count)
end
```

For example, you'll note in box #3 that the average function, which takes a table as input, deals with the possibility that the table might contain non-numeric data (line 6).

In any case, we don't really even need to know *how* the functions work, just how to *use* them. Having these functions and the business constants defined in separate files, means our "main.lua" file can be dramatically simpler than it otherwise might be. For example, to calculate the total price for 3 dozen eggs, the expression is simply:

```lua
total = 3*dozen*priceEach*(1+taxRate)
```

So, our "main.lua" file only contains 4 lines of code:

```lua
require "constants"
require "functions"

total = 3*dozen*priceEach*(1+taxRate)
print("Order Total: $"..total)
```

With the result:

```
Order Total: $11.223
```

Note in box #4 that we are *using* the constants that were defined in a separate file with no need to recreate. Of course, the result in box #5 also illustrates the need to *round* the total. Who is going to pay that $0.003, and how would you? **Bite off part of a penny?** No, we'll use the roundTo() function from "functions.lua":

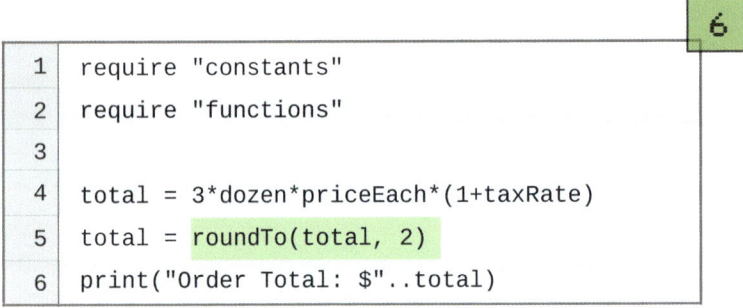

```
1  require "constants"
2  require "functions"
3
4  total = 3*dozen*priceEach*(1+taxRate)
5  total = roundTo(total, 2)
6  print("Order Total: $"..total)
```

Which results in:

```
Order Total: $11.22
```

Ah, that's better. No need to damage your dental-work. This app is available in the Appendix download as "project_mgt_1".

Basic UML

Unified modeling language, or "UML" can be used to visually describe a program class and how it relates to other classes. Although Lua and Corona aren't strictly object-oriented (OO), the use of UML can **still be helpful**. In UML, a class (in our case a *source-code file*) is described in a box, with variables listed at the top and functions at the bottom. Local (private) entities will be preceded with a "-", while nonlocal (or public") ones with a "+". In that way, we can get a "big picture" summary of an application by looking at each of the boxes and how they are related.

Using this system, our simple example (above) with main, constants, and functions would look something like Figure 1. The arrows tell you what file (in this case "main.lua") is loading resources contained in other, support files ("constants.lua" and "functions.lua"). Looking at the diagram, you can really see how organizing resources into separate, supporting source-code files simplifies the code in your main app. In addition, UML makes it easy to **document and describe** your app.

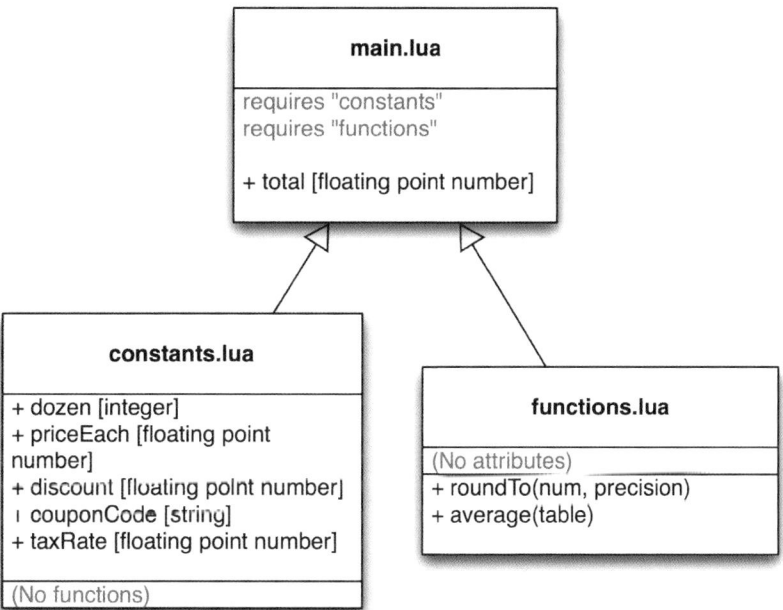

Figure 1: Basic Unified Modeling Language

Extending to the display

Although this first example was simple and only outputted to the console, the basic technique isn't limited to the console. For example, we can add some display-oriented data to our files to display our total onscreen. To make it easier, we'll add a "colors.lua" and "resources.lua" file, along with a resources folder containing an image and a sound effect.

In the "colors.lua" file, I am defining several colors by their name (such as "blue" or "green"), to make it easier to use them without needing to look up RGB codes. It looks something like this (box #8). Unfortunately, there's no easy way to access the colors without using a function to pass them (at least that I've discovered). So, in addition to a list of named colors, there's a "getColor()" function which can be used to retrieve a color using its name.

Inside of "main.lua", we can access a color by name using this syntax:

```
getColor([color name], [alpha])
```

For example, to set the fill color on a display object "o" to purple, we'd use this syntax:

```
o:setFillColor( getColor("purple", 1) )
```

Which is easier than having to remember the RGB values for purple (0.5, 0, 0.5). This app is available in the appendix download as "project_mgt_1b".

```lua
--* color palette for your app:
list = {
    white = {1,1,1},
    lightGray = {.8,.8,.8},
    gray = {.5,.5,.5},
    darkGray = {.3,.3,.3},
    black = {0,0,0},
    red = {1,0,0},
    purple = {.5, 0, .5},
    lime = {0,1,0},
    green = {0,.5,0},
    blue = {0,0,1},
    yellow = {1,1,0},
    aqua = {0,1,1},
    magenta = {1,0,1}
}

--* duplicates/proxies, e.g.,
list["grey"] = list.gray
list["gold"] = list.yellow

-- function to pull color from list:
function getColor(name, alpha)
    if list[name] then
        return list[name][1], list[name][2], list[name][3], alpha
    else
        print("color "..name.." not found!")
        return 1, 1, 1, 1
    end
end
```

A more complex example

These examples are, it may be obvious to say, somewhat contrived. There is no need to create support files that only contain variable declarations or only contain functions. The support files can be quite complex, containing whatever resources you need to make your app work.

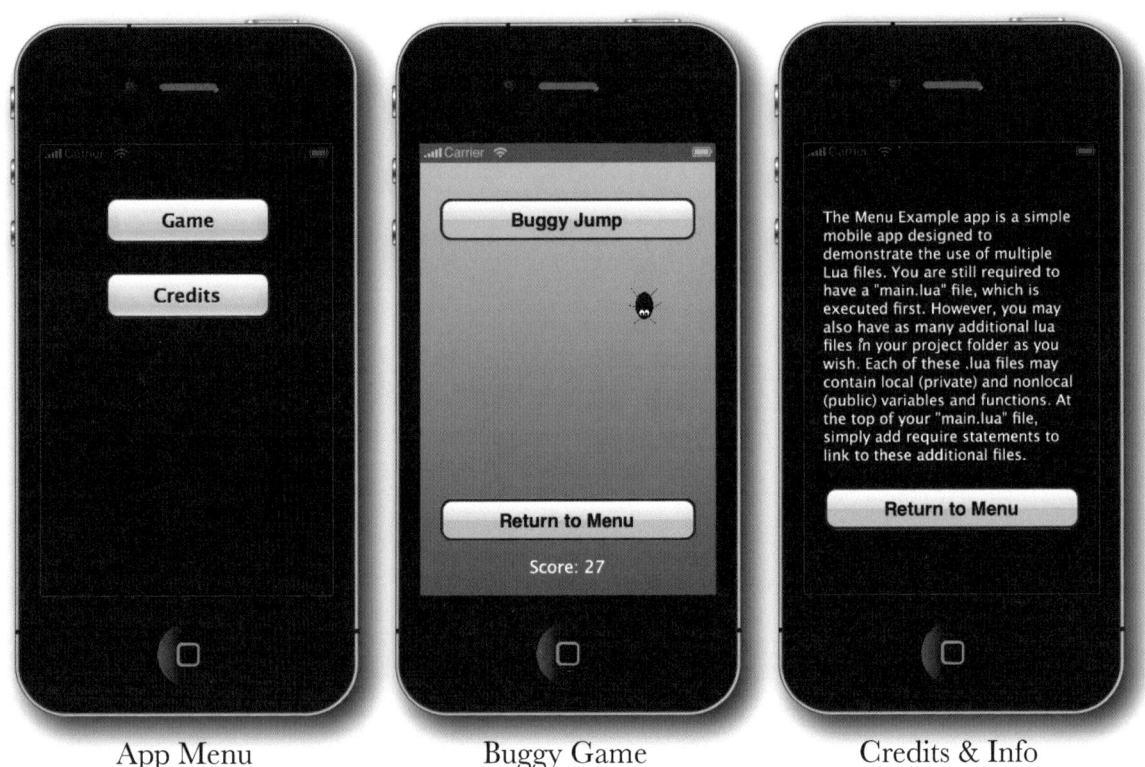

App Menu   Buggy Game   Credits & Info

A buggy encore

How about a slightly more complex example? Let's bring back "buggy", that **lovable software bug**, in an all-new adventure. In this simple game, we'll start by loading a menu of buttons (only two, but that is enough to understand the principles): "Game" and "Credits". When the user hits "Game", the code loaded from a separate Lua file will be used ("game.lua"), and when the user hits "Credits", the code from "cred.lua" will be used (See "App Menu").

You may be wondering why the Lua file for the "credits" isn't called "credits.lua". That's a great question. Unfortunately, "credits" is a **reserved word**, although, if you try to use it, the error message doesn't say anything about that.

<u>Bottom line</u>: Don't create a file called "credits.lua".

So, this app will also use three source-code files:

1. "main.lua" (which will be executed first)
2. "game.lua" (containing code relevant to the game)
3. "cred.lua" (containing code relevant to a description of the app)

For ease, these all need to be created in the same project folder. Inside our "main.lua" file, we will `require` both of the other files.

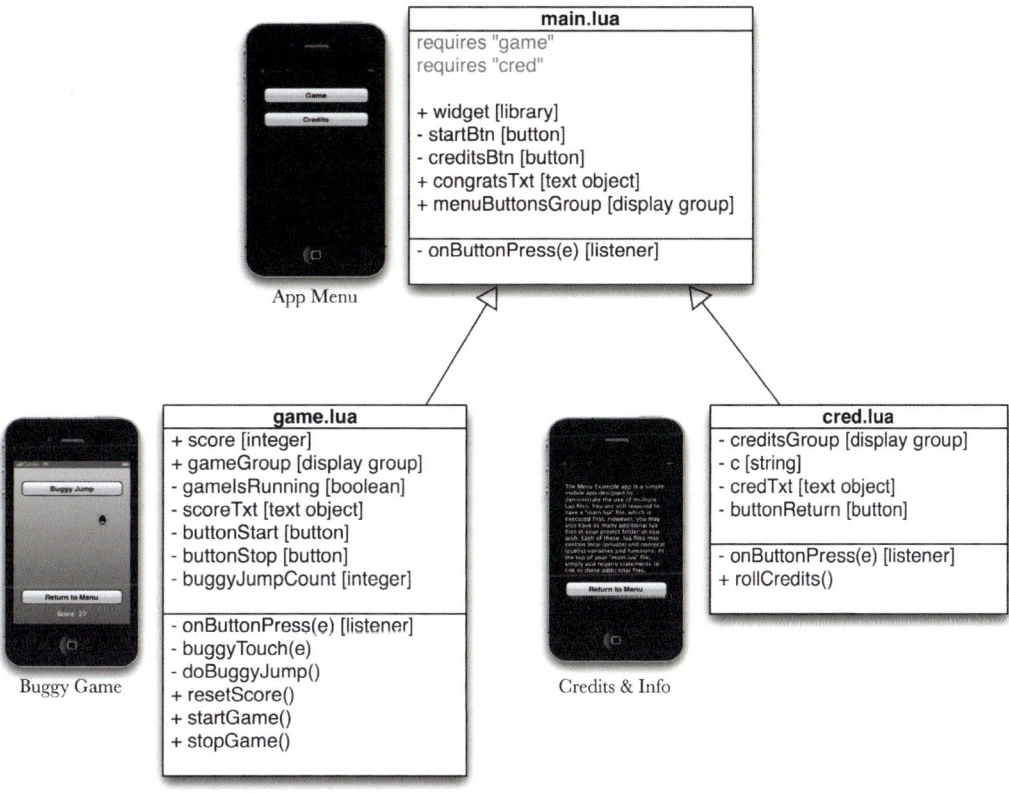

UML

The UML for this new app is slightly more complex than the prior example, but still readily understandable. Remember that variables (or "attributes") are listed first, followed by functions. Each file contains the code necessary to generate its own screen, with the display objects that compose that screen inserted into a display group. Each file has its own display group: `menuButtonsGroup` (for "main.lua"), `gameGroup` (for "game.lua"), and `creditsGroup` (for "cred.lua"). These display groups will be displayed or hidden, depending on the need. The `menuButtonsGroup` and `gameGroup` are hidden by setting the alpha to 0, while the `creditsGroup` is hidden by moving it offscreen.

Scope & privacy

Any items made `local` in the required "game.lua" and "cred.lua" files will be **invisible** to "main.lua". We will not be able to use them in code that we write inside "main.lua". As such, these private entities are for the internal use of the required files.

For example, the attribute `scoreTxt` (a text display object) is local to "game.lua". It is used inside the game to show the player's current score. It isn't used anywhere else, so it doesn't need to be public. It could be made public without *hurting* anything, but that **isn't always the case**.

Like when, you ask? Well, look at the function `onButtonPress(e)`. Wait, which one? There is a function with that name in **all three** source code files. Each file creates and uses one or more buttons and has its own listener defined to handle button presses for those specific buttons. Knowing that, we could code our support files to use unique names, like "gameOnButtonPress( )" and "credOnButtonPress( )", which would allow them to be global. But there's no compelling reason to have them globally scoped. The buttons are only clickable when the UI from the particular support file is visible. There's no reason to think we might need to run the `onButtonPress()` function loaded from, say, "cred.lua" in code we write inside "main.lua".

On the other hand, you might have noticed that the `widget` variable (in "main.lua"), which we have been making `local` in all of our chapter examples, is now global. Why? Because we are using widgets (buttons) in all three files. Importing that library once and making it available to all of the files makes sense.

In general, the rule is to make your variables and function local unless there is a compelling reason not to do so.

Analyzing the code

Lets look at the first chunk of code in "main.lua", since it contains some of the key syntax to examine. This chunk also illustrates some of the differences between the older widgets 1.0 syntax and the newer widgets 2.0 syntax (minor but crucial differences).

On line 1 (box #9), we are setting up our `widget` object, from which we'll be able to create buttons and such. Typically, we have made `widget` a `local` entity, but in this case it makes more sense for it to be global. That way, the code we write in "game.lua" and "cred.lua" can make use of it, without needing to "re-require" it.

On lines 4-5, we are requiring the support files "game.lua" and "cred.lua". As before, these files should be stored in the same project folder as "main.lua", which makes sense.

```
1   widget = require "widget"  --* notice that this is not local
2
3   --* anonymous requires:
4   require "game"
5   require "cred"
6
7   --* local listener function is private to this file:
8   local function onButtonPress(e)
9
10      if e.phase == "began" then
11
12          menuButtonsGroup.alpha = 0
13          if e.target.name == "game" then
14              resetScore()  --* a function in game.lua
15              gameGroup.alpha = 1
16
17          elseif e.target.name == "credits" then
18              rollCredits()  --* a function in credits.lua
19
20          end
21      end
22      return true  --* stops further button press processing
23  end
```

359

Lines 8-23 provide the `onButtonPress(e)` listener, which is the event-handler for the "Game" and "Credits" buttons. Again, it is declared to be `local` so that we can easily use the same function name again in any support files that use buttons.

As always, you need to limit your button handler to a specific button event phase (such as "began") so that your code only executes one time per press. This is done using 'if-then' logic on the event phase (`e.phase`).

The handler function performs three main actions:

1. When either of these buttons is pressed, the `menuButtonsGroup` is hidden.
2. Next, 'if-then' logic using the button name (`e.target.name`) to determine which button was pressed; then, either the game is reset and displayed, or the credits are rolled.
3. The `return true` on line 22 stops the button press from being passed on to any widgets sharing screen real estate with either of these menu buttons.

Chapter resources

• • • • • • • • • • • • • • • • • • • •

In the chapter resource download for this book (www.lillipellilabs.com/mobiledev/download/chapter_resources.zip), look for folder "c".

This folder includes these 3 fantastic apps:

1. project_mgt_1 (constants and functions at console)
2. project_mgt_1b (constants and function on display)
3. project_mgt_2 (buggy jump game)

NOTES

NOTES

Index

A

Algebra, 157
Anchor, 60
Android Emulator, 8, 127, 335
Android Studio, 8, 336
Android Virtual Device (AVD), 336
Android Virtual Device Manager (AVDM), 336
Animation, 84
API, 336
APK (Android Package File), 335
Arithmetic Error, 176
Assignment Operators, 29-30
Audio Table, 85-86, 190-191
AVD (See Android Virtual Device)
AVDM (See Android Virtual Device Manager)
Average (Calculation), 351

B

Background Music, 190-191
bfxr (also cfxr, sfxr), 297
Blast Force, 320
Blast Radius, 316
Boolean, 28, 104
Boolean Condition, 104
Boolean Logic, 104
Bounce (See Physics Body: Bounce)
Branched Flow Of Execution (Branch, Conditional Branch), 33, 104
Build for Android, 334-335
Build for iOS, 343
Button (See Widget Button)
Button Sound Effect, 104

C

Calendar, 255
Calling Statement, 160
Case-Sensitive, 28
cfxr (See bfxr)
Checkbox (See Widget Checkbox)
Chunk, 136
Collision, 197, 289
Collision Event, 290
Colors, 63, 77, 354
Command, 27
Commenting, 39, 185
Concatenation, 32
Condition (See Boolean Condition)
Conditional Branch (See Branched Flow of Execution)
Console, 19
Construct, 93
Constructor, 83, 246
Content Area, 51
Convex Shape, 274
Corona SDK, 2
Corona Simulator (Windows Location), 16, 17
Counter, 114, 134
Curly Braces, 96

D

Damage Attribute, 299
Data Input, 124
Debugging, 175, 176
    Errors Involving "M"
        Mis-Capitalized Code, 181
        Mis-Scoped Code, 181
        Misplaced Code, 181
        Missing Statement, 181
        Mistyped Code, 181

Debugging Mode, 273
Decimal Number, 78, 161
Decrement, 116
Density (See Physics Body: Density)
Diagonal Line, 59
Dictionary, 29
Display Group, 83, 358
Display Object, 71-74
    Circle, 73
    Image, 74
    Image Sheet, 258-259
    Line, 72
    Polygon, 80, 274
    Rectangle, 72
    Rounded Rectangle, 73
    Text Display Object (Label), 48, 81, 94, 221
    Triangle, 273

Display Table, 48
DMG (Disk Image), 10
Drawn2Code,
    aRandomColor( ) (Function), 80-82
    Add Script Object Palette (Object Palette), 19
    Background Music, 191-192
    Design Canvas, 20
    Display Groups, 83-84
    Display Object (Shapes), 71
    D2C (.d2c) Design File, 20
    Event-Handlers,

onComplete, 101-103
onEnterFrame (Runtime), 280
Press, 94-97
Tap, 86-87, 283-284
Touch, 192-194

Flow of Execution (Stack), 88
Generated Code (Window), 20
Gradient (Display Object), 78-79
Hello World Snippet, 19
Image Button (Widget), 100-101
Load Sound (Action), 86
Loop (A Loop That Contains Script Objects), 212
Open Recent, 20
Orientation (Orient Button), 328-329
Physics,
    Add Body, 266
    Friction, 277
    Hybrid Draw Mode, 274
    Irregular Outline (Physics Body), 275-276

Script Object, 19
Script Object Details (Object Details), 19
Script Object Stack (Object Stack), 19
Scroll View (Widget), 257
Setup, 13-17
Shape Button (Widget), 97
Slider (Widget), 154-157
Spinner (Widget), 259
Switch (Widget), 220
    Checkbox, 220
    Radio Button, 225
    Segmented Control, 236-237

Tab Bar (Widget), 249-249
Tap (Listener), 86
Text (Display Object), 86
Text Button (Widget), 94
Text Field (Widget, Native), 125
Transition, 85

Dynamic Body (See Physics Body: Dynamic Body)

E

Error-Checking, 162
Event (User Event), 92
Event Handler (Function), 86, 92, 126, 194
Event Listener, 86, 92, 125, 190, 218
Event-Cycle, 92
Event-Driven App, 91
Exploding Crate, 311
Explosion Image, 310
Explosive Force, 310
Explosive Sound, 310
Expression, 160

F

Filter, 269
Flow Of Execution, 30, 65, 87
Flowchart, 104
Fonts, 56-58
For Loop, 131
Force, 303
Force Field, 270
Fractional Value, 156
Frame Rate, 280
Framework, 3
Friction (See Physics Body: Friction)
Function, 35, 79, 154

G

Gaming App, 4
Google Roboto Font, 8
Gradient, 76
Ground (Physics Body), 266-277, 290-295, 313
GUI (See UI)

H

Hack, 176
Health (Indicator) Bar, 299-304, 318-312
Helvetica-Neue, 8
Hybrid Draw Mode (Physic), 273

I

IDE, 7
Identifier (Also, see Variable), 19, 71
If-Then Logic (See Branched Flow of Execution)
Image, 74-76, 247, 255
Image Sheet, 258
Increment, 116
Incremental Build, 179
Index, 134, 301
Initialization, 155
Install on an Android Device, 338
Install on an iOS Device, 344
Instantiate, 93
Integer Number, 153
iOS Device Simulator, 8, 127
Iron Box (See Lockbox)
Irregular Shape,   Physics Body (See Physics Body: Shape)

J

Java Development Kit (JDK), 7-8
Java Runtime Environment (JRE), 8

K

Kinematic Body (See Physics Body: Kinematic Body)

L

Label (See Text Display Object)
Landscape (Landscape App), 328
Library, 3

Lines of Force, 323
List (see Table or Widget: Table View)
Listener (See Event Listener)
Literal, 28
Lockbox (Physics Body), 271, 289-305, 310-318, 320-326
Logic (See Boolean Logic)
Logic Error, 176
Loop, 35, 79
Lua, 2
Lua Interpreter, 13

M

Malbolge, 26
M, Errors Involving (See Debugging: Errors Involving M)
Microsoft Installer (MSI), 11
Misspecification (Debugging), 176
Misuse (Debugging), 176
Mobile App, 2
Mobile Development, 5
Mobile Device, 2
Mobile UI, 2
Module, 178
Multiple Lua Files, 349, 356

N

Named Variable, 28
Native, 93
Native Library, 123
Native Text Field (See Widget Text Field), 124
Nil (nil), 30

O

Object, 49
Object Dot Attribute, 109
Object Oriented, 26
Object Stack (See Drawn2Code Object Stack)
Objective C, 3

On/Off Switch (See Widget Switch On/Off)
Onscreen Keyboard, 127
Open Source, 267
Orientation, 45
Overlap, 199

P

Package, 334
Parameter, 36, 111, 159
Physics App, 313
Physics Body, 267
    Bounce, 268
    Density, 269
    Dynamic Body, 267
    Friction, 269
    Kinematic Body, 267
    Shape, 269
    Static Body, 267

Physics Engine (Box2D), 265
Physics, Hybrid Draw Mode, 273
Physics Library, 265
Pixel, 45
Platform, 3, 176
PNG Image File, 74, 258
Polygon, 80, 272
Proactive Strategy, 176
Project Management, 349
Programming, 25

R

Radio Button (See Widget: Radio Button)
Radio Button Group, 226
Radius, 269
Random Integer, 78
Range, 157
Reactive Strategy, 176
Require Statement, 93, 349

Runtime, 280

S

Scale, 303-304
Scope, 177, 358
Script Object (See Drawn2Code: ScriptObject)
Scripting Language, 3, 26
Scroll View (See Widget Scroll View)
Segment, 217
Segmented Control (See Widget Segmented Control)
Settings Screen, 167
sfxr (See bfxr)
Shape (See Physics Body: Shape)
Shape Button, 97-99
Simulator Device, 48
Slider (See Widget Slider)
Software Bug, 175, 197
Software Development Kit (SDK), 7
Sound Effect, 105, 296
Sound File, 192, 296
Spinner (See Widget Spinner)
Statement, 30
Static Body (See Physics Body: Static Body)
Status Bar, 64-65
Steel Lockbox (See Lockbox)
String, 28
Stroke Width, 71
Structured Data, 204
Suffix, 74
Swift, 3
Switch (See Widget Switch)
Syntax, 28
Syntax Error, 176
System Development, 38
Systems Diagram, 27

T

Tab Bar (See Widget Tab Bar)
Table (Lua Table), 109, 204
Table View (See Widget Table View)
Tap, 311
Tap Event, 190
Target, 109
Target Point, 195
Test, 179
Test Case, 185
Text Field (See Widget Text Field)
Text Display Object (See Display Object: Text Display Object (Label))
Timer, 200
Tint, 297
Toggle Switch (See Widget on/Off Slider)
Top-To-Bottom, 67
Touch Event (Touch Listener), 104-106, 283
Touch Point, 193
Transition, 84
Triangle (See Display Object: Triangle)

U

UI, 2-3, 53, 112, 142, 228, 238, 328
Unified Modeling Language (UML), 353

V

Valid Expression, 28
Variable, 28
Virtual Keyboard, 346

W

Waterfall Development Model, 38, 177
While Loop, 132
Widget (Widget Library), 93, 123, 181
    Buttons, 94-111
        Text Button, 94-97
        Shape Button, 97-99

Image Button, 100-101

Checkbox, 123, 218
On/Off Slide Switch (Toggle Switch), 220
Radio Button, 123, 225
Segmented Control, 232
Scroll View, 254
Slider, 91, 123, 153
Spinner, 257
Switch, 220
Tab Bar, 245
Table View Widget, 251
Text Box, 128
Text Field (Textfield), 123-128

X
Xcode, 7, 343
Xcode Simulator, 345
XML, 27

Z
Zerobrane Studio (ZBS), 8

Printed in Great Britain
by Amazon